Amanda Hart

SUE ME!

Sue Me!
© 2023 **Amanda Hart**

ISBN: 9781739574406 Paperback

This book is dedicated to my three children, Georgina, Amelia, and Anthony, for they have been my true teachers and motivators to seek the truth.

Foreword
Dee Anderson

Amanda Hart is an intuitive consultant. She is also an accomplished author. This book is one of the most memorable and inspirational reads of recent years, and one that guarantees to move and motivate on so many levels.

As Amanda navigates a turbulent childhood and traumatic events growing up, she finds solace in her spiritual conversations with angels, who she calls The Guys Upstairs. An intelligent and creative way of dealing with her trauma which she demonstrates as a writer in this compelling book.

With my mother Sylvia being the talent behind Thunderbirds, Captain Scarlet, and other iconic series (Gerry and Sylvia Anderson) I am someone who has been brought up not only in a hugely creative environment but with a strong woman as a role model, who has succeeded against the odds in a heavily male dominated industry.

I was excited to be introduced to Amanda, and found her to be charismatic, compassionate, and understanding.

This is Amanda's story, but it is also for everyone, an inspiring tale of overcoming obstacles however immense, and forging a way ahead as a tribute to the strength and determination of the human spirit.

For more background on Dee Anderson please visit www.amazingwonderbirds.com to view her highly successful and entertaining broadcast series.

Introduction

When I was first asked to write my story, I had no idea just how much it would change my life or benefit the lives of others. It was 2008, and a director of the radio station where I was presenting an online show, was standing in the canteen queue in front of me, trying to convince me I should write my memoir. I laughed at how ridiculous it sounded and shrugged it off, telling her that I had no intention of ever disclosing my story so publicly, and more to the point, to benefit who?

Two years later, whilst recovering from surgery to fix nerve damage to my head, I had an overwhelming compulsion to write. From a desperate need to make sense of my life for my children if I couldn't, I asked for a journal to be brought into hospital. And so the first (mostly illegible) handwritten pages of my story started to take shape and form.

I tentatively continued to write in secret on my blackberry phone for two years whilst in a violent relationship and although I had recovered somewhat from the surgery, the story was stirring some long-forgotten calling that I was subconsciously gravitating towards.

Storing the emerging story on my computer at night while everyone was asleep, six of those painstakingly written chapters went missing and I lost faith in the whole process and gave up.

By 2014 however, I was seriously unwell, and about to be made homeless with two small children, to lose my business, our home and everything of any value, through bankruptcy. Desperate to keep a roof over our head, I sought solace in the only source I knew that had bailed me out throughout my life. Through my subconscious, I was shown my part written book in a dream.

And so I started on a path of rescuing my family, holding onto the only lifeline I'd been given. Trusting the message in the dream, I realised it was the only asset I had left in the world, even if it was just a part written book.

Naively, I had thought the process of writing would be a beautiful cathartic creative writing exercise. What I didn't expect was to find myself drawn back into a world of deprivation from my past in order to heal, and then move on to honour what I was truly here to serve.

When I finally emerged from the depths of those challenges when the book was finished, I was not surprised to find myself broken and beaten from the experience. But it was a whole new beginning, a new way of being and a whole other world that was emerging for me and my family.

When I look back at my life the only thing that I know that's real is the fact that every step of the way I have made a series of choices. In my youth those choices took me to a very dark place, not because I wanted that, but because my negative conditioning was my pre-set, which created behaviour that was destructive and detrimental to my wellbeing. I was on auto pilot destruction and choices were made from a place of being powerless.

My journey has consisted of some unbelievable challenges, many of which I chose simply not to write about for many reasons. Some I felt were too graphic to mention, some would compromise people who still exist (and I have no intention and never have had the intention to prosecute anyone for any wrongdoing) and some would affect my loved ones who I wish to protect.

This book has become a journey of choice in itself. The original book 'The Guys Upstairs' was finally published in 2015 and yes, whilst it created a huge impact and changed my life, unbeknownst to me it coincided with the amendment to the Serious Crime Act to incorporate the offence of controlling or coercive behaviour in an intimate or family relationship. That's when I realised that there was no coincidence to my story releasing at that time.

It captured the attention of people in the field of policing, the judiciary, the health sector, journalists, screen writers, literary agents, and those working towards law change in relation to coercive control and domestic violence. Whilst I was all for supporting these changes and being a voice to share my story, I was not prepared for the threats to silence me. After years of vulnerability and control, the irony was that I was being challenged yet again by those voices that dared to silence me. Many were external, but those only amplified the voices within that I carried around with me like internal hostage takers, that I couldn't ignore.

So I pulled the book and shut it down after four months through fear of further pain.

Only recently I was told by a health professional that I can now give myself permission to live. Having emerged after many years of soul seeking and healing, as a healthier, safer version of myself, I knew I was just skimming the surface of life, even though I was making a difference in the world. But it was from a place of safety and compromise. Despite this, I still faced challenges and knew intuitively that I was still not fully living, as I was protecting and hiding from those who'd silenced me in the past.

It was only when I faced burnout in April 2023, six months after my husband had a stroke after our first wedding anniversary, that I was invited to go on a walking weekend break for some respite. I welcomed the break for some clarity and rejuvenation.

Prior to that weekend, I'd planned to shut down my work as a consultant and put all my focus and energy into being with my husband and family, as we had no idea what the long-term prognosis would be. And whilst on that trip, I had a dream.

At first, I couldn't quite trust what I was being shown. But slowly, over the course of that weekend, walking in that natural space, lapping up the beauty of nature, feeling the warmth of the sun on my skin and feeling held, I emerged with a whole new attitude and a choice I knew I had to honour.

I returned renewed and ready for what I knew was a huge time of growth for me and over the course of the months to come, I honoured every aspect of what I was shown to push through the glass ceiling that I had created through fear of being exposed, vulnerable and hurt. I knew unwaveringly that I was ready to stand by my truth rather than hide any longer, not just for myself, but for all those like me who have been hushed, silenced, belittled, bullied, betrayed, and controlled, so that I could finally use my 'whole voice', my whole truth and no longer fear the consequences.

In the past, I had always run from conflict, avoided pain at any cost, even when it was to the detriment of my wellbeing. My inner voice told me that by no longer hiding, I was not only releasing myself from the past, but would be shining a light on those that are ready to release themselves too, to heal their past, present, and future selves. We all have this innate power to change the course of our lives for the better when listening to our heart, trusting in our guidance, and taking a leap of faith into the unknown…even if it looks ugly, makes us face our foes and challenges our fears.

It was therefore inevitable that this book would finally emerge from the process of unravelling my existence and finding what was left of me to present this to you today.

Throughout my life I have been plagued by what some would call bad luck. I know now that luck had nothing to do with it. I've come to understand through years of seeking inner wisdom that what we focus on we attract, and much of that is all housed in the subconscious.

Through all my experiences I have at many times in my life called out for help, reached to others in times of need and spoken out against what I felt was injustice. Not only was it incredibly violating to have gone through some of the experiences at the hands of those who hurt me, but worse was the injustice of those systems and organisations that failed to hear my pleas or take right action to protect me and my loved ones.

When I was a child, teachers, neighbours, police, family members and friends knew of my violation, but no one spoke out and no one acted. As a child I questioned this over and over and, in the end, learned to shut down that voice as it became evidently futile to ask for help. I learned coping mechanisms which was all I could do to survive.

Looking back as an adult I don't blame those I reached out to for help who didn't want to know, nor do I blame the systems or people that failed to protect me. It is through this book however, that enables me to share my story in the hope that people will ask questions themselves so we can cut the cycle of deprivation that lurks in the shadows of our society.

Ultimately, I learned that choice allowed me to find my innate power and voice to help others to find there's. I finally changed the pre-set conditioning of my childhood so that the woman I have become emerged. We all have that power. It is our birth right, our destiny and part of our calling, whatever that may be. And most importantly, it starts changing once we choose to change.

Transparency and authenticity are now at last being recognised as a necessity in many walks of life yet still we exist with vast areas of society that need to evolve. It's not to point the finger or to blame the failings of those that are supposed to be there to help us in society. It is more so for us as individuals to start taking responsibility for our own destinies and co-exist with each other in a more authentic way, which will ultimately encourage overall change.

No one is infallible. Nothing in life is failsafe. We have witnessed so many exploitations in so many organisations, religions, across cultures and continents that have come to light through the media. We can either bury our heads in the sand and pretend that it's not happening, or we take a stand and look at our own worlds, our own colleagues, friends, family, neighbours and ask ourselves, are we doing enough to take responsibility for what we're experiencing in our world, or are we ducking out through fear of challenge or further pain?

There is what we can and can't control in life. Simple as that. What we can control, we need to question through our heart. The answers are always there if we're willing to feel them. What we can't control we need to learn to accept, even when that challenges our status quo, as it matures us spiritually and that's always a win.

Each and every one of us have a part to play in this world, regardless of how big or small that may be. Each one of us is a link in the bigger picture which, when we live authentically through making good choices which come from knowing ourselves, then our lives attract good in all ways. When we fight ourselves through fear, we will never find that peace within and nor so the world around us.

Rather than looking at fixing something external that's going wrong, I've discovered that if we go back to the root cause we can remove the negative habits and ultimately create new positive behaviours that create the world we are destined to live in. We can teach that to children from an early age which enables them to use their mind intelligently to make better choices. Only by going to the grass root level and working with that generation can we consistently start to change through the generations to come.

This is not to say that it is only through education of children that we can change, but through the way digital media, the internet and communication systems over all are changing today. It's inevitable that more and more people are sharing transformative information that can lead to radical change. How we use that information is key. By becoming our authentic self and living our truth, by using our power and our voice, we can share invaluable information that leads to change. But ultimately it is up to us as individuals if we carry that through into all walks of our lives. To make real change though, walking the talk is key.

So, we can either live in fear of what could happen in the future based on what experiences we've had in the past (which no longer exist as it's an illusion) or we choose to become our best potential self by honouring our truth and take action to change our world in any way we can to honour our authentic nature. Only then can we be free and release ourselves from the shackles we've suffered in the past.

Life is a series of choices. Every one of us has choice in every moment of every day. Becoming more mindful and aware of our world is a start. As soon as you choose to change, your world will offer you opportunity.

In 1975, The Maharishi Effect established the principle that individual consciousness affects collective consciousness. Nearly 50 scientific research studies conducted over 25 years verified the unique effect and wide-ranging benefits to a nation produced by the Maharishi Effect. These studies have used the most rigorous research methods and evaluation procedures available in the social sciences, including time series analysis, which controls for weekly and seasonal cycles or trends in social data.

Increased coherence within a nation expresses itself in improved national harmony and well-being. In addition, this internal coherence and harmony generates an influence that extends beyond the nation's borders, expressing itself in improved international relations and reduced international conflicts.

Based on this study I believe that with today's awakening culture we are building a community of like-minded, spiritual, empathically motivated individuals beyond 80 million (over 1% of the world's population), and that collectively will create greater change for future generations to come through united focus.

My aim is to awaken more souls, those without a voice or who've fallen as victims and need a helping hand. We've all had help from those who've inspired us at some point in our lives. It's time to pay it forward and help those who need our support.

If you want to take part in making a difference in this world, then honour your truth, make wise choices from your heart and grab life by the dreams.

Best wishes on your journey.

Amanda Hart

Chapter 1

In every tragedy there's a moment where there's a
possibility for triumph.

Oprah Winfrey

The first time I experienced fear was just before my fourth birthday.

It was 1971 and I sat in the back of my mother's Mini, surrounded by bin bags filled with my belongings. She drove in silence. The only sounds were the hum of the car engine, the noise of passing traffic and my sobs.

"Mummy, please don't take me. I don't want to go!"

She ignored me. I begged her to turn the car around and take me back home, but she continued regardless. I knew she was crying as I saw her hand wipe tears from her face.

"Please Mummy," I begged. "Please don't make me go. I'll be a good girl, I promise!"

What had I done to deserve this? I searched for answers in a desperate attempt to find something to make her stop the car, pull me into her arms, hug me, and never let me go. But she didn't.

I'd only once been scolded. That was when Mummy had left me in the car parked outside the launderette in Muswell Hill where we lived. I'd climbed from the back seat into the front to get a better view of her talking to a neighbour and had accidently stood on the handbrake. The car started rolling down the hill and ran into the back of the car parked in front of us.

Frantic with fear I jumped out of the car and ran up the hill screaming, "Mummy, the car's crashed!"

My mother stepped out of the launderette and found a man shouting and yelling at me about the damage to his bumper – her Mini was jammed against it. I was running for my petrified life towards her as if it were nothing to do with me.

Mum took me in her arms and passed me to a neighbour who hugged me until I calmed down. She then went and dealt with the angry car owner. She didn't speak to me all the way home. When we got to my grandparents' house, my grandfather told me off whilst Grandma consoled my mother.

Later that day when the bar opened (the expression the adults in my family used to say when it was late enough for a drink), and everyone had had their customary late afternoon gin and tonics (more gin than tonic), they fell about laughing at what had happened.

Until then, I'd been raised by my mother and grandparents, and life was filled with pure safety, security and lots of laughter. Our family always laughed, especially when Great Uncle Charlie (my grandfather's brother) was over. He was always cracking jokes and tickling me until my sides hurt from giggling so much.

That morning, Mum had announced that I'd be going to live with my dad. I'd panicked as I didn't want to go, and I hid under my bed. Mum had packed everything I owned, clothes, toys and all my memories, into black bin liners and loaded them into the car as if she were clearing me out of her life for good.

Although my grandparents were usually around in the mornings, on that occasion they weren't around which was odd, so I couldn't plead with them. They would have stopped her. They loved me just as much as Mum. And Aunty Hardwick would have stopped her. She wasn't my real aunty, but she looked after me when Mummy worked at her public relations job, and I loved her like she was my other mother. She made lovely home cooked food and baked delicious cakes and biscuits; things Mummy never had time for. She read me adventure stories and we lay down in the afternoon for a nap together and cuddled whilst listening to *The Archers* on the radio. Life was blissful and I was cherished and safe – until that day.

"Please Mummy, I don't want to go. Please don't leave me," I cried over and over again.

Prior to that day, I'd been to visit my dad a couple of times, but only briefly. Each time I longed to be back with my family as soon as possible. He had a new wife and baby, but his wife ignored me, and I'd felt unwanted each time. I wasn't going to be loved and protected at my dad's and I was petrified.

The drive took two hours and I sobbed for the entire journey. Every now and then, Mum said, "Everything will be OK, sweetheart. I love you."

She didn't convince me as it seemed a pacifier, but I sensed her trepidation in her voice, even at that age.

When we arrived, I screamed harder. "Mummy no," I begged. "I don't want to go, please no."

The daunting large white detached house had ivy growing up the walls, a circular drive and two imposing lions either side of the front door. There was a white van parked on the left-hand side of the drive, which I knew was my dad's.

Mum turned to me in the back of the car, tears streaming down her face. She got out of the car, opened my door, and took me in her arms. "Sorry, baby," she said.

I clung to her, but I knew this was it. Sobbing, she carried me to the front door and rang the bell. She put me down and stood me in front of the door. No-one answered at first, and as I stood there, she went back and forth from the car to the door carrying the sum total of what seemed to have been my little life so far, until eventually the door opened just slightly.

"Go in sweetheart. Everything will be OK, I promise you," Mum said as she ushered me in.

Dad, a stocky, well-built, dark curly haired man with piercing brown eyes, arrived in the hall as my mother walked off.

"Let's go up," he said, taking my hand and leading me up the stairs. "I'm going to show you your new bedroom."

It was a larger room than I was used to with a double bed, fitted wardrobes and a view of a large garden. It smelt funny and there were no toys or pictures. It was a plain white room with a maroon quilt on the bed.

"Wait here and I'll be back," Dad said.

I climbed up and sat on the bed, still sobbing, and when Dad had finished bringing my things up, he said, "Stay here for a while, I've got some things to do." Shutting the door, he went back downstairs.

I lay down on the musty smelling throw, hugging Bunny, my favourite toy that I'd had since I was born. I hated the smell of the room. I lay in a ball on that bed, trusting Mummy would come back and realise what a mistake she'd made. Minutes ticked away and I waited and waited, but she didn't appear.

I sensed something wasn't right in the house. It felt cold and dark although it was daytime. I was frightened but had no idea why.

I could hear voices getting louder. One was my dad's and the other was a woman's. They were arguing. The voices started to rise in intensity and volume. I tried to hear what the argument was about, but I couldn't, so I lay still on the bed.

I felt my body stiffening and my blood running cold as I tried to make sense of what was happening. I buried my head into the throw and covered my ears, drawing my legs more tightly up into my stomach and started to cry again.

I heard a crash and jumped with shock. The voices were muffled, and I could hear furniture falling and the sound of glass and plates breaking. Then I heard dull thuds. Was Daddy hurting the lady? Was she trying to hurt him? Eventually it stopped, and there was silence.

I cried myself to sleep. When I finally woke, Dad was standing over me. "Come on you, you must be hungry. Let's go down and have something to eat," he said with a half-smile. It was starting to get dark by then, but that didn't stop me noticing the huge scratches on Dad's face and neck. I swallowed hard. I had no idea what time it was, but I followed Dad downstairs, reluctantly and cautiously.

He sat me down at a large old wooden kitchen table on a bench in front of a bay window in the large and modern kitchen. He didn't speak and there was no sound of life in the house. I wondered where the woman was. Instinct told me she was there, but out of sight.

Dad boiled the kettle and, without asking me whether I drank tea or not, made me one with three sugars. He placed the mug of hot steaming liquid in front of me and I watched him walk back and forth preparing scrambled eggs on toast. I wondered why Mum and Dad weren't together. I couldn't remember a time when they had been.

Dad put a plate in front of me. "Go on! Tuck in then. It'll put hairs on your chest."

I pondered on this strange statement as I had no idea why he'd want me to put hairs on my chest. Normally, I liked scrambled eggs on toast, but I was in no mood to eat. He sat down to eat his own food and encouraged me to begin. I had no appetite and slowly started to push the food around the plate.

Then a woman walked into the kitchen, ignoring us both. She left after retrieving something from the worktop. It must have been her that Dad had been fighting with. I heard a baby start to cry.

"That's your new baby brother," Dad said, smiling.

We sat in silence eating our food until Dad announced, "I'm going to work tomorrow, and you'll stay here with Sue and Christopher."

I felt light-headed and nausea set in. I felt an all-consuming chill run through my body. I was too scared to ask questions.

"Sue will take you to your new school to meet your teachers and I'll see you in the evening when I get back from work," Dad said matter of factly. "You're living with us now Amanda and we're going to be your family." He said with a nervous smile, like it was supposed to make sense. But nothing made sense to me at that point in my little life.

I nodded in polite agreement. Had I been a bad girl and Mum no longer wanted me? Had Mum left me for good? Would I ever see her and my proper family again? I was too scared and confused to ask.

After tea, Dad took me into the garden. He said he had to lock some of the rabbit cages as it was now getting dark. It was a large square garden separated by four grass areas around a path shaped like a cross that ran up and down and from one side of the garden to another. There was also a perimeter path that surrounded the entire garden, and beyond that borders were filled with flowers, bushes, and trees. A high fence enclosed the entire area.

At the top left-hand side of the garden was a large pond and a huge, majestic willow tree that dipped its branches into the water. On the far-right hand side of the garden was an area full of cages and runs for all my father's animals. The garden was a mass of fruit trees and bushes and with the odd outbuilding, shed, stone statue and a rusty old swing, which was to become a haven for me.

The next morning after Dad had left, I lay in bed listening to my stepmother moving around and talking to her baby. Eventually, she came to my bedroom door and said, "Get dressed and meet me down by the front door." Her voice was cold and harsh, so I quickly got out of bed and looked across at all the bin bags still piled beside my bed.

Having not dressed on my own before, I felt a welling panic. I didn't want to make her angry and I didn't want her to hurt me like she had my dad. I delved into the bag, and the first thing that I found was my favourite dress, the one Grandma had made for me.

I arrived downstairs in the hallway to see her putting her baby in a pushchair. Turning briefly to look at me she said, "Put your coat and shoes on."

Not daring to ask if I could have something to eat, I obeyed. She opened the door and I followed her outside. Once she'd shut the front door and taken the pushchair to the end of the driveway, she turned and looked straight at me.

She seemed so sad. The only other thing I noticed about her physically was her shoulder length, dark brown hair. Something cold and hostile emanated from her. She told me to hold out my hand and promptly gave me a handful of half pence pieces. It was the first time I'd ever been given money.

"This is your dinner money. Don't lose it!" She turned to start walking and threw over her shoulder, "I won't be collecting you after school and I won't be here after today."

I thought she was going to take me to school and leave me there. Apprehension set in and I thought of the story of Hansel and Gretel and the trail of bread in the forest that they used to find their way back home. I needed to do something similar, because otherwise when she left me at school, I'd have no way of finding my way home.

I was proud of my plan. If this sad angry lady was going to leave, perhaps I could get back to Mummy after all. If she wasn't there to look after me, Dad would have to send me back.

I decided to use my dinner money to leave a trail, so I dropped a coin every few steps I walked. We eventually arrived in the playground, and she said dismissively, "Stay here until you hear the bell and then follow the other children." She then turned and walked away.

I stood and watched the children running about, giggling, and laughing. I wanted to be far away from this alien environment and back in the world I knew, but I was fascinated by the excitement and happiness that emanated from these little people all milling about and playing happily with one another. I was temporarily mesmerised by the scene, when I suddenly spotted a girl at the opposite end of the playground wearing a knitted dress exactly like mine! I instantly recognised the pattern and looked down at my own dress. Sure enough, they were identical but mine was blue and hers was peach coloured.

I approached the girl in the peach dress, and she looked at me quizzically.

"Who made your dress for you?" I asked.

She looked down at her dress, realised we matched and smiled at me as she replied, "My grandmother."

12

Maybe last night's prayers had been answered. Grandma had told me that if I prayed my angels would always listen. The girl told me her name was Coral. I thought it was such a pretty name and took an instant liking to her.

When the bell went, teachers came out to collect us and I met my first teacher, Mrs Mustoe. Coral and I were in the same class so found a desk to sit at together. That day we learned to sing *Frère Jacques* and played at shops in the back of the classroom. Coral and I stuck to each other like glue.

That afternoon when school finished, I waited like all the other kids for their parents to collect them. I'd totally forgotten that the sad woman with the baby wouldn't be around to collect me.

"So what's happened to your mummy then?" Mrs Mustoe asked.

"I've only got my daddy now," I said, remembering my stepmother had told me she'd be leaving. I wished my nursery teacher could take me home and keep me there, safe, and warm.

Another teacher came back into the classroom where I sat with Mrs Mustoe and said that they'd tried to call my father, but no one was answering at home. She said they'd have to call the police.

When the police turned up at the school, a policewoman asked me questions. "So why haven't you been collected from school today, Amanda?" she asked.

I explained what had happened when my stepmother announced she was going to take me to school and leave me there.

"So do you know where your father works?"

"No," I said simply and shrugged my shoulders.

"Is everything all right at home, Amanda?"

I told her the truth. I explained what my stepmother had told me that morning and told them everything that had happened since my mother had left me, including the fight I'd heard the night before and how scared I was. They then drove me to my father's house.

When they knocked on the door, he answered. I could see through the hall and into the kitchen and saw a bucket, sponge and half the floor all wet and shiny.

"Sorry I lost all track of time. I was washing the kitchen floor and didn't hear the phone ring," Dad said. "Come in, honey!" he said to me as he gave me a big hug. "Go up to your room and let me just talk to the police and get this all sorted out."

Eventually, Dad came up to see me and sat down with me on the bed.

"Don't worry," he said. "She'll be back in a few days' time. She's just gone to her mother's, but she'll be back."

I didn't want to believe what he was saying.

"From now on though Amanda, don't ever tell anyone our business outside this house again. Do you hear me?"

He didn't seem cross, but his voice was stern and suggestively threatening. I lowered my head in shame and nodded. From that day on, I kept my mouth shut and did as I was told.

For the next few days, my father looked after my every need. He cooked lovely food, took me for walks with his lovely collie dog, Roddy, let me watch television with him and let me help him dig in his garden. He didn't go to work for a few days, and he made me feel cherished and made me laugh at every opportunity.

I met all of Dad's animals: two cats, around twenty rabbits, chickens, ducks, geese, a tortoise, and some fish. We started to bond like a father and daughter should, and I felt a fragment of hope emerging in my new world.

I could see why Mum had loved him as he was very handsome. Feeling very special and chosen, I wished those few days would never end.

About five days later, however, Dad announced, "Now Amanda, I want you to stay in your room until I come back with your stepmother. I'm just going to collect her and bring her and your brother home."

I put my head down and felt sad that the fun would be over with my father, but I nodded to say I understood. Some hours later, I heard a key in the front door. I strained to hear voices and my heart sank as I heard Sue talking to Roddy as he greeted her. I'd started to form a bond with the big shaggy black and white dog that seemed to do nothing but run round in constant circles on the patio in the back garden. This eventually became a metaphor for the repeated cycles of destruction that we all would go through in that house.

That night the air wasn't as tense as it had been before Sue's departure, but Dad was giving all his attention to Sue and Christopher, and I felt excluded. When I made eye contact with

14

Sue, she gave me sinister and threatening looks that sent shivers down my spine.

Dad asked me to spend the evening in my bedroom and I felt confused by his rejection. When the weekend was over and Dad had left for work on Monday morning, Sue arrived at my bedroom door and said in a stern voice, "Get out of bed and get dressed."

She seemed angry with me although I'd heard no arguing that morning so didn't know why. I sensed something was coming, though I had no idea what. She stood with her hands on her hips and started to shout at me, telling me she didn't want to look after me and the only reason I was there was that Mum didn't want me.

"If it wasn't for you, we'd be happy. Your mother doesn't want you because she doesn't love you, so I've been lumbered with you cos you've been dumped here with your father! I've got enough to cope with looking after my own baby. I'm only nineteen and I don't intend to look after someone else's child just cos they can't be bothered!"

I felt tears sting my eyes as she continued to rant at me.

"The only reason I came back here was because your father begged me to but I don't intend to put up with you for long."

I felt terrified and sick. I started to shake and tried desperately to hold back the tears.

"I don't want you here and I have no intention of putting up with someone else's reject. All you've done is cause problems and I'm not prepared to lose my husband and security because of your selfish mother."

Mummy didn't want me anymore because she didn't love me. Pain seared through my heart and tears welled in my eyes. She had abandoned me after all and she was never coming back and to make matters a hundred times worse, Sue hated me and I was an unwanted and inconvenient child.

"You've turned my whole world upside down and because of you your father thinks the sun shines out of your backside. How dare he put you before me and my own son?"

I had no idea what she meant but dared not to ask anything.

"If you think you're going to get away with this you've got another think coming. You're going to pull your weight around this house. I'm not prepared to look after you."

I nodded fearfully as tears began to sting my eyes.

"You're to do everything you're told to do and never, ever tell your father anything about what goes on at home when he's out of the house, let alone anyone else. Do you understand me?" she screamed.

"Yes," I said, petrified by the tone of her voice.

"You are to be good and do as you're told at all times or you'll get punished. Do you understand me?"

"Yes."

I sat and nodded, too scared to do otherwise. I longed for the love and safety of my mother, but I dare not let Sue see my fear and dejection. I swallowed hard to hide my upset, digging my fingernails into the palms of my hands.

Mum had abandoned me because she didn't love me. I wasn't wanted by my stepmother. I had to follow her rules and keep quiet about the daily goings on and, above all, do as I was told. Dad had pretty much told me the same thing about keeping quiet when the police had taken me home that day. All I could do was obey.

Chapter 2

Prayer is more than meditation. In meditation the
source of strength is one's self. When one prays he goes
to a source of strength greater than his own.

Chiang Kai-shek

I learned how to survive very quickly.

Our large, detached house was the only one in our tree-lined road on the outskirts of a moderately busy town in Surrey, fifteen or so miles south of London. From the outside looking in, people would have expected us to be a normal, successful, fully functioning family. My father, an interior designer, worked mainly in Kensington and Mayfair, and spent his weekdays driving to London with his sidekick Paul, whom he belittled at every opportunity.

Dad had a temper and he got what he wanted when he wanted. Working in the beautiful homes of the mega rich, Dad had built his reputation on his perfectionism and attention to detail. Work was in abundance, and Dad's reputation spread, and he had plenty of clients on his waiting list, from Greek tycoons to well-known actors.

During the holidays, Dad took me to work with him to show me what I'd be taking on one day. I hated the hard work as I was always used as another pair of hands for fetching and carrying tools from his van or looking out for the parking meter man. They were notorious around the area, and it was a constant battle to park without getting a ticket.

One of his clients was Joan Sims, the actress best remembered for her roles in the *Carry On* films. She noticed me as a bedraggled, gangly youngster in need of a little TLC. Joan lived in a plush apartment in Kensington.

The first time my father took me to her place to work with him, she was appalled.

"Colin," she said, "What on earth are you doing expecting a young girl like this to work for you? She's not some lackey. She can come and be with me. She certainly looks like she could do with feeding to start with."

My father tried his usual charm, flirting to get his own way, but it didn't wash with her. "She loves to come and work with her old dad," he said, defending himself.

Joan said, "Well, she's coming with me." She took my hand, led me into the kitchen and sat me down to get me something to eat. Dad was cross but he let her take me. Mumbling under her breath she said, "It looks like you've never had a good meal inside you, you poor little poppet."

Later, I got a dressing down for taking advantage of her.

"In future if clients ever question my motives you don't side with them. You're here to help me. Do you understand?" Dad said crossly.

"Yes, Daddy," I said, but I was disappointed I'd probably never be able to have any more time with Joan who'd spoilt me with the delicious food she'd cooked for me and the shopping trip she'd taken me on into Kensington to see the pretty clothes in all the shops. I thought she was my rescuing angel, but Dad wasn't going to give in easily.

That Christmas she brought me some heated rollers. I had no idea how to use them, but it touched me that she'd been so thoughtful.

"Joan, that's far too generous of you," said Dad, "and besides, she's far too young to start doing that sort of thing."

He tried to give her back the present, but she insisted I have it "She's a young girl and one day she'll want to explore her feminine side. What harm is there for her to want to start taking pride in her appearance, Colin?"

I kept the rollers.

Our home was originally three bedrooms to start with, but constantly grew in size and continuous home improvements were the norm throughout my childhood. Not satisfied when he'd completed a project, Dad would soon begin another, so the house was under relentless reconstruction.

We kept ourselves to ourselves. Dad was a successful entrepreneur with an attractive wife and two young children. The walls of our home however hid our house of terror.

Our large garden backed onto a railway line that towered over us on an embankment. I stared into the carriages from my first-floor bedroom window and watched people preparing to get off at the station at the bottom of our road. I longed to be in that world, travelling on that train, anywhere, as far away as possible.

Dad couldn't stand one set of our neighbours. One day he shouted out of our upstairs toilet window, "Oy! There's an elephant got lose in your garden."

He meant the wife who was weeding their garden. The husband came round and knocked on our door. The poor man tried to defend his upset wife who was standing with him on the doorstep, but Dad simply punched him on the nose and said, "Don't you ever set foot near my home again."

Dad said the man was a wannabe policeman as he was only a motorbike courier for the police. Dad had threatened them on a few occasions, so they kept their distance. Though I knew they'd heard my screams on many occasions, they did nothing.

One Sunday afternoon my father walked two doors down to another neighbour with a twelve-bore shotgun and knocked at the man's door. When the man answered, Dad pushed the man so hard he fell back and smashed into a glass table in his hallway. I ran up to Dad to beg him to stop, but he was incensed by a comment the man had made to Sue earlier in the day that implied her children were being abused.

Dad stuck the gun into the man's chest on the floor. "Don't you ever interfere with my family ever again or I'll kill you. Do you hear me?" Then he walked out of the door and shouted at me to get home.

Dad had threatened many of our neighbours on numerous occasions and I began to realise most people would do nothing to cross him. Whenever I saw them in the street, they simply hung their heads. I felt trapped and helpless and wondered if Dad had control over everyone he met.

Apart from being a violent man, he was also an obsessive and a workaholic. If he wasn't working in town he was working on the house or working on our ever increasingly full and bountiful garden of animals, plants, trees, and bushes and eventually, when that wasn't enough, he transformed a quarter of the garden to a vegetable patch.

We spent the summers harvesting and preparing fruit for the winter freezer. It was a laborious task and an added chore to the already huge array of tasks I was given on a daily basis. All the fruit had to be peeled and cored or deseeded, and then cooked down to a stew (which I hated to eat), before being frozen. I sat for hours at a time, peeling apples, and cutting them up whilst Sue put them into a huge cauldron to stew.

Dad's love of breeding small animals grew. He'd started off with the odd chicken and rabbit and built up to a menagerie of small animals, which he bred to sell on. This for me was heaven as I had friends galore. Muscovy ducks and geese enjoyed the pond in the left-hand quadrant of the garden through most of the year. The sound of quacking and splashing was a source of music to my ears amidst the array of different animal noises from pheasants, peacocks, chickens, and cockerels.

I collected feathers from the peacocks that roamed freely and marvelled at their majestic grace and beauty. Our chickens supplied us with a daily basket full of eggs and when they managed to escape, they made me erupt in giggles as I chased them round the garden and back into their pens again.

The rabbits were my favourites as I brushed their fur with my Cindy doll's brush and cuddled them close to my skin. I felt such love and warmth from their little bodies as their innocent eyes always exuded love and I relished being in their company.

Although this was my paradise, it was hell on earth for my stepmother. She despised animals of all sorts as they were dirty and meant work. She didn't like going into the garden and wouldn't clean out their cages or feed them. I was always overjoyed to spend time outside and relieved when thrown out into the garden as punishment.

Whenever my father went to work, Sue would immediately find me and taunt me. "You may think your father loves you, but just remember you're only here because your mother doesn't want you, nor does she care about what happens to you. I'm fed up with him putting you before us. You're nothing and will only ever end up cleaning other people's shit. Now get outside and get those animals fed!" she'd scream at me.

Dad showered me with attention when he was home at the weekend. He was very proud of his little girl. I learned to please him by helping him unload his van at night. I helped him in the garden and was always by his side. And that meant I spent the minimum amount of time with my stepmother.

On Saturdays, I helped Dad to tidy his tools in the garage. Sue rarely came outside the house and Christopher stayed with her indoors, which suited us all. Sunday was a family day. It always ended in a row due to the tension between Dad and Sue. Every Sunday, Dad and I took long walks in the morning with Roddy in the woods. We spent hours there, come rain or shine, and Dad always laughed and joked with me whenever we were out together. It was only then he seemed to be truly happy. Once we were home, anything could tip him over the edge and more often than not, it did.

Come Monday morning, as soon as Dad left for work, Sue visited me in my room. She always started by making comments about how unwanted I was, what a nuisance I'd become and how she hated me for putting her through hell. The more she spoke, the angrier she got, and I just stood and waited for her to finish.

Weekends were my only respite, though she'd catch me if she could if he wasn't around with one of her warnings. "Don't think Daddy can protect you because he's home right now. You wait until he's at work."

I was becoming more and more frightened of her and as the Monday episodes became daily episodes, I found more and more ways to cope, often hiding so I didn't provoke her. She'd usually find me to vent her anger. I tried to pacify her with doing chores before she could ask me to go into the garden to clean out the animals in the hope she'd leave me alone until I could escape to school.

It always started the same.

"Come on daddy's little girl. What're you gonna do now he's not here to protect you? How do you think I feel when he gives you all the attention? He only feels sorry for you cos your mother doesn't want you. She dumped you because you're not wanted and because of her I have to look after you. No one wants you, Amanda and never will. You're nothing and never will be. Now get out and clean up that shit heap of a garden."

She was cruel and spiteful, flicking me and smacking me over the back of my head when I walked past her. Her viciousness began to spiral out of control as she started to hit me more often and with more intensity. It was always the same poison, telling me how I was worthless and would never amount to anything.

She said I'd only be worthy of cleaning up other people's "shit". When she was in an episode, she just lost control until she was completely spent from screaming at me and only when exhausted did she walk away.

From the start, she threatened to beat me with her bare hands if I told my dad what she was doing to me. By the time I was five, she was shouting, slapping, and punching me daily.

She could see the terror building in my eyes on each occasion. She'd say, "I hate you. Because of your mother's selfishness, your father puts you before me and I have enough to deal with having Christopher. Your mother's swanned off with her expensive clothes and fancy job in the city and doesn't give a hoot about you. In fact, no one would notice if you were dead."

And when her voice had risen to a higher level, she'd hit me. The first time this happened, she slapped me continuously on the head, thighs, and upper arms. Then, while screaming, she grabbed my hair and pulled me across the floor. I was caught on the carpet, so she used two hands, grabbing my hair and yanking me until she had leverage, and then she dragged me to a wall.

Holding me by my hair, Sue twisted it round her hand and smacked my head against the wall until she was done. Then she screamed at me to go and clean out the animals. When the physical pain came, it was almost a relief from her painful words. I soon began to learn that on each occasion she abused me, it was only a matter of time before she ran out of steam.

Sometimes the cruelty lasted minutes, more often she could go on for hours. Every day she thought up new ways to torment me. Sue thought up more and more hurtful words and then flew into a fit of rage followed by beating me until she had purged her anger.

Her favourite punishment was hearing me scream with agony as she pulled me along the floor as my hair came out in chunks. Some days she beat my head with her fists and then smashed my head against the floor over and over, finishing by kicking me savagely in my back, stomach, and legs. I held my breath as the searing pain came and each time I hoped I would survive.

When she was done, she sent me to my bedroom and I crawled into a corner with Bunny, crying and praying for rescue. My angels (that I'd discovered at the age of three) were all I had. I begged them repeatedly to save me and prayed to have their protection and to be back with my mother's family where I was safe.

Christopher had fallen into the pond once and I'd dived in and dragged him out. He was only around three or four years old at the time. In her panic, she took him into the house once I'd explained what had happened and she slammed the door in my face. I waited for my punishment, and she eventually came out with Christopher, now dressed in dry clothes, came over to me on the swing and hugged me. I was shocked. She thanked me for saving his life and let me go out with them to the park that day. It was the only time throughout my entire childhood that she ever showed me any affection or kindness.

I often heard Dad and Sue arguing and I knew I'd get it harder if they'd fought. When Dad came home from work, he never knew what he was coming home to. One time he arrived home and she'd not done any of the paperwork he needed for the next day.

"What the fuck have you been doing all day, you lazy bitch?" he yelled at her. "All you do is sit on your fat arse watching crap TV with your son. What the hell do you think I've been doing all day?"

Sue screamed back at him. "Looking after your daughter your selfish bitch of an ex-wife dumped on me."

Dad launched at her and punched her over and over in the head, holding her down by her hair. I watched in terror.

Sue often screamed at Dad about how much she hated her life. "I hate this house. I hate your stinking animals and all the work I have to do and more than anything hate having to look after your unwanted child!"

It only riled him more.

"This wasn't the life you promised me," she complained.

"You're nothing but a selfish lazy bitch and don't deserve anything considering what you've turned out to be!"

Dad expected her to run the home and do his paperwork, and although she often made me do the majority of the chores, he'd come home to see she'd not done any of the work tasks he'd set her.

He had no idea I did most of the work in the house and garden, as Sue told him she did it all. Instead, she sat watching daytime television or having her friends over. If Dad thought the house wasn't clean enough, he'd tell Sue off but the next day she'd take it out on me. The harder I worked, the more she gave me to do.

By the time I was eight, I had to feed most of the animals and clean out their cages before school. Whatever the weather, I washed down the patio to clear up all the dog faeces with Jeyes Fluid. I hated the smell as it clung to my school uniform all day and the other kids would notice and make jibes saying to me, "Look, Amanda's wet herself again. She smells disgusting." I often went to school soaked and cold.

I hated it even more in the winter, as I had to go outside in just my school uniform with no coat even when it was icy and below freezing. Sue took ritualistic and sadistic pleasure in conjuring up ways to add to my torture. I would be outside feeding and cleaning all the animals with an empty stomach whilst I could clearly see her and Christopher having breakfast in the kitchen in the warm.

On a few occasions she left me breakfast. I ate it if I could stomach it but if I couldn't she seemed to relish in forcing me to eat it. She made me eat raw eggs or Weetabix soaked in water or just left it dry in a bowl. She stood over me and smacked the back of my head if I retched.

"Eat your breakfast, you ungrateful child," she said to me on these occasions. I tried to avoid asking for food and dragged out my jobs for as long as possible before it was time to go to school.

After school, I prepared the vegetables for dinner and then set about doing the housework. If I was lucky, she allowed me to use the hoover. Because Christopher was allowed to watch television and she didn't want me to make any noise, she handed me a dustpan and made me start from one end of a room and work my way to the other, picking up every speck of dirt with my fingers.

Our lounge had been extended and was a double sized room. Sometimes it took me as long as two hours to pick up every speck, but if she wasn't satisfied, she made me start over again.

"You haven't touched this room!" she bellowed at me, even though I showed her the dustpan full of fluff. She knocked it out of my hand and screamed at me, "Do it all again and this time I want to see this carpet spotless. Do you hear me?"

I learned in the early days to do everything as thoroughly as possible to appease her. She'd make me wash windows, woodwork, and the insides of all the cupboards and drawers to keep me working long after I'd done all my regular chores. It started to become harder and harder to keep up with my schoolwork.

School holidays were torture and I hated them, especially the summer holidays. Whilst most of my friends were off playing and enjoying time with their parents, I had to do a thorough and gruelling clean of the house daily. I particularly loathed cleaning the woodwork. The staircase was the hardest, as I had to painstakingly wash down and scrub every spindle, making sure I didn't miss a mark.

Whilst I'd learned how to appease the monsters in the house it was the only way I could keep strong to survive. Books became a way of losing myself. Dad had a library of books and I poured over encyclopaedias, reference books and atlases and his African medical book. I knew Dad had lived in Kenya before I was born, as our house was full of African artefacts. I longed for the day I could live in another country, far away from the savage battles between my father and stepmother and the fallout that I received as their punching bag.

When I'd first arrived at that house I found security in my dolls, toys, and books, but my belongings soon began to go missing. Eventually, all I had was a few books left with pages missing, torn, or sabotaged with permanent marker pens. The toys I could handle but my books were my escape to another realm of safety and happiness.

Sue's mother was a traveller who'd settled in a council house. Sue, the eldest of five children, all with different fathers, was ambitious and nothing like her siblings. Dad had little respect for Sue's mother and had no qualms about letting her know. I heard him say to her, "All you are is a ponce on society. You're lazy and I can certainly see where your daughter gets it from."

Sue's mother tried to lash out at my father, and I witnessed him punch her full in the face on one occasion. She dropped to the floor and then he walked out with me scurrying behind him, terrified.

On one of our trips to Sue's mother's house, I found some of my toys and dolls. That's when I realised that Sue had been giving my precious possessions to her brothers and sisters. Dad certainly wouldn't have done it. If I got new clothes or toys from Mum when I visited her on rare occasions, they soon disappeared. I quickly learned not to get too tied to anything.

Dad often reminded Sue of how lucky she was and heard him often in arguments shout at her, "If it wasn't for me you'd still be in the gutter where I found you. Your life would be nothing without me so don't you ever forget."

There was a love hate relationship between Sue and her mother. The only time I saw Sue show fear was when she was in her presence. I felt sorry for Sue, though I didn't understand why considering her behaviour towards me. Her mother disowned her once saying she'd sold out to better her life.

"You've sold out to us, Susan and you'll have to accept the consequences. If you think you're better than us, then you don't need us."

We didn't see her mother again throughout my childhood.

While Sue was in her own inner turmoil and dysfunctional world, she couldn't take my garden or the animals away from me and she couldn't take my father's books either. These were my solace. She did sometimes sabotage his books and told him I'd torn the pages. When he questioned me, I would plead with him I hadn't, but invariably he would think it was me and then I'd be asked what punishment I wanted. As if that made it any better.

Dad showed his authority through punishment. If I did anything that didn't comply with what he wanted, he felt it was necessary for me to undergo a beating so I would learn. Sue found numerous ways of getting me into trouble with my father so that I would get double punishment from him or her.

His choice of punishment was with a large cane, a stick, a large wooden ruler, a belt or his open hand. I could choose. He'd push me to make a decision, or he would decide himself if I was too petrified to answer him. Regardless of what I chose, he used each weapon until I bled. The first time was an immensely terrifying shock and I thought I was going to die.

"Amanda, I've told you to choose so just get on with it and it'll be done with," he said.

I pleaded for him not to hurt me.

"Right, OK. I'll choose," he would say and frogmarch me to my room.

"Pull your pants down and lay face down on your bed."

"No, Dad, please don't hurt me."

He yanked my pants down and despite me begging for mercy and the screams of terror that came from me for what was to come, he ignored me, too fuelled by his own fury and pushed me face down onto the bed, pulled up my skirt and started to whack me on my buttocks. I screamed, terrified by the searing pain. Without even taking a breath, he came down hard with another lash. He whacked me on the same spot ten times, and when he was done, he simply said, "Now, perhaps you'll learn by this and in future behave."

And then he left the room.

Mostly he hit my open hand, repeatedly whipping me over the same spot until a wheal appeared and eventually the skin broke. When he beat me on my bottom and thighs, I found it

26

difficult to sit for days. After he beat me in the house, he always made me stay in my room. I began to hate my room.

No-one ever spoke about the punishments. After I'd been beaten, I was called down for dinner and had to sit with Dad and Sue and watch TV as if nothing had happened.

Harder still was trying to swallow the foul-tasting food I was served. My father's fascination at living off the land extended to skinning and gutting our rabbits and invariably they ended up, bones and all, in a stew with our garden vegetables. I hated the smell, and it made me heave to taste the flesh of my dead friends, but this infuriated Dad. He made me sit for up to three hours until most of my food had gone. I retched at every mouthful.

"You should be grateful to eat from what I've produced. Not many children get to eat fresh food, you know," he would say.

Winters were harder to bear as Sue rarely let me wear warm clothes. When I was sent out into the garden, I sat huddled in the shed where all the animal feed was stored to keep warm. Dad often threw stale bread out to our animals – a bonus to me as I could eat it. When there was no bread, there was nothing to eat unless I could sneak into the fridge when Sue went out. She didn't often leave me alone in the house and sneaking food was risky.

"Have you been in the fridge?" she asked one day.

"No." I said protesting my innocence.

"You little liar, you. I know you've stolen food. How dare you."

And then she beat me, even though I hadn't taken anything. I learned it wasn't worth the risk.

Sue took great pleasure from making me climb into scalding baths. I was too frightened to complain, so I bit my lip and endured it as long as I could. If she felt I hadn't suffered enough, she set about me with her fists. One day she dragged me out of the bathroom, tearing at my hair and dragging me around naked to humiliate me. Every opportunity she had to humiliate me, she took.

I was constantly at her beck and call. I didn't mind looking after Christopher, in fact, I loved it as I was able to give him all the attention she didn't. I read him stories and made the most of playing with him as I got to play with his toys and read his books.

As I got older, Sue's cruelty increased. She locked me outside for longer and longer hours in extreme cold conditions or starved me for longer periods. I wrapped myself in Dad's dust sheets that were stored in the garden shed and stole food whenever I could, careful not to get caught.

Every time I was beaten, I wondered if I would survive or if she would lose it completely and someone would eventually find my broken body and the truth would finally be revealed. But I was never to have that mercy bestowed upon me, despite begging for it to end. Death seemed my only escape and I prayed daily for the end to my harrowing daily nightmare that I lived.

I wasn't allowed to play at friend's houses, unless Dad was at home, and very few came to mine, but my best friend Coral and a few of my very dearest friends knew of my situation at home. Some of their parents knew what was happening, but my friends told them not to say anything or it would be worse for me, so everyone kept quiet.

I prayed someone would tell the police or report Dad and Sue, but the neighbours were fearful of my father and didn't dare provoke him. They must have heard the screams, the terrified gurgling and my calling for help, but no one came. No one ever dared.

When Dad and Sue rowed, it eventually became a fight leading to him punching her and meant I'd get it twice as bad.

"It's all because of your precious daughter we're like this." I heard her scream over and over.

"If you touch her, I'll kill you with my bare hands!" he would respond, and he hurt her more, each time getting more brutal than the last.

My faith in my angels grew as I got older. I prayed every night and was left little messages during the day to let me know they were there with me. I couldn't have survived without them. The only reason I was alive I believe, was because of my prayers.

I prayed every night and begged my angels to let me go and live with my mother, but the moments of seeing her were too few and far between. Every weekend I spent with her, all it did was reaffirm my panic and terror toward the lead up to my return to the house of horror. Every weekend I spent with her, it got worse and all it did was make her became more resistant to my pain.

My mother and father were completely different. She was warm and generous, an outgoing, confident woman, and she had an awesome power no man could match. I never heard her say a cross word. She always maintained such dignity and command over any situation.

"Guess what we've got planned for you this weekend, sweetheart. We're going to all your favourite places and you're going to get some super treats."

When I had the chance to stay with my mother, I was collected on a Friday, and whisked into London to eat at a swish restaurant surrounded by my mother's friends. Saturdays and Sundays were always much the same. We shopped for clothes or spent time in a box at some racecourse, starting with a champagne breakfast, which led onto a champagne lunch before the day ended with afternoon tea and more champagne. We spent Saturday evenings at a restaurant until the early hours. Alcohol, food, and money flowed freely, and I was in awe of the bubble I was in for those few days of complete and utter indulgence which was the absolute opposite to my everyday life. This only happened when Dad would let me go though. Sometimes, it was as rare as every six months.

Sundays were often quiet as Mum and Brian, her new long-term partner worked off their hangovers and read the newspapers. The only relief was that she finally had stability with one man, as I'd met numerous men who seemed to resent her having a young child around, so I relished the peace and quiet they wanted and spent my time drawing and colouring. Mum's new man, Brian, was as generous as she was and had told me once when we were in her lavish office that Brian had pursued her after seeing her photograph in a national newspaper.

"Why were you in the newspaper, Mum?" I asked.

"It was an article about me being the tenth highest paid businesswoman in the country," she replied nonchalantly and showed me the article proudly.

I was amazed at how casually she mentioned it and wondered if she felt shame about how she'd put her career before her own child. I already knew she was important in the public relations world as her colleagues adored her and she commanded such respect from them all. To top it off, she was gorgeous. She had legs up to her armpits and the face of an angel. And although she ignored my cries of mercy to have her rescue me, she was my mother and to me she was beautiful inside and out. She reminded me of Jennifer Hart out of *Hart to Hart*, my favourite programme at the time. She always dressed to impress with amazing suits and high heels and was the envy of women and men alike. I fantasised that one day I would be with her and then become just like her.

Her PA, Irene, was like a Barbara Windsor clone. She was lovely and funny and always wore bras that were far too small to make her cleavage stand out more. One Christmas Mum bought Irene a present as a joke – a leather-bound chequebook holder with *Poor Sod* on it as Irene always commented on how poor she was. Irene saw the humour behind it as Mum had one herself, but her engraving on hers was *Rich Bitch*.

Yes, she was rich, but she was the loveliest person in the world to me and everyone who knew her. Her sense of humour captivated people and wherever Mum was, there was laughter. She was everything I yearned to be.

In the early days I told Mum what was going on at home in the hope she'd not make me return to my father. "Please Mum, don't take me back home. Sue hurts me every day and Dad beats me if I'm naughty," I cried to Mum.

She cried, too, but replied, "I can't take you back sweetheart. Your father would be furious with me and I'd never be able to see you again."

Whenever I begged her to let me live with her, she pacified me by saying, "Darling, I can't upset your dad. One day soon you'll be able to live with me, I promise."

I got it into my head that when I was eight, I would be with my mum, so every time I was with her, I counted the months, weeks, days and hours and relished the time we shared together until eventually I would be returned to her. When I turned eight, I realised my hopes though had been for nothing.

"Mum, I'm eight years old and you promised me I would be able to come home," I cried to her.

"Darling, I tried to talk to your father but he's adamant you're not to leave until you're an adult. There's nothing I can do about it."

My dreams were shattered from that moment. I couldn't bear to think of having to live another ten years under the same roof as my father and stepmother.

"You're going to have another brother or sister." Dad announced shortly after that weekend. I prayed for a girl and when Maria was born, she was an absolute joy. All I'd known up to then was my brother who was nice to me when he wanted to play, but he was becoming brutal like Sue when she egged him on. It wasn't his fault as Christopher was just appeasing her in his own attempt to survive, but she began to entice him into her sadistic rituals to ridicule me. Christopher sometimes told tales on me, blaming me for something he'd done. I knew he was scared of her, as sometimes she'd beaten him, but not often. The threat was always there though. Sometimes, Sue and Dad argued about whether Christopher was his child.

"Why the hell has he got blond hair and blue eyes when both you and I are dark?" he asked Sue one day.

"How the hell should I know?" she replied.

The only person my father liked in Sue's family was her grandmother. Sue behaved when she was around, so we sometimes had her to stay. One night when my father was at a boxing match at the Albert Hall, I sat on the staircase listening to Sue talking to her grandmother in the living room.

"I can't take any more, Gran. He treats me like I'm scum and like he's doing me some favour."

"I've told you this before, Susan. You're luckier than you realise. Look at your mother and your sisters and brother. You have so much, and you still bicker on about wanting more. You watch it, my girl. He may just call your bluff and then what would you do?"

"Gran, I have no idea what to do! I know it was ridiculous seeing Colin and that other guy at the same time, but I didn't know for sure whose baby it was. I knew Colin would offer me a much better life, but it just hasn't turned out the way that it should. What the hell do I do now?"

"Well you've pretty much made your bed now, so you've just got to darn well lie in it, girl. Just remember, Colin will give you the life you could never have possibly had so hold on to him and just let this go. Christopher is his, so just accept it."

I crept back to bed and hoped they hadn't heard me.

One night I heard Dad shout at Sue, "I told you I didn't want any more children. I know damn well why you've done it, to secure what you know you could lose."

She screamed, "If you try to get rid of me Colin, I'll take you to the cleaners and take everything you've got, and you know it."

Three years later, Sue fell pregnant again with Sarah. Soon after that, I heard my father yell at her, "Amanda comes first in the pecking order in this family, then my dogs, my other children and lastly you."

Sue never let me forget that one, as she ramped up her punishments.

Roddy died when I was around the age of about nine. That was the first time I saw Dad cry as he buried his beloved dog in the garden. When he came into the house, Sue was in the kitchen and from my bedroom I heard him shout at her "You evil bitch. You know damn well the reason he's dead is because you beat him."

She yelled back, "I don't know what you're talking about. How the hell is it my fault?"

"You never loved that dog, and you were always jealous I gave him more attention than you. He was loyal and loving and you're just cold and callous and evil."

Dad nearly killed her that morning. Then one day he announced to me, "I'm getting us some new dogs so they can look after us. Your dad has a lot to protect now so you won't have to worry, we'll be safe."

He chose two dogs that could look after themselves. I knew that they would turn on her if she tried anything as they were hunting dogs, a pair of Rhodesian Ridgebacks, bought to guard us. Sue hated them even more than Roddy. These were tough hunting dogs from the wilds of Africa used for hunting down lions in packs of six. However, they had a unique intuitive connection to children and were very protective.

Sue starved them when Dad wasn't around, and she locked them away in the downstairs toilet. I never saw her dare hit them though. One day Pete, the eldest, was left alone with Maria whilst she was teething, and she bit through his ear. He ended up with five stitches, but he never batted an eyelid. I was impressed by his loyalty and protectiveness towards our family despite how Sue treated them.

As I got older, I realised I had a mind of my own and I wanted to make my own decisions. I was a young teenager when I decided to run away from home. It was harvest festival time at school and we'd been asked to take in tins to donate to charities for the elderly. Armed with several tins of spam, tomatoes and soup that were out of date, I decided to take the opportunity to run away.

I didn't turn up for school that day and the school phoned home to report me missing. Sue eventually found me walking along the roadside at a local walker's spot after my teachers questioned Coral and found out where I was heading. I was cross with Coral for betraying my trust, but realised she didn't want me to be homeless. That night Sue relished in the beating my father gave me. He didn't once ask why I'd run away, but he told me if I ever tried again, I'd suffer more.

I made several attempts further after that to leave the house of hell.

As Sue had three children to look after now, she wasn't prepared to let me go. My chores had quadrupled as I nursed babies, washed, and ironed clothes, fed and bathed the children and still had to clean the house and garden and prepare food for the evenings. Her children were allowed to be kids, while I was a responsible little person with a multitude of duties. They got to watch children's TV and play. Unless I was looking after them, I didn't get to indulge in anything that allowed me to be a child. They had tea after school, sandwiches, and cakes, while I cleared out animal hutches or did chores which were never ending until my father came home from work at night.

I imagined I was Cinderella and loved reading Hans Christian Andersen's fairy tales to my brother and sisters. I thought that one day I'd meet my handsome prince so I could live happily ever after. I believed that when I was old enough, the boy of my dreams would whisk me away and my life would become beautiful.

Drawing and reading allowed me to immerse myself in my imaginary world. I spent hours creating beautiful pictures and reading stories. I had no toys so when I played with my little sisters I made the most of dressing dolls.

One Christmas when Maria was about five, all the family were round at ours. Uncles, aunts, cousins, and Nan as the head of the family, had come to enjoy the festive season. We'd all sat down to eat, excited to be together. My cousins and I were very close. There was much laughter and excitement that day and constant giggling between Claire and I (who were more like sisters). Often we got told off for irritating the adults with our constant laughing over every little thing! But that day everyone was on top form.

We all prepared to tuck into our Christmas meal when Nan suddenly piped up, "Oh, I haven't got a knife and fork!"

Sue looked at Maria and said, "I thought you laid the knives and forks. Why didn't you lay some for Nana?"

Maria innocently said, "Well you said she ate like a horse, so I didn't think she needed them, Mummy!"

Silence spread through the room and after what seemed like an eternity of silence as we all held our breath, Dad blew his top and banished Sue from the meal. That day was the best Christmas Day we ever had as Sue spent the entire rest of that day in her bedroom whilst us kids played and laughed and made the most of every moment of freedom.

As the years went on, Dad and Sue's fighting became worse. One day I saw him take her by the hair and drag her across the floor, threatening to kill her with his fist in her face.

"You think you can hurt me you fucking bitch. I know what you're doing, and I won't let you destroy me. If you ever fucking hurt my child or my dogs, you will not survive. Do you understand me?"

She fought back with fists, hands and teeth, and Dad kicked and punched her until she was motionless, curled up in a ball on the floor.

That was the first time I realised he was aware that she was abusing me.

Chapter 3

If you cannot get rid of the family skeleton, you may as well make it dance.

George Bernard Shaw

Once I was at secondary school, I realised that my family was far from the norm. Perhaps I wasn't to blame after all.

I watched other girls rebel against their teachers and saw how this seemed to give them power, especially popular girls like Paula. She always had a smart answer for everything. Up to that point I'd been a very good girl, just like I'd been taught. But I realised there was a way of taking back the power that had been stripped from me at home.

Having four children in the house tested Sue beyond her limitations, but I did all my chores and went beyond, asking her constantly if there was anything I could do to help. This helped to appease her and while I was working for her, she left me alone.

In the strangest way I'd learned to cope with her volatile behaviour by loving her and feeling pity for her. She was after all a mother, and I felt for her when I saw her hold her children close and wished she'd love me like she loved them. I still felt love for her as I knew it was my only hope of staying alive.

Dad was working harder than ever as his business was growing. Whenever he and Sue argued, Dad told her she'd be out on her ear if she threatened his empire or those he cared about. She'd always respond that she'd take him to the cleaners if he tried.

He was even bold enough to rub her nose in it by goading her when he was on his way out to meet some other woman. As he became more successful, he'd often disappear, suited and booted in his tux or his masonic regalia.

Dad always wore a gold signet ring with a diamond in the shape of a star. He told me it was a King Solomon signet ring which brought him great power and because he was a thirty-three-degree mason I would always be protected. I had no idea what that meant but hoped he was right. His social network was broadening, and he had friends in high places, including a beautiful woman he was besotted with who he claimed was from a very wealthy Indian family.

She was exotic looking and sometimes my father would take me to see her in her palatial surroundings. I knew she was far wealthier than anyone Dad had ever known. Her sitting room was adorned with solid gold elephant ornaments the size of my father's dogs and she always wore huge diamond necklaces, bracelets and rings and beautiful traditional silk clothes.

Her name was Yvonne. Her British father had passed away some years before, but her mother, a short and very warm and friendly Indian woman, was often there when I went to see her with Dad, and it was obvious they both adored and respected him.

"Dearest Amanda," Yvonne would say when we arrived. "Colin, your daughter is getting more beautiful by the day. I do hope you're looking after her well."

Dad was constantly at functions with important people. It was becoming the norm for him to go out on many nights and weekends. As I made the most of my time with him watching him shave and dress for an evening event, he would talk to me about where he was going.

"You watch your old dad tonight. I'm at a boxing match at the Albert Hall and there'll be a lot of important people there so watch out for your dad as I'll be in the front row."

I hardly ever got to watch TV when Dad wasn't around so knew I'd never get the chance to see him. When he questioned me the following day I said, "Sorry Dad, I was too tired to stay up and had to go to bed early."

I was always making excuses to cover up for why I couldn't do the things he thought I would be doing in his absence from the house.

When I was eight, Dad sat me down with the family for a meeting.

"We've just been informed by our accountant, we are finally millionaires," he told us proudly.

I thought he was going to tell us something positive that would change my situation. It certainly wasn't going to improve my life and I felt disappointed and disheartened more than anything.

Although Dad was teaching me to achieve great success in life, it conflicted greatly with his proclaimed spiritual ethos. It smacked hypocrisy with his great proclamation of wisdom to me that he constantly reminded me of - "It's not what I gave you, it's what I taught you that counts!"

I felt disturbed by this statement as I felt all he was really teaching me was that you should take anything you want in life and bugger the cost to others.

As I got older, and he got richer, every Saturday we all got dressed up and drove up to London, to Harrods, Peter Jones and Selfridges, Dad's favourite stores. I loved our trips to London and said to Dad that when I grew up I wanted to be a window dresser. I was in awe of the beautiful displays in the windows, especially at Christmas.

He replied tautly, "Don't be so bloody stupid. You'll never become a millionaire like your dad dressing fucking dolls!"

Dad developed a fascination for collecting silver and filled three huge cabinets in our living room with beautiful and unusual pieces of every kind. He also collected antique pieces of furniture which we travelled all over the country to collect and his appetite grew more and more for beautiful material things. He felt a desire for handmade cut crystal which he spotted one day in Selfridges and bought boxes of it by the dozen.

Every time Sue threw them at him, he went and bought another dozen to replace them. Dad didn't buy things in singular. When he bought china dolls, he bought every one he could find in the collection. They, like the crystal, ended up one by one in pieces in the kitchen bin. We would often go to Saville Row for his suits and shirts, and I spent many weekends watching him satisfy his desire for beautiful things.

As his increasingly glutinous lifestyle changed, so did his drinking. Dad drank the best scotch and smoked the best cigars – every night. I felt uncomfortable as he got louder and crasser. I was a young developing teenager and he'd started making suggestive comments. I tried to avoid being around him at night when he drank. After plenty of whisky he would often remark, "Come and sit with your father now. Come on. Tell me all about your love life. Have you got a boyfriend yet? I can see the boys must be giving you the eye now!"

He wouldn't let me go up to my room. Instead, he made me sit with him on the sofa and watch TV whilst he drank. As he got drunk, so he got lewder. "So, now you're wearing your teenage bra, have you got the boys sniffing round you yet?" he would say in a suggestive way. I hated his comments.

His insatiable appetite for life included deep sea diving or water skiing on his V8 engine power boat every weekend. We spent most of the summer down at the coast whilst he went diving on wrecks with his new diving buddies. Even his boat was a status symbol having belonged to a client which he'd acquired as part payment for a job. As it had been used in British power boat racing it was adorned with a huge Union Jack on the front. To me it was just another one of my father's statements to show his ego infused drive to show his wealth and status.

We were always on some adventure or another to satisfy my father's insatiable lust for life and anything he could acquire along the way; he would take ownership of if he wanted it.

The more he earned, the more he consumed. He'd drink a bottle of scotch or brandy in a night and the evenings would often end in a drunken row between Sue and Dad while the rest of us took refuge in our bedrooms.

I felt protective of my younger step siblings. Sue sometimes lost control with Christopher every now and then over his bed wetting which he still did up to about the age of eleven. She would beat him if he'd wet the bed and scream at him how vile and dirty he was. She never touched the girls though.

My faith in my angels got me through and I felt it was only down to them that I was still alive. It was during the darkest times I felt them closest. In my cold dark bedroom, I cowered in the corner behind a curtain. There, I prayed to my angels and told them how afraid I was and how I wished to be with my mother. I felt as if someone was hugging me, as if huge wings were wrapped around me and gently cradling me. Often, I heard voices gently reassuring me that everything would be OK. *Amanda, we're protecting you and everything will be OK. Please trust us and know we'll get you through this.*

I'd thought as a young child the abuse would last a few months and then I'd be yanked out of my hell. As it continued the voices reassured me. *Amanda, we're with you every moment of every day and that's how you get through. You will understand one day just how much but you have to trust us and know you're stronger than you think, and everything will change. Please trust us.*

I had no idea who "us" was, but I knew they were my only true friends.

I'd stopped telling Mum about Sue's behaviour as she had buried her head in the sand completely. She couldn't deal with it and despite me begging her to take me away from my abusive nightmare, she would always say she was powerless. I didn't believe her but wanted to as it was all I could hold onto.

Weekends were an opportunity for my mother to repent as she included things that she felt I would love to appease me. We went to pantomimes at Christmas, *Skating on Ice* shows and theatre trips. For me it was it was an incredible feeling of escapism and fantasy to be with two adults having as much fun as I was. While my mother knew the truth of my real life, I suspected she hadn't ever dared reveal what I went through to Brian. I knew Brian would have rescued me instantly and would have threatened their relationship with him knowing the truth, but I felt a ridiculous loyalty towards my mother to keep our sordid secret, to protect her from the shame of it. And so the secrets, lies and abuse continued.

Whilst I was with my Mum and Brian, I fantasised that we were a family and lived together. We still regularly went to eat in beautiful restaurants at weekends and went racing and sometimes I was allowed to go on holiday with them – which was the icing on the cake for me.

We went to grand hotels or resorts in beautiful locations in Spain or Gran Canarias. We'd stay at Five Star hotels where I could have anything I wanted and eat everything I desired. It was bliss. Mum and Brian spent their days around the pool drinking cocktails and I had a pool to swim in. Life was fun on those holidays, and I could have anything I wanted, so I made the most of it.

By sixteen I was almost at breaking point as I had held on in the hope that I'd one day go to live with my mother which she'd continuously promised me and never honoured. I was heartbroken when Mum again said it still wasn't possible and I felt an all-consuming rage that I'd held on for nothing after 13 years of hope of escaping, realising I'd been duped and deceived year after year, for nothing.

One day, when I was begging her for an explanation as to why she wasn't letting me come to live with her, she announced "I thought your father would let you come and live with me, but he won't let you leave until you're married."

I was sixteen and there was no hope for me anymore, so I started to rebel. What the hell had I got to lose? I started to sneak out of the house to meet my friends. My best friend Paula introduced me to smoking and although I hated it, it gave me power over Dad who detested it and had said he would kill me if he ever found me smoking. I learned to be careful. Dad had told me a long time before, "If you're going to do anything naughty, make sure you don't get caught." And even though it was figurative and was the rules he lived by alone, he had made it clear that I was never to behave like him, or I would know about it. And that meant punishment.

He'd often beaten me if he thought I'd been dishonest, even if I hadn't. I however, was beyond caring about what punishment I would receive by the latter years of my childhood. If I disobeyed, I was punished. If I was good, Sue abused me anyhow. There was no respite, so I found ways to grab the moments of freedom that I could to hold onto what little power I had left in me.

One day my friends and I shut ourselves in the upstairs girl's cupboard, on the first floor, inside the toilets in our school. It was sports day and Paula, Katy and I decided to go and have a cigarette after double needlework whilst everyone was running about getting ready for Sports Day.

"Come on," Paula said. "Everyone will be out on the field, so we won't even get noticed."

And so we'd sneaked into the cupboard with only fifteen minutes to spare until we had to get to double maths which we all hated. To our shock and disbelief, we heard the caretaker come into the toilets. We crouched down to hide among the boxes of loo rolls and heard him turn the lock in the door and walk straight back out again. Panicked, Katy tried to jump up and alert him to us being in there, but Paula grabbed her and covered her mouth. As we heard it go quiet, Katy erupted into tears of panic and claustrophobia.

We were locked in that cupboard for almost two hours and managed to get through a packet of ten B&H, finished off the tapestries we'd started earlier in needlework that morning, burst two water pipes climbing down through a grate to the downstairs boy's cloakroom cupboard and flooded most of the entire ground floor of the school.

We were greeted by our headmaster, at the door of the downstairs cupboard in the boy's toilets when eventually the caretaker turned up with the key. We'd managed to climb down into the cupboard below but in doing so had caused utter carnage. We were sent home with letters to each of our parents with a list of all the damage and repairs necessary and a stern addressing of how punishment will be left to the discretion of our parents. We were petrified. I told Katy and Paula I'd have to run away.

I phoned Mum from a phone box and begged her one more time to let me come and live with her, but she told me I had to go home. I loathed to but did as she requested and waited until Dad had got home, unloaded his van, and had his evening meal. I even waited until he'd had a few drinks. Eventually, when I couldn't take the suspense any longer, I handed him the letter. By then he was enormously drunk.

He read it and looked up at me with his eyes reddened from too much alcohol and said with a slurred voice "Go to bed. I think you've probably gone through enough with the school and hope you've learned from this."

I ran to my room before he changed his mind. I have no idea to this day why on earth I went unpunished. All I felt was that somehow my angels had protected me as I should have had the beating of my life and may well have never survived.

Chapter 4

I just wish I could understand my father.

Michael Jackson

I idolised my father because of what he'd achieved and how charismatic he was. He told me constantly that I was his number one.

It was hard to believe I was his special girl when I was getting a beating on a regular basis by him and my stepmother and conflicted with what he did to make me feel cherished. He often referred to me as his son. I didn't always mind, but it sometimes grated on me. He even nicknamed me *Bwana* which he told me meant "slave master" in South Africa. I had no idea why.

I followed him everywhere and took every opportunity I could to go to work with him during the school holidays. When I was stuck at home with Sue, I was the only child waiting by the front door when he came home at night. I helped him unload his van, made us both a mug of tea, and then ventured out into our garden for our evening stroll.

I walked proudly by his side as he surveyed his crops and animals, the plants he'd lovingly grown, the seeds he'd sown and all the hard work we'd put into it. I listened to him eagerly as he made notes to himself, telling me what he needed to tackle in the garden in the upcoming days and weeks, and I relished being his personal assistant and privy to his passion and love of nature.

We sometimes got carried away, especially in the summer, doing small jobs around the garden tending to plants and shrubs until it was time to go in for dinner. He was forever changing the garden layout. He would transform parts of the garden into an allotment and for growing vegetables, and bring in more and more animals, building runs for dozens of pheasants or chickens at a time. Life was never dull. It was always changing, and I was constantly in awe of this man with his insatiable appetite for life.

One day, I was going through the loft and found a chest. I opened it to discover a vast treasure of medals and cups and discovered Dad had gained medals for boxing, running and martial arts as well as pictures of him, including articles in saved newspaper clippings. I also found a letter from the Queen for outstanding bravery when faced with two burglars in our home.

I asked my mother about what I'd discovered. I wondered why Dad had hidden them away and was worried he'd be cross with me for finding them. Mum told me he'd been pulled out of the army due to his extraordinary sprinting speed and placed with an athletics team to train at Mitcham Athletics Club. During a judo competition, he'd broken his ankle and lost his big chance to run for his country in the Olympics. I felt sad for him and wondered if it was why he drove my brother and me so hard in our own training.

Dad had made Christopher become a sprinter. When I went to watch Christopher train at Crystal Palace, the young girls of his age looked like little old women. Dad didn't bat an eyelid. At that time Steve Ovett and Sebastian Coe, both Olympic gold medallists, were training at Christopher's club. This fuelled Dad's ambitions. When Christopher was about nine, our family doctor told my father if he continued to push my brother, it would do him irreparable damage. Christopher was training so hard he was getting severe growing pains as his muscles were developing far too quickly.

My father had ambitions for me too. I'd learned to swim when I was five. We'd been to Brighton for the day and Dad had taken me into the sea near the pier, all the way to the end of it. I remember it towering down over me. I clung to his neck and wrapped my legs around him, frightened of the huge vortex of water being sucked forcefully around the great struts that supported the pier.

Without warning, he took me off his back and told me I was going to swim back. I panicked. I'd never swum before and went straight under. Dad pulled me up and shouted at me. "Come on, Amanda. Show your dad you can swim."

I must have drunk half the sea water that day as I went under and forced myself back to the surface, doggy paddled a few strokes, then went under again and again. I made it eventually to the beach, exhausted, frightened, and relieved.

As soon as we got to the beach, Dad made us pack up our things and insisted we drove straight to Cheam swimming baths back in Surrey where he booked me into a swimming club and made me go into the pool for my first swimming lesson that afternoon.

From then on, I was in swimming clubs for the school, Brownies and then Guides and as I got older, I joined Leatherhead Swimming Club, where I trained regularly. I hated the smell of chlorine, hated lane swimming, the boring, repetitious back and forth training, but I loved entering galas, as racing was easy for me. I was always leagues ahead of everyone in my age group.

That was until I was a teenager and my energy levels dropped through over-training and lack of food. Dad fed me two tablespoons full of butter mixed with sugar before training to boost my energy levels and never understood why I was so underweight. After training, he made me drink Guinness to boost my iron levels although I hated it.

One of the dreaded roles I had to endure twice a year was when Dad made me dress like a boy in dark clothing with a hat on to hide my hair and I would go with him to Smithfield Market before the sun came up, even on a school day. It was a male dominated environment, and he didn't want to draw attention to me, so I wore clothes that made me look more masculine.

Dad was very protective of me which seemed a dichotomy of messages to my young self. Protected fiercely from others but for his own obsessive perverted gratification. It wasn't until I was 14 that I realised that he had been sexually violating me from the age of three, but as it had always been introduced in 'play', I felt it was normal.

At Smithfield, Dad sourced the family's supply of meat for the coming months – a whole lamb, pig or a cow and several boxes of chickens. After returning home at about six in the morning, I had no choice but to help with the endless chopping and bagging of meat to put into our three chest freezers in the garden sheds. It was ironic to think we had so much food, considering I hardly had any of it myself.

Sometimes, in the dead of night, I was driven off to someone's back garden where they had a huge outbuilding or warehouse. I always wondered what I'd walk in and find. Most of the time it was filled with boxes and men were standing around chatting and smoking. Sometimes the buildings were full of rails of clothes, sometimes boxes of jewellery and sometimes alcohol. Each time, the stash was huge and very obviously expensive.

I always felt odd in these grown-up situations as he treated me more like his wife than his daughter. I never dared speak up, nor challenge him as I was terrified of the consequences.

"Don't speak to anyone, even if the men talk to you. Do you understand me? Above all, don't ever tell anyone about this. This is between you and your dad. You got it?" Dad said on one visit.

I nodded, too scared to contemplate what would happen if I didn't comply. I kept quiet and didn't even tell my friends about our late-night visits.

Dad's drinking was getting worse to the point of him sometimes losing control of his bodily functions. One Sunday evening, he was so drunk and laughing so hard he wet and messed himself in front of us all. He was in his dressing gown and the sight horrified and repulsed me.

I first noticed Dad having to face the effects of his drinking when I found him in agony trying to pass a kidney stone. We were alone in the house together and I was so scared I ran into my bedroom and hid as he was reeling in agony and shouting for me to help him.

"Amanda, please don't leave me. Come and help your dad, please." I heard him calling me from the downstairs toilet.

Having never seen him like that before, I panicked. He was screaming out in agony and asking me to help him. I thought he was dying. But I hid in my room until the shouting and screaming stopped.

When it finally went quiet, he came up to my room to see me. I couldn't explain why I ran, but he seemed to know.

"Amanda, where the hell were you? Didn't you hear me screaming? I just wanted you to be there with me. Look what your dad's just passed through his penis."

I was shocked when he showed me an enormous, jagged crystal. I was more shocked that he expected me to help nurse him through his agony after what pain and suffering he had me endure almost daily.

About a year later, when I was about fifteen, Dad disappeared for a few days. I didn't know what had happened until he returned, and I saw his face and arms scraped and scratched. He sat me down and said, "Your dad got knocked down by a car when I was unloading the van in the road. It was dark and he obviously didn't see me, but I'm OK."

I looked into his eyes, and I knew instantly that he wasn't telling me the truth. We had a big circular drive and he'd rarely had the need to park on the road before so couldn't understand why he'd park so far away from his garage. He'd always parked just in front of it on our drive.

He disappeared a second time and this time, just before he went, he asked me to go to work with his employee to keep an eye on him whilst he went into hospital for a while. He said he was OK, but I knew something wasn't right.

Throughout the summer holidays, I went up to London with Steve, his new employee. I wasn't able to do much except fetch and carry, but I was so happy to be free of Sue if only for a few hours a day. That summer I started to spread my wings as I explored London, fearless and in awe of everything a big city had to offer. As long as I was back before we had to load up to go home, Steve let me come and go as I pleased. London was an adventure. I felt alive for the first time in my life.

I'd started hanging out with a new bunch of friends when I entered secondary school, and though they were probably not who I'd have chosen if it had not been for my home life, they offered excitement and adventure. Breaking the rules whenever possible was daring and risky. Dad didn't approve of my new friends and often embarrassed me by letting them know in no uncertain terms.

I remember the first time I was invited to a party, and he insisted on driving me there and picking me up. When we arrived at the house, it was obvious the party was in the garage and Dad drove up the drive to within a foot of the wide-open garage door with his lights full on.

There must have been 40 or so kids in there who were stunned by the sudden light shining into the garage and they all tried to shield the light from their eyes as he dazzled his full beam at them. Embarrassed, I said, "Thanks, Dad, I'll see you later then," and went to get out.

"Where the fuck do you think you're going?" he said as he roughly grabbed hold of my clothes and pulled me back into the van. "You've got another thing coming if you think I'm leaving you here with this lot." He got out of the van and shouted, "Whose party is this and where the hell are the parents?"

I was mortified as I could see their terrified faces. Dad looked at all the blank faces, no-one wanting to take ownership for the obviously unsupervised party with young teenagers drinking alcohol. Shaking his head in disgust, he walked back to the van, got in and we drove off. I was petrified about how I was going to deal with my friends at school on Monday.

From then on, I was teased for having such a strict father. The boys made snide comments when walking past me in the corridors. "Your dad's a nutter. I hear it runs in the family."

I didn't feel I was able to be who I really was when I was with my friends, but I tried to mimic their behaviour to fit in. It worked, but at a price. I was often the one who'd have to face doing things I didn't really want to do. I was often asked to do dares such as steal sweets from Woolworths for my friends, say rude things to adults in the street to make them laugh or annoy shopkeepers.

We went out in cars, driven by people who didn't have a licence. I watched films Dad wouldn't have let me watch and tried to please my peers, so I'd be accepted, even though I hated what I was asked to do. Each time I felt an undeniable nagging in the back of my head telling me I had to stop, but I knew my friends would become my enemies if I tried. I then began to play truant.

I should have been settling down with my revision as we were taking O-levels, but I hardly ever went to school while he was in hospital. I just couldn't deal with the thought that there was something seriously wrong with him. It was just more uncertainty in an already unstable and unpredictable world made of sand.

That summer when dad seemed better, we spent almost every weekend with my Dad's best friend Mick and his family. They were diving buddies, so we'd often all go to the beach. While Sue and Val (Mick's wife) sat and chatted on the beach, I went off with my brother and we hung around with Mick's twin sons, Graham, and Terry.

It was love at first sight for me and Graham. For both of us it was our first love. The intensity we felt when we were together was sometimes overwhelming. We spent every moment we could holding hands, sitting, and chatting and laughing and kissing for hours. Those first kisses felt like lightning bolts shooting through me. We were besotted with each other and every opportunity we had, we spent it together.

I thought about Graham endlessly and counted the days until we could be together. I thought we'd be together for the rest of our lives. Fortunately, as Mick and Dad were diving training at

Leatherhead during the week where I was swimming, Graham and I got to see each other quite often.

After we'd been together for over a year, I thought when we were old enough, we'd eventually marry. He made me feel nothing I had ever felt before. It was mind blowing and made everything I had to endure worth every moment I was with him. I felt I could achieve anything all the while I was with Graham. For the first time in my young life I felt heart stopping, breath taking and all-consuming infatuation, admiration and he was my first innocent love. I believed this was the love and freedom I had prayed for, delivered to me in a secure package called Graham, to carry me off into a future of happiness and peace.

One day we were camping on yet another one of my Dad's deep-sea diving weekends and while the men were all off on the boat, I was at the campsite with the women and all the kids getting ready to head to the beach. Sue slammed Graham's hand in the sliding door of our VW van and the screams we all heard suddenly emanating from Graham sounded like he was in excruciating agony.

"Mum!" he screamed. "Mum, help me."

"Oh Christ, I'm so sorry Graham. I didn't know your hand was in the door," Sue said in a panicked voice. I looked at her and it immediately dawned on me that she was being dishonest in such a palpable way and wondered if she had shut the door on his hand on purpose.

Graham was holding his injured hand by the wrist with his other hand and jumping up and down in agony. "Mum," he screamed. "I think my hand's broken!" He had tears pouring down his face.

Alarmingly, that was the first time I saw his hand. My mind searched to understand what I'd seen. He only had three fingers and I couldn't fathom what I was seeing. He always walked with his hand in his back pocket, and it dawned on me that he hadn't lost two of his fingers in the door and must have only had 3 fingers prior to the accident. That must have been to disguise his hand, but I was so used to the way he did that. I'd always thought he looked so cool, but he'd been trying to keep it secret from me. When he saw me look at his hand, he instantly ran away.

When he had finally calmed down, I went over to where he was with his brother and mum. Graham and Terry had their backs to me, and I could see Graham urge Terry to come and speak to me. As Terry approached, his head was low and he said,

"I'm sorry, Amanda, but Graham doesn't want to be with you anymore."

I stood with my mouth open. "Why on earth not? What have I done?"

Terry just shook his head. "My brother's always been really embarrassed to show his hand. He was born like it. When he met you, it gave him a chance to be a normal kid as you didn't know about it. I know you love him for who he is but now you've seen his hand, he'll never know if you love him for that reason or out of sympathy and he can't stand knowing that."

Terry hugged me and walked away. Graham looked over his shoulder at me and I never knew whether his tear-stained face was due to the pain of the injury or from letting me go.

I was broken-hearted, crying every night when I was alone with my thoughts, trying to work out what I'd done to deserve this. As the months went by and winter came, the weekends ceased.

I felt I could never fully let my guard down and love again like I'd loved Graham. I spent every moment I could going over all the happy memories we had shared together. I thought he was my prince, who'd save me from my wicked stepmother, but my dreams were shattered, and my hope was gone. Time eventually healed the pain and my second boyfriend appeared in my life when Dad was becoming ill again. I didn't quite know the extent of my father's illness, but I started to panic about school and tried to settle down.

I'd stayed on an extra year and was due to study interior design at Redhill College. Dad naturally assumed I wanted to take over the family business, and I hadn't protested through fear of upsetting him. Being good at art and enjoying it was a bonus, but I wanted to escape my home life as soon as I could.

My best friend was a girl called Peta and she was going out with the best-looking boy in Coulsdon. When they finished and he asked me out, I thought he was winding me up. Paul was the son of a self-made builder and had his own car. He was eighteen and I was sure Dad wouldn't approve. But something had changed in Dad since his illness and he was more accepting of me having friends, even a boyfriend, encouraging me to go out and enjoy myself.

When I asked permission to go out with Paul, he said he'd let me go on a date as long as he met him first. He insisted on him coming with us for a walk with our dogs to Banstead Woods.

Paul was very different to us. He was into his car and always immaculately dressed. When he showed up in his bright yellow escort, I cringed, especially when he got out wearing his best leather jacket, shirt, and trousers.

As he got out of his car, Dad said, "Never trust a man who wears white socks!" and walked off.

We went for that walk, Paul, slipping and sliding all over the place in his brown slip-on shoes and us in our wellingtons. Although Dad didn't like him, he let me go out for dates with him as long as I was home at a respectable hour. The problem was, Paul was older and wanted more.

Dad was soon back in hospital, but this time he told me what was wrong. He had a brain tumour and was going to need more treatment as the treatment before hadn't worked. Nothing got the better of my Dad and I assumed he'd overcome it.

What would happen if I lost him? What on earth would I do? Sue would get rid of me straight away. I was only seventeen and had no backup plan, no future path, home, or security to support myself.

Eventually, I gave into Paul's pressure and agreed to sleep with him. I was losing Dad and needed Paul more than ever. One night at his house, he took me up to his bedroom.

"Come on, Amanda, we've been together for months now and you know you can trust me," he said, constantly pawing at me.

"Paul I just don't think I'm ready for it."

"Look, once it's over and done with we can get on with our relationship."

He started to take my clothes off. It felt wrong and I didn't feel good about myself, but I guessed it would mean he'd stay with me. After losing Graham, I wanted to try harder to keep this relationship, especially with all the uncertainty around my father. Even though I'd always had an image of what the first time would be like, I was dejected and disappointed and felt vulnerable after the deed was done. It was cold, quick, and needy on his part and I felt used and deceived, but I hoped he'd keep his word.

Paul was very close to his sister, and I'd been invited to go with his family to her wedding. Dad had just gone back into hospital, and he asked me through Sue to go and see him the very day of the wedding.

"Please Sue. I need to go to the wedding. I've told the family I'll be there. I'll do anything you ask if you'll let me go."

I don't know why but somehow something wasn't right with Paul and I had to be there. Sue insisted I went to see Dad. I went begrudgingly, thinking I would go to the reception in the evening as a compromise. I was worried Paul would get fed up with my strict father and thought going to the reception would at least pacify him.

When I got to the hospital, Dad looked weaker than I'd seen him before, but I assumed he'd had the operation and was on the mend. He was different though. He was spiteful and cruel as soon as I arrived. "So, you chose your new boyfriend over your father I hear," he spat at me as soon as I walked up to him in his bed.

I looked at Sue who gave me a satisfied grin. *Bitch*, I thought. "No, Dad, it's just I've never been invited to a wedding before, and I told the family I'd be there." I sat down on his bed.

"Do you know how ungrateful you are?" he said. "You should put your father before anyone. I've given you everything. Do you hear me?"

I left in tears and wondered why he'd bothered to ask to see me. I didn't realise this was part of his condition. Sue dropped me at the reception, and I tried my hardest to fight back tears as I raced in eagerly to see Paul. He was dancing with his best friend's girlfriend Heather when I arrived. He seemed to be in high spirits and had by then, had a lot to drink. Although he acknowledged me briefly, he continued laughing and joking with his friends and family and hardly spoke to me for the rest of the evening. I assumed it was because his sister was moving away to live in another county straight after the honeymoon and that was affecting him. He cried when she got in the car to leave with her new husband.

Shortly after they'd gone, he wanted to leave and several of us got into a taxi to go home. I sat in the back with Paul's best friend, Tom, in the middle and his girlfriend on the other side of me. As we drove home, Tom was silent. His girlfriend Heather was chatting to Paul and comforting him. The conversation started to get quite strange as Paul was talking to Heather intimately as if they were an item.

I looked at Tom in confusion and he shook his head and looked down. Was there something happening I didn't know about? Why was Tom letting them talk that way? It was as if the two of them couldn't contain themselves in their own intimate bubble anymore and it had spilled out to make it obvious to anyone and everyone. Alarmingly, the penny dropped as they were blatantly rubbing our noses in their infidelity with no regard to how Tom or I felt.

We eventually stopped outside Heather's house. She and Paul got out and starting kissing on the pavement right in front of us.

"What on earth are you doing, Tom, letting your best friend kiss your girlfriend?" I asked incredulously.

He just put his head in his hands and said, "She dumped me tonight. They've been wanting each other for months, so what can I do about it?"

"But you've been together for two years now and Paul's supposed to be your best friend!"

He looked up at me as if someone had robbed him of everything. "So you can understand how bad I feel right now then, yeah?" he said and then looked away.

Tom was dropped off next in silence and then we arrived at Paul's house. We got out of the car, and he turned to me and said, "I would walk you home, but I lost my sister tonight so I'm going in."

With that, he walked up to his front door without looking at me once. Walking home, I felt as if I'd been kicked in the stomach. I felt foolish, rejected, used and alone.

Two months went by, and I was doing anything to avoid school and found things to help me escape my life as I was past caring. Dad was in and out of hospital. I was not only having to do more and more tedious chores at home, I was also trying to keep Dad's business going by helping on Saturdays and helping with unloading and checking the van when it came home with Steve at night.

I had to go to school but hated all the pressures because Dad was now very aggressive, moody, and unpredictable. I was supposed to prepare for college, but I avoided schoolwork, feeling it was futile.

I started to hang out with teenagers much older than me and soon met Justin. Just like me, he was looking for a way to escape his parents. His father was an air crash investigator and very eccentric. His mother was eccentric too and rescued greyhounds and collected old Fiat 500s, which were piled up on their driveway.

We met through mutual friends at a pub one night. I liked his quirkiness and confidence and we started to go out regularly with the group. Eventually we were an item and spent every moment we could together. Although we were very different, we both needed to escape our home lives and sought solace in each other's need to make a life for ourselves outside our parental homes.

Dad was in the kitchen one evening and Justin dragged me in. Dad was in remission at the time and had always told me he'd never let me leave home until I was married, so I was petrified Justin would upset him.

Justin simply said, "Colin, I want to get engaged to Amanda so we can get married."

Dad was sitting on a chair at the kitchen table, and I could see he was not the man he used to be. Tearfully he said, "Justin, I give you my blessing but if you ever hurt her, I'll hurt you worse. And don't get any ideas about her moving out until she's married. I've got plans for this girl to get through college and take over the family business."

I was shocked that my father was so approving, and I know Justin was, too. Elated Justin said, "Of course, I totally understand and thank you, Colin. I promise I'll look after her."

Even though I agreed with my fingers crossed behind my back, I wasn't having any of it. I didn't want to stay a moment more than I needed to in that house. Dad went back into hospital a few weeks before I was to start college and without telling my family, I got a job in Croydon under a YTS scheme, intending to run away with Justin just as soon as I could. He was doing well as a heating and ventilation engineer, so I didn't need to earn very much.

I bided my time until the day I was legally old enough to get a mortgage. One month after my eighteenth birthday, I managed to get a flat with Justin in a rough area in South London. I'd started working for an insurance broker and loved my newfound independence. Sue thought I went to college every day, but I was travelling into Croydon to work. It was the first time I had money. Not only did I have control over something Dad and Sue knew nothing about, soon I would be able to move out.

Almost two weeks before we were to complete contracts on our flat, Dad was rushed into hospital for the last time. That was my chance and I had to take it. We planned to move into Justin's parents' house for two weeks until we could move into our new place. I waited until Sue was out and then filled Justin's car with all my things. Just as we were about to leave Sue returned to the house.

"What the hell do you think you're doing?" she said shouting at me directly into my face.

"Justin, just go and get into the car," I said.

"You're not going anywhere until your father hears about this," Sue said.

I went into the house to get my last bag. Sue rushed past me into the kitchen. As I went to walk out of the front door, she came rushing into the hall with a knife from the kitchen drawer. "You leave this house and I'll hurt you so bad you'll wish you were dead," she screamed at me. And then she lunged at me.

I ducked and she toppled forward dropping the knife on the floor. We both ran towards it, but I grabbed it first and turned it on her. Poking it up to her neck, I said, "That's the last time you ever threaten or hurt me. You're nothing but a despicable, cruel bitch. You're on your own now to look after this house and all the shit I've had to put up with. How you gonna cope with everything when I'm gone … I guess one of your own kids will have to become your slave."

Sue said nothing and just looked at me with fear in her eyes. I knew she wasn't frightened of me. She was worried about what Dad would do if she let me leave home.

"Even though those kids are yours, they're still my brother and sisters and I'll miss them, but one day they'll leave you, too Sue and then what will you do?" I knew I was pushing my luck, but she didn't move and nor did I.

I threw the knife on the floor, knowing the look I'd given her was enough. Then I walked out of that house for good. I smiled and felt the sun shining on me. *I made it.* I thought. *I fucking well made it!* I was finally free after 15 years of entrapment, abuse and slavery.

Justin and I felt like we were on holiday at his parents' house, holed up in his room and only coming out to go to work and use the bathroom. We spent every possible moment in bed, and it felt good to do as I pleased for the first time in my life.

We moved into our one bed maisonette with very little, but it was so exhilarating for both of us. Since leaving home, I'd completely disassociated myself from all my friends. I couldn't risk Dad finding me. I missed my friends, but my freedom was more important. I started my new life spending time only with Justin and his friends who made me feel very grown up.

One day Justin and I were out in Croydon and happened to bump into a girl I knew from school, Beverly. I'd been round to her house a few times as a child and my father had dropped me off there once. She said, "Your father came round to my house recently and he said you'd gone and asked if I knew where you were."

I'd assumed, like Sue, he'd be pleased to be rid of me. She looked smug that she'd bumped into me.

"We must keep in touch. I don't really keep in touch with many people from school. How about you?" she asked.

"No, no one really," I said awkwardly but didn't really want anything to do with her, especially if she'd recently had Dad round at hers looking for me. I didn't trust her. She wanted my phone number and insisted we kept in touch. I awkwardly gave it to her even though we'd only briefly been friends at school. I didn't know what harm it could do back then but eventually I would grow to learn she was a dangerous and manipulative pariah.

We met up a few times, though I didn't disclose where I lived, but she started to become clingy, so I started putting her at arm's length. I was far more interested in my new friends I'd met through Justin, so I cut contact with her.

When Justin and I moved into our new flat, we got a rescue dog and one day I was out jogging with him, when he suddenly saw a cat on the other side of the road and darted under my feet, knocking me flying. I broke my ankle. A kind woman drove me home, but the next day I went into hospital and ended up with a cast on my leg. I decided to call my dad as by then six months had gone by and I missed him dreadfully despite what he'd put me through, which confused me, but I think it was missing family and that sense of belonging (even if it was dysfunctional), that was at the root of my loneliness. He wasn't cross at all but wanted to see me straight away. I was surprised and melted somewhat into a sense of believing he had reformed as he had missed me and realised the error of his ways.

"Hon I've missed you so much. Why didn't you tell me where you were going? You're my girl and I just need to know you're OK," he said. I wasn't sure if it was a trap but was so relieved to have him be kind to me, I ignored my instincts to run.

"Dad, I didn't want you to be cross with me, but Justin and I are fine, and we just want to get on with our lives."

I was pleased to speak to him, though, and hear him back to his old familiar self, so I told him where I lived. When he came to collect me the next day, I heard him before I saw him. As I looked out of my window of my upper floor maisonette, I saw a car driving towards my home, a ridiculously distinctive spotlessly clean white Audi Quattro convertible, with the roof down. Dad was driving with my sister Maria in the passenger seat. As they pulled up, the music was blaring, and I heard both of them singing a Dolly Parton track at the tops of their voices.

Because of the area I lived in, I was mortified as he got out of the car, dressed in all white with linen trousers and open necked shirt to match – and, of course, a medallion necklace. He looked like Elvis with his white shoes to match, his jet-black curly hair and dark glasses. Embarrassed by what seemed to be his midlife crisis shining for all to see, I couldn't quite make out where his new guise had materialised from, as I had always known him to be very down to earth and sophisticated, even when he was working. It was as if he was wearing some kind of front or costume to hide himself behind.

He was armed with flowers and chocolates and despite the initial shock, he was my old, best version of my dad again, so brilliant, funny, and loving. I was thrilled he was back in my life and thought I'd made the best decision.

"Come on, girly, your sister wants to see you so I'm taking you to see your nan and we'll all go out for lunch."

We left with me sitting in the back, crouching down low out of embarrassment. It was a beautiful day. Dad was on form and had us all in stitches. Nan was buoyant and positive rather than her usual grumbling and moaning self, and my sister was adorable. I missed them all so much and wished I could be back with my cousins, aunts, and uncles too. The afternoon was over too soon and when they left me at my home, I felt a very deep sense of loss.

Within a few weeks, stuck alone in the flat whilst Justin was working, I started getting stir crazy and wanted to get back to work. Every time I spoke to Dad on the phone after last seeing him, he was off with me and seemed to revert back to his angry, bitter self – critical and aggressive.

Justin and I were starting to bicker and spending less and less time with each other due to the fact I couldn't get around much with my cast, and Dad started putting pressure on me to ask him to leave.

"He's a nobody, Amanda, and you know damn well you needed each other to leave home. Face it. You both bought this flat for the wrong reasons and as I'm your dad, I can help you get out of this. No one else will."

I hated the way my father seemed to know everything and still had power over me, but I realised even though I'd escaped my family home, I had no one to help me in the outside world except for Dad.

Justin didn't seem bothered our relationship was failing and I guessed he was miffed at my letting my father back into my life. After a few weeks, my father insisted I handed my half of the flat to him and said he'd pay Justin off.

Justin was no longer meeting his monthly obligations with the bills and was starting to get spiteful with riling me up and arguing. I started to despise him and vice versa and we avoided each other at all costs. We started to fight like cat and dog. In fact, we'd started soon after moving into our flat together. There was no rhyme or reason why it started to me at the time, but later I came to realise that we both resented one another as we were not together for the right reasons. Eventually we came to realise we were escaping our dysfunctional family homes.

I finally phoned Dad and did as he asked, as I was scared of not making the mortgage payments. Justin left like a shot to live with his best friend John when Dad paid him off. It was all done in a matter of days as Dad had a solicitor who'd been with him for years and would do anything for Dad at the drop of a hat.

Dad came to the flat the day Justin left, and to my shock he brought Sue.

"So, you little bitch, now you've caused so much trouble, you just get on and sign the papers. You have no idea how much suffering you've caused. I'm sick and tired with looking after you. Just get on and sign this flat over to me and I'll deal with this like I've always had to," he shouted at me as if I were someone who he loathed and needed to get rid of.

I signed the papers just to get him out. I was shaken by how much he seemed to resent me.

"Do you know how much trouble you've caused me since you were born? You have no idea how much. You'll have to suffer the consequences now, you little bitch, all on your own."

After that, I didn't hear from Dad for several weeks. Justin had gone but I was trying to make the best of my new job. I was even studying at night at secretarial school to improve my skills. I'd got back in touch with my best friend from secondary school. She'd gone off the rails a bit since leaving home. The eldest child of a strict Catholic family, with nine siblings, Juliette was a wild child. Having had to do too much at home as a child like myself, she'd accepted a dare at her workplace and married a work colleague for the hell of it after knowing him for only three months.

Life was fun and we were always at parties, but I felt lonely. I had hardly any contact with Mum, as I wanted to punish her for not keeping her word and leaving me with Dad. So when I got the call from Sue to come to the house *now*, I knew it was serious. I was absolutely petrified on the bus. None of my siblings were there and the house had a deathly feel. No sooner had I entered, she turned to me and very calmly and directly, told me, "Your father is dying and it's all because of you. He's got an inoperable brain tumour and he's only got a few weeks to live so I've called you here to see what you've done."

My chest felt suddenly crushed from the pain of the blow she'd hurled at me, but I wouldn't give her the satisfaction of letting her see how her shocking news affected me. I stood firmly and as still as I could as she went on.

"Because of all the worry you've given him over the years, it's made him sick, and you'll have to live with that, you cruel girl you! Now go in there and see what you've done." She pointed towards the living room door.

I obediently walked through the door, petrified of what I was about to face, and there in front of me was a man I didn't recognise. I stood and scanned him for a moment. Sitting there on the sofa in front of me was an old and sallow shrunken version of the man I knew.

I walked over nervously. "Hi, Dad," I managed eventually. "I'm here!"

He tried to speak and couldn't. I noticed the struggle on his face and in his body. He started to cry. Tears welled up and flowed down his face and I wanted to hold him. He reached out to touch me, but as I walked towards him, Sue entered the room and rushed towards me, saying, "Enough! It's too much for him. You have to go!"

All I could do was tell Dad I loved him with my eyes as I stared at him in disbelief. I held his gaze for as long as I could, then I turned and walked away, determined not to show her any emotion. I longed to tell him I loved him, but Sue pulled me by my arm and frog-marched me out of the room. When I looked back, his head was down, and he was sobbing uncontrollably.

As we reached the front door, Sue yanked me round and turned to face me and said, "There, see what you've done! You've upset him again. I hope you're happy with yourself!"

And with that she threw me out the door and shut it in my face.

Chapter 5

It's not what I gave you, it's what I taught you that

counts.

Colin Stanley Golledge

For days I walked around under a cloak of confusion, numbness and grief, unable to register what had happened. I had no one to turn to. I'd lost contact with all my friends. I tried to speak to Justin on the phone, but he told me he didn't really care what happened to me. I was on my own.

Sue had a key to my flat and I couldn't sleep at night knowing she could appear at my bedside whilst I was sleeping. Justin eventually let me sleep on the floor in a spare room at John's house where he was living. The two of them found it entertaining to ridicule me and constantly make snide comments whenever they could.

I tried to ignore their remarks as much as possible, but they hurt. I said I would only be staying for a few days to get my head straight as I couldn't stay in the flat anymore. The truth was I had no idea what to do or where to go.

I'd arrived with only a few bin bags of clothes and had left the remainder of my belongings behind. My room at John's was cold and empty and it added more emptiness to my already diminishing hopes of a new life. There was no furniture, only a carpet and curtains. I gratefully accepted the space even though it was freezing, and I had to sleep on the floor.

I had food poisoning shortly after moving in, which was debilitating in a strange and cold environment with no creature comforts whatsoever. Alone, feeling rotten and dejected by the world, Juliette called me to say she'd passed her driving test that day and wanted to go out for a drive. She picked me up around ten o'clock in the evening from John's house. Justin and John were on one of their pizza and get pissed nights and didn't even comment when I told them I was going out.

We set off in the direction of Gatwick airport as we knew we could get a coffee there late at night. Juliette was in her element driving and full of high spirits. She chatted enthusiastically about how she'd annulled her rebellious marriage within weeks and was now off exploring pastures new. I envied her enthusiasm. We arrived just before midnight as it took Juliette a bit of time to get fully accustomed to dealing with traffic at night and driving without an instructor. After parking the car, we entered the airport in search of coffee.

"So now I can drive I just want to get the hell out of here," she said excitedly. "I'm fed up with this place. Croydon's a hole and has nothing to offer me. I think I might even go abroad."

"Where will you go though? How will you get a job? Juliette, you won't know anyone," I said, concerned.

"Oh don't worry about me. I've met a guy recently, who's absolutely gorgeous and we've talked about nothing else but travelling the world together."

"Wow," I said. "I wish I had your guts. Aren't you scared though? How long have you known him?"

"Amanda, I'm done being scared."

I admired her courage and wished I could be brave like her. I decided to tell her about the systematic abuse that had occurred, not only from my father and stepmother, but also the five other men who had taken advantage of me sexually, including a cousin of mine and my best friend's brother. She was horrified but not surprised, as she always suspected I was repeatedly beaten, but the sexual abuse was beyond her understanding.

We talked into the early hours of the morning. That night, it was as if a light came on for me and Juliette had become the voice of my angels, and something awoke in me. I suddenly felt lighter after everything I had shared and felt a sense of freedom ensue as if I had removed the shackles that were holding me down. Eventually, we set off to head back to South London. This time though, the journey was filled with a hint of hope and promise.

When we eventually arrived back at five o'clock in the morning, I opened the door quietly and crept in to collect my belongings. I'd decided to pack a small bag and go to my grandparents in North London. I knew if anyone would, they would take me in, and I'd be safe. It was my only hope for a fresh start. Once I'd made the decision, I was exhilarated. Juliette waited in the car for me and as I finally packed the last things in my holdall, Justin walked in, still half asleep.

"What the hell are you doing?" he said.

"I'm going away," I said calmly and walked past him towards the door.

"No, you can't leave. Where the hell are you going? I won't let you! Amanda you can't leave. You've got nowhere to go. Who'll look after you? I'm sorry I've behaved badly. I didn't mean to, but you don't love me anymore and I still love you. Please stay, we can sort this out."

He started to panic as he could see I was serious. I'd stood and listened to what he had to say and simply turned away and continued towards the front door as he followed me closely. Ignoring his protests, I walked out of the door and up the front steps to the roadside. He was close on my heels, and I could see Juliette sitting in her car about a hundred yards down the road, double-parked with the engine running.

"I'm sorry all right. I just wanted to punish you for hurting me. I know I've been horrible to you lately and I know it's been hard with your dad and all that, but I just didn't know what to do. John's my mate and I guess I was just trying to play it cool."

Justin was now shouting and seemed to be oblivious to the fact we were outside. I eventually turned to look at him. "It's too late and you've done too much damage, Justin. I'm going!"

I pushed past him and ran to the car where Juliette was now revving the engine. As I jumped in beside her and threw my bags in the back seat, I shouted, "Quick! Drive!"

As she slammed her foot down on the accelerator, Juliette laughed at Justin. I looked in her side mirror and could see him running up the centre of the road after us, tears streaming down his face as he shouted my name over and over. He was waving frantically, crying out for us to stop and tell him where we were going. I tried to ignore him and glancing back one last time, I wondered if he ever did love me or had just needed me like I'd needed him. That was the first I'd seen him show any true emotion and it was too late.

As I hugged Juliette at East Croydon Station and we said our last goodbyes, we both knew I wouldn't come back. It was half-past six in the morning. I stepped onto the train and sat down. I took a deep breath and realised for the first time since I'd been taken from my home at the age of three, I was going back to where I would feel safe, cared for, and loved. A warm feeling washed over me as I began to feel the barriers of survival coming down and hope take their place. I vowed to make a new start and make up for all the years I'd suffered.

I arrived at my grandparents' flat at half past eight in the morning. My heart was fluttering in anticipation of what they would say when they saw me. I felt warmth and optimism rising in my body. Deep down, I felt they'd receive me lovingly but the voice in my head kept saying, *But what if they don't want you, then what will you do? Remember what Sue said about how none of your family wanted you?* I tried to ignore it and kept walking.

The back door was open as I rounded the corner to my grandparents flat and I heard BBC Radio Two playing in the kitchen. The familiar smell of a mixture of cigarette smoke, toast and tea filled the fresh morning air. I could hear their laughter and babble of conversation and as I approached the back step, they both stopped in their kitchen in mid conversation and gasped, "Amanda!"

For three weeks I lived in bliss and harmony with my grandparents, feeling loved, secure, and cherished. I got a cleaning job to tide me over, but I hated it as it reminded me too much of growing up. My grandfather collected me from the house I was working at after my third day and refused to let me go back.

Mum spoke to me on the phone a few times asking me what my plans were. At that stage I had none. I was just relieved I'd escaped from my old world and was making the most of being with my grandparents in their flat. On the third week of my stay, Mum turned up to speak to me and told me Bob, her new partner, had said I could live with them. Even though I didn't want to leave the security and love of my grandparents, I knew she was right. The flat was far too small, and I was sleeping on a camp bed in the living room. Mum and Bob had a three bedroomed house, a typical new build in a very up market area in Buckinghamshire where all the gardens were manicured, and the neighbours all got on. The house was immaculate, and everything was where it should be. There was order and quiet and nothing moved. To me, it felt more like something likened to the film The Stepford Wives, cold, ordered, and loveless.

When I moved in, I felt uncomfortable at first, as I didn't know where to put myself, so I spent most of my time in my new bedroom. Mum seemed happy to have me there. Bob I wasn't so sure about.

Within a few weeks, I managed to get a job at a company on the trading estate just outside their village, selling spares for electronic equipment to airlines and broadcasting stations, including the BBC. I worked for a small sales team with a lovely lady boss named Irene, who took me under her wing. She commanded respect and order in her team and everyone liked her. Irene gave me more and more responsibility and nurtured my eagerness to make a fresh start with sensitivity, even though she knew nothing about my past. I looked up to her as a role model.

I started driving lessons soon after moving in and Mum and Bob helped me to buy my first car. I felt ashamed of my past and worried if anyone knew about it, they'd judge me and treat me differently. I tried not to think about Dad, although I missed him terribly. Apart from my new work colleagues, I knew no one. I had even cut off contact from Juliette, worried Sue would find me if I let anyone know where I'd gone.

I'd been introduced to one of Bob's younger work colleagues, Gavin. Bob and Gavin both worked for Bryant and May. They were based locally but travelled all over the country seeing customers as salesmen. Gavin was a tall, good looking thirty-something who looked a bit like one of the three musketeers. He took an instant liking to me and took me under his wing as Bob had said to him, "Look after her."

He soon became a good friend to me. In fact, I called him my guardian angel. Although he was good looking, he was certainly not my type – he preferred blondes anyway – but there was something endearing and protective about how he treated me. Gavin loved being surrounded by women and I was like a younger sister to him. He was a social climber and terrible flirt, but I could see deep down he was a sensitive soul and had vulnerabilities.

Before I moved into my mother's, I'd not taken much notice of my appearance. Watching Mum getting ready for work and dinner parties had always fascinated me, and I started to borrow clothes from her vast wardrobe that made me look a lot older. I enjoyed dressing up and wearing make-up and started to take pride in my appearance, even though I felt ugly inside.

Gavin started taking me out with another close friend of his, Marianne, and the three of us became inseparable. Gavin had a different girlfriend every week, always blonde and slim, but

Marianne and I went with him wherever he went, regardless of who he was dating.

Marianne was plain, short, dumpy, hyper-intelligent and a little opinionated at times. She was a chain smoker and didn't hold back when expressing her feelings about people, but she was strong, and I admired that in her.

Mum said one morning, "You're going to have to lose a little weight if you're going to find yourself a nice boyfriend!"

I was only nine and a half stone! I didn't think I was overweight but when I looked in the mirror, I couldn't help but see my father. He had the upper body of a boxer and the thighs of a sprinter, and I'd unfortunately taken after him in the body department. It wasn't a good look for a young girl wanting to look feminine and sexy. Mum had done a bit of catwalk modelling when she'd worked as a buyer for Harrods in her youth and had legs up to her armpits. I'd drawn the short straw having inherited my father's genes.

I felt awkward at home as I was so different to Mum and Bob, and I felt they'd taken me in out of duty. I started to avoid being at home and spent all my time at work or going out partying with Gavin. We got into all the best clubs and drinking establishments. The more I was out, the more I didn't have to be at home when Bob got home from work. We were chalk and cheese, and I was uncomfortable around him. When I passed my driving test, I was so excited to at last spread my wings. It felt as though I'd been thrown a lifeline. But all this changed one day when I got home from work to find Bob waiting for me in the hallway.

"Come and sit in the lounge, Amanda, I've got something I need to tell you."

I followed him into the lounge half expecting him to ask me to leave or find fault in my partying lifestyle. Instead, he just calmly said, "Your father's died."

I slumped down on the sofa, wanting to ask questions but too frightened. He continued, "Well, you weren't close to him anyway, were you."

I had no idea where that had come from but assumed Mum had told him this. I wanted to leave the room and scream and cry, but I just sat staring at him.

Bob explained that a policeman named Harvey, one of Dad's closest friends, had come to the house to tell me the news that evening before I'd got home. He wanted to give me the news in person, but Bob had insisted he would inform me and would get me to call Harvey. I felt robbed that my father's best friend hadn't been able to break the news to me personally.

Soon after, Mum arrived back from work. I immediately got up and went to her in the hallway, Bob following. I told her Dad was dead and she burst into tears. We hugged each other, crying together.

Bob was clearly uncomfortable with this and after a few seconds said, "What are you crying for?"

"It's Amanda's father!" she answered, glaring at his coldness.

Bob walked off. I couldn't get out of the house fast enough.

"Don't you think you should stay at home tonight?" Bob said when I declared I was going out.

"Why? I want to be with my friends because they care about me," I shouted at him.

I didn't go and see my friends. Instead, I went and sat in my car in a quiet place where no-one would disturb me and cried until I was exhausted and drained.

I phoned Harvey the next day when I was alone in the house. I remembered him as one of my father's dive buddies. He'd managed to find me when I'd applied for my full driving licence. Harvey helped out with lots of the arrangements for the funeral but wasn't happy with the lack of effort when it came to finding me. I sensed there was more as he seemed hesitant when talking about my dad's wishes. He mentioned perhaps I needed to get legal advice, but I didn't question why.

I had to go to my father's funeral. I knew once it was over, I would run straight back to Buckinghamshire and not look back, but even so the thought of going petrified me. My grandparents offered to go with me as Mum was too intimidated by Sue. It was an awful day; one I'll never forget.

I arrived at the house to be greeted by my uncles. My brother and sisters were there but didn't seem to want to even look at me, let alone talk to me. I suspected Sue had given them instructions to keep me at arm's length. I stuck to my grandparents like glue. When the funeral cars arrived, Sue got in the lead car with her children and her family.

I was ushered to the last car after my uncles and cousins. Although we were surrounded by people, it was evident to my grandparents how frightened I was as I trembled continuously and clung to them for support.

The funeral was simple, but a blur and I did my best not to shed a tear. Sue sat composed the whole time showing no emotion and my siblings sat rigid next to her too like little clones. After the funeral, we headed back to my old home and my uncle put his arm around my shoulders, guiding me into the house. It was a small token of reassurance. I found a seat where others were congregating in the very room where I had last seen my father. The memory of him, crumpled, crying like a child on the sofa, flashed through my mind and I wondered how long he'd had to endure his illness and suffering.

I'd only sat for a short while in the lounge when Maria came in. I put my arms out to hold her, but she just looked down at the floor and said, "Mum said she wants you to leave now."

A lump rose in my throat. I knew that was the end and smiled at her reassuringly. I couldn't speak. I simply nodded although I knew I'd probably never see her again. As I rose to leave, my uncle got up and instructed the family to leave. He simply nodded and said, "I think it's time to go."

Outside we hugged and said our goodbyes, knowing we'd probably never see each other again. We all departed in our own cars and drove our separate ways. Some weeks later I was sent a copy of my father's Will. Almost everything had been left to Sue including the half share in my flat, although my siblings had all been left something in trust for when they were old enough.

I wasn't even recognised as his daughter, which shocked and hurt me. It wasn't that I wanted any wealth; I just thought he'd leave me something so I could make a fresh start. It made me question whether he had ever loved me at all.

Shortly after the funeral, I drove down to see my Nan. She'd always insisted us kids called her Nana as she was quite old-fashioned. Nana had lost lots of weight and looked very withdrawn when I arrived. I wasn't surprised as Dad had been her number one son.

While Nana and I sat sipping our tea, she told me she'd been up at the hospital quite a bit right up until Dad had died and had been witness to the comings and goings. She said his solicitor had been called in by Sue three days before he died to change his will. Nana had known his old will because she'd always been involved in all Dad's business affairs, but when he became ill, Sue had taken over. Nana said the solicitors were in cahoots with Sue. I had no reason to doubt her, but I wished she hadn't told me.

"I don't understand, Nana, why didn't you tell someone?" I asked, shocked by what she was implying.

"I did, I told your Uncle Derek and Don, but they refused to get involved."

Not one member of my family was prepared to stand up to this. Nana tearfully continued, "Sue's put your father's business up for sale and she's even had his dogs put down. I'm sorry, darling, to tell you like this, but you need to know."

I burst into tears as I knew my father would have been heartbroken to lose his dogs and I loved those dogs just as much as he did.

Before I left, Nana added that Christopher was now helping her out at the house and Sue was speaking to her on the phone on a regular basis. I couldn't believe how my Nan had defected, considering she had always loathed my stepmother and had very little to do with Christopher or the girls as it had always been dad and I that visited and helped her every week. And I had been the only one out of the siblings that stayed over at hers where she taught me to knit and crochet, make ice cream and home-made jams, and tended to her garden. Nana was not only a traitor, but also a hypocrite. It had to be about money. I felt abandoned and betrayed and was better off without them all.

After leaving my Nan's, I went to the flat to collect some belongings. Because I was scared Sue would be there, I'd phoned Justin to ask him if he could go there with his old key and check it out first. I wanted it to be my last visit. Justin seemed so warm and kind. He said he would gladly meet me at the flat and check the coast was clear. He called me when he got there and I arrived shortly after with my heart in my throat and rushed in the door, slammed it shut and put the chain on.

It was strange seeing Justin. That day he seemed so caring and apologetic, so I agreed to stay over and have a meal with him and leave with my things in the morning. He said he'd have to get some work things, so he was going to nip out and while he did, I decided to have a bath. Shortly after he left, there was a knock at the door, and I assumed he'd left the key so put on my dressing gown to go and open the door. No sooner had I opened the door than Sue lunged at me pushing me to the ground.

I fell back against the staircase, conscious I had nothing on under my dressing gown, and scrabbled to cover myself and get a footing. Someone behind her, a balding, younger looking man, pulled her off me as she started to punch me. He told her in a stern but calm voice to keep cool, and as he held her back, I made a dash up the stairs and into my flat. Sue raced up and caught my legs, pushing me to the landing floor. As she got to the landing, she kicked me several times and I winced in pain as I cowered.

The man grabbed her shouting, "Sue, stop it. What on earth do you think you're doing? Leave her alone and calm down for God's sake."

"No I won't!" she screamed still trying to pull away from him and grab at me. "This is my flat and I want her out now. Get out, you little bitch!"

I got up and ran into the lounge, but she got free and ran at me with fists flying. I couldn't defend myself because I felt vulnerable in only a flimsy dressing gown. Sue punched me over and over in the face. I stood firm and let her get it out of her system.

"Get out. Get out. Get out." She screamed with every punch, spitting, and going red with rage. "I hate you, you little bitch. I wish you'd never been born you worthless piece of shit."

The man rushed for her and grabbed hold of her arms and shook her to snap her out of her frenzy. He dragged her, half kicking and screaming, to the other side of the room and held onto her as her anger decreased. "What on earth's got into you Sue? You've lost it completely."

I tried to stand up, wincing from the painful bruises and cuts to my body. I tried to catch my breath and watched him shaking her. He looked shocked as if he'd never seen her behave like that before. He pulled her up and marched her towards the top of the staircase as I looked on. She reluctantly complied and just spat her last words at me "Just make sure you get out of my flat and never come back you little whore."

I didn't utter a word and watched her descend the stairs first with him close behind. The man turned to me as he left. His look seemed to be a silent apology for letting her do this to me.

Justin arrived back shortly after she left but didn't look as shocked as I'd expected when he asked, "What the hell happened?"

He could see I was bruised and bleeding. I looked into his eyes and realised what he'd done. He'd told Sue I was going to be at the flat and left to let her deal with me. Shocked and scared, I went into the bedroom, locked the door, hurriedly dressed, and grabbed whatever clothes I could pack. Justin made no attempt to beg me to stay and I walked away from my flat, from him and my life to go back to Mum's. As I glanced back, he was sitting on the sofa with his head in his hands.

Something that day told me I would never be free until I cut off completely from everyone connected to my upbringing. I had to remove myself entirely from my old life if I were to survive but I had no idea that Sue would remain with me for much of my adult life, causing destruction, devastation, and pain far beyond the years of my childhood.

Chapter 6

Only the broken-hearted know the truth about love.

Mason Cooley

I had no real direction in my life, let alone dreams or aspirations. I let Mum and Bob guide me reluctantly. I was working locally as a sales assistant. Mum had helped me to work on my appearance and behaviour to become more feminine. For the first time, I started to take an interest in clothes, and I found the whole process liberating.

"Perhaps you need to go on a diet to make yourself lose a bit of weight, darling," Mum said seemingly frustrated by my undesirable appearance. So, I starved myself in an attempt to become what Mum thought was acceptable. I felt if I got to the right size, I would find the happiness she proclaimed I would find.

Mum growing up as a child during the Second World War had no choice but to live on rations. My grandmother had fed her milky puddings and stodgy foods. When she'd become a teenager, Mum had taken drastic action to lose weight to become what she saw as the ideal woman. From then on, she was conscious of her weight and hardly ate during the day, eating only one meal at night. I wanted to please Mum and assumed a woman had to be very slim to be successful in life. So I started to watch Mum's behaviour and copied her. When she came home from work, she opened a bottle of wine while cooking and when dinner was served, we had very small portions.

What I later noticed was that Mum filled herself up with cheese and nibbles while cooking. I thought it wasn't good to eat much in front of people, so I started eating in secret. I would starve myself for three days until I felt sick and faint and then binge on chocolate bars, cakes, and bread for a day. This created a crash and burn effect, so I often ate when I was very low and starved when on a high. Outwardly I was outgoing, confident, and fun. None of my friends or work colleagues realised the agony I was going through or that I had developed a serious and uncontrollable eating disorder.

Mum had told me when I moved in that someone famous lived in her road. "Darling, Lewis Collins happens to live on one of those large farms down Denham Lane, just near the club you go to. You used to adore him when he was on *The Professionals*."

Gavin had already mentioned Lewis often popped into the country club for a drink. "Don't worry, my gorgeous girl, you. I'll introduce you to him when he comes in. He will adore you, I just know it!" Gavin said teasingly.

Gavin used to take me to the private bar at Winkers Farm Country Club where the wealthier and trendier set drank. I found it a little intimidating, but being with Gavin I was accepted. One evening I went to Winkers Farm with Gavin and Marianne. We walked into the private drinking area and there, sitting on a bar stool, was Lewis Collins surrounded by a crowd of people chatting to him.

I instantly felt very self-conscious when I spotted him. You couldn't help but notice him, he was oozing Elvis energy! I was mortified as I was wearing my long three-tiered skirt and a little white embroidered top and, although it was my favourite outfit, I wished I was wearing something more sophisticated. Feeling like a little girl, I made my way to a group of friends as far from Lewis as I could possibly be. My heart was racing, and I felt angry and self-conscious with myself for being so unprepared. Gavin had no qualms and went immediately up to say hi to Lewis.

I decided to pretend Lewis wasn't there and not even glance in his direction. I stood as far from him as possible and hoped he wouldn't notice me, and I'd have a chance on another occasion to look my best. I tried to act as nonchalant as possible but then my worry head butted in and said, *What the hell is he going to see in a little girl like you? Look, he's surrounded by people adoring him and all the women's eyes in the club are focused on him.*

I felt utterly foolish to have even considered the gorgeous Lewis Collins would notice me and I tried to relax. Then Gavin came striding towards me, dragged me towards the bar and announced, "Lewis, meet my very good friend Amanda! Amanda, this is Lewis!"

I said politely "I'm pleased to meet you, Lewis," and offered my hand to shake. He simply took my hand, raised it to his lips and kissed it whilst looking at me with his dark hypnotic eyes, grinning at me naughtily. I blushed heavily and tried to hide my embarrassment.

"Gavin tells me he's very protective of you and doesn't let you out of his sight? Is that right?" he said as I tried to recover.

His gorgeous brown eyes bore through my clothing as he looked me up and down. I imagined myself running my hands through his thick curly brown hair and his confidence gave off an air of sensuality which oozed from every pore of his body. I could smell his aftershave and thought I would never be able to get that smell out of my nostrils again. I drank him in without giving anything away as I replied in my coolest voice, "Yes, he's my guardian angel!"

It was obvious Gavin felt very proud to introduce me as his special friend as most people thought of him as a player. As his platonic friends, Marianne and I were like a protected species. Marianne liked this arrangement as she wasn't a girly girl.

We made small talk for a while. "So I understand you live locally with your parents. Is that right?" he asked me, still grinning.

"Yes." I started to stutter, unnerved by his demeanour. "Yes, my mum's in PR and my stepfather is in sales."

When I could hold it together no more, I made my excuses and headed for the ladies. Standing at the sink, splashing cold water on my face, and trying my utmost to do something more glamorous with my hair, I saw Tink, the lady who worked behind the bar, walk in. She came straight up to me.

"Amanda! Lewis wants you to have this." She handed me a piece of paper, smiled, winked, and then walked out. With my heart in my mouth, I opened the piece of paper and was astonished to see his name written on it with *Call me at five tomorrow* and a phone number on it.

My knees felt weak, and beads of sweat started to form at the base of my spine. Standing alone with my mouth open like a guppy fish I looked in the mirror not knowing what to do next. It was hard enough to have made small talk at the bar with him. How the hell was I going to phone him? I returned to the bar and mingled with some of the regulars not once glancing at Lewis. However my insides were in knots, and I felt an exhilarating rush of excitement mixed with bouts of nausea every time my mind wandered back to the piece of paper in my pocket.

As soon as I got home, I spilled the beans. "Mum, you're not going to believe this, but I met Lewis Collins tonight and he's given me his phone number. He wants me to phone him tomorrow."

"You're kidding?" she said open mouthed. "Has he asked you out on a date then?"

"No, Mum, and I've got no idea what he wants," I said, shaking my head.

"Well, I'm sure you'll find out tomorrow, darling. It must be that he wants to ask you out. What other reason would he give you his phone number for?"

Mum was obviously excited as she contemplated me going out with someone famous and couldn't wait to tell Bob. I had no idea then that Lewis was forty-two and only two years younger than my stepfather and the same age as my mother, but Mum was obviously happy because this was what she always told me she hoped for me – to find a nice man to look after me, and Lewis ticked all her boxes.

The next day, I made the call with Mum's encouragement. I tried to waft Mum and Bob away as they hovered around me like flies. I made the call with them both standing next to me, ears pressed up against the phone in order to catch the whole conversation.

Lewis answered promptly and, although I was very nervous, I found it easy to talk to him. "Hi, Amanda, it's so good to hear from you. I do hope you got home all right last night. I wasn't sure you'd call me."

"Well, Tink said you wanted me to call, and I dare say I was a little intrigued as to what you wanted to talk to me about," I said.

Mum was beaming at me with her thumb up, obviously pleased with how cool I was playing it. We chatted for several minutes until he said, "The reason why I wanted you to call me was because I'd like to take you out on a date if that's all right with you. Don't worry, I'll be bringing a couple of female friends of mine as chaperones, so you can tell your parents you'll be well looked after."

He went on to tell me he wanted to take me out the following weekend and asked me to speak to my mum for her blessing. Embarrassingly, Mum shouted, "Yes" before I even asked her, so it was evident she was listening as he could clearly hear her. When I came off the phone, we all jumped up and down screaming with excitement, including Bob. I was in fairy-tale heaven.

74

Lewis arrived to collect me promptly at seven o'clock the following Saturday. When he rang the doorbell, Mum threw open the door with a glass of bubbly in her hand. She asked him in, and I could hear him politely introducing himself and explaining his plans for that night, and felt a warmth flow through me as I made my way downstairs. To my horror and embarrassment, I saw Mum's dinner party guests had all emerged from the dining room and were hovering in the hallway, glasses in hand. Lewis gazed up at me, obviously amused, and his cheeky smile melted me on the spot.

Our first date was at a local country club with two other ladies he introduced to me as chaperones, which I felt was extremely thoughtful. I wondered if it was because he was aware of my age and naiveté or he was just very old-fashioned. Either way, it was evident to everyone we met that night he was proud to show me off.

When we arrived, I was introduced to the owner of the club, several of the staff he knew personally and his friends. Everyone else in the club looked on at a distance, knowing they were in the presence of a sexy iconic star, and I felt on top of the world. That night he asked me on a second date. I was so flattered he wanted to see me again.

"Would you do me the honour of coming with me to Prince Andrew and Sarah Ferguson's wedding ball next weekend? It's at the Grosvenor Hotel in London. I know it's a little short notice but if you can get yourself a long evening gown, I'll make all the arrangements for us to stay in London over the weekend. That of course is if your parents approve."

"I'm sure they'll approve, Lewis. I'll ask my mum to help me find an appropriate gown."

He winked at me and continued. "It's a tradition that the future princess organises a ball the night before their wedding. She then invites all her favourite guests and then doesn't turn up. You may well find the place will be teaming with celebrities so I hope you can handle it."

"Of course I can. I'm sure it'll be an amazing evening," I said, although my stomach was in knots.

He told me we'd be attending another party the next day which was an invitation by a man called Benny Lee who owned Shepperton Studios.

Mum took me to an evening-wear hire shop in our village and almost instantly I fell in love with a peacock blue, beautiful full length evening dress which fitted like a glove. With its tight bodice and gentle layers flowing gracefully to the floor, I felt like the princess I'd always longed to be.

When Lewis picked me up to take me into London, I was all packed and ready to go. In fact, I'd been ready with dress and suitcase in the hallway long before he was due. My hair and outfit looked a little ridiculous as I was in a jogging suit with my hair tussled up in ribbons and curls piled on top of my head which I'd had styled at a chic salon. I started to backtrack and wonder if I'd made the right choice of outfit.

When I opened the door, Mum and I were surprised to see an old Renault 5 parked outside on the drive. *Oh well*, I thought, *Can't have it all*. I guessed his white steed couldn't accommodate my bursting suitcase all the way to London anyhow.

The journey seemed to fly by. He was full of compliments as he'd noticed how much effort I'd made with my hair and dress, which almost took up the entire back seat of his car. He was very upbeat and his banter throughout our journey made me realise he was looking forward to spending the weekend with me. I was in heaven. Before I knew it we'd arrived at our hotel and he left me to get dressed in our room while he went down to the bar. When he returned, I was finishing off my make-up and he gave a warm sound of appreciation as he checked out my appearance.

I had my back to him looking into a full-length cheval mirror as he arrived back in the room, and he stopped to look at me through the reflection. I smiled and looked down as he commented, "Beautiful!"

Nervously, I sat next to him in the black cab on the way to the ball and we talked a little about his life. "Look, Amanda, I know you're a decent girl and that's why I invited you here tonight. I know you're not interested in getting celebrity status like all the usual girls I meet and that's what struck me about you!" he said. "I don't want to draw attention to us, and the place will be swarming with paparazzi. You're too nice a girl for that mob to speculate who you are, and I don't want to ruin what hasn't yet begun. So, when we arrive, we'll get out of the cab at separate times and head to the door, I'll be waiting for you in the foyer. That way they can't photograph us together and they'll leave us alone."

When we arrived at the venue, we lined up in a queue of cars arriving at the steps of the Grosvenor Hotel. There was a huge mob of photographers and people surrounding the guests entering the hotel. Lewis gently squeezed my hand and winked at me. I was nervous and didn't want to disappoint him. I made sure when I got out, I walked away from Lewis so we couldn't be photographed together. As soon as we got inside, he grasped me by the arm, turned me towards him and held me firmly by my waist. He smiled at me appreciatively and said, "Thank you, Amanda. You did brilliantly." I melted under his gaze but revealed nothing of what I was feeling at that moment.

Guests were pouring in through the main lobby area and we were directed upstairs to a private function area for a drink. I wasn't fond of alcohol, but on this occasion felt the champagne would calm my nerves. Celebrities were mingling with other guests, and it all felt so surreal. I didn't want to forget anything so drank in every detail to store it all forever in my memory. As I stood with Lewis, who was smiling and greeting everyone he knew, I felt he was proud I was on his arm, but no-one spoke to me. I guessed my age had a lot to do with it. Feeling slightly self-conscious, I prayed to feel included. At that moment Paul Daniels the magician with his wife Debbie McGee on his arm, walked up to me.

"Hi, my name's Paul Daniels and this is my wife, Debbie. Don't suppose you can introduce me to Lewis, can you? I've got a request to make!"

I smiled sweetly, introduced myself and then turned to Lewis who was just finishing a conversation with someone. "Lewis, this is Paul Daniels and his wife Debbie. Paul has something to ask you!"

Lewis squeezed my hand which was still draped over his arm, gave me the cheekiest, sexiest grin and turned to give his full attention to Paul. Paul then got into a deep conversation about Lewis donating a bow tie to the celebrity memorabilia he had at his restaurant. Lewis agreed and was flattered Paul had asked him.

It was a spectacular evening. Being seated at one of the many elaborately dressed tables with Barbara Windsor, Gareth Hunt and Jess Conrad amongst many others had me gushing in awe at how lucky I was. When the late-night DJ started to play his music, Lewis asked me to dance. I thought at some point the clock would strike midnight and Cinderella would have to leap off home. But no, the wicked stepmother existed no more, and this prince was real.

We danced until it was almost the end of the night. In the taxi to the hotel I asked him what room I'd be staying in. He smiled at me and nodded "You'll be sleeping with me, Amanda, but don't worry. You don't have to do anything you don't want to do if you're not ready."

It shocked me as I wasn't prepared, and I wondered if I'd disappoint him by saying no or yes and getting it wrong. I considered my options and decided as I'd had such an amazing time and he was so considerate of my needs; I would just say "yes" regardless. I felt nervous and yet excited at the prospect of fulfilling my girly fantasy. I decided to give myself to him even though I didn't feel I was capable of knowing what to do with a man of his age. I felt all I could do was try to please and enjoy the moment.

The night in our hotel room was not how I'd imagined, but I put that down to an excess of alcohol on his part, and his age. Still, I felt special as he'd chosen me, so how could I let disappointment shadow my moment?

In the morning, I hurriedly had a shower and got ready for the party the next day. While we were having breakfast, I listened to Lewis talk more about his fascinating life until we eventually left to head up to Shepperton Studios. On arrival we were greeted by Benny Lee, the owner, and his entourage who welcomed us into a hugely decorated room full of red, white, and blue balloons. Many guests were already there enjoying a late breakfast with champagne. All eyes were on me as Lewis and I arrived.

We spent the entire day and evening there, eating and drinking. Champagne flowed continuously and it was obvious to me Lewis loved to drink. At one point he said, "I loathe occasions like this, but you've just got to do it in my trade."

I could understand why.

We were taken by Benny in a golf buggy round the various film sets. It was a long day and equally long night, and when it was time to leave I realised Lewis had drunk heavily all day but was nonetheless getting into his car to drive home.

We drove back to Buckinghamshire and though he was incredibly over the limit he seemed completely in control so I didn't worry as much as I should have done. When we got back to his home, near to where I lived, he took me up to his room.

It was a huge room with several windows due to the shape and size of it with a large bed in the middle and one end of the room was filled with stuffed toys. He smiled cheekily as he saw me looking and said, "These are from my fans from all over the world. My sister Val and bother-in-law John live with me and manage my affairs. They deal with all my fan mail and gifts as I've still got a huge following from Germany and other parts of the world. I keep the gifts as I feel humbled they still follow me."

I felt oddly uncomfortable to think women from all over the world still sent him gifts even though he'd not worked in television for some time, but realised I'd have to start getting used to his life if I wanted to be a part of it. And I did.

It was an odd cold room, sparse and olde-worlde, and it seemed like the life had been sucked out of it. I could see it had probably been a grand room at one point, with its copious amounts of space and huge ensuite bathroom overlooking the grounds but something had died there, and I couldn't put my finger on it. It felt a little morbid, like the room was in mourning for a loved one.

Climbing into bed with him that night I felt the best had happened and something was amiss. He fell asleep almost the moment he got into bed mumbling he was tired. I felt rejected, but turned over and went to sleep myself. I assumed his copious alcohol intake had taken its toll.

In the morning, when I went down into the kitchen I was greeted by Val and John who were sitting at the kitchen table with two German girls.

"Hello, Amanda. It's lovely to meet you. I'm Val, Lewis's sister and this is John my husband. This is Brigitte and Claudia, two sisters who are fans of Lewis and camping in our garden for the summer."

They were all tucking into a breakfast of eggs and toast and Val told me how the sisters were great fans of Lewis and had followed him for years. I was amazed at his generous appreciation for his fans and Val and John seemed so down to earth. I immediately liked them, especially the girls.

"Ah, so you're Amanda. We're so happy to meet you and hope we can become friends," Brigitte said.

Lewis eventually let them have one of his rooms to stay in, as he felt for them camping in the grounds of his home. The family had taken to them as they were so young and incredibly loyal. The girls had been invited to a few places with him, which I'd guessed had stroked his ego.

"They're here every year so becoming part of the family," Val told me "Lewis felt it was only right to offer them a room as they've saved all year to come here to see him."

I was overwhelmed with the girl's dedication to him and likewise the way Lewis and his family honoured them with inviting them into their home. Val introduced them as future chaperones and I took comfort in this as they were more my age and I understood from what she was telling me Lewis had future intentions for me.

When I was dropped off home later, I was surprised Lewis still wanted to see me. "So, Amanda, did you have a good time this weekend?"

I bit my tongue, so I didn't gush how amazing and fairy-tale like it had all been. "Yes, I've had a wonderful time, Lewis, thank you!" I said, keeping it simple.

"Then I'll give you a call and we'll arrange to go out again soon then." He kissed me firmly on the lips.

I saw Lewis nearly every day after that. He'd pick me up in his car with the German sisters and we'd head off up to Winkers Farm or Hazelmere Country Club and spend the entire evening there, often until the early hours of the morning.

I struggled with this as I worked at Hayden Laboratories full time but made up for it by catching up on sleep when I wasn't seeing him. I was lucky enough to be able to wear Mum's clothes and so had a vast wardrobe of sophisticated and expensive outfits to choose from.

Lewis didn't work. He spent his days sleeping and his nights drinking. Val confided in me one day. "He was engaged to a woman called Melanie for five years and was besotted with her, but she left him for another man, and it crushed him. That's when the drinking started, and his career nose-dived."

I felt for Lewis and for the whole family. I wanted then more than anything to be his salvation. He'd not had much work since leaving *The Professionals*, and although Val and John managed him and he got auditions, he was podgier than he had been some years before and it was starting to get round he had a drink problem.

He'd had an audition just before I met him for the new Bond movie, but Pierce Brosnan got it because he was taller Lewis said. Lewis spoke of it often, and I sympathised with him as he regretted missing a key role that would have set him up for life. Since then, he seemed to have given up.

Lewis was passionate about life and especially skydiving and asked me if I'd like to watch him one day. As the summer progressed, I was with him all the time and often alone, as it was obvious by then the German girls had been a cover at the beginning to hide our relationship. As the months rolled on, he was keener to spend time taking me out alone and didn't worry about us being seen together.

He drove me to a private sport parachute club, Weston on the Green in Oxfordshire, and that was the first time Lewis introduced me to his sport by taking me up in a glider. I'd never been in a small aircraft before, let alone a glider. It was exhilarating but like being strapped into a flying coffin.

We did five loop-the-loops, one after the other and from that moment I was addicted. Every weekend I travelled with Lewis to the drop zone and watched him skydive. I found it exciting and was such a relief to see him in his element – alive, passionate, and stimulated.

He proudly introduced me as his girlfriend to all his club mates who eyed me up and down. It was obvious from the looks on the boy's faces that they thought, *Good on you Lewis* and the girls thought, *I can't understand what he sees in her*. I was always dressed in jeans, a jumper and my wet weather gear, no make-up and hair in a constant look of weatherworn distress. No wonder they were speculating as to why our relationship existed.

At night, the drinking took over in the clubhouse and went on into the wee small hours, with Lewis surrounded by his sky diving buddies, most of whom were air force personnel or stewardesses. His lovemaking was short and sweet, if at all, followed by open-mouthed snoring, so different from the sexy man I spent my days with, but I was besotted with him and accepted his shortcomings feeling this was either his age or his drinking. Either way, it didn't matter. The fact I was his girl meant the world to me.

The summer was magical. We were together all the time. I didn't see my friends as much, as my life was absorbed by him, but he always dutifully made sure I was home when I needed to be. Life was a roller coaster of laughter and partying.

One morning as we were heading off to Weston for a weekend of skydiving, he took me out into the outbuildings on his farm and showed me his two beautiful bikes. These were obviously his babies and a glint in his eye revealed he'd not spent time with them in a long while. "I want us to go up to Weston on my bike this weekend together. Val and John can follow us in the car with all our belongings. What do you say?"

I looked at him nervously.

"It'll be OK, I promise you. I've even got leathers for you to wear." Like a boy announcing his new toy, he disappeared into the house for a moment and when he reappeared, he had a beautiful all in one woman's leather bike suit.

He told me it had been made for Melanie, his ex-fiancée, and he'd kept it. He still had the Ducati he'd ridden in the film *Who Dares Wins*, which was his pride and joy, but as it was only a one-seater, he took me out on his other bike, which was equally as fast, noisy, and powerful. The leather suit fitted like a glove.

That day I clung onto him proudly on the back of his bike, feeling I was melding into his body. He rode the bike with such expertise and confidence, and when we hit the road works, he ignored the queuing traffic and swung the bike into the coned off lane and accelerated past the flabbergasted people sitting dutifully in their cars. He pushed the boundaries, and I loved it.

One day he dropped me back at my house on the back of his bike and Mum came out to greet us. She was gushing over his amazing bike, and he started to tease her. "Come on then, Val, why don't you come and have a spin with me?" he said. Mum was clearly excited, and Bob and I looked on incredulously, but Lewis persisted. "Come on, put the helmet on and I'll just take you round the block." As usual, when Lewis turned up at our house many of the neighbours suddenly appeared, pruning, and tending to their gardens. Mum finally agreed and popped on my helmet and jumped on. He rode at top speed out of our close with her screaming and wailing on the back.

When Lewis returned, he looked at me with his cheeky grin, winking at me as if to say, "Your mum's hooked!" I admired his confidence to take people out of their comfort zone, including my mum, and hoped it was to impress me.

After several months of being together, I was concerned my period hadn't started and I told Lewis. "I think I might be pregnant," I said after weeks of worry. He wasn't cross as I'd expected, but immediately told Val. "Don't worry," he said, "we'll take care of everything. It'll be OK."

Val quietly arranged for me to go to their Harley Street doctor, and I had a pregnancy test. It came back as negative, and everyone was relieved. Lewis had confided in me several times he wanted a boy and I thought, if I were pregnant, I could make his dream come true, but deep down, I knew I wasn't old enough for him. Not once had he said he loved me although I'd told him I loved him at the end of the summer. He'd hugged me that night and held me tight which made me feel he must care for me.

As the weather got colder and the sky diving season finished, out of the blue he turned to me one day and told me he'd been given an acting job in Australia. I knew he was gently saying it was over.

He told me it was a six-month theatrical role, which he'd taken as he needed the work. He'd been bankrupt since I'd met him and made no illusions about it. Val and John had been managing his finances and he was just about holding onto Moap's Farm, his home. Whenever we went to Winkers Farm or Hazelmere Country Club drinking, everything was done on a tab which Val and John dealt with as Lewis never carried money. Val had told me he'd drunk himself into debt and as they'd given up good jobs to manage him when he was doing well, they had no choice but to keep going until he came back up out of the deep water, he was in.

"Amanda, I know we've had a wonderful time together and you do know I'm very fond of you, but I start rehearsals in three weeks."

I felt sudden panic and loss well up inside me.

"I care for you very deeply and if you were older, I would have that boy with you but you have your whole life ahead of you now. You are worth so much more and need to spread your wings. You need to start living and one day you'll find that special someone. I promise. You're still so young. Spread your wings and find a nice young man of your own age and enjoy life. Don't you dare wait for me to return. The last thing I want is for you to waste your life. Go and live it and enjoy. Much as I want you to be there for me when I get back, I don't want you waiting for me, pining. I just want you to get on with your life now, Amanda."

He hugged me and walked away. I then plunged into a transient state of grief and mourning, and my world was empty once again. It was as if at long last I'd met, fallen in love with my prince and then lost him.

Chapter 7

Do what you fear and fear disappears.

David Joseph Schwartz

I made a decision. I was either to creep out of life's existence or drag myself into a new one. So shortly after Lewis had left, I planned to do a parachute jump. The day drew nearer, and I had to prepare. It was a weekend course of a mixture of practical and theory at Weston on the Green. There was a large crowd of us, and the training was strict. The camaraderie was highly charged and positive, so I felt I was doing something that would make me feel I belonged.

On the Sunday of the jump, we nervously lined up to wait for the plane to taxi onto the runway and take us up. Two lads had dropped out through nerves and the instructors took plenty of opportunities to keep us relaxed in readiness for our special moment. We had to pass all the training as only we were in control of the jumps and had to be perfectly prepared. We all filed onto the aircraft like sheep as we'd rehearsed meticulously in the hanger. Dressed in our jumpsuits and with our parachutes perfectly packed on our backs we all felt the adrenalin kick in and the fear was obvious on our faces.

It took a good five minutes to reach the right altitude. There was no side door on the aircraft and the sound of the wind rushing past us and the increasing cold as we reached the right altitude heightened our anxiety. We were all linked up to our static lines and told to move towards the door one by one. We'd all reached that moment and wanted it to be over and done with as quickly as possible. One at a time we moved to the edge of the plane, dangled our legs over, arms crossed over our chests, and ran through our drill of shouting commands to let the instructor know we were exiting.

I don't know how I managed to let myself go but an automatic response took over and I leaned forward and tipped myself off the edge of the aircraft. For that first second, there was nothing as my brain tried to register what was going on. Before I knew it, I was shouting out the commands and with an almighty thud, I pulled on my harness straps, my parachute opened. Then there was silence except for the sound of the wind whistling in my ears and round my chute. The sound of the aircraft engine and rushing of wind had subsided to a gentle whistle as the wind carefully carried me through nothingness. The exhilaration was overwhelming, the biggest buzz I'd ever had.

I pulled myself into touch again and talked myself through the process of using the windsocks to guide me down to the drop zone. I didn't allow fear to come into play, just focused on trusting that, if I followed everything I'd been taught, I'd land in the correct place and land without breaking anything. Constantly assessing my speed and direction and using my guidelines to turn me this way and that, steering myself nearer and nearer to where I needed to be before attempting to land, I aimed for the centre of the drop zone. Moving from the thrill of actually exiting the aircraft and my chute successfully opening, I had to move to the most important part — landing.

The postage-stamp sized fields neatly laid out beneath me were getting bigger and bigger. Soon cars became visible on the roads below. When I realised it was almost time to land with about fifty feet to go, I turned into wind over the drop zone. It was crucial to get it right as the landing was the equivalent of jumping off a ten-foot wall. One wrong move and it would be a broken ankle or worse.

I was coming in fast as the blades of grass became visible and I tried to remain calm and remember all I'd been taught to land as safely as I possibly could. As my feet finally touched the ground, the landing felt harder than I'd expected. A huge judder shot up my body, but I remembered to let my knees bend to lessen the impact and do the dive roll I'd practiced umpteen times.

I'd done it!

I felt elated as I looked around and saw all the other guys around me landing and busily scraping up and gathering their parachutes. I pulled the silk and lines towards me, bundled it into my arms and proudly walked with everyone to the end of the drop zone. I was on such a high I wanted to do it again. That day I signed up for a parachute-training course.

Every Friday I drove to Oxfordshire straight after work and left last thing Sunday to get back for work the next day. My weekend was consumed with parachuting lessons and partying when night fell. I was at last one of the gang! The people at Weston were grounded, wholesome characters, risk takers, adventurers who were always out to get the biggest buzz. Who wouldn't want to be with them after the upbringing I'd had? Most of the guys were RAF boys from the local airbase, Brize Norton, and the girls were mainly air stewardesses. The group was three-quarters male, and because they were addicted to their sport, they tended to be single. It wasn't for the lack of being unable to get a girlfriend, just that they lived on airbases 24/7.

Shirley, one of the eldest girls, was in her forties. She always flirted openly with all the men, including Lewis, and never really got anywhere. I'd sensed from the onset she felt threatened by me, so when one of the instructors asked me out, even though I wasn't particularly keen on him, I guessed she'd feel appeased by me being unavailable! For some reason, I felt threatened by her. I hated conflict. I assumed it was because she reminded me of Sue, as Shirley was very judgemental of the other girls at times and could be downright cruel behind their backs. I didn't want to upset the apple cart, so I tried to step back and let her feel she could freely flirt with whom she wished and walked away when she started on one of her rants about another club member.

Try as I might, I couldn't get Lewis out of my system. Though this new guy was a gentle giant and very courteous, he didn't make me feel the way Lewis had. I started to resent going out with him and so finished the relationship. I then attracted one man after another, but none of them had the maturity or charisma Lewis had. None of them came close. I was hooked on being at the drop zone every weekend but wanted to progress and do what the big boys did, so I decided to sign up for an automatic free fall course and learn how to skydive to make myself feel more accepted into the club.

I started with a tandem jump with an instructor and knew I'd made the right decision. Soon I was jumping out of aircraft at twelve thousand feet. Now I felt I was really part of the gang, even if we were a bunch of misfits come together to escape. I had this deep yearning to belong to a family, a community, even if it did come at a cost with the risks we took to get our fixes.

One day I jumped with a head cold even though I'd played it down. We were all told not to jump with a cold because of pressure building up in the head, especially going through the last three thousand feet, but I was so determined to keep going I went ahead without telling anyone.

That day it was a normal jump as any. I exited the aircraft with two trainers and a cameraman. After falling for nine thousand feet in freefall, I opened my parachute at about three thousand feet. Usually, when our parachute was opened, we'd do a few spirals where you pulled down hard on one side of your lines, which would make your parachute spin so you'd drop faster, or you could just allow yourself to coast up and down wind, guiding yourself eventually onto the drop zone. If you got it right, when you pulled down hard on both break lines, you'd flutter down and tiptoe onto the grass. This day however, everything went as always until I reached that crucial last three thousand feet and then I felt extreme pressure in my head. It was so painful, and I tried to guide myself down as slowly as possible, gliding on the wind rather than spiralling, to slow the descent and reduce the agony. As I came into land, I felt myself feeling faint and then there was nothing.

I had managed to get down safely enough but lay on the grass a little too long for comfort, according to some of the instructors who ran over to me. Instead of taking my helmet off, they took me to the debrief centre and rather than sympathy and a cup of tea I got a damn good rollicking about not taking responsibility when they discovered I had a cold. Word got round and soon it was known how I'd risked myself and other skydivers who I could have hurt by passing out in free fall. At speeds of a hundred and twenty miles an hour, a collision could be fatal. That weekend I went home with my tail between my legs.

Because of the vast expense of the sport, I was also working at Hazelmere Country Club as the owner, a fellow skydiver and one of Lewis's friends, had given me work there several nights a week. The pay wasn't brilliant, but the tips were good, and I was used to the lack of sleep anyway. After the cold incident, I took a reality check with what was going on with my life. I was working day and night to pay for a sport that was taking me over and the highs and lows were taking its toll on me. And since Lewis had gone, my eating disorder had worsened dramatically. I decided to walk away from the sky diving and stop working at the club and try and find something to earth me and help me feel I belonged. It was the end of the parachute season anyhow and I felt the break would do me good and was starting to get myself into a more civilised routine of work and seeing friends again.

It was close to Christmas when I got a call out of the blue from Lewis. He said he was finishing his stint in Australia and soon to be on his way home. He asked me to join him in Stockport for a weekend as he was playing Buttons in pantomime. John and Val drove me up there to the venue and we all stayed the weekend.

Lewis was so excited to see me, like a young boy. He was on top form and in great spirits. I was wonderstruck by how much he came alive on stage. He'd lost weight and was almost back to his fighting weight of yesteryears, but something was missing.

After Saturday's performance, we headed off to a private party in a club in Rochdale, hosted by the comedian duo Cannon and Ball. It was at that party I realised how alone I felt. These people were strangers to me. I felt lost in a sea of faces, all laughing with one another in their private huddles that I would never be a part of. They were not my people. I felt ridiculously young and naïve, unworldly, and disconnected.

That weekend, I said goodbye. Lewis realised I meant it and we said nothing about seeing each other again. I was in a better space and felt more assured about what I wanted from life. I decided to take time out for myself and booked a couple of 'weeks' holiday in Tolon in Greece. I needed to spread my wings from the safety net of those who had become my custodians. It was I that had created the net in Lewis, Gavin, my mother, and her husband, but it was filled with holes that was letting me hang precariously, threatening the possibility of me falling into another black hole that I did not want to visit.

It was at the beginning of the season in 1987 and I was twenty. I arrived excited, scared, and hopeful as I'd never been away on my own before, let alone abroad, but something had guided me to do this, and I knew it was right. As soon as I arrived, I bonded with the three holiday reps. Over the next two weeks, I found the bond between us strengthen. Louis was the tiniest man I'd ever seen. Worn and leathered from too much sunbathing, his wrinkled complexion tarnished a once good-looking guy, but he'd aged considerably from too many fags and far too much alcohol. Living from one resort to another he'd worked for years on the holiday rep scene, and it showed. He was an old timer, but he had a great personality and the girls loved him. The two girls, Charlie, and Carol were gorgeous in every way, beautiful, slim, and tall with curves in all the right places and of course, were in their element as all the boys loved them. They were good girls. They didn't go out with holidaymakers, and I wondered how they sustained this respect for their roles considering they were still young, attractive women. It turned out they both had boyfriends back home but liked the long-distance relationship thing.

I had an amazing time during that fortnight as the girls and Louis took me to all the best clubs and bars, to the best water sports and on the best excursions and I fell in love with the lifestyle and people there. When it came to the end of the holiday, the four of us were in tears. It was then Louis said, "Look, we've needed a fourth rep out here for some time. Why don't you consider working for us? You'd be great with the holidaymakers."

"I would love to, Louis, so long as it would be definite work as I'll have to resign from my job." I felt a surge of excitement and hope surge through my body once again, like the thrill I'd experienced being around Lewis and I knew in my heart I had to grab the opportunity.

"I'll have a word with the bosses, but I can guarantee you have a job here. Can you start in two weeks?"

I hugged him with all my might for the chance to leave the UK and make a fresh start.

Louis contacted his firm and they let him officially interview me, which comprised a drink in the local cocktail bar. I then returned home, told Mum, handed in my notice, and booked a flight to return in a fortnight. Mum was concerned I was giving up a good job, but I told her I needed a change of scenery and to make it on my own for a while.

Two weeks later, I was travelling back out to Greece with sixty passengers ready for my new life. I chatted excitedly to all the passengers around me, telling them I was going to work for the company as an airline rep and would be travelling back with them to the airport when they left. As we arrived at Athens airport, however, we got the shock of all shocks. The airline had gone into liquidation. This meant we were all stuck at the airport as none of the coach drivers would come and collect us through fear of not getting paid. What had started an exciting adventure and new chapter in my life was suddenly a living nightmare. I now had no job, nowhere to stay and probably no means of getting home. As passengers got wind of the fact, I was an official rep, they began to approach me to create a rescue operation for them.

By chance, I'd kept a cocktail stick with a phone number on it of Dionysus Bar, the bar where all the reps hung out. I phoned, not expecting anyone to be there as it was the early hours of the morning, but the bar owner, Yannis, answered.

"Yannis, it's Amanda, the new rep! I'm at Athens Airport with sixty passengers I've just flown over with, and we've just been told the airline's gone into liquidation and don't have a coach to collect us. Is Louis or the girls there?"

"Don't worry, Amanda, Louis and the girls are here and are trying to do something about it. I'll pass you onto Louis."

Louis came onto the phone and said, "Amanda, don't worry. We were told late last night. The coach company informed us they weren't sending their men out as they were worried about not being paid, but we've managed to organise another coach who've agreed to fetch you all. When it arrives, you'll just have to do your best and get all the passengers on the coach and when you arrive here, we'll sort them out this end. Please don't worry, Amanda, we'll sort this mess out and everything will be OK."

I wasn't totally convinced, but to make the best of it I went back to the passengers and told them we'd all be picked up as soon as possible and their holidays would go ahead. I managed to convince them they'd have their flights home. We were fortunate as we were the last flight out. Others who'd booked and paid would lose their holidays. Everyone started to calm down and started to chat about how lucky they were. As the coach arrived, a cheer erupted, and we all poured out. Three hours later we were in Tolon. I was exhausted from the responsibility of having to take on a role I wasn't prepared for, though I accepted that I and the dodgy coach driver, whose coach was equally as dodgy, had no choice but to get on with the job in hand.

It was five in the morning when the weary passengers were greeted by Louis and the girls. As they ushered them into hotels with promises of an afternoon meeting to reassure them their holiday would be just as planned, I went into Dionysus Bar for a coffee. Louis eventually walked in to greet me whilst the girls continued to deal with all the questions arising from the guests.

"What's going to happen, Louis?" I asked.

"I don't know!" he said, and sat and sipped his coffee, trying to weigh up the odds more than drawing any conclusions from what had happened. "It seems this next two weeks are our last working for the airline and then Charlie, Carol and I are out of a job. I'm sorry, Amanda but the airline has told me you haven't got a job either. Don't worry though, we'll work something out."

The girls and Louis all had a flight home in two weeks to see the last passengers home. As I'd not officially started, Louis suggested I shared with him and the girls for the duration of their stay and then I'd have to fend for myself. Having taken little money out there as I was expecting a salary and soon to start earning, I realised I was in dire straits. Yannis had been hovering at the bar and he came over to us and asked if he could speak to me. He asked me to meet him in his brother's bar further up the street in private later that morning.

I was sitting outside in the already blazing heat drinking yet another cup of coffee when Yannis arrived. He sat, ordered a coffee by snapping his fingers in the air at his brother, and proceeded to tell me his proposal.

"Look, Amanda, you're in a predicament and so am I. My wife, Jackie, has just sent our English nanny home. Paula was staying with us at our house looking after our daughter Nicola, but I got caught sleeping with her and my wife is furious. Jackie told me to find a nanny and quick. I know it's not what you came here to do, but if you became Nicola's nanny, you'd have your own room and food, and everything taken care of. You'd have free drinks at the bar anytime, free access to all the clubs here and, of course, free water sports. What do you say?"

I was flabbergasted by my lucky recovery landing on my feet like that after such a shock, so I replied a little dumbstruck, "Yes, I guess it's meant to be, Yannis. Does Nicola speak English?"

"A little. Baby English. She's only four."

I recalled seeing her on my previous trip and remembered a pretty little blonde girl in a blue dress. I thought it would actually be much more fun looking after a little girl than dealing with problems and irate holidaymakers.

"You only have to look after her three mornings and two afternoons a week. The rest of the time is your own and we'll pay you twenty-five pounds per week. It's not much to live on, but enough for all you need as we'll pay for everything else. What do you say? It would mean starting today as we both need to work."

I felt it was meant to be. "Yes, of course, Yannis," I said without hesitation, feeling my lucky angels were hovering close and orchestrating my windfall.

So, I moved into my new home and met my new family. It was a far better deal than working for the airline anyhow, as I only had to work fifteen hours a week and when Jackie arrived home at night from the bar, I could go out and meet my friends. Louis and the girls were thrilled with my good fortune, and they tried to stay by finding cleaning jobs (the only other jobs apart from nannying available to Brits in that area). When I got to know the family, I realised my good fortune as Jackie and Yannis were the wealthiest family for miles.

I spent my days with Nicola down on the beach or dressing her up to go and have an ice cream at her uncle's bar. The rest of the time, I spent with my newfound friends on the beach. Nicola hardly spoke English as her parents always spoke to her in Greek. I had to therefore learn baby Greek to communicate with her, but I grew very fond of her and loved how my wonderful opportunity had given me this great pleasure of looking after this gorgeous little blonde girl.

During the summer, while it hit temperatures of forty degrees, Yannis taught me to water-ski, and I spent every opportunity paragliding off the back of his powerboat. I found a whole new bunch of friends, so I was out every night at the bars and clubs. Although I didn't drink much, I had a passion for dancing, so I spent all night on the dance floor. Life was magical and exceptional in every way I could wish for. I felt I had found my Nirvana.

The sun filled days were consumed by sunbathing, swimming, water sports, new friends and of course, little Nicola whom I adored. I met up with the other English nannies and our children played on the beach together as we made sandcastles for them and dug tunnels.

Yannis was a challenge as he was constantly trying it on. I'd have felt flattered had it not been for the fact he looked like an ageing rock star, and I wanted my job too much, but it kept him amused and I avoided him as much as possible when alone.

October finally arrived and all the tourists were disappearing, the reps from all the other airlines were setting off for home and I had a flight booked to return courtesy of Yannis and Jackie. As the bus stopped to collect me to take me to the airport, Jackie and Nicola came to see me off. I dared not cry as I didn't want Jackie to know how fond I was of Nicola, but instead gave them both a big hug and leapt onto the bus and grabbed a seat.

From the bus window however, looking down, I felt a rush of apprehension and loss as I looked at that little girl. But it wasn't Nicola I saw. It was the girl I once was, being left abandoned by my own mother. The feeling was overwhelming and intense, and I recognised then that my own younger self was there still inside me, alone and fearful of being abandoned. I shut it down as soon as I felt it, not letting it take root, too frightened that if I did, I would leap off that bus and never leave her.

Numbed by my internal ache, I watched Nicola who was crying and reaching out to me as we drove away and I wondered how many nannies she'd have throughout her childhood and for that matter, how many more would Yannis have?

Chapter 8

Ambition has one heel nailed in well,

though she stretch her fingers

to touch the heavens.

Lao Tzu

I arrived home in the UK to be greeted by Mum. I'd missed her but didn't relish the lack of freedom living with her and Bob would bring. However, reality was that I had nowhere else to go.

"So Amanda, now you're back home, what're you intending to do workwise?" Bob asked no sooner had I arrived back at their house.

"Have you thought about a career? How about working for the airlines if that's what interests you?" Mum said.

She had a point. I did need to focus my efforts into something more substantial for the future.

"You've had a great summer, but perhaps you need to start thinking about making something of your life now." Bob said.

They claimed they both had my best interests at heart, but at that stage I still had no understanding of what I really wanted to do. I felt they needed to encourage me to find a sustainable job so that I could move on from living with them, and likewise, I felt the same.

The airlines did seem like a logical starting point. In a matter of days, we'd discovered British Airways were doing a major recruitment for their contract handling division at Heathrow. I couldn't decide if it was a sign or a stroke of luck.

I had no idea what contract handling entailed but phoned up for an application form. When it arrived and I read all the details, something stirred within me. A mixture of excitement and fear surged through my body as I thought about the benefits and enormous opportunities of working at the airport. This was a serious role with serious training needing serious people. I was suddenly thrust into insecurities galore and battling with a voice that haunted me from childhood saying, *Don't be so stupid, you won't be good enough. Who'll want you anyway?*

Over the next week, Mum nurtured my spirit and appeased my nagging doubt and built me up to realise I had every opportunity to be recruited. I spent hours putting my application together and focused on putting all my efforts into wishing and praying as I had as a child.

I spent every day envisaging myself already as one of their employees even though I knew it would be a long drawn-out process and a vast number of applicants. In the meantime I started scouting the local papers for something to do while I waited. Although the odds were stacked against me, I had a gut feeling I'd get the role.

I found a job going at a quaint local historic inn, a very popular spot for the community and tourists alike. The advert asked for someone to help out in the office to do the books. I got an interview that afternoon and I went down to the Greyhound Inn and walked in to find chaos. Mr Milne and his wife were running about like headless chickens trying to deal with decorators and people milling about fixing pumps and equipment behind the main bar. Mr Milne apologised for being stressed and explained they were under pressure to get the place fully operational.

He sat me down near the Coach Bar where a few elegantly dressed businessmen drank, the main bar being more for everyone else. We had hardly started the interview when a gentleman came over and asked if he could be served. Desperately looking around for help, Mr Milne then turned to me and asked me if I'd ever worked in a bar before. I shook my head, but he said, "Don't worry, the German gentleman will tell you want he wants. He's always here!"

With that he took me over to the bar and introduced me to the two gentlemen who were sitting on the bar stools and told them I'd be serving them, but they'd have to help me! Nervous at being drafted in to help out in this way, I smiled and politely made conversation while being told by them how to pour their drinks.

Harold, a tall German man with a handlebar moustache and expensively dressed country set clothes, sat on the bar stool in the corner. John, a short, roundish, and portly gentleman, was a recent widower. The two of them were part of the group that was to comprise my future regulars.

The bar was only wide enough for four people to stand side by side. I imagined it had been very busy in its hay day until things changed and the new managers were eventually called upon to breathe new life into the place. I ended up working a whole shift that day and enjoyed the idle chitchat and warm smiles I was getting from behind the bar. Harold and John sweetly helped me by telling me how to pour the drinks, measure, cut the fruit, find the ice, and use the dishwasher. They even knew the prices. It turned out to be a very enjoyable day and when I finished Mr Milne said, "I don't suppose you'd consider running the bar for us? You've obviously got a knack with the customers and I'm sure you'll be great with our regulars."

As it was only short-term, I thought, *Why not?* and started the next day, eager to take on a new challenge. The bar was supposed to support the restaurant with drinks, but it had become an exclusive gentlemen's club for local businessmen. It had dwindled in numbers over the years to almost nothing, but as the refurbishment finished some of the regulars were slowly returning, plus new customers from further afield.

I lovingly transformed that dusty little dated bar into my own sparkling oasis. My regulars were fascinated with me as I was in my early twenties but dressed in an elegant, sophisticated manner, far beyond my years. The *suits*, as I called them, were a mixture of solicitors, accountants, and directors from various local firms. I was treated with the utmost respect and was in my element with such constant flattery. Harold and John were there every day without fail and the bar was often used for meetings and social gatherings. Eventually Mr Milne had to recognise the bar was a growing, viable concern in its own right.

As the weeks went by, I realised I was a listening ear for many more of the regulars. I was the one they turned to when they had work issues, family squabbles, relationship difficulties and strife in general, and I always instinctively knew what to say to make them feel better. I became a regular agony aunt, but always remained composed and professional, even when they flirted outrageously. There was one customer in particular, a solicitor, also named John, who often made comments implying he wanted to take things further by getting to know me better on a personal level, but I never indulged him, as I had no interest in a relationship with anyone, let alone a married man. Gavin would often grace us with his presence, and I was also inundated with the usual crowd of his impeccably dressed friends. Gavin was always surrounded by beautiful people with amazing jobs, so Mr Milne was over the moon having them as customers.

British Airways accepted me for an interview and my grandparents took me along to a very formal meeting with a panel of people who asked me numerous questions. I was very nervous as I wasn't good at speaking about myself, especially to a panel of people staring at me from across the room. I was told there were twelve places to be allocated for contract handling. This meant the people who were chosen could be posted to several different airlines in a number of roles. I wanted the job more than ever when I heard how varied and exciting the life of an agent would be – especially as then British Airways was the elite airline. The uniform alone was worth almost two thousand pounds per agent over their work life as it was designed by the Emmanuels who had made Princess Diana's wedding dress. All staff were treated to top hotels when travelling and had free access to clubs like Stringfellows in London.

Several weeks after my interview, I was called to a second interview and then I got called for a medical. Finally, I got a letter offering me a post and a start date for a twelve-week induction followed by a supervision process of a year before finally joining this elite group. Only twelve of us had been chosen out of fifty-two thousand applicants we were told, which made me feel incredibly privileged.

I was to start in the spring, so I made the most of a magical Christmas and the months I had until I left to start my training. Leaving the bar was very sad for all of us as my regulars had become like a family to me. When Mr Milne told me I'd put the place on the map, I felt a huge thrill of pride.

Chapter 9

Things come apart so easily when they have been held
together with lies.

Dorothy Allison

The day I started my training, I was on cloud nine. Two days before, Mum had taken me to a local garage so I could buy a car. When we got home, Bob told me I'd been ripped off by the deal and was paying towards an extortionate finance plan and I should have gone to him. I would have done, but found it hard to ask him for help. I kept out of his way as I always felt like I was an aggravation to him. British Airways was going to give me more freedom. I met my new colleagues, and we were all just as excited as each other, almost like we were on some reality TV show.

We were introduced to our trainers and given a schedule for the next twelve weeks. It was very intensive and comprehensive. I had homework. Tons of homework. I had to learn every major airport around the world, the codes for the airports, and brush up on my geography. We trained in hangars learning flight attendant safety procedures, the computer system and how to use it for check-in and arrivals, customer service in great depth, and even terrorist training and airport safety. I was chosen to fly to Bremen in Germany, shadowing the captain and co-pilot with them in the cockpit. I even went through all their flight procedures with them for pre-flight in the airports, their exclusive lounge and then the flight itself. It was a unique experience, and I was treated with respect and courtesy by all the crew.

The weeks wore on and we were eventually given our uniform to start feeling our way into our role. We even had actors come and work with us and were filmed role-playing scenarios so we could learn how to deal with irate passengers and plausible challenging situations. As staff we were diverse in every sense and trained to work for over forty airlines at a drop of a hat and trained accordingly. Once training got under way, we became aware we were now connected globally and had the world at our feet.

When we started to work out in the airport itself, some of us started planning trips away with our concessions. As we worked shifts, we had three or four day breaks in between each set of six days working, and so time off could be worked in our favour with a day or two of added holiday. My first trip abroad was with one of the girls whom I'd befriended, Tina, and we went to Malta. She was a bit of a party animal and was boy mad, constantly on the prowl. I felt uncomfortable with this but ended up tagging along. When we returned, I realised most of my colleagues were party animals and so this started a roller coaster year-long time of partying, travelling and working long hours to subsidise the lifestyle.

I could work back-to-back sixteen hour shifts of overtime so my earning capacity was vast for a girl of my age. My eating disorder had got very extreme by then, however. It was inevitable that Michelle (another colleague I befriended) and I gelled at that stage, as we both seemed to have similar traits, her being a bulimic and me a binge eater, neither admitting our individual disorders to anyone including each other.

Since starting my new job at the airport I never got to see any of my friends in the village where I lived because airline life had taken over. I spent most of my time working or partying with my colleagues. Jumping onto jumbos to pop over to Dubai to buy a pair of Ray Bans sunglasses was becoming the norm and life was getting out of control.

I was never shocked or surprised by what life at the airline conjured up, from irate businessmen I managed to appease to stroppy celebrities who held up flights for their own convenience. I checked in Lindsey de Paul on a flight once and was stunned by her height. She was so petite but very down to earth – unlike Samantha Fox, the former Page Three model from the Sun who made an aircraft late and was so flippant towards our crew when she finally arrived. "What's all the fuss about? I'm here, aren't I?" she said as she finally arrived at the gate, breezing past us with a smirk and having no idea how much she'd cost the airline in lost revenue from missing the flight slot. We dealt with them all.

On one shift, I was on the customer service desk in arrivals, which was the most boring allocation of all. We usually just sat and read a book. That day George Michael appeared with his entourage and stood a few yards away from me whilst others collected his luggage and loaded it onto the trolleys.

He was muttering to an older man he was travelling with, and I was trying my hardest not to look. I popped my head up every now and then and surreptitiously gazed around the baggage hall as if conscientiously searching for stray passengers. After a while the older man came over with a brief case and popped it down on my desk.

I asked if I could help him and he surprisingly piped up, "George Michael wondered whether you'd like a signed autograph of him. I'm his manager!"

He opened his brief case and I saw it was filled to the brim with pre-signed photographs of George. I don't know what upset me more, the fact George hadn't come and asked me himself or the audacity he had to think I automatically wanted one. I answered, "No thank you, but I'll take one for my mum!"

He stood open mouthed and passed me a photograph as I smiled sweetly at him. He then shut his case swiftly and darted back off to George. I didn't even give him the satisfaction of looking at it — until he'd left the baggage hall, of course.

On one occasion I was meeting a Singapore Airlines flight, which was invariably a pleasure as the people and crew were always so courteous and grateful. As the aircraft door opened, one of the first passengers to emerge from the aircraft was Boris Becker the tennis player. He had a bag slung over his shoulder and without any warning walked straight up to me and said, "Here! Would you like my sunglasses?" I gave him a huge smile as he handed them to me. He kissed me on the cheek and walked on up the jetty as if it was the most natural thing in the world to give away a pair of Ray Ban Cats. I was one of three girls standing there that day and felt so elated he'd chosen me to give them to.

I treasured those glasses for years. Life was certainly in the fast lane – Stringfellows and the Hippodrome every weekend, champagne and smart dates with decent cars and men with money and power, all of whom seemed to have personality bypasses as they were so egotistical, so they never made it past the second date.

I was hardly ever at home and could no longer relate to my family as life had become a succession of highs when I was travelling and working and lows when I was at home. I crashed and binged or starved and depression slowly started seeping in.

To combat the lows I fixed myself with more highs. It was endless cycles. I started staying at friends' houses and hung around with Michelle and Steve from work. We'd party late, sleep at theirs and go to work as they were both nearer to the airport.

Then I got a pelvic infection and ended up in hospital having a laparoscopy to investigate my stomach. Mum and Bob were away on holiday, and I tried to deal with it alone, scared by the revelation of the damage I'd done. The doctors found I'd damaged my right fallopian tube as my body was rebelling against my terrible eating pattern. I was told I would likely find it difficult to have children and might be infertile due to the damage caused.

I told Mum the news when she returned home, although I avoided the mention of my eating disorder. She started crying at the mention of me never giving her grandchildren which I found hypocritical as she was the least maternal woman I'd known. And when she finally calmed down, she poured us each a glass of wine and she concluded that at least I wouldn't do anything stupid by getting pregnant out of wedlock.

Not having to worry about contraception, she had convinced me I could at least get on with my life. I felt she was relieved for me, wishing it had happened to her when she was my age. I tried to suppress the reminder of her giving me away and got on with my life, but it was becoming shallow, empty, and lonelier.

Outside of work I had all but lost any friendships I had, and happiness was fleeting as my enthusiasm and adventurous nature was becoming overridden with quick highs and long lows. Life had become too many long hours working to feed my lifestyle, strangers at parties, lonely hotel rooms and too much of what wasn't good for me. Above all, I lacked love and affection.

Having not had a boyfriend for some time I was feeling pangs of need for someone in my life. One night Michelle and I had been invited to a ball for the Barcelona football team in London. We got a cab there and were pretty miffed when she'd mislaid the invitation. From memory only, she tried to guide the driver to where she thought the venue was. We drove around and eventually ended up at a club instead, followed by a trendy all night cafe. Stephen and his younger cousin were sitting at a table there.

Michelle was always on the pull for a pilot or someone with an equally financially successful role. Stephen was full of flannel, though his younger cousin seemed compliant and quiet. Stephen was not good looking by any means, and certainly not my cup of tea, but it was obvious from the onset Michelle was after the younger of the two and wanted me to go along with her plan.

"Come on, Amanda, these two look like they can buy us a drink or two. What have we got to lose? The evening's been a dead loss as it is, so perhaps they could turn out to be a couple of real catches," she said, eager to find out.

I knew the drill, so chatted with them, and listened to Michelle. "Yes, so we both work for British Airways and can pretty much fly anywhere we like and stay in the most amazing hotels. Sometimes we just can't decide which party to go to and it all depends on whether we've been to that country before or not." Michelle said.

The boys seemed to take it all in and I did my usual nodding and smiling in agreement at how wonderful our lives were. Something didn't feel right. I wanted to go home but Michelle persuaded me to stay.

"Well girls, I guess you both want to continue the evening. Why don't you come back to our little pad in West One for a nightcap?" Steve said.

When we arrived at their home, Stephen bragged about his twelve-roomed house and his Porsche 928 parked outside. I was a little in awe of him as he seemed so young. He told us he was a successful salesman in the West End, making fifty thousand a year and living the life of Riley!

He was very ambitious, had the gift of the gab and seemed so adventurous in spirit so I weakened and fell for his charm. We spent the weekend (innocently, as I was not physically attracted to either of them) with them, laughing and chatting and going out around the West One area to eat. In that time, Stephen worked his magic.

Chapter 10

When you stretch the truth, watch out for the
snapback.

Bill Copeland

Stephen was clever in how he lured me in. I started to fall for his wit and charm, and he chipped away at my insecurities to nail the deal. He'd mentioned I was OK weight wise, but he could see I'd be stunning if I tried harder. He showed me pictures he carried around in his briefcase of his ex-girlfriend who'd been an underwear model. He said he'd transformed her by putting her through a gruelling aerobic exercise regime. I too could be sexy if I gave it a try.

Within three weeks, Steve had me hooked. He never seemed to be at work when I was off shift, so we started to spend all our time together. One day he wanted to sing to me when we were alone. It felt cheesy and awkward at first, but I thought it was charming. After a while I realised he just loved to hear the sound of his own voice.

Steve talked of adventure and his goals and dreams, always quoting the mega rich and the most expensive cars as aspirations of his own. "I came to London to realise my dreams, Amanda, and you are part of that dream. With you I can achieve anything I set my mind to."

I felt flattered. I thought he was inspirational as no one had spoken to me like this since Dad. Within no time he'd influenced me into believing his ambitions were mine too and I started to get enticed by his talk of his business ideas. Within weeks of meeting him, I was planning a business abroad hiring out jet skis to tourists on the beach. Stephen had convinced me it was a money spinner and his lifetime ambition.

He told me his bank manager had told him to put together a business proposal and financial forecast for him to consider a loan. I was surprised and shocked by the speed at which he'd taken on the idea, but he said time was of the essence. The next time I saw him, he told me his bank manager had told him his income wouldn't cover the initial loan as it was tied up in flats in the West End. It made sense to me. He was living there in the West End. Well, in a fashion. He was actually sleeping on a mattress on his cousin's floor on the ground floor flat of the building. He'd convinced me it was so he could maximise his earning potential with the other flats he owned in the building.

"My bank manager's turned me down as I'm too financially involved with all my London properties. Amanda I've got to look at the long term and need to consider all my options, but it seems my bank manager doesn't want to risk my properties for what he calls a gamble. I can't believe it. After all the figures I've put down, I can't believe he's letting this opportunity pass me by," he said.

I tried to console him and when I suggested going to my bank instead his eyes lit up and he told me I was a genius. Within a week we were both sitting in front of my bank manager asking for a thirty thousand pound loan.

As soon as the money went into my account, Steve wanted to start spending it, taking me to boat shops and marine centres to purchase the equipment we'd need. He said we better go and get the licence we had to have to work beforehand and therefore I'd need to book us a week in Greece.

I had no more holiday left, but once the wheels were in motion, I didn't seem to be able to stop it. He got refused in Greece and didn't get the licence. Steve said Plan B was to go to Portugal instead but as time was running out, we'd just have to apply when we got there. I was uncertain as it seemed too risky, but he'd booked our tickets.

I took Steve to meet Mum and Bob. They were shocked and open mouthed as Steve sat in his cream business suit (looking more like Don Johnson from Miami Vice than a West End top executive) and I could see they were not happy. Mum disliked him immediately and Bob asked him questions he failed to answer.

"So, Steve, what guarantees have you got this business will work and what experience do you have in this area?" Bob asked.

"Well I can't guarantee anything for sure and I've seen how much those guys make on the beaches so know it'll be a good earner."

"Darling, you can't give up on your career now. You've got so much going for you." Mum pleaded with me. "Besides, you've only just met each other, what if it doesn't work out for you both, what then?"

Mum and Bob begged me to reconsider what I was doing.

"Amanda, you've worked so hard to get this position at BA, don't throw it all away now on a whim," Bob said.

But I needed to escape the loneliness and isolation I felt. Steve was offering me adventure; an opportunity, and he seemed to genuinely want me and saw I had potential. "I believe in Steve and believe this will work. He's shown the bank the business plan and they think it will work too so why shouldn't I go for my dream?" I pleaded with them.

Bob simply said, "It's not your dream, Amanda, it's his and I'm afraid it will all end in tears. He's nothing but a clown."

I left that day on bad terms with my family and soon after left my career, too. I handed Steve control of my funds and prepared to leave for Portugal, but something stuck in my throat, and it felt like fear, not excitement.

Having spent a small fortune on jet skis, Steve decided not to buy the windsurfers after all as he'd spotted a bike he wanted to buy and claimed it would pull in the punters and was a better investment. The bike was at a long narrow garage wedged between houses on a busy road in South London. Steve said he'd driven past it one day and spotted the bike of his dreams, a fluorescent pink and black bike. He'd already spoken to the owner (a nineteen-year-old) about purchasing it.

When I went with him to see it, the garage was a hive of activity. Trucks were driving in and out and the place was full of bikes and cars with men working on several of them at the back of the workshop as well as the front. Steve's bike was out on the pavement in readiness for him to see it.

He convinced me he would ride this new bike of his down to Portugal whilst I could drive our new jeep full of our equipment. The jet skis were going to be shipped direct. The young guy, Barry, seemed very knowledgeable and commanded a lot of respect from the many much older guys working there. He seemed to have a rapport with Steve, so I put two and two together and worked out Steve had been visiting the place for some time.

He negotiated a price with Barry and the day we arrived to buy the bike, Steve opened his trusty briefcase, full of piles of money in bundles.

"Yes, I'm an entrepreneur and just about to set off to Portugal to run a jet ski hire business, aren't we, honey?" he said turning to look at me. I was gobsmacked by his arrogance. "We're renting a large villa for the summer and you're certainly welcome to come and visit us any time you want while we're down there," he said.

Steve thrived on telling strangers how rich and successful he was. He always told me afterwards it was merely business practice to get better deals. I always felt embarrassed by his role-play, thinking people saw him as untrustworthy and the closer it got to leaving for Portugal, the more I started to panic, wondering if I'd made a huge mistake.

We visited the garage several more times before we finally left as there were a lot of adjustments to be made to the bike. Each time, Steve told the boys his stories. On the last day, Barry announced he would love to take us up on our offer and come out for a holiday with his girlfriend. Steve realised he'd given the address to Barry as the bike needed spare tyres and he'd ordered them to be delivered to our new address in Portugal, so he couldn't go back on his offer. In the jeep on the way home he said, "Don't worry yourself. Barry wouldn't dream of coming out to stay with us, he's all talk. It's just what guys say to each other when we're doing business."

I wasn't convinced however as Barry came across as someone far more intelligent than he let on. The day we set off, I started to feel unwell, which was not good timing to say the least. The jeep was packed with our luggage and smaller equipment and now, with Steve's insistence, we had a huge stereo system put in the jeep – again, apparently for business purposes. The jet skis and larger equipment had been shipped and we were due to pick them up when we arrived in Portugal. The tyres for the bike likewise had been sent. I didn't understand why it was imperative to have Barry supply the tyres when he'd made the deal on the bike.

"We could have purchased tyres in Portugal," I said.

Steve shrugged it off and said, "These guys respect me and want to make sure the bike has the best. Remember that back tyre's a nine inch and we're not likely to get that in Portugal so easily."

We set off on the ferry to Santander in northern Spain, a twenty-four-hour crossing, leaving my world behind and hardly speaking to my family, let alone saying goodbye to my friends.

106

Steve had monopolised me from the start making sure my time was with him as much as possible and so I'd hardly seen anyone other than him. Deep down I sensed things were not adding up.

I was ill the whole way across to Spain. The sea was choppy, and the ferry was constantly rolling. There were several floors on the ferry and Steve decided to spend the entire time on the lower deck in the cinema whilst I sat freezing on the top deck, trying to focus on the horizon. When we arrived, he planned to ride off ahead of me which I wasn't too happy about as I'd never driven abroad before and was completely on my own if anything happened. We didn't even have mobile phones.

We agreed to meet enroute and then he sped off on his pride and joy. I drove the jeep down through Spain and headed out towards the west coast of Portugal and marvelled at how smooth the roads were that flowed through beautiful pine forests and thought it must have been a huge bonus for him on his bike. Funnily enough, I didn't feel lonely or scared at all. The feeling of being in such a natural environment reminded me of that familiar feeling of being in my garden as a child and how protected I felt.

Although I felt ill, I was happy to have the scenery and peace in between each stop. As we headed into Lisbon, I was feeling worse though and when we booked to stay in a hotel, I fell into bed and stayed there without venturing out to explore at all. Steve disappeared into Lisbon to explore and on his return showed me he'd bought some gold from a guy in the street for five hundred pounds.

He was convinced it was real but when he scratched at the surface with a knife, it turned out he'd been sold duff gear which he was livid about, but he still wore it anyway. Looking flash with his new jewellery to highlight his wealth, he felt he looked a million dollars. I felt he looked more like Derek Trotter from *Only Fools and Horses*! I was slowly but surely losing respect for him and becoming concerned for my future.

Struggling on alone on my journey, I continued down to Albufeira whilst Steve sped off on his new baby. All I could do was stop when nausea overwhelmed me. Finally, we arrived at our villa. It was far too big for our needs, but Steve had convinced me it was necessary and said it had a garage for our equipment, which was essential. I spent the first few days in bed and eventually convinced Steve to take me to the doctors.

I then found out to my utter shock I was pregnant.

Steve told me without hesitation I'd have to get rid of it as we had a plan, and a baby certainly wasn't in it. He took me to several places to ask about abortion and was told each time it was illegal to perform such a procedure in Portugal. He even tried to find an illegal method, but in the end, having exhausted our options, he gave me an ultimatum. I would have to go back home and have the baby terminated or leave him. It was my fault I was pregnant and certainly not his.

I'd been convinced I couldn't have children. I fought with the realisation that if this was my one and only chance, I didn't want to lose it. I also knew if I chose to keep the baby, I'd have no home, no prospects to work even if I could and I'd have the sole responsibility of a baby. Furthermore, I would be in debt to the tune of £30,000 and Steve would be off like a shot.

I was hurt and angry. I felt cheated and cornered, lonely and fed up with being ill day and night and just wanted my mum. Steve made it clear we could no longer afford to fritter money. The hypocrite had been spending my loan money like water and so far we had absolutely nothing to show for it. I phoned Mum who arranged a flight home for me and set off home for the termination. I felt so helpless. When she collected me at Heathrow airport a few days later, I hugged her so tight. I didn't want to let her go.

I realised I'd made a dreadful mistake with Steve, but I'd made my bed so felt I had no option but to lie in it. The termination was booked. It was a cold and practical process and I remember every moment of it. The unexpected grief that came after was overwhelming.

I knew I had to return to Portugal to try to salvage this farce of a relationship and make something work, even if it was just to get my loan paid back. Mum tried to convince me over and over not to return. It was the hardest thing to do to say goodbye to her as she dropped me off at the airport and it was then I realised that I had no-one in the world but Mum and Bob, two people who were so far removed from being my people. I wondered if I would ever find my people, and most importantly, anyone I could love and trust.

Chapter 11

One may outwit another, but not all the others.

François de La Rochefoucauld

After two weeks, I returned to Portugal, hoping Steve had organised our licence and collected the shipped jet skis ready for us to start earning.

I certainly didn't expect to see what I met at the airport. Steve walked towards me clad in luminous pink and black Lycra skintight shorts and sporting his new all over orange glow tan, topped with a bright orange and purple sports jacket. I hardly recognised him. Though I knew nothing about fashion, I was sure it wasn't just me who was stunned by the calamity of colours that walked towards me. But he looked as confident and contented as the cat who'd got the cream.

"Hi, you OK?" he said when he saw me, kissing me on the cheek.

"Yep, fine thanks. You're looking tanned. New clothes?" I asked raising my eyebrows and wondering how much his outfit had cost.

"I thought I better look the part on the beach. I know the bike stands out, but this will certainly get me noticed with the jet skis."

I nodded, too weary to bring up money.

"So, how did it go then? I take it it's all done?" he said.

"Yes, it's all done, Steve."

He gave a big sigh of relief. I was shocked at his insensitivity, but equally didn't want to talk about it. As Steve drove, I looked out of my passenger window, thoughts drifting in and out of my mind of what could have been if I'd had my baby.

"Guess what," Steve said excitedly. "While you were away, I found a gym hidden away that's used for athletes who stay here on holiday."

I turned and said, "Oh yeah?" not really listening.

"I just happened to be out walking one day and looked through the fence of what looked like a running track and saw a caretaker. I called over to him and asked him what it was, and he told me it was a gym and track for athletes. So we got friendly and as no one was using it he let me have a free pass for the entire fortnight you were away."

I turned to him and looked at him beam.

"Yeah, I've been getting a tan and preparing to look the part. Hence the O'Neil and Nike clothes so I'm all ready for the beach."

I sat in complete silence. My grief started to give way to anger, and I dared not tell him how repulsed I was by him. The clown had fully emerged.

"And you'll never guess what else? Whilst you were away, coincidentally I bumped into a crowd of guys I used to go to school with. There's ten of them all staying here in Albufeira. I think it's going to be an amazing summer."

A coincidence?

When I finally met them, I realised the only thing they had in common was none of them wanted to work. Steve was in his element with a large audience to play to, and he told them again and again what a successful entrepreneur he'd become since school. I watched their eyes light up at the prospect of a free lunch. Steve thought he was the leader of the pack. They played their role well, egging him on to his face. Behind his back was different. Steve sat so high on his own pedestal; he had no idea what people really thought about him. Ian kept them under control. He was quietly assertive and had a technique of pulling the girls who were leaving for the UK the following day, so he had an endless source of totty and very few complications. I liked him as he was honest and quiet. Away from the boys and his pulling sprees, we became friends.

I finally managed to convince Steve to go to the captain of the port. On his return he announced the man required £75,000 for a licence and the application could only be put in for the following year. I was livid.

"How could you have not checked the most fundamental part of the business plan? You just kept saying it would be OK. I felt all along it wasn't OK. Now what the hell are we going to do?"

He simply shrugged and looked down.

"Steve, come on now, please talk to me. Don't just leave this with me. What are we going to do?"

"Amanda, I have no idea. I guess the business is a nonstarter. We'll just have to hang out until the money runs dry and then get jobs."

Something told me he wasn't bothered at all by our predicament. I realised at that moment he'd had no intention of making our business work. He'd simply fed my bank manager a plausible plan for the sake of getting the money and spent what he could. He certainly had the gift of the gab, but I'd never seen any evidence of his so-called success.

From that moment, Steve started to spend money like water and withdrew a large stash of cash every day, carrying it around in his briefcase. I didn't know which was worse: the fact his dress sense was just so dire or the fact he liked people to stare at him. His luminous orange vest and orange trainers stood out more as his tan increased to a deeper carrot orange. I could hear comments from passers-by, but he seemed to be immune to sniggers in the street.

The boys in his gang were in the habit of smoking cannabis and Steve often joined in. As they had little money, they got Steve to supply them. He found a source in a young American boy, the son of a Portuguese surgeon, who was staying in one of the villas next to us. I'd tried it when I was eighteen with Justin but hadn't liked feeling out of control so hadn't tried it since. Watching the boys getting stoned was unpleasant, and I left them to their hours of mind-rotting indulgence.

Most of the time they'd spend the day smoking, and the evenings were spent smoking and drinking. Life was just one long party at our expense. The boys treated me as one of the lads. As time wore on, I got more and more concerned about our finances. Steve said he was working out another business strategy. All I could do was wait and worry. The money was pouring out of our account and, when we were almost out, Steve convinced the bank to forward us on a further loan. I couldn't believe he'd got away with it.

"Steve enough is enough. Somehow, we have to start making provisions to pay this money back. The spending's got to stop. I can't sleep at night with worrying about it." "Don't worry, Amanda, I've got a backup plan and am going to lose the jet skis and claim for them on the insurance."

I was by then starting to get scared of what lengths he'd go to con people and was concerned he'd leave me with all the debt and run a mile. I decided to play along and agreed with him until I could get home and leave him for good. I'd somehow have to find a way to pay back all the money. He very quickly burned through the next lot of money, so I suggested we got jobs as timeshare touts, stopping people in the street and inviting them into the resorts to listen to sales pitches. It was hard work but there was little else available. After three weeks Steve walked away, giving up. We were down to our last few hundred pounds. Then out of the blue we got a call from Barry who told us he and his girlfriend would be arriving in a few days. I'd completely forgotten about them and started to panic.

Steve said "Don't worry, I've got another game plan. I'm going to sell all our equipment. It's still brand new in the garage."

"Who's going to buy the life jackets and all that stuff we've brought over?" I asked.

"I've been having a word round here with the locals and plenty of guys will buy our stuff. The jet skis I'm still going to claim on the insurance for and sell them across the border in Spain."

When we went to meet Barry and his girlfriend at the airport, I noticed how odd they looked together. Sharon towered over him, a huge and rather unkempt looking woman.

"Oh, that's great. Barry didn't tell me you were a skinny bitch," she said.

She was a rather large and unkempt looking girl. Barry and Sharon looked a very odd couple as I expected him to be with someone who was as immaculately groomed as he was. By then I'd lost weight through worry and sickness and had dropped a couple of dress sizes. I felt self-conscious with her comparing me in such a condescending way and it touched a nerve with Steve constantly reminding me that I could be a 'stunner' like his ex-girlfriend if I put my mind to it.

"So, I guess you have nothing to do but work on your tan all day out here," she said.

I simply answered, "I don't actually like just sitting in the sun, but you can't help but catch it when you're in it all day."

No sooner had we arrived at the villa and showed them to their room, they started to argue bitterly. I heard her accuse Barry of fancying me! When we went out that night, we tried to get along as best we could.

For the next week we put up with snide remarks, rudeness, and sulks from Sharon. Barry never rose to it in front of us, but behind closed doors the arguing was no holds barred. When they finally left, Barry thanked us and told us we were welcome to come to stay with him on our return. We had no plans to see them again.

It was inevitable we would eventually have to return to the UK, as all the money had gone bar a few thousand pounds which Steve acquired through selling our equipment.

"Come on, Amanda, it'll be easy. Let's just do this and get rid of the jet skis. We can get at least half of what we paid for them and then we can put a claim into the insurance company for them as if they're stolen."

This time I put my foot down. "No, Steve, I can't do something like that. I'm just not used to the way you work. I couldn't live with myself." I walked away from him to stop his pleading.

He was faced with no choice but to sell them anyway and accepted next to nothing for them. We finally arrived back in the UK with nowhere to live. I was too ashamed to ask my mother for help and didn't dare tell them how much I was in debt, so in a brief phone call I let them know we were coming home to buy a house and settle down. Mum asked lots of questions, but I managed to skip over them, although I desperately wanted to go home and be as far away from Steve as possible.

We drove to Anglesey in North Wales, a small fishing village where one of Steve's five sisters, Jackie, lived. She let us stay with her even though space was limited, and money was tight. Steve had offered her a wad of cash to put us up for a while. Nicky, her teenage son, loved having his uncle to stay.

Steve wanted to buy a house and said he was going to apply for a mortgage. Barry had been in touch, and asked if we wanted to stay with him, saying he could do with the money. I'd thought he ran the garage in South London and was doing OK, considering how many people he had working for him. Something about the offer didn't feel right though.

Steve had contracted dysentery the last few weeks we were in Portugal. He was losing weight rapidly and didn't dare see a doctor. Rather than live rough at his sister's, he took Barry up on his offer. I was scared. I wasn't sure why, but I didn't feel comfortable going there.

We travelled back to South London to Barry's plush two-bedroomed first floor flat. Everything was fresh and new and at first it seemed like we had landed on our feet. Steve lent Barry what was left of my money as Barry said he needed it to invest in something short term, although Steve was supposed to be using it as a deposit for a house.

At first Barry made us feel very welcome in his flat and was grateful for the loan, but this changed when Sharon started to turn up nearly every day.

"Get rid of them, Barry. Why are they here? You still got the hots for that skinny bitch?"

Steve and I could easily hear her from our room and Barry seemed frightened of her.

When she left, he said to us, "I'm sorry guys, she's just a little insecure, but just to keep the peace, do us a favour and stay out of the flat when she comes over. You can both come back at night when she's gone, but it's just to stop her kicking off."

I was fed up with her constant nastiness and Steve could hardly get out of bed, let alone drive around all day. We found it harder to find places to go to until we could go home to bed. It was exhausting. In fact, it was so difficult, we'd often drive up to Wales so Steve could sleep, as he'd lost a huge amount of weight and looked very gaunt and weak. He was obviously seriously ill. Barry often didn't return our calls when we phoned to see if we could return to the flat. This wasn't working. Steve left a message to ask if we could have our money back. There was no response, so we left another message and yet another. Still nothing.

"I don't know what he's playing at, Amanda, but I don't think Barry's got any intention of giving us that money back. We've got to do something as it's all we've got left." Steve said.

"Like what? If he doesn't want to give it back, then he won't. You can't force him," I said, wanting to walk away from Barry and his girlfriend.

Steve came up with another plan. "Look, we'll take Nicky with us, hire a van and go to Barry's and take some of his furniture. You know how much his living room furniture must be worth."

"You can't do that, Steve, it's stealing," I said, shocked.

"Oh don't worry. We'll just take it and hold it for a while until he pays us what he owes us and then we'll take it back. Simple."

I was scared out of my wits, as I didn't believe we should be messing around with someone like Barry, but Steve was convinced he was just a grease monkey and not the owner of the garage as he made out. I felt Steve had no idea who he was messing with. Steve told me I had no choice but to go along with the plan. Jackie was shocked by Steve involving Nicky and told him he was out of order expecting me to go with them too. Steve convinced us both I had to help shift the furniture as he needed as many hands as possible.

Nicky, Steve, and I drove all the way down to Barry's flat in a hired van to do the deed. I felt sick the whole way there, but Nicky and Steve were high on laughter and scheming to get the money back. They thought the whole thing would go like a dream. I felt the complete opposite.

Barry was at work when we arrived. Nervously, we loaded Barry's plush leather three-piece suite and glass dining table onto the van, together with our belongings, and drove down the road to a phone box to make a final call.

Steve left a message on Barry's answerphone saying we'd taken his furniture and if he wanted it returned, we needed our money back and then we'd be straight. Immediately he got a call back and I could tell by Steve's face he was scared. He told us Barry had said we were in big trouble, and as he held his head in his hands in the van, I sat in silence.

Steve told us we'd drive back to Anglesey and sell the furniture. Sod the consequences. We drove back to Anglesey. I sat with my head against the side door window looking out as the world passed by and wondered where it would all end. Deep down, I felt something terrible was going to happen.

Chapter 12

Survival means doing what you have to do in order to live, and sometimes that means thinking smart rather than working hard!

Chris Ryan

We stopped along the way at a couple of service stations, the boys in high spirits by then and Steve bragging how he'd outwitted Barry.

"Steve, don't you think it's all been a little too easy for you to just walk away with Barry's belongings?" I said. "I know you're confident this'll work, but something just doesn't feel right."

Steve decided to pull over and sleep in a layby and arrive at Jackie's house in the early hours of the morning.

"Steve, I'm worried about Mum," said Nicky. "Are you sure nothing's going to come back on her?"

"Will you both stop being ridiculous," Steve responded. "I know exactly what I'm doing."

As we pulled into the layby Nicky started to panic. "Steve, we really should have stopped and called Mum from a service station to warn her that if Barry phoned, she should say she'd not seen you for years. I don't think it's right she has to be involved in case anything happens to her."

Amazingly, Steve then admitted, "Actually, I gave Barry Jackie's phone number a while back. Don't worry though, Nicky, there's no way he'll think we're going to hers. It was just a contact number for him when I bought the bike."

"Why didn't you say? Why the hell have you put my mum in danger?" Nicky shouted.

"Nicky, calm down for God's sake. You know damn well I'm not going to put my sister in any danger. Barry's not going to come out of London for a bit of furniture. He'll get in touch when he realises I mean business and give me the money back if he knows what's good for him," Steve shouted back, but Nicky and I weren't convinced.

I told them both to pack it in, as Steve would have to make amends and sort this mess out himself as it had gone too far. Still, Steve was adamant that he would not go to Jackie's until the next morning.

None of us could sleep. Not knowing conjured up all sorts of scenarios, but nothing prepared us for what we were about to walk into. We decided at seven o'clock it would be safe to go to the house. We drove and parked a few roads away from Jackie's, and Steve decided it would be safer to slip round the back and through the back door, even though it was obvious the village was quiet and still and no-one was about.

As we entered Jackie's living room, we found Jackie in the middle of the floor on her knees, sobbing her heart out, rocking backwards and forwards and hugging a cushion into her stomach. The room had been ransacked. Steve fell to his knees, put his arms around his sister and asked her what had happened. It took her several minutes before she'd calmed down enough for us to understand her.

"I was watching Coronation Street earlier this evening," she said struggling, to get her words out between sobs, "when I got a phone call from someone saying he was your friend and wanted to pop up to see you as he happened to be in Wales."

"Go on!" Steve said, still holding her by the shoulders.

"I had no idea who he was, but he came across as charming and seemed to know so much about you when I asked him questions. He claimed to be an old school friend of yours, so I gave him my address as he said he wanted to come up and surprise you. I'm sorry, Steve. I thought you'd come home to a lovely surprise." She began to wail.

Jackie had returned to her television set, expecting to relay the message to Steve on his arrival about his friend's impending visit. She eventually got ready for bed, deciding we were all going to be late. She knew we could get in as we had a key. As she was climbing the stairs, the back door burst open and in ran a horde of men built like brick outhouses. One ran to the front door, opened it, and in ran more men. She was petrified.

They were all shouting and running around frantically calling for Steve. Some ran upstairs whilst others started turning over furniture and opening and ransacking drawers and cupboards. Jackie froze on the spot as Barry, a very different Barry to the one we'd described, pulled her towards him and shouted, "Tell me where Steve and my belongings are!"

He held her by her dressing gown with his fist, her face close enough to his she could feel his breath on her. She genuinely had no clue as to where we were. Barry threw her back on the sofa telling one of the men to watch her, and he ran upstairs to join the others. After a few minutes of banging about and rummaging of drawers and cupboards, they came downstairs, arms laden with cameras, watches, jewellery, TVs –anything of value they could find. As they reached the living room, they placed everything in a pile in the middle of the room. Jackie begged them to leave.

"Please don't take my things. I have nothing of value. Those are mine and my son's and nothing to do with Steve."

One of the men came towards her as if to shut her up. "Please don't hurt me."

"If you're not careful, lady, we'll all get our fill and sort you out good and proper. What's your brother going to do about that then?" one of the men said, prodding and poking her and pulling at her clothes. She wet herself through fear and he laughed at her.

Nicky saw red and told Steve to leave his mum alone. He got down on his knees to hold her as she sobbed. Steve then stood up and backed off. "I'm sorry, Jackie. I had no idea they'd come here. I'm so sorry," he said. "I'm sorry."

Barry had been fuming by the time they'd checked the house and there was no sign we'd been there that evening. He turned to Jackie and said, "Tell Steve that as soon as he gets here, he's to turn around and drive back to the lock up and return my furniture or he's a dead man."

Jackie sobbed hysterically and nodded in the hope he'd just leave.

"Tell him, he's a very stupid man as he's crossed with the Yardies and for us to have to come out of our territory, he's got to pay! Tell him, he has no choice. He doesn't realise what he's got himself into, so he better do as he's told as I don't want to have to come back to this hole again. Do you hear me?"

Jackie continued nodding to appease him as much as she could and counted around twenty men exit her front door with all our belongings, including everything she had of value.

As Barry left, he threw over his shoulder, "This is payment for our inconvenience, tell him!"

Jackie ran to the window when the last one had gone and slammed the door shut, putting the chain on, even though she knew it wouldn't hold them back if they wanted to return. As she looked out the window the whole of her street was awash with pick-up trucks with flashing orange lights. It looked like a scene from some American disaster movie. They all got into their trucks and drove away. Once more, the village was quiet and still. Jackie cowered in the middle of the room half expecting them to come back. She didn't move for the next few hours.

"You've gone too far this time with your corrupt and greedy ways. When are you going to learn that all you do is hurt people?" I said to Steve, seething at what his poor sister had gone through. I could see Nicky was holding his mum to hold back from attacking his uncle. He was livid.

Jackie spat at Steve. "I'll never forgive you for letting me and my son become involved in your despicable criminal dealings. Now get out of my house."

"Well it's your fault for telling them your address and believing it was a friend of mine. What do you expect?" Steve said incredulously.

This just made Nicky and Jackie angrier.

"You weak and spineless man you," yelled Jackie. "Just go and get lost. You have no one who's going to help you now. And what about poor Amanda? What the hell have you got her involved in? Why don't you do everyone a favour Steve and just get lost. Amanda, you're staying with us!"

"Well what the hell do you think I'm going to do now, Jackie? You've grassed us up and I've got to have someone drive the jeep as I've got to drive the hire van down to Barry. So she'll have to come with me to drive me back." Steve said as if I weren't there and didn't matter.

Eventually, to get Steve out of their house, I told Steve I'd go, but I wasn't going to take the rap for what he planned. Jackie said I should leave him, but I realised it was too late. I should have left him when we returned to the UK. I'd got myself into deeper water with this man and had nowhere to live. I couldn't tell my family I was in debt with no money and no prospects and was now in trouble with a gang from London. I had no choice but to keep moving on with him.

We left immediately. I asked him what Yardies were, and he told me they were from Jamaica and usually involved in criminal activities. That didn't make me feel any better, but it explained why this young boy had so much respect from the others. I felt as Barry and I had a good rapport going, he'd let me be and Steve would get away with a rap on the knuckles. I obviously had no idea how things worked in their world.

After another five-hour journey back into London, as we neared the lock up I felt my stomach wanting to purge itself of its contents. I tried to concentrate on the practical side of driving and staying calm, but I felt petrified.

We parked a few streets away in our individual vehicles to go over our plan.

"We'll just pull up outside the lock up and leave the keys in the van," said Steve, and then I'll jump in the jeep with you, and you drive off as quickly as possible. You got it?"

When we finally arrived at the lock up, as Steve got out of the van, a man came out of nowhere and took the keys from him and frog marched him into the lock up. I was stunned by the speed in which it had happened and sat open-mouthed. Before I could react, a man opened my driver's door and told me to hand him the keys and go with him into the garage too.

I wanted to scream and run, but nothing came out. People were walking along the pavement, but no-one seemed bothered by what was going on. We were both manhandled into the eerily empty lock up. Petrified, we were told to stand together as one of the men started to talk on a radio.

We heard the man say, "We've got them and the furniture's safe." Then there was a movement back by the door and more men started turning up. I realised we were now trapped inside. I looked at Steve, but he ignored me. Anxious voices discussed what they were to do with us.

Within a few minutes, trucks and bikes were turning up from all directions and men were pouring into the lock up. One man was darting about as if he was on some kind of fix and didn't quite know how to release his heightening anxiety.

Suddenly Barry turned up and the doors were immediately shut behind him. He walked straight up to us shaking his head and tutting with an angry smirk on his face. "Steve, you stupid man, you. Don't you realise you've now got to face the consequences?"

Barry ushered us deeper into the dark lock up, which was now devoid of any vehicles and looked ominous with a door up leading to a grease pit underground which he pointed towards.

"There's your stuff, Steve, if you want it," he said, pointing at the darkened pit.

"You're all right," Steve answered.

"No, I insist! Why don't you go and get it, Steve?"

Steve shook his head, petrified. The men formed a circle around us, and Barry approached us both, taking off our jewellery, telling us it was "inconvenience pay".

The psyched-up man kept coming over to me, stroking my hair and skin. I reeled back, but that seemed to excite him more. Barry was busy questioning Steve. "Why did you do it, Steve? After all I did for you, why did you take what was mine, man?"

Steve silently shrugged his shoulders.

"What's all this shit about you lending me money? What the hell do you think I need from you, you pussy?"

Steve at last answered "Don't worry, Barry, we've got your furniture outside and won't say anything about the money. Just let me go."

Barry smirked, and the psyched-up man started touching me up more intensely. Barry turned to one of his boys and said, "Take her into the office and lock her in." He turned to the pest and said, "Leave her alone and get over there."

I was asked to sit on the chair in Barry's small office and the man left and locked the door after me. There was a glass panel at waist height so I could still see what was going on. The men were tormenting Steve, not hurting him, but taking great pleasure from frightening the wits out of him and all I could do was watch and wait. Eventually, they started walking Steve towards the front of the lock up and someone came and let me out. I was told to stand outside the office door and wait. Barry was with Steve at the lock up door and I heard him turn and say, "Do you want to collect your girlfriend, Steve?"

The psyched man approached me again as soon as I was released, licking his lips in delight and he started rubbing his body up against mine and pushed me into a corner. I screamed and called out, "Steve, help me! Don't leave me here, please!" but he just turned and looked at me and continued to walk away.

I panicked and struggled to get away from the man who was now breathing his rancid breath down my neck and running his hands all over my body. I knew if I didn't do something to escape, I'd be in serious trouble. All of a sudden, there was a commotion at the door and men started pouring out. From what I could make out by the shouting, they'd sent Steve off in the jeep, making him think he was free to go and now they were going to play cat and mouse with him.

When only a few men were left in the lock up, Barry walked back in with a few of his sidekicks. He walked straight up to me and pulled the increasingly aroused man away from manhandling me.

"Get out with the others and find Steve and do what needs to be done!" Barry bellowed at the man and then Barry took me by the arm, pulled me into the office and sat me down.

"Now listen to me, Amanda." Barry started, "When you both arrived in London, we had no idea which way you'd come in. So all my men were positioned at all possible entry points with their trucks, waiting for you both. They were on radios to communicate with each other so as soon as they spotted you, they followed you in to check you didn't back out. We were watching your every move. Steve was so frightened out there just now before we let him go, he wet himself right in front of us on the pavement. And you know, when I asked him if he wanted to save his girlfriend from being raped and subjected to all kinds of torture, Steve just begged to be spared himself."

I sat open mouthed.

He continued, "What sort of spineless shit of a man does that? He's not worth touching, especially on our patch, but he'll get his reward when we catch him later. Don't worry. We'll never do anything on our turf to draw attention and as before the men will follow him to a safe place and then deal with him!"

Tears streamed down my face as I realised not only had this man conned and used me all these months, but he had left me with twenty men (that I'd counted) to be abused, raped and probably to die.

Barry told me to go to the van, get in it with two of his men and they would drive me back to his home. He followed us on his bike. The journey was short, but it seemed like time had stopped and I was in some horror film.

Barry had decided I would help unload the furniture back into his flat and then find out my punishment. When we arrived, he made me carry chairs and cushions indoors and kept an eye on me constantly. Eventually when it was all put back, he sat me down on the sofa and spoke to one of his men on his radio. Thunder crossed his face as he listened to the man on the other end.

"What d'you mean he's disappeared? How can he disappear?" he shouted.

When he'd finished ranting, he spoke to the two guys in the flat with us and told them the boys had gone to all the exit points they thought Steve would leave by, but he never passed any of them.

He told the man on the radio to keep looking until he was found but also to do it quick before he left London. Barry then turned to me and said, "Do you know how much trouble your boyfriend's caused? You have no idea! We never leave our patch unless we really have to and because of what he did, we had to get that furniture back straight away."

I was bemused as to why a three-piece suite and dining set would cause a gang of Yardies to react the way they did. Then the penny struck, and I realised why they'd gone over the sofa so meticulously when it was back in the flat — there was something stashed in it.

"I'm sorry for being so stupid and helping Steve to do this to you," I said.

"I've always had respect for you, Amanda, and liked you from when I first met you but couldn't understand why you were with such an idiot." He then asked me for my mother's phone number.

"Why?" I pleaded. "Please don't phone them, you'll worry them."

Barry explained that he was going to tell my mother some home truths about Stephen and then explain she wouldn't see me again but that I'd be OK and looked after. When he called my mum, I could hear her begging to speak to me, but Barry calmly said I was starting a new life and put the phone down. I was terrified.

"I never liked him, but he was such a prat. I thought I'd play with him at first and when the opportunity came along to see what he was up to in Portugal, I took it," Barry said.

"But why?"

Barry smirked. "Because he was trying to have one over on me and it was the principle of the thing! Look, I didn't set out to punish you. We were after Steve so now this is all over, I'm going to look after you and give you the life you deserve of respect and security."

I realised that he wasn't inviting me. He was telling me. He spoke as if it had been planned all along. No wonder his girlfriend felt threatened by me. She obviously knew what he was feeling better than I did.

Barry went on to say, "We look after our own and now, as you're mine, you'll live with my mother for a while, be given a job and gain respect amongst our community and eventually be my girl!"

Frightened to do anything but to appease him. I went along with what he was telling me. I knew I needed to bide my time. I had no idea what the alternative was if I refused. Suddenly the buzzer went from the main door outside. We all jumped as it was by now the early hours of the morning.

Barry jumped up and went to the door, pressing the intercom and we heard his girlfriend loud and clear shouting at the top of her voice.

"Where the hell is she? I know you've got her in there, you bastard. Let me in right now, Barry!"

Barry shouted back, "No one's here, you silly cow, except for my boys. What the hell do you want?"

"I know she's in there cos I've been told, you liar. You wait till I get hold of her!"

Barry transformed into a quivering, frightened young boy, turned to me, and told me to get in the bathroom and lock myself in, quickly shouting over his shoulder, "Don't worry, I'll get rid of her!"

I swiftly made my way into the bathroom, heart pounding, and heard Barry and his boys exit the flat and run down the staircase to stop her from her ranting and cursing. As I heard the main door open, I heard Sharon screaming and lashing out and assumed the boys were also taking a pounding or trying to restrain her. They must have been trying to get her away from the building as the noise decreased.

Then I realised I had a chance to escape. Unlocking the door and running out of the bathroom, I ran round the flat looking for the van keys and found them on the work surface in the kitchen. Heart racing and feeling sick, I sneaked out of the flat, down the stairs and out the main door.

The van was parked about a hundred yards away and as I started to make a run for it, I heard Sharon scream after me, "There she is. There's the bitch!" and with that she tore away from Barry and started running towards me. Barry and his boys raced after her and Barry shouted, "Stop. Leave her alone." I froze.

Without warning, a fist landed in my face and knocked me back onto the grass. Sharon went to dive on me and hit me again, but Barry and the boys pulled her off and held her back, telling her that was enough. I pulled myself together and mustered enough strength to make a last attempt to run.

I got up, grabbed the keys that had fallen out of my hands and said, "Thanks, Barry, I take everything on board that you said and will get myself a new life away from Steve."

I looked at him one last time as I got up then turned, ran, and jumped into the van. I knew he wouldn't try to stop me with her there, but I had no idea if he would try to follow me or have me followed. Having never driven the van before, I clumsily tried to thrust the key in the ignition, missing it several times through panic. Eventually the engine started, and I raced off the estate. I drove as fast as I possibly could for several miles until I felt I was alone.

I couldn't go to my mum's house or friends as they wouldn't understand, and I wouldn't be safe as Barry would find me there. I knew the only option was to head to Jackie's, so I headed back up to North Wales. Terrified and angry, alone and confused, instinct drove me forward. Then I looked at the petrol gauge and realised I was almost out of fuel.

With no money I'd never make it to Wales. A service station was coming up and I knew I'd have to come off and find some way of generating money. All I had was a twenty-pound note I always kept in my sock for emergencies and two signet rings that Barry had thought were worthless. I planned to sell them to someone to get some extra cash.

I parked up and sat for what seemed like an age. As I looked around, I wished I could jump out of my life and into the life of any one of those families hurrying to get supplies and continue with their journeys.

Eventually, I pulled myself together and got out of the van. My legs felt like jelly and almost buckled beneath me, but I pushed myself to move forward. I went in through the main doors, looking behind me all the time in case I was being followed and suddenly, there parked right outside the main entrance, I saw our jeep.

Thinking I was imagining it, I stared. I walked slowly towards it as it dawned on me that Steve must be here. But how? As I peered in through the passenger window, there he was curled up on the seat like a cat. I hammered on the window. Steve woke, startled, confused, and obviously frightened by the sound. He sat bolt upright and for a moment, stared back at me, unable to register that it was me standing there, glaring at him through the passenger window. Then he hung his head in shame.

Why on earth was he there?

Chapter 13

Worse than telling a lie is spending the rest of your life
staying true to a lie.

Robert Brault

Opening the door, Steve sat staring at me, still with his mouth open.

"Why did you leave me?" I asked. "Why did you abandon me and leave me? You knew those men were going to hurt me. Why would you do something like that?"

He sat and cried and put his head in his hands. I walked round to the driver's seat and got in. I let him sob until finally I said I wanted to know the truth about him and if he dared lie to me, I would hand him over to Barry personally.

He started by telling me when he was taken out of the lock up earlier that evening, he'd frozen and couldn't go back for me as he was too scared. Barry's boys had threatened to hurt him and when he'd wet himself, they'd laughed and told him to get in the jeep and get out of London and never make any contact with them or me again.

"I'm sorry, "he said. "I just assumed they'd talk to you about leaving me and I know it's no excuse, but I was scared shitless. I know it was cowardly to leave you alone to face the consequences of what I've got you into, but I was too petrified to know what to do. I was so scared, I couldn't even drive, so I pulled into a petrol station and cried. I realised the fuel tank was almost empty, so I put enough in the jeep to get me away from London and then sat for a while wondering what to do."

What on earth had I ever seen in him?

"As I was filling up, I noticed all the trucks from the garage, driving the way we'd originally driven in to London. I wasn't sure if they noticed me, so I decided to turn the jeep around and risk going back past the garage and head out of London in the opposite direction just in case they came after me."

I nodded and told him what Barry had said to me about searching for him out of their territory.

"All I had was the twenty-pound note, hidden in my sock to get petrol and when I thought the coast was clear, I drove a way out of London they'd probably not even think of."

As Steve had once been a courier in London, he knew the streets well. Once he'd finished, I relived my experience to him whilst he sobbed quietly, more for himself I guessed, than me. I asked him to tell me the truth about himself and his past or he'd live to regret it.

It turned out that when I met him, he was unemployed and had come to London from Wales, hoping to make money by selling some knock-off jeans, but failed. He'd had high hopes of being an entrepreneur, but his lack of business sense and having been a big fish in a small pond inevitably led to failure. Sleeping on the floor of his cousin's rented flat as he was broke, he certainly wasn't the highflying sales executive he'd first told me he was, and he didn't own the building but was living off his cousin for food and lodgings. The Porsche outside simply belonged to a neighbour. He happened to be out the night I met him hoping to meet some rich older woman to scam. I happened to be in the wrong place at the wrong time.

"I've never really had a decent job and learnt from a young age I had the gift of the gab, so mostly lived off women who had money in the hope I'd one day have a lucky break."

I felt nothing but disgust for how he'd lied to me from the day I'd met him and his parasitic way of living off others. "So why," I asked, "did you fool me into thinking we could make a go of this business venture? Was it just a plan to get money out of me?"

"I know, I'm sorry. I fed you a story to try and impress you and Michelle, and once I'd started, I just couldn't stop. I did believe though you were different and would be so good for me. I thought you were the one to change my luck but I was too frightened to lose you as I needed you. So I made up the business plan to give us a chance to be together for a reason."

He hung his head in shame. I wanted to slap his face, but he wasn't worth the energy.

"What are we gonna do?" he kept saying.

I couldn't go back to my family after what I'd put them through, and Barry knew where they lived so he'd find me anyway. I had no friends to turn to now, no home, no money, only debt and a gang of Yardies looking for me.

Steve piped up we could go to his other sister's house in Wales, the one who didn't talk to Jackie. I decided to leave the keys in the hire van and phone the company and let them know where it was when I could get safe enough away. When I got back into the jeep Steve was looking at me expectantly.

I turned the engine on, looked at him and said, "I have nothing left in my life now thanks to you! I would walk away this very moment if I had any choice but I don't. To say I've lost all respect for you is an understatement, but I have nothing now and that's the only reason why I'm staying with you. Do you understand me?"

Steve nodded and I turned away from him in disgust.

In the darkness, I drove in silence back up to Wales, tears streaming down my face as I grieved the loss of my mum who I felt I would never see again. I couldn't muster any words to say to Steve and he knew he'd lost me as a partner. Now it was survival and all we could do was hide and hope Barry and his mob wouldn't find us.

Chapter 14

The ultimate lesson all of us have to learn is
unconditional love, which includes not only others but
ourselves as well.

Elisabeth Kubler-Ross

We arrived at Barbie's in the early hours of the next morning.

"What the hell have you got involved in this time Steve?" she said as she opened the door to us. "Do you know half the village knows about this Yardie gang you're involved with. Jackie's been shooting her mouth off to everyone about the fact she was burgled and nearly raped because of you." She was fuming and waving her hands. I thought she was going to pummel him.

Barbie was a loud, larger than life and opinionated woman, with a deep husky voice and she evidently wore the trousers in her relationship with Christopher, her partner. Her house was secluded which was probably why Steve chose to take sanctuary with her. As she didn't have a spare bedroom in her small bungalow, we slept on the living room floor, although we were made to feel welcome to stay as long as we needed.

I was relieved by her agreeing to help us and had no choice but to sleep with Steve in the same bed, although I'd lost faith in him and didn't relish pretending to still be in a relationship with him.

Barbie made spaghetti for us that first night whilst entertaining us with stories of her escapades with Christopher. "Christopher and I were down the Menai Straits two nights ago when it was windy and managed to get several radios off the boats which he's managed to sell already."

I wondered what the relevance of it being windy was to do with it and was surprised at how blasé she was about taking people's equipment, but I daren't ask questions.

Later, Steve explained that they regularly burgled the rich English people's boats that were moored on the Straits when it was windy as it masked any noise as the masts made a heck of a racket in the wind.

After dinner, Barbie took me into her bedroom to find me some clothes. "I'll give you some of Mandy's clothes. She's my daughter and more your size. She's outgrown them since she's had the baby," she said handing me a bin-bag full. "Sort through that and leave what you don't want, I won't be offended." She then started rifling through Christopher's clothes to find some for Steve. She pulled out a couple of shell suits and T-shirts along with some underwear and said, "That'll do him. Chris is a bit of a fat bastard but Steve'll cope."

At first, we were constantly on edge and never opened the curtains at the front of the house. We were so frightened of being spotted that we crawled on our hands and knees out of the living room to go to the bathroom and back again. Even though we were remote, we were sitting ducks if Barry and his gang found us.

As days turned into weeks, we nervously made our way to the back of the bungalow and started to spend time with Barbie and Chris in the kitchen. It was a relief to have the sun shine on us and as the view was of the hills and fields as far as we could see, we felt somewhat safer. As each day passed, we had more and more hope of survival, and seeing the natural landscape around us gave us strength.

Daily we thanked our lucky stars and as the weeks rolled on, we started to hope that we were going to make it. Steve was often low and would moan "Well if they catch us, they're going to do serious damage to me as it was me who mastered the whole bloody thing and committed all the crimes. It's all right for you. You'll probably get away with it as you're a girl."

Steve kept promising to change. "If we get through this, Amanda, I promise I'll make it up to you."

Barbie and Chris didn't work and were involved in all kinds of petty crime, such as burglary and fraud, to make ends meet. They were just like Steve and had no intention of working. I liked Barbie though as she made me feel safe, and even though we never left her home, it felt like we were protected. She, unlike Steve was strong.

We'd left some possessions behind at Jackie's and Christopher eventually went to collect them. On his return Christopher said Jackie had asked lots of questions, but Chris said to her, "Steve phoned me and asked me to collect some of their stuff and I'm taking it down to London when we arrange where to meet."

She asked where we lived, but he simply said, "I have no idea, Jackie, and I don't really care. I don't want to get involved. I'm only doing this to help Barbie."

Steve said he couldn't trust Jackie anymore. "I reckon she knew all along that it wasn't an old school friend of mine and that it was Barry. I think she told him where she lived cos she was jealous of what we had. She's always been a jealous cow."

Chris replied that she was certainly angry that we'd not even been in touch with her and left her on her own not knowing if those men would be back. She told him she was petrified at night, but Chris said, "I suspect Barry's been in touch with her and threatened her to tell them if you guys materialise." That was even more worrying.

Steve's mother, Stephanie, who lived with her sister in Norfolk at that time, decided to come and stay with Barbie, too. When she heard what Steve had done, she felt she had to come and sort things out. His mother was a large and homely woman and at first, I warmed to her as she was very cross with Steve and most protective of me by telling him off for his stupidity and hugging me to assure me I was safe.

"Steve, because of what you've done, you and this poor girl are likely to be on the run for the rest of your lives. If you're caught, you're both dead. You do realise that don't you!" she said.

Steve nodded with his head in his hands, and I listened glumly at the obvious.

"So as your father and I raised you to be a good and honest human being and because I believe God will protect you, I think you should do the right thing and get married. If you both die, then at least you'll both go to heaven together and that at least will give me peace of mind and should too for both of you."

No sooner was it suggested than plans were put into place. We had to leave the protection of the bungalow, which was very scary. The day we married we got into the car, lay down on the back seats and once Barbie had driven for several miles, and it was clear we weren't being followed, we cautiously sat up and tried to act as normally as we could.

We'd had to arrange a licence (which Barbie and Chris had helped us with) and find something appropriate to wear. Barbie had hired outfits for each of us under false names at a fictitious address with no intention of returning them. I found myself wearing an incredibly ugly and cheap synthetic white dress.

Barbie drove us in her car to the registry office. It was a dismal grey and cold day, and I was miserable too. Miserable because I was marrying a man I didn't love, for reasons that served only him and his mother, but with nowhere to go I felt I had no choice but to go along with his family's wishes.

Barbie and his mother had planned for us to move to Manchester after the wedding. They'd found a house for us to rent and had planned to take us there for us to make a fresh start.

It wasn't the big wedding that I'd always hoped and wished for. I wasn't surrounded by my family and loved ones. I had no feelings of ecstatic overwhelming love and happiness for my future husband. It was a cold and emotionless ceremony with Steve petrified for his life, adding a distinct air of despondency and despair to the already dire situation.

We moved to a council house in Manchester that had been applied for by the family on our behalf. It was a far cry from the isolated bungalow in the Welsh hills. We were on a huge estate near the airport, and when we arrived Steve applied for benefits to live on. I signed on at a temping agency. Our house was basic but felt like a palace compared to what we'd endured for the past few months.

Steve was paralysed mentally and emotionally and couldn't leave the house unless he was collecting his benefits. His excuse for not looking for work was because he was too scared of getting caught by Barry. He became more and more of a hermit, watching TV all day. I was starting to get fed up with him being so negative and depressed.

Feeling lonely, and desperate I decided one day to phone Beverly from a phone box. When she answered I was elated. It was the first time in months I'd spoken to a familiar voice. "Hi, Bev, it's Amanda," I said when she answered.

"God, Amanda, are you still in Portugal? I called your mum's house a few months ago and she said you'd gone off with some guy she didn't like, to live there."

I told her some of what had happened, and she was clearly shocked, but it felt so good to just talk to someone who knew me. I felt she was the only one I could tell. Whenever I could, I called her without Steve knowing. She insisted I stayed in touch as she was worried about me. I didn't reveal where we were though.

After six months, Steve was still unemployed, and I needed more than the hopelessness our life had become. I sat him down and said, "I've been in touch with Beverly for some weeks now and I'm sure she's safe as she has no way of being connected to Barry. Can I just ask her to come up and stay with us for a few days, please?"

"As long as you are very careful and don't give her the address. Then she can come up. You'll have to meet her from the coach station and bus it back here."

I nodded, thankful that he'd agreed.

When Beverly arrived, I welcomed her like a long-lost friend. We went into Manchester on that first day and had a pizza and spent the day catching up. It was such a relief to talk to someone about our situation. We both ate until we could eat no more that day, relishing in the common understanding that food was our comforter.

"I've had problems with food since my accident," she admitted. "I craved anything to take away the pain but now I'm stuck on these bloody pain killers and anti-depressants and can't get off them. Valium's the worst. I just can't cope without it."

The weekend was spent consuming anything we craved such as cakes, chocolates, and sweets. It was incredibly indulgent and offered light relief after months of fear. I had become very thin, and Beverly said, "You really need building up, girl. You've got so thin and gaunt."

I agreed with her. She gradually gained my trust, and I opened up and told her everything about Steve and how he'd conned me. We planned to keep in touch, and I said I'd call her whenever I could.

When Beverly left, I started to bond with Steve. I guess I felt sorry for him at some level and felt compassion for his fears. At least I knew the truth and he no longer lied to me. I thought about my future and what would become of us. We couldn't go on as we were. I'd managed to get a temp office job which was only a bus ride away. One day when I came home from work, I sat him down to talk to him.

"Steve, I want to have a child. I know we're not in love but we're making the most of this situation and as we are husband and wife, all be a loveless marriage, I'm no longer prepared to live my life without love. I know if I have a baby, then I can feel love again."

He looked at me, shocked.

"I don't know about you, but I can't go on with life without feeling that connection with another human being. I just want to nurture and feel that unconditional love in my life." I said, hoping he'd understand.

"You must be joking. What the hell do we want to complicate things for by adding someone else to the equation for?"

"We've been here in Manchester months now. If Barry was going to find us it would have been by now. I think we're safe and I want a family to love."

Although he said no to start with, Steve eventually realised that he may lose me and that a child would keep me with him. Reluctantly, he agreed.

I became pregnant sooner than expected. At first I thought I'd caught a virus as I was sick every day and couldn't get out of bed. Then when the doctor came to see me, I found out I was pregnant and was over the moon.

We'd been at the house for nearly a year and nothing bad had happened. There'd been no sign of Barry or his gang, so I phoned Mum up to tell her the news. She broke down on the phone when she heard my voice. "Amanda, I thought I'd never hear from you again. How are you? Are you OK? Where the hell are you, sweetheart?"

"Mum, Steve and I are married and we're having a baby."

She cried all over again. "Amanda, I'm sorry but I'm still angry that this man has turned your world upside down and isolated you from everyone. You had so much going for you and was on the verge of making great changes to your life until he came along."

I told her I was OK and that I was trying to make a life for myself, and without Steve knowing I promised to keep in touch and phoned her every week. It felt wonderful to have my mum back in my life.

Something seemed to wake Steve up once I was pregnant. He found the motivation to find work, but the type of work he'd chosen – selling time share – brought the old Stephen out again. He was working for commission only with about twenty other reps. He came home every night full of enthusiasm and talked endlessly about his ambitions and soon went back to his old ways, spending money on clothes for his image and telling stories to his colleagues about his past "successes". He would often come home late at night, drinking out in Manchester with his team, so I spent long days and nights alone, knowing no one else in the area. He bought himself Hugo Boss suits and a brand-new Renault Turbo, which completed his new image. I didn't care. At least he was working and starting to earn money legitimately.

I focused all my attention on my growing belly, while he focused on his newfound career and associates. Within a few months we'd moved into a house Steve said he'd bought in Gorton, near Moss Side. I never asked Steve how he'd bought the house, I was just grateful we had security. It wasn't in the nicest of areas, in fact the surroundings were drab and run down, but it was a large, terraced home and in no time, we were decorating and transforming our own nest.

We made a nursery for the baby. Somehow, deep down I knew she was a girl with blonde hair, although I had dark hair and Steve was a redhead. Steve was bringing money in at last and would often come home and show off his rewards.

"Look hon. Guess how much is here," he said, beaming at me as he threw a wad of cash into the air and watched it land all over the duvet.

We were in different worlds as I lived every day reading and planning for my baby to arrive, with the nesting process. Towards the end of my pregnancy, Stephanie contacted Steve. She was finding it increasingly difficult to live with her sister in Norfolk and wondered if she could live with us. Steve, true to form, compromised by asking for his inheritance up front. With a few weeks to go before the baby was due, Stephanie moved in. She was different this time and not as friendly towards me like she had been when I met her at Barbie's, and she ignored me most of the time but spent every moment she could with Steve.

She was so proud of her son who had his own house, great job and baby on the way that she insisted on cooking every night. Steve came home loving the attention and I found bit by bit I was just seen as a baby machine as Steve insisted I just sit and let Stephanie look after him. I felt I'd lost my identity in my own home. I'd leave them to it at night and retire early to my room as I felt I was in the way.

She made it perfectly obvious that I could never compete with her love for Steve by saying, "Steve is my baby and we've always had that special bond. He knows how to make his mum happy." Too tired to contemplate competing for his attention, I found solace in knitting for my baby.

136

Georgina Stephanie Louise l'Estrange (pronounced le trage) d'Ormain was born on the 28th of October 1990 after four days of labour. When she arrived, I lay awake looking at her as she slept through for over eleven hours.

I was amazed, fascinated, proud and scared all at once. I fed her myself, insisting the nurses give her nothing so that I could build her immune system up with my own milk. When I took her home, I felt I was the proudest mum ever.

Stephanie wanted to give me advice on everything, so I tried to be fair and let her have her way. When Georgina was five days old, my family finally came to see me – my mum, her husband, and my grandparents. It was a special day for me as Steve had at last given in and let them visit us.

When they left, I didn't feel as low as I thought because of having the most beautiful little girl to love and adore. She'd turned out to be dark haired which I found strange as the pictures in my mind had been of a little blonde curly headed girl.

When Georgina was one month old Steve announced, "I'm going to have to go to Portugal to work for a while. I've been promoted and they need me there for a while, but Amanda, it's huge money and we'll be set, I promise you."

He'd stopped making the big money he had at the beginning and was no longer top salesman and told me he was on the wheel, which meant he was on the downturn for a while until the wheel took him back up again.

"I've got to do something radical and accept the promotion Amanda. Don't worry, I'll send money back to you to support the family," he said trying to reassure me.

I knew though he didn't want to bond with Georgina as he spent most of his time out of the house and hardly ever gave her any attention. I felt we had no choice as he'd spent all the money his mother had given him, including all he'd earned at the time share company.

Though Steve had said he'd send money on, nothing came for weeks. He hardly ever called so I phoned the resort and spoke to a colleague who let the cat out of the bag. "Yeah, Steve's OK," he said when I asked after him. "In fact he was salesman of the week last week again. He's a generous guy, your hubby and every time I'm out with him he's always buying drinks for everyone."

I was stunned. It seemed he was living it up on a champagne lifestyle out there with his boys, living the single life. He'd hardly phoned home since he'd left, and times were getting hard as I'd had to apply for benefits.

Every day, I walked to the local shops with Georgina in her pram, proud as punch. In the window of the local pharmacy was a picture of Cybill Shepherd, the actress who had played Maddie Hayes in *Moonlighting*. Her hair was golden blonde, with short curls that framed her face and that's how I'd seen Georgina when I was pregnant, so I nicknamed her Maddie!

Finally, after several months, Steve came home. His money had run out and his partying was over. On his return he insisted he wanted time with me and so he encouraged his mother to visit one of his sisters on the Isle of Man. I was horrified that he suggested she took my baby girl with her.

"I can't possibly let Georgina go to the Isle of Man with your mother, Steve. She's still so young and I've never had more than a few hours away from her. How will she cope?"

"Look, she's only going to go for a few days, and I think the break would do us both good. We need it, Amanda. I haven't seen you for months," he pleaded.

Eventually, I grudgingly gave in. When they left from Manchester Airport, my heart felt heavy, and I felt choked from her leaving me. Steve was adamant he wanted to rekindle our relationship, and for Georgina's sake I decided to make a go of it. That was until I realised his true intentions.

Steve had always had an insatiable appetite for sex, but his experimentation sometimes pushed my boundaries which I would not tolerate. Since he'd come home, he'd pushed me for sex, but I wasn't interested as I just didn't have that sort of connection with him anymore.

Then he started talking about being with another woman and I was horrified.

"Come on, it'll spice up our sex life. God knows we could do with it," he said.

"I don't know how you can ask me Steve. It's sick." I said, disgusted he'd even contemplated asking me. It made me wonder how he'd coped in Portugal. I knew he must have cheated on me whilst he was away, and to be honest, I didn't care but this was different. He wanted me to know about it. He went on for days and all I was concerned about was getting my daughter home. It had been a week since they'd left, and we'd heard nothing.

I pushed Steve to contact his mother as I had no phone number for his sister. Eventually when he spoke to his mother, he told me that when he'd spoken to her on the phone she told him she'd been poorly and that's why she'd not rung. She would have to travel back the following week. This terrified me as I wasn't sure she was telling the truth and worried she would keep Georgina out there and not return. Something didn't feel right. This though gave Steve more opportunity to badger me.

He talked relentlessly about sex day and night. When he told me he'd organised a prostitute to come to the house, I wanted to walk out there and then. I would have if his mother hadn't had my baby, but I hoped that if I gave in, he'd leave me alone.

I wondered if he was telling me the truth about Stephanie. I wondered if perhaps he'd phoned her and told her to stay longer.

That night he made me sit in the cupboard under the stairs so I could view his performance! The doorbell went and his setting of music and candles made me realise he was deluded enough to think this girl would be wooed by him. As he brought her into our living room and sat her down, I heard him talking to her as if they were on a date. I couldn't bear to look let alone listen, so I kept as still as possible and hugged my knees in an attempt to block out what was happening. I heard her say, "You do realise you're paying for this, don't you? Shall we get on with it?"

"Oh, yeah, sorry. Do you want me to pay you the money up front or after?"

"Now would be good."

I covered my ears and screwed my eyes shut tight though I could still hear them. When she'd finally gone, I climbed out of the cupboard. Firmly I said to Steve,

"That's the end now Steve. I want my daughter back and don't think you'll ever get to sleep with me or go near me again, cos you won't. You disgust me and I have no idea how low you will stoop for your own gratification. I'm done with you. You get used to sleeping on the sofa from now on." With that I left him staring at me as I went up to my room and locked my bedroom door.

I was twenty-four and felt I'd been through a lifetime and could never trust anyone ever again.

Chapter 15

Violence is the last refuge of the incompetent.

Isaac Asimov

The debt collectors finally caught up with us in Gorton and so one night we had to load the car up with what we could. Steve put the keys through our letterbox, and we drove back to North Wales leaving our lovely home.

We stayed with Barbie for a while. This time we were even more cramped with a baby and all our possessions. Steve said he'd sort it. Miraculously, he managed to purchase another house, although he'd left his job and we had no income. The new house was a new build in a remote village on the North Welsh coast. It was a chalet, very small and fuelled only by a coal fire. But it gave us security and we were helped by handouts from the family to start with.

I loved the coastline and the surrounding hills and spent every day walking Georgina in her push chair with our new dog – an Alsatian we'd got from a rescue centre called Jack – who ran alongside me loyally on our daily walks on the beach. Jack was beautiful and I trained him to do all sorts of things which amused Georgina no end. That was until one day I found Steve in the kitchen on all fours with his head in the dog bowl teasing Jack by making out he was eating his food. Jack was sitting about a yard from the bowl looking at the food intently.

"Look!" Steve said as I walked into the kitchen with Georgina in my arms. "I'm teaching Jack not to go near his food until I say."

Suddenly, Jack went for Steve and bit his face. Steve threw the dog out into the garden and, watching through the window, I saw him pick up a piece of timber and smash it down on Jack's back. I ran outside.

"Don't," I screamed. "Don't hit him. He didn't mean to. You provoked him."

Steve looked me straight in the eye and said, "Take him to the vet and get him put down or I'll kill him myself!"

Tearfully, I phoned the vet and made the appointment and the next day I sat with Jack on my own in the reception praying for him to forgive me. I had no choice but to tell the vet he'd bitten Stephen and I was concerned for my young daughter, but I knew if I didn't, Jack would suffer greater torment. Tears poured down my face as I watched my friend and companion look up at me. I held onto him hoping he'd understand. Steve was beyond my forgiveness. I hated him for what he'd done to my dog. I loved Jack unconditionally like Georgina and I found it heart-breaking to have to do what Steve had asked me to do.

The next day, grief stricken, I made an appointment to see my GP. I felt so low and even Georgina's sweetness couldn't pull me out of my pain. As I sat down to talk to my doctor, I told him how I felt. I didn't give details but hoped he'd give me some tablets to help make me happy. I was surprised when he asked me where my family were as it was evident I needed to be with them. I told him they were down south and he suggested I went back to my family for good. Up till then it hadn't struck me that I could. I was brought up to believe if you made your bed you had to lie in it, and when I had permission to change that, I woke from the spell that had held me tied to a man I'd never really loved.

Steve was waiting outside the surgery, and I was shocked to see him there. I think he knew I had come to the end. He'd never shown interest in my personal needs up to that point, but that day he seemed to sense I was serious. We sat on the wall outside the surgery, Georgina asleep in her pushchair, and I said to him very calmly, "I'm leaving you to go and live with my family."

He simply nodded his head whilst he held his hands together in a prayer like manner in front of his face. I continued feeling hopeful. "I want to take Georgina with me. You can keep the house and all our possessions. I don't want anything," I said, hoping he'd let me go without a fight. I knew he was relieved as he'd gain everything we had and let go of all responsibility towards myself and our child.

The night before I left Steve cried and begged me to stay begging for forgiveness, but it was far too late. I organised transport and left to go and stay at my grandmother's flat down in London as I'd planned. My grandfather had passed away two years before, so it was very strange to be with just my poor widowed grandmother in their home. Those first few weeks were filled with love and tenderness. All the familiar smells of toast and tea, fags and lavender were still there, the sound of BBC

Radio Two still played in the kitchen and we sat in blissful warmth instead of the cold I'd battled with continuously in Wales.

I soon found a flat around the corner from Grandma's and enrolled at college to do a travel and tourism qualification so I could get back into the travel industry. Once I'd completed that, I applied for jobs immediately. It was hard to find a job that would suit a mum with a young toddler and so I took a job in a call centre to make ends meet.

Mum hadn't been around to help as she was so engrossed with her own responsibilities, and she seemed to stick her head in the sand when I told her what I was going through. I felt alone. Mum had been headhunted and was now managing PR for the whole W H Smith Group which, with all the travel, demanded much of her attention. Grandma became my surrogate mum. Every day I took her out somewhere to shop or have a coffee. She especially loved our trips to Asda to people-watch over a cup of tea and when we got home, we'd watch our favourite programmes together.

I found a wonderful local child minder, Yolanda, and once my divorce had finally gone through, Mum said she'd help me to buy a small new build flat near my grandmother's. Steve didn't have anything to do with us as he'd met a girl in a nightclub three weeks after I'd left him and moved her in with him almost immediately.

I found out when he called me one evening when he asked my advice about how to cope with his new relationship. "Amanda, I know this may come across as a bit too much for you to cope with but I'm hoping you'll give me some advice. Heather, my new girlfriend, suffers from depression and because I can't afford to pay for the mortgage on our home, I wondered if you would know how to help us as I need to know about how the insurance works."

I couldn't believe he wanted me to advise how he and his new girlfriend could find a way to pay for the mortgage on the house. I told him I had no idea how to help him. He never spoke to Georgina on the phone, let alone came to see her or enquire about how she was doing, but I knew he had what he wanted so why would he?

I was working full time. Yolanda had become a friend and Grandma, Georgina and I had a wonderful time together whenever we could. Georgina and I had a beautiful flat which I decorated, and life was starting to show promise.

One evening, Georgina was in bed asleep, and I was in the living room on the exercise bike I'd won as a raffle prize listening to the TV, when I heard a loud cracking noise. Suddenly, there was a second cracking noise but even louder this time. I quickly got off the bike and turned the TV off and at that moment, heard a third and more violent cracking sound occur. My heart was racing. This time, I realised it was coming from my window. I threw open the curtains and looked out. On the next level down to the side of me was an Indian looking man screaming hysterically at me. I stared at him wondering if he was having an episode of some sort and then opened the window and yelled at him.

"Excuse me. I don't understand what you're saying. Are you talking to me?" I asked him shocked by his reaction towards me. From what I could see, he was smartly dressed in a suit and was a short and very thin man with what seemed like a billy goat beard. That seemed to exasperate him even more and I heard a torrent of abuse unleashed at me. I was feeling scared and worried Georgina might hear him, so I went to shut the window. As he saw me do this, he shouted, "Wait!"

I opened the window again and even though he seemed to be fuming still, he started to shout his grievance rather than scream like he had before. "I'm sorry but I just can't deal with the continuous noise coming from your flat. I work long hours in the city and can't deal with coming back to this every night."

He said my music was far too loud even though it was turned down enough for a sleeping child in the next room and I'd only recently acquired the bike.

"I'm so sorry," I replied. "I had no idea. It's no louder than normal as my daughter's asleep in the other room. Why don't I switch it back on so you can hear for yourself how loud it is?"

With that he started apologising profusely for his outburst. I was relieved but still unnerved and as he was my neighbour, I thought I'd better get on good terms with him.

"That's quite all right." I said, but he wanted to apologise over and over again.

"I'm so sorry. Perhaps I've overreacted," he kept saying. "It must be these walls that allow the sound to travel. I do hope I haven't offended you, especially if you're a woman on your own."

I felt uncomfortable and wanted to end the conversation as soon as possible so just said what I could to appease him. The next day he appeared from nowhere and approached my car. I felt scared but tried to compose myself as he got nearer. He started mumbling apologies yet again. I just wanted him to leave me alone, but he was so insistent.

"Hi, I'm so sorry about last night. My name's Imran and I just feel awful about how I treated you last night. Please, let me make it up to you, after all, we're neighbours and need to resolve this."

I just smiled and waved him an acceptance as I tried to get into my car, but he continued.

"I'm sorry. Can I make it up to you and take you out for a drink to show you I'm not the person you witnessed last night."

"Honestly, you don't have to do anything to make up for it, I'm fine. I'm sure you're a lovely person but I don't go out often as I have my daughter to look after," I said, hoping he'd leave me alone.

He didn't seem happy with that and kept pushing me to get the answer he wanted. In the end I said, "OK, perhaps we can go for a drink sometime, but can I let you know when as I've got my daughter to think about?"

The very next day he was at my car again when I got home, insisting on making our date official. He was standing there with a bunch of flowers and a limp smile, looking like a child who'd been caught robbing the sweet shop. For one moment I looked at him differently. So I said, "Thank you. Yes, OK, I'll go for a drink with you as long as we put this whole thing behind us and never bring it up again."

He was quite a small man and seemed physically no match for me. What harm could he do? A night out would be a welcome relief to my routine of work, children's TV, and trips to the park with Georgina.

The next evening we set off in his car and he took me to a rough area in North London that I hadn't visited before, and realising I felt uncomfortable, he said, "Well, I've brought you here cos I'm anti-white and so like to stick to my own territory." I thought this was an odd thing to tell me considering he was taking me out to atone for his bad behaviour, and his tone was a little snipey and came across as sinister. But I tried to push it aside to get the evening over and done with.

We sat in a corner of a pub, and I listened to him tell me all about how successful he was as an accountant working for the government. He told me how he cared for his family and that they'd returned to Guyana, and he'd suffered at the hands of white people because they mistook him as Asian.

"I'm a West Indian man through and through," he said. "My mother and father abandoned me to go back to Guyana and left me here to cope with these white people."

I felt increasingly threatened as he got more and more frenzied as he described his family rejection of him and so I just tried to nod and smile sympathetically in agreement, hoping the evening would end quickly.

"My ex-girlfriend who was white betrayed me for a white man and so you can understand why I don't trust white people," he said, which unnerved me even more. He was unleashing his pent up anger and resentment and I couldn't make out if he was wanting to purge his past or was making me aware that I was included in his hatred.

I wanted to get away from him as soon as I could, but I had little money and no transport and was reliant on him getting me home. I told him as little as possible about myself and hoped he just wanted to download on me. Finally, he took me to the car to return home. He was by then, thick with rage. As we got into the car I said, "Thank you for the drink tonight. I do hope we can remain friends."

He immediately turned on me. He sounded again like he had the first night I'd ever set eyes on him and seemed to think I'd strung him along and was now dumping him as though we'd had some long-term relationship. As I got into the car and sat as far from him as possible up against the door, I tried to fathom out what had happened.

"You whore; white women are all the same. You lead us men on and then think you can walk away," he said. "You scunt hole you. You're nothing and just some dirty white girl trash."

I turned to get out of the car. He grabbed my arm though and twisted it until I felt it was going to snap.

"If you dare to leave me, I'm going to break your arm, bitch. You're mine and if you ever dare try to leave me now, I'll hurt you so bad you'll wish you were dead. You're a very stupid girl if you think you can try and escape me. I know where your grandmother lives and if you try anything, I'll deal with her," he said menacingly. "I've got underworld connections and belong to a gang in Birmingham. Don't think you can run from me, you whore."

I was in shock by his threats. He added, "I'll find your daughter and take her if you dare to disobey me as I know where your childminder is and can easily arrange something to take your child out."

I was petrified and felt physically sick at the prospect of anyone touching my daughter. I stopped protesting and prayed this man would end up apologising like before.

"If you tell anyone including your family, friends or the police, we will have no choice but to hurt those you love," he said. He then drove me back to his flat. Then he turned into a grovelling, sweet talking man who then tried to feed me his mum's favourite food he whisked up in his kitchen. He told me how he was going to look after me and cherish me.

And then he raped me.

He eventually let me leave his flat and I walked home to the next block where I lived. When I got home, I climbed into the shower for hours as I cried uncontrollably. Eventually, exhausted, and emotionally drained, I climbed into the single bed with my daughter and held her in my arms all night.

For those next two weeks, Imran continued to call and torment me with the same threats. If I dared to show any rebellion, he would raise his voice and make more threats. I felt powerless and trapped.

"You have nowhere to run to, bitch, as you've been seen out on a date with me in a public place and I've got several witnesses, hence why I took you into my territory. The police won't believe you as it will just come across as a domestic," he said.

I was so scared of what he'd said that I kept going to his flat and each day prayed for some way out of this man's grasp. He made me feel sick, but I had to protect those I loved. He always seemed to be one step ahead of me, cornering me into stopping me from having any freedom or power over him. I kept this away from Georgina and my family. I cried at night when my little girl was safely tucked up in her bed and wondered why I had attracted yet another untrustworthy man into my life, this time though with the traits of my father and step mother all rolled into one.

Chapter 16

If you must hold yourself up to your children as an
object lesson, hold yourself up as a warning and not as
an example.

George Bernard Shaw

I knew I had to do something to stop Imran's power over me. It had only been going on for two weeks, but it seemed like a lifetime. He had started to punch and kick me and then he'd become childlike and beg for forgiveness for his appalling behaviour. This was followed by tears of grief while he purged to me how painful his existence was as a young boy growing up and then he raped me. I was too exhausted and frightened to fight back, so I switched off and became numb.

I phoned Steve to ask if Georgina could come and stay with him for a break in an attempt to get her away from the situation.

"Amanda, I don't think that's a good idea as Heather's having issues as she can't have children of her own. It would be unfair for her to have my child in the house, don't you think? I'll discuss it with her and see what she says but I doubt it," he said.

I was surprised when he called me back the next day. He'd spoken to Heather, and she had agreed to have Georgina for a holiday on the proviso she would have more than just one-off contact with her. I wasn't OK with that at first, because up to that point Steve had had very little to do with his daughter. I felt uncomfortable with his digging as he said, "So why the need for her to go on a holiday right now? Why does she need to be so far away from you?"

I explained I was having trouble with an aggressive neighbour but gave little away and hoped that would suffice. Imran was by now telling me he wanted us to move into his flat with him. He kept telling me I was his woman and would remain his always. When the situation became unbearable, I phoned Steve again. He asked me what I really wanted. I was angry at his game playing as he was telling me one minute he'd have

Georgina to stay and the next he said he didn't want anything to do with her. I eventually said I'd sign an agreement if it was the only way he'd agree to have her. He said that would suffice as it would reassure Heather I'd let her see Georgina on a regular basis and not just use them to help me get out of a jam. I felt the agreement would be a useless piece of paper with no merit whatsoever and once I'd dealt with Imran by going to the police, it would all finally be over.

I sat watching television to dull the noise in my head. Tears poured down my cheeks and I just couldn't hold back my pain. Georgina got out of her bed and came into the living room. She came over to me on the sofa, gave me the biggest hug and said, "It's OK, Mummy. Everything will be all right!"

I threw my arms around her and held her as tight as I could. I sat her on my lap and gently told her she was going to have a little holiday with her daddy. That night I took her to bed with me and held her all night long until we rose the next morning to leave for Wales.

I'd stuffed a bin bag full of Georgina's clothes and toys and got us into the car before I could change my mind. I'll never forget the journey as I drove Georgina to Wales in the early hours of that morning whilst no one else was on the road. As I looked at my baby girl on the back seat, cuddled up in her pyjamas under her duvet with the black bin bag beside her, memories flooded back of the day my mother had driven me to my father's. Georgina was the same age as I'd been.

I rang Steve from a service station and told him we were on our way. He said he'd changed his mind.

"What do you mean, you can't have her now?" I screamed down the phone in panic. "You've got to have her, we're almost at yours. I can't go back with her Steve. I've got to sort this mess out or it'll make it worse for us if I go back."

Steve seemed to enjoy my suffering and need of him by mocking me on the phone. "So, you want me now, do you? I guess I'm not as indispensable as you thought!" he said.

I pleaded with him to help me. In the end, he said he'd meet me at a layby, as Heather didn't want me to come to their house. Within half an hour, we were parked up and Steve pulled up in a sports model BMW, emanating his typical message, oozing with ego. He walked towards us and impatiently opened the back of my car, grabbed the bag off the back seat and told Georgina to get in the front seat of his car. My legs went to jelly.

Something screamed at me to get back in the car and drive away with Georgina and not look back, but my fear was too great. I held onto her with a hug I felt I couldn't let go of.

"Baby, you'll see Mummy sooner than you know. It'll only be a couple of weeks and soon you'll be home again and safe with Mummy, I promise you."

She stared at me with bewilderment and frightened eyes and then cried out to me and flung her arms around me. "Mummy, don't leave me, please don't leave me!"

Tears poured down my cheeks as I tried to reassure her and all Steve was shouting was, "Come on. I've got things to do!"

I held her until he'd switched on the car engine. He slammed his car door shut and shouted at me again "Come on for fuck's sake, Amanda, I've got to go. Get her into the car, now!"

I picked Georgina up, carried her to Steve's car and put her in the passenger seat, even though she clung to me desperately. I struggled to release her arms from around my neck and put her seatbelt on and as I shut the door, I saw Georgina's face pressed up against the window, arms stretched out for me, screaming, and begging for me to take her home. I took a huge deep breath as I watched in slow motion as he put his foot down and drove away from me.

I watched the car until the last second. That was the last time I saw my little girl.

Chapter 17

Ever has it been that love knows not its own depth
until the hour of separation.

Kahlil Gibran

The flat was cold and empty when I returned alone and instantly there was a knock on the door. As soon as I opened it, Imran ran in as if he were about to steam into a pile of guys outside a nightclub. He was fuelled and ready for the attack. I stood back and watched him run into every room. All the while he was screaming at me, "Where the hell have you been? I've been waiting hours for you. Why didn't you tell me you were going to be so long? Where did you go and what the hell have you been doing that took you so long?"

His voice was reaching that hysterical high-pitched scream I'd heard on the first occasion I'd met him.

"You fucking white bitch, how dare you do this to me. Are you that fucking stupid that you think you can get away from me? Whores like you are two a penny. How dare you try and defy me. I've told you before, if you dare to trick me, I'll kill your scunt hole grandmother and daughter and let them bleed to death!"

I couldn't believe somebody could be that vile. I froze. When he realised, we were alone, he pushed me into my bedroom. Somehow, I gathered the strength to face him head on.

"I'm not going to let you do this to me anymore," I yelled as I ran for the front door.

He flew across the bedroom at me with a kick and suddenly I was on the floor struggling to breathe. As I landed, I felt crippling pain in my chest and found I was gasping for breath. I thought my lungs had collapsed. The pain was instant and incredible, and I felt panic set in. As I curled into a ball, he kicked and punched me from behind. I was locked in that room for over six hours that day as he continued to curse me over and over, saying, "You've defied me and so you're going to have to learn to do as you're told. When are you going to learn, you white trash you! Your grandmother's a sitting duck. After I've raped her, I'll slit her throat just like your bastard child."

He seethed with demon eyes and a rabid expression I'd never experienced in anyone before. He randomly slapped my face hard in between bouts of kicks and punches until he was emotionally exhausted and anger turned into pain.

"You don't understand how hard it's been trying to live here without my parents! Why the hell did they have to leave me? I'm their son. Because of them I get called an Indian. I'm not Indian, I'm from Guyana and I hate them for leaving me. Because of them I suffer. My ex-white bitch girlfriend left me, too. You have no idea what it's like to be me. You think it's all right to go around thinking your life is just great. Well it's not. Your life is mine now and I'll make you pay for all that's happened to me and then you'll understand just what it's like to live in fear."

I was beyond pain and expected him to finish me off for good, but he burst into tears and begged me for forgiveness. I sat huddled in the corner of the room with my arms around my knees and listened to him. I thought I was in for it, but his mood changed and then he raped me.

Eventually, in the early hours, he left my flat. Before he left, he said, "You're going to have to go to hospital to get that checked out. Make sure you tell people how you've fallen out the loft hatch tonight onto some ladders and that's how you've hurt yourself. You may think you've taken your daughter somewhere safe, but I guarantee I'll find her within days. I've got the connections remember? Don't you ever think you can cross me again as next time, you'll be lucky if you can breathe at all. You got that?"

I nodded and prayed he'd let me be.

"Right, so when can I see you next?" he said as if nothing had happened. "I've got to go away for a few days on a business trip from tomorrow so will be back in three days. You best make yourself available."

I stayed in my flat for a few days, telling work I'd had an accident. They insisted I went to hospital, but I played it down. My breathing difficulties continued for several days and for weeks the pain was incredible. I didn't answer the phone when it rang, but my grandmother called me continuously. When I eventually answered, she insisted I went to see her.

He'd called to my flat on the day of his return and coincidentally my mother was on the phone. I spoke to her as calmly as I could whilst he watched me like a hawk. I started to get emotional, and Mum asked if I was OK. I said, "Yes, Mum, I love you."

She knew instantly something was wrong and said, "Amanda, what's going on? What's wrong?"

Tears emerged and ran down my cheeks and Imran simply approached me, took out a knife from his pocket and ran it over my hand. I stifled my sobs and said I needed to go and put the phone down, understanding his warning. I was bleeding profusely as he'd caught a main artery and he took me to hospital. When the doctor saw me in accident and emergency, Imran told me to say I'd caught myself with a steak knife. Ironically, that day the doctor had little help and asked Imran if he'd help stitch me up. He looked at me proudly as if he was in complete control over me and mocked me as he helped the doctor stitch my hand.

I'd called Steve's house the day after I'd left Georgina with him but no one answered. The next day when I called, a stranger answered and passed the phone to Georgina. When she came on to the phone, the first thing she said was, "Mummy I'm hungry!"

"What do you mean you're hungry, baby?" I asked.

All she kept repeating was, "She only gave me cornflakes."

"What do you mean, you've only had cornflakes? Do you mean you've only had them once or only had cornflakes and nothing else to eat other than that, sweetheart?" As she was four, I had to intuitively understand what she was saying.

"I'm hungry, Mummy. I had cornflakes but nothing else. I want what you make."

I gathered she'd not been given anything other than cornflakes since I'd dropped her off. Warning bells were ringing.

"Darling, where are the adults in the house?" I asked.

"I don't know Mummy. They keep arguing and fighting. I think they're upstairs now."

"Georgina, who's the lady who answered the phone to Mummy?"

"It's just a lady."

I assumed it had been Heather, which was worrying as my daughter hadn't been told who Heather was. "Georgina, listen carefully to Mummy. Has anyone hurt you in any way since you've been there, darling?"

152

"No, Mummy. I just sit in my room all the time. I want to come home Mummy. Please don't make me stay here anymore. I don't like it here," she said, starting to cry.

I told her to go to her room and cuddle her cuddle cat and I'd come to get her. I told her she'd be safe and warm soon and Mummy would cook her favourite dinner and she shouldn't be scared. I promised her I'd be there as soon as I could. I rang my grandmother and told her I was coming over. When I got there, I revealed what I'd had to endure over the past few weeks and why I'd taken Georgina to her father's. Grandma sat there open mouthed as I poured out all the horrific and sordid details. We hugged and I felt as if my power was returning as I felt her love. We spent the day together planning and decided to speak to Mum. When she got home from work, I called her.

Mum was equally shocked but suggested Georgina was safe for now and I should stay at my grandmother's and this man would realise I'd left my flat and perhaps leave me alone. I felt she thought I was exaggerating. Against my mum's advice, Grandma and I decided it would be best I phoned to tell Georgina I was going to get her straight away. When I called there was a continuous tone. I rang over and over and it was the same. Eventually, I tried the operator and found out the phone had been disconnected.

Grandma calmed me down and told me to ring Mum who suggested Steve probably hadn't paid his bill and I should write to him so he could phone me. After there'd been enough time for him to receive the letter, I waited all day for him to ring.

At six o'clock that evening, I called Mum and said, "I've had enough of waiting, Mum, I'm going to drive to Wales to get Georgina."

Mum told me to phone the police instead. Grandma wasn't so sure and thought I should go and get her regardless and I was confused. I loved my grandma, but my mum was a woman of the world and should know best.

"What if you get there and he's disappeared somewhere with her?" Mum said.

I worried if I phoned the police would they do the right thing? Or should I do nothing and trust it was just a problem with Steve's phone? I eventually decided to phone the police. They informed me they'd go to Steve's house and some hours later they rang me and told me they were satisfied Georgina was happy and it was a marital dispute, so I should get in touch with a solicitor.

"What the hell do you mean marital dispute?" I screamed down the phone at the policeman.

The police officer was polite but firm. He said Steve had told him Georgina had been given to him as part of a custody arrangement and it wasn't a two-week break as I suggested. The policeman said I needed a solicitor if I disputed this.

"No, please you can't do this to me. She's not safe there. That wasn't what we agreed. You check out his house. He's a regular cannabis user so how can that be good for my daughter's well-being? That house they're living in was obtained through fraud. Surely that tells you the nature of what the man's character is like? And he's defrauding the government for benefits because he's told me that, too. Isn't that enough?"

It was obvious the policeman wasn't interested, and he repeated he was satisfied Georgina was safe and I'd have to get my own solicitor to help me as it was a domestic incident and not a criminal incident. Even when I told him I was concerned about the mental state of Steve's girlfriend, he just kept emphasising the same thing.

"Steve has told me she has volatile behaviour when she's out of balance. Don't you think that's enough to look into?"

"Don't worry, miss, we'll contact social services tonight and get them to check your allegations out," he said.

I had to eventually explain to the policeman why I'd taken Georgina to Steve's in the first place and his comment was she was probably better off where she was. He wasn't interested in all the other offences, so I came off the phone feeling as if I'd been punched and kicked harder than I'd ever been hurt before.

Grandma had no way of consoling me as my world had finally come apart well and truly at the seams. A police officer came to see me. I was so angry that I was ready to tell the police everything Imran had done to me. After all if it hadn't been for him, my daughter would be safely tucked up in bed and we'd be safe in our own home together.

The policeman said he couldn't do anything about my situation as we had no proof Imran had persistently targeted and followed me. I had no proof he'd threatened me, and I couldn't prove I hadn't willingly had a relationship with him. The police said it was a grey area and it was hard to prove rape in relationships. I was put in touch with Victim Support, but felt it was a brush off. More so, I was concerned if Imran found out I'd attempted to report him, I would be in huge trouble.

The police said all I could do now was to keep away from Imran and report any future threatening behaviour so they could gain evidence for any future attacks. I was desperate to be with my little girl and had to deal with the incessant panic and feeling of wanting to scream inside and I had no way of channelling it.

I stayed at my grandmother's and wouldn't answer my mobile until it ran out of charge as my charger was at my flat. Imran had then somehow found my grandmother's home phone number, although it was ex-directory, and started to call us. When I answered, shocked he'd got our number; I just put the phone down as soon as I heard the hysteria in his voice. My heart was racing.

My grandmother was fuming. "You let me answer next time he calls. I'll certainly give him a piece of my mind."

He phoned back straight away, but she told me when he answered he spouted vile insults at her and threatened to hurt her if she didn't pass the phone to me, which she didn't. He phoned over and over again and Grandma would not give in, nor leave it to ring as this was her only lifeline, she told me, and she didn't want to show him she was scared.

We had the number changed when we called BT and reported him, but somehow, he found out the new number. Over the next few days we were bombarded day and night with threatening calls until we called the police again who said until we had evidence of threats, they could do nothing. We changed our number four times and, in the end, BT could then show we were being hounded so then decided to monitor the calls to record the number of times he contacted us to build a profile for the police. At least BT and the police were taking it more seriously, but still he left no evidence.

I tried to leave my grandmother's flat one day to sneak to mine to get some things, but he was watching our flat and as soon as I tried to get into my car in the car park, he jumped me from behind. I struggled but he was too strong for me, holding my arms behind my back and pushing his body weight against mine. He held me against the car to show his power over me. He was more livid than I'd ever seen him before and screamed at me, "What the fuck do you think you're doing, bitch? Don't you know you're getting dangerously close to the mark? You come back with me now or your grandmother's life ends! You got that?" He grabbed my hair and yanked it backwards, knocking my driving glasses off my face and smashing them into the ground with his foot.

"Do you know where your daughter is right now?" he asked.

I shook my head.

"Well I do, lady and you're in big trouble, cos I even know where your whore of a mother lives, too."

I struggled with all my might and finally got free. He ran down the street after me, but luckily my grandmother lived in the same road as our local police station. As I got nearer to the station, he retreated shouting venomously, "You watch your back, bitch. Don't worry, though, I'll get you when you're sleeping."

As I glanced quickly behind, I could see him fuming and his face showed how deadly serious he was. I ran into the police station, gasping for breath and told them he'd caught me outside and threatened to kill my family. A policeman eventually made his way outside to search for Imran, but I knew it was a waste of time as he'd be long gone. Imran was always a step ahead of the police. I was taken home to the safety of my grandmother's flat and was reassured the police would do all they could once they had evidence.

Days became weeks and eventually I had to resign from my job as I'd begun to make excuses to avoid going to work. I loved my new job as a legal secretary with a firm of solicitors, but Imran had called on a few occasions and they'd mentioned they didn't want to attract anything nasty into the workplace. He was beginning to corner me, so I spent most of my time inside my grandmother's flat feeling like a trapped bird. Each time I'd tried to go to work, I found him waiting outside which petrified me. He threatened over and over to sabotage my credibility with my employers, and I didn't doubt him when he'd started telephoning my workplace.

I had no choice but to confide in my boss who was sad to let me go but realised I need protect myself and family. I visited two solicitors to initiate proceedings to get my daughter back. On both occasions, once the solicitors realised I had problems with Imran's obsession, they informed me I would need to find a solicitor who specialised in my particular case to try to get my daughter back.

I felt disheartened. I sought solicitors as far from my address as I could. No matter how far I went, Imran somehow found me at some stage on the journey and proceeded to threaten me. On one occasion in broad daylight on a busy high street in North London, he tried to drag me into his car as I walked past his car not realising he was in it. It was broad daylight and busy with people walking by. I thought he was crazy to try to do it so publicly, but he didn't care there were witnesses. It just made him more vile and irrational as he was angry at how he couldn't fully use his power over me. On that occasion and on several others, he said he had a knife in his pocket and he would kill me if he had to, but I chanced it by hoping he was lying and ran each time. He couldn't chase me as he knew someone would apprehend him for sure and he knew it would be a big mistake. The police would then definitely have evidence against him.

I began to feel paranoid about where he was whenever I ventured beyond the sanctuary of my grandmother's flat and hardly slept at night for fear of being stabbed in my sleep. Whenever Imran threatened coming to the flat to hurt us, we informed the police but each time he was smarter and quicker than us and wasn't caught as by the time the police arrived, he was gone. On several occasions, they arrived with firearms to protect us as he'd threatened to come to the flat to shoot us, but he never materialised. I didn't know what was worse, knowing where he was or not knowing where he was. He played with my mind, and I was petrified.

Christmas was coming and I'd been without my little girl for several months. Imran tormented us daily with calls or by coming to the flat to frighten us. I was now seeing my fourth solicitor who took on my case but again pondered over the complexity of all the aspects within it relating to losing Georgina and Imran's abuse and stalking. Up to that point, each solicitor had expressed they could only deal with one aspect.

I was deteriorating emotionally and mentally, living each day in the hope Steve would change his mind and bring my daughter home, but each day was a hopeless repetition of the day before. I wrote to Steve constantly in an attempt to jog his conscience, but he never responded. In the end, the solicitor said that as I'd signed an agreement that allowed Steve and Heather to have parental responsibility for my daughter, I would find it hard to fight them. I was told I should accept Steve had legal rights to Georgina, too, and I may have to accept that because of Imran, she would be better off with him. When I heard that, I decided to forget the legal system that was failing me and find another way myself. Time was slipping away fast and the longer it took, the more advantage Steve had over me. I explained to each solicitor what Steve's intention was and they agreed with me, but it came down to proof and until we could go to court, we couldn't fight our case, which would take time to put together. I couldn't wait any longer.

Steve and Heather had moved away from where the police had originally found them. It was only through contacting a neighbour of theirs that I knew this. I wrote to all the neighbours in the road where I knew Steve had lived, asking if they would contact me if they knew where Steve and Heather had moved to with my daughter. I hoped someone would have news of where they'd taken her.

Two people wrote back out of nearly forty. One neighbour said Steve and Heather had moved away some time ago with my daughter and they'd often questioned the oddities with the family situation with Georgina arriving so suddenly. They wished me well, being concerned for my daughter's welfare and offered further help. The neighbour next door to where Steve had lived wrote in more detail. They explained they'd seen all the comings and goings and had always been concerned for Georgina's welfare. They wrote they'd often come home to find her outside in the street on her own which immediately brought tears streaming down my face. They'd taken her in sometimes and fed her as she was cold and hungry. When they asked her where her friends were, she'd told them she had none and when they asked about her parents, she said she'd lost her mummy, and her daddy was always out.

The lady who looked after her apparently was always in the house, but Georgina was often sent into the garden to play, but as it had no fences she would explore. The kind neighbours warned her to stay close to home or go in and see them, which she often did. They offered to help me in any way they could and said I could stay with them if I wanted to come and look for my daughter, and they even offered to help look for her themselves. I was touched by their kindness.

The next day I answered the phone when Imran called. It was the first time in weeks he'd heard my voice and at first, he was shocked. Then he spoke softer and calmer in an attempt I suppose to encourage me to continue to talk to him.

"What do you know about my daughter? Where is she?" I said in a strong and demanding, no nonsense voice. I was suspicious my daughter's disappearance was linked to him as he'd threatened over and over he knew where she was and he was going to hurt her.

He was silent for a moment and then said, "I can help you."

"I don't need your help – you've done far too much already. I want to know if you have anything to do with my daughter going missing."

He was strangely quiet and willing to listen.

"I just want my baby home. I don't care what it takes. I just want this all to end. You need to leave my grandmother alone too. I can't take any more of this. If you tell me where my daughter is and leave my grandmother alone, I'll do what you want," I said.

Within a couple of days, I'd convinced Mum and Grandma I would fool Imran temporarily to convince him I would want to be with him to help me find Georgina. He'd told me if I went back to him, he'd leave my family alone, including my grandmother, mother, and daughter.

Grandma thought I was taking too much of a risk and I'd end up getting seriously hurt or worse. Even Mum seemed desperate for me to find another way as she feared the danger I'd be in, but I was adamant I would do anything to find my child and as we'd run out of options, I would have to become the bait to save Georgina. I didn't even care what he'd do to me. Inside I was dying anyway without my daughter.

The plan was to run as soon as I had the information, get my daughter, and move to a location where Imran would never find me. How naïve and desperate I was. Mum was horrified at my decision and Grandma tearfully begged me to stay.

It was now eight months since I'd lost my daughter. Imran had constantly professed to know her whereabouts. He'd managed to track me down wherever I went, had the obvious contacts to find out ex-directory phone numbers and seemed to know our every move. I assumed he was behind Georgina's disappearance or had traced them in an attempt to hold an ace card against me. Either way, I had to risk it. I knew full well I would be beaten and raped but felt too numb to care.

When I met Imran for the first time in months, he treated me like a long-lost lover, telling me about all the wonderful things we would experience together now we'd been reunited. "I've managed to find us a new love nest so we can make a fresh start," he said.

I thought he'd completely lost the plot. I felt only repulsion and disgust towards him. I went with him, bag in hand, expecting it to be a lie, but just like he'd said he moved us to a basement flat in a converted bank which still had bars on the windows. When I realised what he was doing I panicked. Below ground level, with no access points other than the barred windows and locked door when we were in the room, I realised what he planned to do with me.

All the room contained was a bed, an oven, fridge, and a few bits of bedroom furniture. It had a dingy bathroom attached and that was it. There were two windows that looked out onto a wall that framed the drive which descended to the back car park behind the building. He'd obviously sourced the place to contain me with minimum contact to the outside world. There was hardly any daylight in the flat and the room was dark, damp and dismal. He told me he had to learn to trust me again so we'd had to move into that flat until I could prove worthy of going back to my own home. Until then, he would not reveal the whereabouts of Georgina so I would have to do my utmost to please him. He constantly told me how he'd terrified Steve and Heather and they'd run to a secret location, but he knew where that was, down to his sources. He seemed so smug and pleased with himself and I couldn't understand how he thought I could possibly want a relationship with him. I concluded he was utterly mad.

I'd promised my family I would let them know I was OK and stay in contact, but Imran took my phone the moment I'd met him and informed me on that first Monday morning he'd be going to work, and he'd lock me in so he'd know I couldn't possibly contact anyone.

I panicked, feeling an overwhelming sensation of claustrophobia. The thought of being left alone in that room every day was too much to bear. When he left, I searched high and low for anything to help me escape but there were no keys and no way of getting out. Having no TV or radio I had nothing to occupy my mind, so in the end, finding some paper and a pen, I decided to write to ease the pain and mind turbulence.

For the first few nights he returned, he brought food in and was mildly pleasant. I started to question his objectives saying, "So how long do you intend to keep me imprisoned then?" but that just seemed to infuriate him. I fought back when he demanded sex, but this seemed to excite his sick and sordid mind and he took great pleasure in beating me.

He often took away my glasses before he went to work so I had trouble focusing, which made my world feel even more closed in. One night he'd ripped them from my face and stamped on them, breaking the arm on one side and told me, "You won't be needing these, bitch. I'll tell you what you can see and can't see." When he'd gone, I managed to find some Sellotape to bind them together and hide them.

After a week locked in the flat, I found a spare key in one of his overnight bags tucked into a side pocket. I realised he must have left it by mistake as he'd not been so careless before. I decided to take the risk and try and get to my grandmother's before he got back that night. It was a long walk from South Barnet to Southgate, but I had no money for a bus. When I arrived, Grandma threw her arms around me. She begged me not to return, but I told her I had to until he revealed to me where Georgina was. I told her I'd be back every day and Grandma took me to the opticians to get some new glasses which this time I hid so he couldn't destroy them. I got a copy of the key made and replaced it before he returned that night without him suspecting. Every day I left the flat as soon as he went to work and returned in plenty of time before he got home. As the days started to become weeks, I started to push more and more for news, but he was not budging until one day, he suspected I'd been out and all hell broke loose.

"You've been out of this flat today. I know, you bitch. How the hell have you managed to get out?" he screamed at me.

I knew somehow, I'd given something away but didn't know what so said as calmly as I could, "What the hell are you on about? How can I have got out of here if you lock me in every day?"

He looked doubtful and I wondered suddenly if I'd been spotted outside, and it had got back to him. "The guy who lives on the ground floor said he saw you coming from the flat today and asked me if I was living with someone as he'd assumed I lived alone until seeing you," he said in a terrible rage.

And then he beat me black and blue, threatening to kill my grandmother and Georgina as I'd now betrayed him beyond measure. He went through the entire flat and all I had until he found the key I'd hidden. When he left the next day, I smashed the fire alarm, and this alerted the landlord to the flat. In the confusion and panic of everyone leaving their flats, he opened the door with the master key.

"Why the hell are you locked in here?" he asked.

"I'm sorry, my boyfriend accidentally locked me in, and I didn't have a key," I said, desperate for him to believe me.

I ran for my life without looking back, all the way back to my grandmother's five miles away. When I arrived, I called the police and the same kind officer who had built a rapport with us, came to see me. I told him where I'd been and what I'd been through. He wanted me to go to Women's Aid and I refused, saying I had to stay with my grandmother to protect her. I didn't want to go to Women's Aid and be a victim. I just wanted to protect my family and find my daughter and I didn't feel being locked away at a refuge would help anyone, least of all those Imran was targeting.

The officer was becoming almost a friend. I promised him I'd stay clear of Imran. Although the police were compiling a dossier of the amount of calls BT had recorded, it still was not enough evidence to convict him of anything. My bruises were evident but not having witnesses and having gone to this basement flat of my own free will did not add up to a prosecution. And Grandma wasn't herself. She looked very withdrawn and had lost a lot of weight over the last few months. I knew this time we had to stop Imran once and for all and was determined not to let him win.

The calls started up once more and even though I begged my grandmother not to play his game by answering the phone, she wouldn't give in to him. BT had already started to get evidence for the police, and this started up again. At one point they recorded over five hundred calls in one day, another time over three hundred and fifty which finally helped to build a case against him. My grandmother had an old-style phone with no answer machine service, so we allowed BT to monitor and record from then on in the hope it would lead to a conviction.

Imran had totally dedicated his life now to intimidating, hounding, and frightening us. On several occasions we had armed police at the flat to protect us, but they could never find him in time. Grandma and I were terrified as he seemed to constantly avoid capture. Instead, he pursued us even more relentlessly as if his appetite for cruelty were increasing. I managed at last to find a solicitor who would deal with my case as she specialised in this type of situation, dealing with victims of harassment. I hated being portrayed as a victim but that's what I'd become.

It had been almost a year without my little girl before we started the court process to get her back as we'd had to go through the Salvation Army and the Missing Person's Bureau to find Steve and Georgina. When at last we started to put a case together, I found every time I left the flat to go to see my solicitor, Imran would appear somewhere along the journey to attack me. Sometimes, he had no qualms at how he treated me in public. On one occasion, he found me in London and as I tried to cross the road, he grabbed me by my hair and tried to drag me to his car. Most people ignored us and walked away, but some men took umbrage to seeing a man hit a woman and one approached us.

"Oi you, you fucking bully. Want someone to deal with your own size, do you?" a man said who seemed incensed to see what Imran was doing to me.

I was desperate for help and screamed to him to help me. As the man approached to tackle Imran, he let my hair go and I ran. I didn't look back to see how the man dealt with Imran, but I was so grateful he'd stood up to him to protect a stranger.

Imran never approached my grandmother when she went shopping, but we knew he was watching her. Often, the kind police officer would pop in out of concern for us to see how we were doing when he was on his way home from duty for a cup of tea with us and keep up with Imran's daily antics, but there was nothing we could do to stop him. The policeman assured us a law would soon be passed that would allow him to act on the evidence so far and we would not have gone through this in vain. He asked us to be strong and hold out.

At last the day came for me to go to court with a barrister. I wanted Mum to act as my character witness, but my barrister said I should have someone unbiased, so I asked Beverly who was really the only person I'd kept in touch with. She jumped at the chance of a trip to Wales. However, I had to pay for her travel, food, and accommodation.

I felt I was going with a stranger as she was changing and becoming quite a judgemental and angry woman, which she said was down to her reliance on prescribed drugs. She was cross with the world for her downfall in life, but I needed her to help me as a character witness and hoped she'd pull through. I listened to her drone on endlessly as we left London on the train, wondering if she had any idea how much my family and I had been through. When we arrived in Wales, she wanted to go out and party. I wanted to sleep so I compromised and brought her a meal which she made the most of. Beverly admitted she hadn't worked for years and told me she was claiming from the NHS for the pain she constantly had from her car accident. She was very proud she'd put a large claim in for compensation.

That night my barrister arrived, and I met with her to go through the formalities. It seemed straightforward.

The next morning I felt sick to my stomach but forced some cornflakes down me at breakfast. Beverly tucked into a huge full English breakfast and as my barrister arrived from her room to have a coffee, Beverly sprang up and announced to us both she suddenly had a migraine and had to go back to the room.

The barrister and I looked at each other worriedly and I dashed after her. The taxi was due to take us to court in fifteen minutes. I found Beverly on the bed with the curtains shut, claiming to have a migraine. I asked her if she was all right, but it was obvious it was all an act. I was panic stricken.

She said she was too ill to go, and I'd have to go without her. I begged her to come but she turned on me and said, "Get out you selfish bitch! It's always about you isn't it! I'm sick, so go and deal with your daughter on your own. At least you have a daughter. I'm never going to have that chance and you damn well know that."

I asked her, "Why are you doing this, Bev?" but she just ignored me. It didn't feel right. "Don't you see how this will mess up my chance to show I'm a good mum?" But she kept silent. When I said I could have had family to be my witness but chose her as she was a friend and would be less biased, she turned to me and said, "Just go, and leave me alone!"

I left, sobbing, feeling alone, and let down. I got down to the lobby and explained to the barrister what had happened. She said we had to go. I prayed Beverly would change her mind and come after us. We arrived at court and in the reception area sat Steve and his new girlfriend. My hands were sweating, and I felt sick to think I had no one to support me.

When finally we were in front of the judge, my barrister explained my character witness was at the hotel and was unwell. Steve's barrister claimed what my barrister had said was untrue, and Steve was concerned about Georgina's safety as I'd travelled up with my boyfriend who wanted to kill my daughter.

I was enraged but knew my barrister couldn't stand up for me as she'd driven up and I'd arrived with Beverly by train. I had to admit I was being harassed by Imran. The judge said he would have to give Steve the benefit of the doubt to protect Georgina.

We were dismissed and I broke down crying with disbelief. In the taxi on the way back to the hotel, my barrister said she felt Beverly must have planned this from the start and asked if she knew Steve or had any way of contacting him. Beverly's migraine had miraculously disappeared when we returned to the hotel. On the way home on the train she acted as if it was no big deal. I sat in a daze for the entire journey and felt so weak and helpless, I just wanted her away from me. I didn't even have the guts to question her motives. When I got home, I felt I had nothing left to live for as I'd lost my one and only chance to get my daughter back.

Chapter 18

It is not in the pursuit of happiness that we find
fulfilment, it is in the happiness of pursuit.
Denis Waitley

During the next few months I tried to come to terms with what had happened. A new children's act had been passed which put emphasis on protection of children's rights and this was hindering our case. As far as the law was concerned, as long as Georgina was looked after by a responsible parent, she was OK.

I had one communication only in the post after that first Christmas from Heather, stating I shouldn't send presents as they would provide everything Georgina needed. I could however send money instead. By then the police were deeming Imran to be a stalker which they were taking seriously, even though he slipped through the net every time through knowing his rights.

The police were convinced Imran's high connections were a fabrication to keep us controlled and fearful of him. They didn't believe he had the ability to harm us through other people. They felt he was most probably mentally ill, but couldn't be sure until we had enough to arrest him. It was his unpredictable and emotionally volatile behaviour that suggested this. They were concerned he was more likely to lose it completely and then cause serious if not fatal harm to us. They didn't believe he knew where my daughter was, and in fact were happier she was out of the equation.

I cut off all contact with Beverly as advised by my solicitor. She was obviously unwell or had a hidden agenda and had taken the opportunity to take out her bitterness and jealousy on me.

Imran's continued daily threats and sudden appearances whenever I left the flat were beginning to take its toll on us, especially Grandma. The only good bit of news we had was the police were sure an act would be passed in the near future which would give more powers of arrest over those who harassed others. We never gave up fighting to get my daughter back but were told by my solicitor it was harder working with a Welsh jurisdiction as they would favour Georgina staying in the area where she'd grown up.

Eventually, two years had passed since my daughter was taken by Steve. Two years of threats and abuse. Two years of watching my grandmother become frailer. I knew she couldn't go on forever like that and it felt like Imran would at some point break us and win.

I became Grandma's carer. She wouldn't let me leave as she felt whilst we stuck together, we'd win as a family. Grandma and I though coped even through the darkest days. At one point, we didn't sleep as Imran had threatened to burn our flat down whilst we were in our beds. Getting out of the flat was even more difficult as he would always find me. He must have left work as he had so much time on his hands to hound us and the police were finally preparing enough evidence to prepare for when the new act came into being.

At long last, Parliament passed the Protection from Harassment Act in 1997. I was encouraged to prosecute Imran for theft and rape, but I couldn't fight any more. Within a few short months of the Act being passed, Imran was arrested in the early hours of a summer morning, one of the first to be arrested under the Act. Though I was only thirty, I felt sixty years of age by then.

I'd sold my flat, which I got hardly anything for as I hadn't had it long, as I couldn't keep up the payments on the mortgage. I'd gone into the flat one day when I felt it was safe enough to do so and found it completely empty. Imran had stripped the place of furniture, ornaments, clothes, and everything personal to me, including all my photos and precious things. I told the police I just wanted him out of our lives for good and couldn't face another fight to prosecute for theft. It was as if he wanted to keep battling me to keep me in his control.

When the police came to see us, they were smiling. Apparently, when Imran was arrested, he lost his temper, and when he was eventually questioned in custody, he'd cried like a baby. He'd begged for forgiveness, put his hands up to all his wrongdoing and confessed his obsession with me. He'd said he was bitter about his ex-girlfriend leaving him for a white man and felt betrayed and felt if he controlled me, I wouldn't have the chance to betray him. When the police had asked him if I'd willingly had a relationship with him or he'd forced me, he hung his head in shame again and burst into tears. He was given a three-year suspended sentence and an order was placed on him so he couldn't come near me.

This was at long last an end to a very dark time in our lives. It took months before I could travel anywhere and stop looking over my shoulder. I was too scared he'd break the order, but each day was a bonus not having to worry when the phone rang.

Grandma was getting increasingly frail and within a few short weeks of him being arrested she passed away after the hospital staff tried to revive her. I cried for days and stayed in the flat alone, begging God for answers. God and my angels had all but gone in my mind and the only consolation at that time was that Mum and I spent time together helping each other through our loss and making arrangements for the funeral.

I felt it was my fault she'd died.

I stayed at my grandmother's flat as it felt it was the only connection I had to her, but my days were filled with nothingness. Mum called often to keep my spirits up, but I was full of self-pity. I was still waiting for social services to do what they needed so I could apply for contact with Georgina. I hadn't seen her, let alone spoken to her, for several years and I couldn't imagine being happy ever again.

Since I'd become an independent adult, my life seemed to mirror how I'd been raised as a child and somehow, I had unwantedly attracted one piece of bad luck after another. Mum suggested I went to college and focus on something productive, so I started an accountancy course to give me structure.

My classmates seemed nice enough, so I started socialising with them to get myself out of my flat. My confidence was building, and I started to speak to the man who lived above our flat. Michael was a very private and quiet Greek Cypriot guy and soon a friendship started to flourish. I invited him to a small birthday party and was impressed he alone stayed when it had finished to help me clear up. He was an electrician and Grandma had often said, "It's a shame you didn't meet Michael before Steve. He's a nice, honest young man."

I'd always found him very attractive and only ever said hello to him in passing. His calm and passive approach to life was very alluring. I just wanted peace and so we started to form a strong bond between us. We never dated, just slowly slipped into a routine of him coming home from work and me joining him to watch television in his flat. Life became a haze of grief and stillness as my life slowed down to nothing.

Chapter 19

The power of intuitive understanding will protect you
from harm until the end of your days.

Lao Tzu

Michael was from a traditional Greek Cypriot family. When I went to his sister's house, I was swept into the kitchen with the women and children while the men stayed in the sitting room, deep in debate about the state of the country and the world at large. It was like putting warm clothes on after coming in from the rain.

One day, shortly before I was due to finally go to court over Georgina, Mike and I pulled up at McDonald's to grab a bite to eat. I froze in terror. There in front of us was Imran. As soon as I saw him, he caught my eye. Michael wanted to go and deal with him. I'd never seen him angry, and I held him back.

We watched as Imran talked to his girlfriend and when he finally left, which seemed to take forever, I started to breathe again. I could see how scared Imran was as he was obviously aware he was breaking the court injunction against him. Equally, I could see he was scared as I was with Michael. We did nothing. It was enough for me to see I was sitting in my own power and showed him no fear.

I told Michael it was thanks to him my life had changed for the better. But I was still struggling. When I was alone, the darkness would return. The only way I felt I could deal with the pain was to give into smoking which I sadly did, this then in turn increased the intensity of my eating disorder more and more so. As Michael smoked cannabis, I fell into the habit, too, and found it numbed the pain. I felt weak giving in but hoped it would be a temporary crutch to ease the suffering.

Eventually I got my day in court, three years after I'd lost my little girl. The judge looked at me solemnly and said I'd been caught up in an unfortunate set of events which my ex-husband had taken full advantage of. Although it was evident then what had happened, he was going by social services' recommendation that the child remain with her new family as it was not clear as to what she'd been told about her mother.

The judge said Georgina was now calling Ruth, "Mummy" and it was clear that disturbing her would have a long-term detrimental effect. I was choked and sick to my stomach as I listened to his words. I felt I was in some horrible nightmare. I'd never thought I wouldn't get her back.

The judge made Steve stand as if he wanted to emphasise his words. He told him because he'd chosen to do what he did by taking Georgina in the most manipulative and cowardly way, he'd have to live with the responsibility of her until she was old enough to leave home. He went on to say one day she'd go looking for her mother and find out the truth. Until then, she was to remain with him, and he would have to live with the consequences of a rebellious teenager when she was older.

The judge seemed very much on my side. He even apologised to me and said I could send letters once a month to Georgina and have a photo and school report once a year, but if Steve thought any of the letters were inappropriate, then he could stop her from seeing them. I begged my barrister to take this further, but she said we had to accept the outcome. She simply said, "Copy every letter you write to her as one day you may have to show them to her. I doubt he ever will."

I went into a rapid decline of a smoke-fuelled binge that lasted months. Hardly leaving the flat, I gave up and felt everything that was good in my life had died. As the weeks turned into months, I managed to play the happy girlfriend when with Michael's family, but when alone I stewed in my grief and despair.

I prayed I'd smoke so much I'd not recover and slip gently away to be with my loving grandparents. Although I didn't consciously realise it, I was praying for a way out and crying for an angel to rescue me.

It was by then four years since I'd seen my little girl and I finally started to realise I might never see her again. However, I never gave up hope and each letter I sent every month was written with the intention to send a secret coded message to my daughter, if by some chance she'd managed to read them or get hold of them in the future. As the months rolled on, I knew in my heart Steve and Heather were probably throwing my letters away. I continued regardless and copied every one of them.

My divorce with Stephen had finalised. He seemed to have got everything he wanted with no qualms of how it affected me.

One day, flicking through the junk mail, which was all I ever got those days, I noticed a flier. It offered the opportunity to have a numerology report done to help me to understand why negative things happen and how I could improve life.

I'd always been fascinated by the Jonathan Cainer horoscopes Grandma read to me. We were both Capricorns and they always seemed spookily accurate. I felt a surge of hope and light shining through me. Scraping together the twenty pounds to pay for the report, I sent off for it as if I were applying for the job of my dreams. Every day I checked the post to see if it had arrived. A week later, the booklet arrived containing much more than I'd anticipated.

The report summarised me as a person. Numerology, a science based on understanding the relationship with numbers based on our names, date of birth etc., allows us to see what we will face in life. The report highlighted my personality, my weaknesses, faults, and strengths with possible outcomes. I was amazed how by giving a few details I had received a comprehensive overview of who I was and what I'd been through. It was scarily accurate.

Finally, there was an in depth forecast for my future and I poured over every detail like a child with a new Christmas present. It certainly highlighted my struggles and plights. However, when I read about my future, it seemed miraculously different to my past. I finally read about my personality traits, and something seemed to register deep inside.

There was a flicker of hope for the future, as the person the report described was successful and a confident, popular, and compassionate person. The report showed all the ideals I longed for but certainly didn't match who I was then in the slightest. I was confused. I felt perhaps it was an enticement to give me hope for the future and I'd have to pay out in some way to find the solutions, but it didn't ask for any more money.

I scanned thoroughly over the report once more from beginning to end and this time, I made a note of all the characteristics about me I disliked. When I looked at the list, which was extensive, I was shocked at who I was and how other people must view me. I felt ashamed as this wasn't me – I felt it was simply who I'd become because of my circumstances. Why had I become that scared, lonely, vulnerable, and threatened individual when all I wanted was a happy life?

I decided to write out the list again but this time from the opposite point of view. When I read, *I have no interest in worldly issues or current affairs,* I wrote on a new piece of paper *I have great interest in worldly issues and current affairs.* I went through the whole list like this and when I felt the positivity from this exercise, I made a point of reading the positive statements on the paper to myself several times a day, especially before I went to sleep at night and first thing in the morning.

Something started to stir in me. It was as if I was waking from a deep sleep and started to become intrigued by spiritual subjects and research them more objectively to find ways to make myself better. The more I researched, the better I started to feel, and I started to have a glimmer of hope for the first time in years. Although I had no idea what was happening, something was lifting and, although darkness still prevailed, a flicker of light was beginning to shine through.

I felt my invisible allies working in parallel with me more closely and the more information came to me and gathered momentum, the lighter I felt. The problem was I was only able to feel this when I switched the computer on and was plugged into a website relating to spirituality or when my nose was immersed in a book on the subject. When the book was closed and the computer was off, I returned yet again to my black hole. I didn't know how to deal with the extremes.

Even writing a letter every month to my daughter didn't take the edge off the immense pain I was feeling and in some ways I wished she'd died. Knowing I'd never see her again was too much to deal with. At least I could work towards closure if she didn't exist, but she did, and I didn't know how to function being a mother with no child.

There were so many times when I was beside myself with grief, I felt the only way I could cope was to consider leaving this life. I felt cornered, trapped and in immense pain but something kept pulling me towards having faith my angels were there for me, just as they were when I was a child. The reality was I could never give up the hope of seeing Georgina one day as I made a commitment to keep going regardless for her sake.

I felt perhaps my angels were back with me somewhere, but because of the fog around me I couldn't see them like I had when I was a child. When I was a young girl, I'd felt their wings folded around me like arms holding me close. I was cross as I wondered why they'd got me through my hellish childhood, but I'd had to go through the loss of my daughter alone. The need for answers was stronger than ever and I pored through as much information as I possibly could to find solutions. Eventually, I realised they had been with me, but it was just that I was too closed down to realise.

Patterns started to emerge. Every time I needed the answer to something, it would appear in a form I could understand clearly. It started to increase the more I paid attention. A pattern of coincidences was forming to show what I was attracting was exactly what I needed to be on my path. This seemed to become commonplace as I started to feel there was a power there once more. It felt though like I'd been given a Ferrari having only just learned to drive, and I just had to trust I'd get to know how to deal with its power.

I felt the amazing energy around me that had protected me as a child. It was returning and guiding me, showing me the way through the jungle of insight to find what was specifically relevant for me. The pendulum of my life started to swing daily. As I woke, pain drove me to get up and find solace in anything spiritual which got me through my day-to-day life.

I only had very sporadic contact with Mum as she was going through the pain of losing Grandma, but I noticed she was drinking more than she used to. I didn't have the strength to help us both through our grief, so I chose avoidance, which was my way of dealing with it. Michael was aware of my suffering, but in some way I didn't put pressure on him as I was engrossed in my need to reunite with my daughter. I was there for him when he came back from work at night and as our first Christmas came upon us, we started to feel a little magic was coming into our lives.

For me it was my spiritual findings (something he didn't really want to know about but accepted) and for him it was allowing him to do what he wanted, including smoke. We even started to speak about living together and once we'd talked about it, the momentum just carried us forward. This gave me even more hope as I believed my newfound friendship with spirituality was guiding me to a better life.

I was finding it more and more difficult to smoke as it conflicted with my spiritual beliefs, and I found I wanted to be healthier and better. I knew at a deeper level cigarettes and cannabis were stopping me from moving on with my life and I started to feel repulsed by them. I also started to notice food was becoming less and less of a problem. Slowly but surely, I could feel myself becoming healthier and happier.

Michael was taken out of his comfort zone when I asked him if we could try to stop smoking together, but I told him we had a real chance to live a happy and fruitful life if we gave it a go. We agreed we'd make a start on New Year's Day.

Although I prayed every day and had done over the past few years as intensively as I had done as a child, my experience was different as an adult. As a child, I'd often seen and felt my guardian angel, but it had just felt normal. At that time as an adult, I was aware of many different angels and other beings that I could only sense but not see.

When I connected with these beings, it was like I was discovering old friends and I found myself addressing them as if they'd known me for lifetimes. I yearned for them to come closer and worked hard every day searching and seeking for enlightenment to clarify their existence and give me hope for the future.

New Year's Day wasn't what I'd hoped it would be. Michael lasted no more than a morning and then walked out on me after our first ever argument. He couldn't give up the drugs as he'd agreed. I was hurt and angry but stayed on my own that day and determinedly stuck to my end of the bargain.

He returned later that evening after an all-day binge with his friends and apologised. He promised me he'd give up before we moved in together but needed more time. I gave him that chance as by then I was on a defined and focused spiritual path of faith towards my end goal which incorporated a healthy and holistic lifestyle.

By then I'd seen enough to convince me what I believed in was real as whenever I questioned situations in my life, I received messages that proved I was getting help from a higher source. Each time I prayed for answers, they came. Each time I asked for guidance, it arrived and every time I cried out in pain and asked for some hope all would be well, I was shown glimmers of light at the end of the long dark tunnel.

I was determined to turn my life around, but I didn't realise Michael would never stop unless he believed in himself and no matter how much love I showed him, it would never be enough.

Chapter 20

Blessed are the hearts that can bend; they shall never be broken.

Albert Camus

By the end of March 1998, we'd sold our flats and bought a bungalow on the outskirts of Hertfordshire. I hoped that our relationship would carry us through to our retirement. I could see myself with Michael for the rest of my life because he was so easy going and grounded. I hadn't really figured that the cannabis had a lot to do with his relaxed manner.

We'd moved to a town only ten minutes down the road from where we had lived before, so we were near enough to family and all we knew. I'd stuck to my end of the bargain by giving up smoking as I could see hope for our future. Michael promised to give up when we moved in, and I gave him the benefit of the doubt. Somehow, he always found an excuse not to.

The bungalow was in desperate need of renovation which excited us both as we took it on as a project. That summer, I spent every moment of daylight transforming the hugely overgrown garden. My grandmother would have been proud of me, I thought, as I'd never had any yearnings to be a gardener. However, my spiritual awakening was encouraging me to explore my creativity in the nature kingdom. I realised that being outside in the garden, I was working creatively which I could feel was beneficial to my emotional well-being.

I started to work for Michael, doing admin for his business, and worked on the house getting it renovated slowly but surely. We started building a life together. I still craved answers to justify why I'd suffered so much for most of my life and went on course after course in holistic subjects, such as reiki and crystal healing. Michael was willing to let me go on any courses I took comfort in, feeling it was serving me to find answers to my loss as he could see how much it helped me.

The more answers I found, however, led me to only ask more questions. The more I learned, the more I needed to learn, but I still couldn't find the solutions I needed to understand why I'd attracted so much bad luck in my life. I was impatient to learn anything that could help me.

That first six months was bliss. For the first time in my life I was creating a home for myself. But the distance between Michael and I was starting to become evident as we were not as close as we had been. We weren't talking as we used to and we certainly weren't going out and having fun as all our efforts were focused on renovating the house.

I was spiritually maturing, and Michael was still caught up in his addiction, which conflicted with my beliefs and made me feel resentful. I'd managed to stop smoking, so why couldn't he? I knew he'd smoked since he was eighteen, which was fifteen years, almost half his life, whereas I'd only smoked a matter of months.

Michael and I talked about having children. Not sure how it would affect my feelings towards Georgina, I was cautious about starting a family. I knew he took other drugs such as cocaine, though I chose to ignore this, feeling once he gave up the cannabis, he'd give it all up. While we tried for a baby, he continued to try to give up, but nothing was happening.

One day I read an article in the *Daily Mail*. It was a full two page spread about a woman who'd worked in the city on the money markets and gone to Australia for a holiday after burnout. It was there she went for a massage by a woman who told her she'd change her whole life and become a healer. The woman, Anya, was shocked but felt she was being told the truth.

She arrived back in the UK and gave up her hugely rewarding job in the city to become a healer and set up a practice in the King's Road. I was intrigued and needed to see her as I felt she was an ordinary everyday person who had a unique gift. I made an appointment and travelled up to her clinic. When I went into the reception, it was very clinical but relaxing. I was very nervous as I questioned what on earth I was doing and I certainly knew Michael wouldn't understand why I was drawn to her, but I just trusted my instincts.

Anya came out to the reception area when my appointment with her was due and introduced herself. I followed her into a very clinical room with a couch and a small desk with a chair. She asked me to get up on her couch and close my eyes and relax and explained she wouldn't touch me, but I might feel energy. She would work at healing my energy field and would explain her findings after the session. I was completely trusting as I felt the *Daily Mail* wouldn't do a two-page spread on her unless she had credibility.

At first, when I shut my eyes, I felt calm. Then I started to feel energy moving up and down my body. Eventually I could feel it moving so dynamically I started to feel a little perturbed. But suddenly a voice came into the room and said *We're just fixing your right fallopian tube.* But it was in the voice of Kenneth Connor from the *Carry On* films which made it seem more surreal. I was unnerved because no one other than my mother knew my right fallopian tube was damaged and I had no idea where the voice had come from.

After the session, Anya asked me to get up off the couch and sit with her. "Well, Amanda, I know you're a vegetarian but not a very healthy vegetarian and this is the leading factor behind why you're not getting pregnant," she said. "You need to boost your protein levels and I suggest you leave here and have a burger."

I laughed as I craved one like she wouldn't believe, but I was still shocked at what I'd heard.

"Oh and by the way," she continued "We've fixed your right fallopian tube."

And that just floored me. How the hell did she know my fallopian tube was shot to bits? More to the point, how on earth had that voice told me it was fixed? I realised something profound had happened. Sure enough, not only did I fall pregnant, but it was within a few days. We were so excited.

I'd trusted Michael up to that point, but my pregnancy was much like my first with constant nausea and feeling completely exhausted. As I became more housebound, it played on my hormones, and I questioned his lack of time at home as he started to be out of the house for longer and longer each day. I became anxious and insecure when he disappeared with his clubbing friends. Every now and then he came home in the early hours telling me he'd been at a men's only, all night drinking club. I was concerned.

I started to feel rejected as I felt I was no longer attractive to him, and his affection towards me started to diminish. I was getting huge, and he slipped up a few times by saying to me, "I can't stand fat women. There's something gross about them that makes my skin crawl." I was desperately unhappy when he'd said that and assumed that was the reason, he no longer found me attractive.

As the baby was developing and getting bigger than average, it was determined I'd have a caesarean before term. Amelia Maria was born on the 19th of May 1999. She weighed nine pounds 9 ounces, but she didn't clear her airways for several hours after the birth and although I begged the staff not to take her from me, their hospital policy was to give her antibiotics just in case she had an infection. They then had to grow the cultures over forty-eight hours to determine whether she had an infection or not, but if she didn't then she would have had the medication needlessly.

I was angry and cried to Michael to support me, but he felt the hospital should intervene. I was adamant they'd mess up her immune system and refused adamantly, but she was taken from me regardless as it was hospital policy. I knew giving Millie (her nickname) medication in that way at only a few hours old would affect her. Sure enough, after forty-eight hours and all the antibiotics they'd pumped into her fragile little body, they found out she wasn't ill after all and concluded as she'd been delivered by caesarean section and not naturally, she'd not been able to clear her airways properly. Eventually, she'd cleared her airways herself. I was so upset with them and knew my instincts had been right and I was determined to listen to my inner voice in future. I was getting more in touch with myself and so I used holistic and natural products to help with my little girl's start in life, administering healing I'd learned through my training courses.

Millie was certainly never a replacement for Georgina, but she was a gift from God to help me fulfil my yearning desire to be a mother. She was different to Georgina in so many ways, but the love was just as strong, and I knew I could love them both. I still missed Georgina who was by then nine. Steve still ignored my letters. They moved address which they notified me of because the court insisted on that, but that was my only communication. Eventually the yearly reports and photographs stopped, and communication dried up completely. I contacted social services to ask them to help me and they insisted I get in touch with a solicitor as it was no longer their problem.

As Michael was working, my solicitor said she would have to charge to deal with our case, but the fees were astronomical, and I knew Michael could ill afford them. I was no longer entitled to legal aid and the solicitor suggested Georgina would probably be in touch with me within a few years to find me anyhow.

She tried to console me with the fact it was only a photograph and school report and said I should hang on to hope and wait to see how she dealt with this as an adult. So I gave in but continued to ask for photos in my letters in the hope she got to the post before Steve and Heather.

The first six months of Millie's life were blissful, and her proud father was with her constantly, though Michael showed no affection towards me. We'd become more like brother and sister. I hoped perhaps when I'd lost my baby weight, he would feel something towards me again. I held on as I did love him very much and more so since having Millie.

Her christening was a huge, over the top affair. We took over an entire restaurant with over sixty of our close family members and friends and I was so proud to be part of a real family. There was live music and amazing food and speech after speech. Even Michael came out of his shell for once, gushing at being the proud father. I felt all my dreams had come true.

Michael and I were growing further apart though. We only came together when we worked on the house or went out with our daughter. Otherwise, we led separate lives. I wanted to reignite the passion in our relationship, but he was happy to just go to work and sit in front of the TV and smoke when he got home at night. I felt life was passing us by. I needed something to make me feel good about myself and started to exercise at the local leisure centre with a few new friends I'd met through my post-natal courses. They were very different to me as they had no understanding of my spiritual awareness, so I kept that side of me private. I still attended more courses which deepened my spiritual wakefulness.

Slowly as I started to form new friendships through my baby friends, I told them my beliefs which surprisingly they wanted to know more about. They were intrigued with me and asked individually if they could come to me for healing sessions which I enjoyed. At first, I just dipped my toe in the water as I felt a strong calling in that area, but I didn't have the confidence to take it further. They seemed to enjoy it and started to give me feedback about the changes occurring in them. Word got around and I attracted a lot of mums wanting advice and guidance. It was all new to me and I really didn't have much confidence in what I was doing, but the insight that came to me created a definite positive effect in the ladies I advised.

Soon I was getting donations which helped me to buy crystals and remedies to assist my newfound interest. Michael wanted nothing to do with it. "I thought this healing stuff was to help you. Why've you got all these women coming to the house?" he asked one evening.

"Michael, I know I can help these women and it's what I want to do now," I said, hoping he'd understand. He just dismissed it as something he didn't want to talk about, and I was disappointed he didn't value me in that way either.

I found people were genuinely getting relief and help from my sessions as they would come back to me to clarify the changes in them and so ask me to help them further. At the beginning, many of the women came to see me with fertility problems or reproductive issues, such as hormone imbalances or menopause problems. Not only did they overcome those initial problems, but other issues in their lives also seemed to naturally right themselves. For the first time in my life I'd found something I was passionate about, enjoyed wholeheartedly and felt rewarding.

Millie was only nine months old when I fell pregnant with Anthony. Michael and I had wanted two children and had planned it from the start, but as Millie was still a baby, I'd planned to go back to college to enhance my studies with a view to working when she was old enough. I was even taking the pill. I felt however it was meant to be as in some way the universe knew what was best for us. Michael was happy and for a while we started to feel connected again.

One day when all was going well, I suggested we should get married as I was now divorced from Stephen. I asked for practical reasons to give my children security. I longed for the beautiful white wedding I'd always dreamed of as a girl, but Mike wanted something understated, so I agreed to get married as he wanted, in secret. I felt he was ashamed of me. We planned to head off to Gretna Green with Millie in tow and Anthony in my tummy. I was having debilitating bouts of nausea once again, so we planned to break up the journey and stay in places enroute. Mum had always said she wanted to one day be able to wear her hat and be the perfect mother of the bride and I felt I was robbing her of her chance yet again but honoured Mike by not telling my family. At the last minute however, Mike told his sister, which I felt was completely unfair as I wasn't allowed to tell my own family.

Mike's sister without hesitation announced she was inviting herself and her family along. It seemed to defeat the object of getting married in secret. And I didn't like the fact his family was allowed to attend but not mine, but although I protested, Mike said we had no option but to let his sister attend. As we travelled up to Scotland, I questioned whether our love was strong enough. We were very different individuals going down separate paths, but I convinced myself it would bind us together as a family and was best for our children.

I felt sick constantly due to my pregnancy. The weather was very warm which brightened the occasion, but as Anna, his sister arrived I felt suddenly very low. Within a few short hours, it was decided Anna's husband Stavros would give me away. I felt awkward as he hardly ever said a word to me being a very shy man, but I couldn't say no, or I would offend everyone. Everything that could go wrong that day went wrong.

Our room had several problems. There was no cot for Millie. It wasn't the beautiful room with amazing views that we'd been told and was very cramped for three of us. The flowers never turned up for the wedding although we'd paid for them in advance. When the lady arrived to do my hair and makeup on the day, she made me up to look like something out of a horror movie and I just wanted to cry.

When Michael's family arrived in Scotland, he withdrew from me completely. I felt a huge distance between us. I felt if I were closer to home I would have left, but I couldn't, and we went through the service as best we could. That night we couldn't even get a seat in the local pub where we'd agreed to celebrate. The tension between Michael and me was obvious. The main room of the pub was filled with celebrating couples and their families and was alive with happy cheers and laughter. Being a Greek family and out of their comfort zone, both Michael and Stavros felt out of sorts. We managed to get some food for Millie and her three cousins and focused on them for as long as we could. By then, Michael and I weren't even talking.

Finally, I announced I was putting Millie to bed. Escaping to our room, I felt so sad and alone and wondered what on earth life was going to be like if we couldn't bear to be with each other on our wedding night. That night I slept with Millie while Michael slept in her cot bed.

Throughout the pregnancy he was hardly around, and I spent most of my time at home with Millie or with friends. Because of how Michael felt about my weight, I was determined to change my appearance and win back his heart once I'd had Anthony. Throughout my pregnancy we were doing a loft conversion. The whole house was disrupted and so all our furniture was in our bedroom where we had lived for the duration of my pregnancy. We still had no roof on the house, and it was cold, damp, and smelly. Michael was hardly there, and I felt abandoned.

Two weeks before I was due to have Anthony, I left Mike. I was in so much despair at not feeling any love or affection from him and had hoped Anthony's arrival would bring us together. I went to stay with Mum and Bob for a few days, taking Millie with me, feeling I needed to get away. I wrote Michael a long letter to ask him to make a choice as he just didn't seem to want to be with me. I poured my heart and soul out saying how much I adored him, hoping he would open up. We spoke on the phone, and I felt he wanted to make a go of things for the sake of the children, and yet again he promised to give up drugs. I went home and two days before I gave birth, the roof was finally fixed.

Anthony Colin was born on the 10th of the 11th month 2000. The date seemed appropriate somehow. Millie was born with all the 9's in her birthday representing 'endings' and Anthony was born with all the 1's and 0's marking 'beginnings and potential for manifesting dreams'. I knew then that my children marked a huge significant turnaround in my life, but I wasn't prepared for how it would happen.

Mike was so proud I'd given him a son that everything seemed to start working for us again, but it wasn't long before I realised it was only the children that made him happy, not me. One night he was off his face more than most nights and he made a comment about some people on TV. "God you white English people are so different to us."

I was shocked and questioned him about it and he said he'd been bullied at school for being from a minority culture and so hung out with others like him. Since then he'd found it difficult to mix with us English people. "So why are you with me then?" I asked.

"I guess I knew it would upset my father so I could get my own back."

I felt the floor go from under me and the man I desperately wanted to show love to had thrown his hardest punch. I'd been a fool to trust him. We argued and because he'd at last purged himself of his guilty secret, he said, "Amanda I found you in the gutter just to get back at my father. You're nasty with your disgusting past and being married before. What the hell did you expect from me?"

Colin and Valerie's wedding (my parents), 1966

Amanda (aged two) and mum Valerie, 1969

Amanda (aged three) and Valerie, Muswell Hill, London, 1970

Amanda (aged nine) and Valerie, Berkhamsted,
November 1976

Amanda (aged sixteen) and Valerie Berkhamsted, 1983

Left to right: Arnold Clift, Eric Hart, Amanda Hart, Andrew
Clift, Pat Hart, Val Hart, Chalfont St Peter, 1987

Bob and Val Clift's wedding, Amersham, Bucks, 1990

Left to right: Amy Thomson, Pat Hart, Steve D'ormain,
Georgina D'ormain, Linda Thomson, Arnold Clift, Val Clift,
Amanda D'ormain, James Thomson, and Eric Hart, December
1st 1990

Georgina D'ormain and Val Clift, 1991

Pat Hart, Eric Hart, and Amanda D'ormain – Mum's 50th birthday, 1992

Georgina D'ormain, Amanda D'ormain, Val Clift, Pat Hart

Georgina and Amanda, 1993. One of the last photographs taken
before she disappeared.

Chapter 21

Being defeated is often a temporary condition. Giving
up is what makes it permanent.

Marilyn vos Savant

After Michael's revelations, things never got back on track, although to the outside world we were the ideal family. We continued with life with a cloud of truth hanging over us. I struggled to deal with it while Michael found it easier now, he'd purged himself and I knew how he really felt.

We spoilt the children as if to compensate them and the more we spoilt them, the harder the façade became for me to deal with. Every Wednesday, the mothers from my little group of friends had a weekly meeting at one of our homes so the babies could get together, and we could chat as mums. At first, it was great. It was a network, a lifeline, and a chance to have fun with mums, learning together. However, it wasn't too long before the backstabbing started. I was in the kitchen making tea one day and one of the mums came in and said to me quite out of the blue, "God, I never realised how Louise had such a big conk. What the hell does her husband see in her? He's supposed to be earning a fortune in the city. I wouldn't have thought she was his type".

I avoided responding. After that occasion, she then nicknamed one of the larger ladies, "Big Al" and so it went on. Each time the group separated into smaller numbers, it was a chance for each one of them to have a dig at the others when they weren't around. I felt drawn into the banter and joined in to feel included. I hated it, as I knew they were talking about me behind my back, too, but I desperately wanted to be accepted.

When it was my turn one Wednesday, I had a sudden feeling of claustrophobia when they were all there sitting on the floor in my living room. They were like predatory vultures waiting to pick one victim off at a time. They were well on their way towards ostracising one of the girls who happened to be absent, and I left them to it as they all laid into the absent victim. I went into the garden and stared at them through my patio windows. I felt they were picking us off one by one, and suddenly felt protective of the poor girl who had no way to defend herself. I couldn't handle it anymore, and walked back into my living room and announced I wanted them to leave. I'd had enough. Enough of people lying and their cheating and spitefulness and pretence. I wanted to stop all the hypocrisy. They looked at me as if I'd gone mad, and I knew I'd given them plenty of ammunition to slaughter me as their next victim. But something had snapped, and I couldn't tolerate pretence anymore. And so I'd outgrown more friends.

Mum was seeing less and less of us. Her drinking had got worse and whenever I spoke to her on the phone she slurred and repeated herself. I couldn't blame her. I knew how much she was hurting from losing her parents and thought perhaps losing Georgina had triggered guilt from memories of giving me away as a child.

Truthfully, I had no idea what was going on for my mother internally as she was a closed book. Too manufactured from a life of investing in her aspirations to achieve great success and recognition, it was evident that her increasing alcohol dependency was the result of deep inner emotional instability which she was not willing to face. Sadly, she didn't recognise the destruction this was creating to an already fragile relationship with me.

The straw that broke the camel's back finally came when we heard our closest friends had lost their little girl in a tragic swimming pool accident. Panis, one of Michael's best friends, was married to Sue who was English. They'd moved to Cyprus for a better life and Sophie had drowned in the family swimming pool soon after they'd arrived. The funeral was back in the UK and was almost too much to bear watching all our friends weep. For the first time, I saw Michael shed tears. The funeral was packed with mourners and at the graveside elderly relatives were collapsing and wailing.

It was a scandal in Cyprus as their news had covered it as a tragic accident. A finger was pointed at the authorities as her death was blamed on the appropriate equipment not being in the right place at the right time. An investigation ensued looking at why so many children died from drowning in swimming pool accidents in Cyprus up to that time. I understood the heartache Panis and Sue were going through and their need for answers.

However, the situation became an international drama which incensed the Greek Cypriot community in the UK. Their culture was all about community. I wholeheartedly respected that, but it also highlighted my separation from my own family. I left the funeral early, leaving Michael with his friends and family.

I couldn't face going home, so I went to see Terry, my personal trainer, someone who wasn't connected to anyone and who I'd made friends with recently. He was eight years younger than me, and I felt safe having a secret friendship, as he was unlikely to be a threat to anyone or know anyone connected to my family. I turned up at the leisure centre and said, "I'm sorry Terry, I just didn't have anyone I could go to and hope you forgive me for interrupting you at work."

"It's OK, Amanda. What's happened?" he asked in concern.

"I don't know what to do. I've worked so hard at becoming strong and you know that more than anyone. I can't cope with my marriage anymore, especially after today. I love my children, but I just can't continue with this loveless marriage."

He seemed to understand and certainly didn't judge me for asking for him to listen to me, let alone what I had to say. I'd increasingly confided in him about my marriage whilst having training sessions at the leisure centre. It was the only time I could be truthful about what I was going through.

Terry seemed to genuinely care and want to listen, so I felt safe. As he was a man, I felt he would see things objectively and help me understand what to do about Michael. The fact he listened meant the world to me. I didn't stay long. After half an hour or so of purging myself, I had to return home as Michael would wonder where I was.

I felt I had to then turn to family for help but couldn't quite muster the courage to tell my mother I wasn't coping as I didn't want to disappoint her, so instead, I contacted a cousin who I hadn't seen in a while and went to see him. He lived in Northampton, a bit of a trip from where we lived, but I went when Mike was at work. James wasn't there when I arrived as he'd had to work late, but his partner was. Although I didn't know her very well, she welcomed me into their house and offered me tea and sympathy while we waited for James.

"Sharon, I know this may sound harsh but I'm contemplating leaving my husband," I said. "The only problem is I have nowhere to go where I can be safe. Michael's threatened to take the children from me and take them to Cyprus if I leave him and

I'm petrified he'll do it. I've lost Georgina and can't risk losing Millie and Anthony – it would kill me. I just need somewhere to take them temporarily whilst I sort out where I can move us so we can be safe."

"Well actually, I know you think James and I are OK, but we've been having difficulties for some time," Sharon responded. "He's never home and always with his band and I've recently discovered he's addicted to cannabis. I don't know what to do as his behaviour has become so erratic lately and I've got to think of the long-term effects that this will have on Charlie."

I was shocked and disappointed as he was such a bright, intelligent boy when we were kids. I sympathised with her as they had a baby and had only been together a short while.

"Don't worry," she continued. "Come and stay with us. It would probably do James some good to see what he's doing to himself, and it may wake him up. I've tried so hard to convince him to stop, so if he sees you're serious about leaving Mike because of his habit, it might trigger him to quit."

While I worked out a plan to leave Michael, I asked if I could move some of my belongings into their house. James called Sharon to say he wouldn't be returning that night, so I left the bags with her and drove home. The next day was a Sunday, and we were due to go out as a family with twelve other couples and their children. The washing machine had broken down and I told Mike I'd go to the launderette to get the washing done whilst he bathed the children. As the leisure centre was over the road, I popped over to pay for the children's swimming lessons. I was standing in the queue at reception when I got a call on my mobile from James. He went into a rant of angry accusations I couldn't make head nor tail of. Embarrassed, I left the queue and went outside to speak to him to ask what on earth he was on about.

"You know damn well what's wrong!" he shouted at me. "Sharon's going to leave me, thanks to you!"

When he'd returned home, they'd got into an argument. Sharon had said she'd finally had enough and threatened to leave and James assumed I'd instigated this. I tried to explain Sharon had been kind enough to offer us a place to stay and presumed he'd be happy, too.

"Amanda, you don't get it. Why the hell would I want to help you if Sharon's leaving me? I don't want anything to do with your separation. In fact, if you don't collect your belongings from my house within an hour, I'm going to phone Mike and tell him you're having an affair. I'll make sure I destroy your relationship like you've destroyed mine," he shouted.

I begged and pleaded with him to let me get my bags the next day when Mike was at work. James and I had always had a close friendship and to hear him threaten me in this way was upsetting. I assumed Sharon had told him about my confiding in Terry and knew James was using it as a weapon to get back at me. "Please, James, you have no idea how difficult this is for me. If Michael thinks I'm leaving him he's threatened to take the children to Cyprus, and I may never see them again."

"Good. I don't care. I could lose everything because of you. She never considered leaving me before until you got it into her head. I don't want anything to do with you. Come and get your stuff or I'll call him."

It would take at least three hours to drive to Northampton and get back. I didn't know what on earth I could use as an excuse for being out so long. Without wasting any more time, I jumped in my car and started heading towards James's house. I put my foot down and drove there as quickly as I could. Then my phone started ringing and I looked down at where it was resting on the seat beside me and realised it was Mike. I wasn't surprised as it was almost eleven and we were due to leave at midday to meet our friends. I couldn't answer as I was driving and had no idea what to say to him anyway, so I kept going, tears streaming down my face.

James called and I stopped to answer. He told me all my bags were in his car and Sharon had thrown him out, so he'd meet me in a layby. When I arrived, he opened his boot and unloaded my bags. He threw them on the road as he took them out one by one and hurled abuse and accusations at me.

"After your little chat yesterday, according to Sharon it seems she's suddenly found her power and found the strength to make a new start with Charlie thanks to you. Why the hell did you have to interfere? Now I've got no home and no family. I've a good mind to tell Mike anyway, so you'll lose your kids and see how it feels."

I silently packed my bags into the car. I tried to calm him down, but he just wanted to focus all his anger on me. I felt at that moment I'd never see him again and I felt sad. Trying to keep as calm as possible, when I'd finished loading my car, I turned to him and said, "Goodbye James! Do yourself a favour though and get off the drugs!"

This sparked an increase in his rage, but I got into my car and drove off, watching him in my mirror as he continued to hurl insults at me. I had no idea what to do with the bags and knew Michael had called several times, but I wasn't ready to speak to him. I stopped when I was some distance from James and sat with my head in my hands. I suddenly thought of Beverly, who I knew had moved to the outskirts of Hertfordshire and decided to call on her as she had no real connection with anyone I knew. I called Beverly and she told me to come straight over.

It was weird to see her settled in a small new build house on a quiet estate. I'd always known her for the dark dismal places she'd lived in alone and the house seemed too normal for her, and it was surprisingly tidy too. She hadn't lived there long. I met her new husband John for the first time as I arrived. He was her first real boyfriend. She'd never really had any interest in men as far as I knew. In the past she'd always ran men down constantly, hated sex and lived only for her food and other addictions.

She announced she'd met some guy on the internet the last time we spoke, and within six months she'd married him. She'd only met him a few times but had told me he was in his forties, lived in Glasgow with his mother and told me as he was a virgin, she'd mould him into what she wanted him to be. "He's perfect cos I can make him into anything I want and do whatever I want."

When I met him, I immediately sensed he must have deep insecurities as he was treating Beverly like his mother. Beverly took me into the living room to sit down to talk and he hovered around her like she was a queen bee, asking her if she wanted food or anything brought to her.

When John sat next to her, he gazed at her like a little boy and kept putting a stuffed toy into her face as though he wanted her attention. She ignored him and talked to me as if he weren't there. I felt uncomfortable with this man being treated like a circus animal. Beverly sent John away so we could talk. She winked at me to show she had complete control over him like a dog.

I poured out my story and Beverly suggested I stayed the night, but it was obvious to me John was unnerved by me being there. Eventually I called Mike to tell him I'd had enough of all the arguing and had decided to stay with Beverly to think about what to do. He was understandably cross and made me feel ten times worse by saying, "What sort of awful mother leaves her children like that. You can't just up and leave when you want, Amanda, you've got responsibilities. Anyway, I've got to work tomorrow, so you'll have to be here."

"Please don't shout, Michael, they'll hear you," I said. "Can you just please tell them Mummy's away for a few nights with a friend and will be back in a day or so?"

Beverly was sympathising one minute and then the next I got the impression she was mocking me. Unnerved by her behaviour, I phoned Terry and asked if he would come and see me. I knew he'd understand and wondered if I'd made a terrible mistake in asking Beverly for help, as I'd felt compelled to confide in a woman for support. But I was starting to feel she was relishing in my predicament.

When Terry arrived, we went for a walk outside for some time as I told him the day's unfolding events. He said I should perhaps think about making a break from Michael then as it had all come to a head, but I was too frightened of what to expect when I got home.

The next day, I could hear Beverly whispering with John and sniggering. I'd been feeling unwell for several months at that point and had been told by my GP I should deal with it but had put it on the back burner. I'd spoken to a specialist who suggested I should go to hospital immediately, so as I felt unwell, I decided to go to the hospital the next day.

After I'd dealt with this, I planned to go home and tell Mike I was leaving him. I felt the stay in hospital would give me time to think. Beverly smirked at me when I told her what I was going to do but reassured me she thought I was doing the right thing and she'd be there for me when I came out of hospital. I had no choice but to trust her. I phoned Mike and told him I needed time out to think things through and would return on the Tuesday. I spoke to my children and tearfully told them Mummy missed them and I'd soon be home, and then I left for London with nothing but a wash bag and a change of clothes.

I was operated on that evening. It was a small op to repair damage caused when I was with Imran. I emerged bruised and weary on the Tuesday morning, relieved it was done, but not so happy I was to go home and face the music. When I walked into the car park, I stopped dead in my tracks as I looked around for the car, but it was nowhere to be seen. I walked round the whole car park and then rushed back into reception to report my car stolen. I called the police, and they told me to get a friend to collect me and they'd start searching for it. I phoned Beverly from my mobile to tell her what had happened. "Bev, someone's stolen my car. I can't believe it. Can you please come and get me?"

To my utter horror, she venomously spat at me from the other end of the phone. "I contacted Mike and told him exactly what you're planning to do. I've told him everything – that you're planning to leave him, take the kids and you're with that guy, Terry."

I couldn't believe what I was hearing. "Why? Why would you do that? What have I done to deserve that? I don't understand … and anyway, what has Terry got to do with it? He's just my friend."

"Well, I told him if he wanted the car, he could collect it from the car park where you've been staying, so I gave him the address. I told Mike you're leaving him for another man, and he must do everything he can to protect those children and his assets."

I felt that stab of betrayal like a knife to the heart once more and my life felt like it was imploding in slow motion.

"Your bags are all out in my front garden for you to collect. Oh, and just to let you know, I don't give a damn about you and never have. You've always had it easy, Amanda. Life's always dishing you out favours and I'm fed up hearing about your spiritual bullshit. You've got everything I can't have and it's not enough for you, so see how you survive now."

Then the line went dead.

I phoned her back, but it went onto voicemail, so I left her a message. I begged her not to abandon me as I had nowhere to go, but she never responded. In a matter of days I'd lost everything. I knew calling Michael would be like throwing myself into the snake pit. I realised if he'd taken the car and left me at the hospital, he would have had to involve his family to look after the children. That meant that was the end for sure, especially if they thought I'd left him for another man.

Everything I'd attempted to do to protect my children had backfired as foolishly I had let more people betray me. It didn't seem to matter where they resided in my life – friends, family, neighbours, I seemed to be a magnet to be destroyed.

I walked away from the hospital, cold, hungry, and terrified. I headed for the station but when I tried to get money out of the cash point, my card had been cancelled. I only had one hope left. Terry!

Chapter 22

*Remind thyself, in the darkest moments, that every
failure is only a step toward success, every detection of
what is false directs you toward what is true, every
trial exhausts some tempting form of error, and every
adversity will only hide, for a time, your path to peace
and fulfilment.*

Og Mandino

Luckily, Terry was home. In tears, I explained what had happened and he said he'd come and pick me up. Within an hour, I was in his car and heading up to Beverly's. We arrived at the house to find all my stuff on the front lawn. I rang the doorbell and went round to knock at the back door, but she didn't answer. When we loaded the car, I found a note she'd tucked inside one of the bags. The letter wasn't what I expected. She admitted that it was time to part company, and she had to get on with her life. She said she had to be strong and told me I'd be OK as I was one of life's survivors.

Terry drove to his sister's house so I could have a place to stay. Although I'd never met her, Terry assured me it was OK, but when I got there, I panicked and felt I couldn't be left alone in a house full of strangers. She was a nice enough girl, and very generous to offer to let me stay, but I couldn't sleep at a total stranger's house, especially feeling so low. I told Terry I had to go to a hotel so I could be alone and near to the children. I chose a hotel at South Mimms, the only service station on the M25. It was only five minutes away from where I lived.

When at last I was alone in the dark and dismal room, I sat on the bed looking out of the window at the view of the vast car park. I sat for what seemed like hours and contemplated my dilemma. I phoned Mike but got no answer. After several attempts, I got hold of him and he simply said, "I don't want anything to do with you as you're probably with another man right now."

"Don't be so ridiculous! If you're referring to Terry, yes, we're friends but he's got a young girlfriend."

Michael didn't say anything.

"For God's sake, Michael. I'm down the road in a hotel waiting to come home but only you can decide what you believe. Come and see for yourself if you're so sceptical."

But he didn't believe me, or rather he chose not to believe me. "So why would Beverly phone me to tell me you're having an affair with another man if you're not?" he asked in a matter-of-fact manner.

"Why do you believe her when you distrusted her from the start? Why believe her now?"

"You disappeared on Sunday to go and see Terry, didn't you?"

I then felt I had to tell him the truth about what happened that day and my intention with my trip to Northampton to ask for my cousin's help.

"I'm sorry, Amanda. It just seems too far-fetched for me. How do I know you've been to see James and Sharon? It seems all too convenient."

I sighed and asked him to check out the truth with Terry.

"No, I'm sorry, Amanda. I just don't believe you and think you've been staying with him. I don't want to see you anymore."

I couldn't believe what he was saying.

"I'm moving my mother and father into our home and they're going to look after the children until I plan what to do, but you won't see the children again."

He put the phone down even though I started to beg and protest. Ashamed and defeated, I sat until it went dark feeling numb and beaten. The voice of my stepmother rang loud in my head, mocking me, reminding me I was a useless waste and a worthless human being. As I faced myself there in the dark with those spiralling thoughts of destruction, I resigned myself to concluding that I had only ever and would only ever attract people who took advantage of me. Worse still, I let them.

Too ashamed to speak to anyone else, I decided to disappear. I had nothing else to live for and nowhere to go. I knew how very protective Michael's family were and I knew his threats were real. I felt I had failed at every relationship that I'd had since childhood and the worst was failing my three children. I was an unfit mother and should have realised that my own mother and stepmother's behaviour throughout my childhood should have been a warning to me back then – I wasn't worthy to mother children.

Crushed and demoralised, I knew I had to leave the country as that would mean no one could find me. I found a Yellow Pages in the room and going with the physical action with no focus on anything other than disappearing, booked a flight to Sydney, Australia. Mum had given me her credit card details for emergencies, and I thought as I was never going to see her again, she wouldn't lose her rag at me if I paid for the hotel and flight on it. I felt she was already too ashamed of me anyway so using her card wouldn't make much difference.

I booked the flight and left what I didn't need at the hotel. I got a train to Heathrow and all I had left in the world was my passport and clothes in a bag. I withdrew some cash out of a savings book belonging to the children. That further added to my shame, but I knew I would need all the money I could lay my hands on. I phoned Terry one last time from the airport and asked him if he would collect my things from the hotel. I told him I'd paid for the room in advance for another day and asked if he'd keep the bags for me. I then asked if he would write a note to Michael in a week's time to let him know he could collect them. He said he would help, asked where I was going, and I told him I was leaving to start a new life.

"You take care of yourself, Amanda, and if you ever need me, just call."

I aimed to give myself one week before I did the deed. For the first time ever I felt no fear or pain, just a numbness, a peace, a knowing I was going home. I cried tears of regret at the airport as I said goodbye to Terry on the phone. Not because I was going to miss him, as he'd been a good friend, but because I would never see anyone again, especially my children, family, and friends. He wished me luck and I struggled to put the phone down. I pictured myself at my funeral and was saddened to think probably no one would attend knowing what I'd done to my children. The shame drove me deeper into despair and made me more determined to end things once and for all. I certainly couldn't deal with any more heartache or pain in my short and sorry life. I'd just run out of fight.

The flight over was long and the films they showed were all ironically based on marriage break ups and issues with children.

When I finally arrived in Sydney, I walked calmly out to a taxi and asked the driver to take me to where all the Brits hung out. He took me to a guest house in Coogee, which wasn't too pricey. I felt safe and warm there instantly and said I'd stay for one week. But once in my cheap and dated, basically furnished basement room, I plunged once more into crippling isolation, loneliness, and fear, reminding me of my tortured life as a child and with Imran, locked behind closed doors. I felt the light in me was gone, my angels had given up on me and it was finally the beginning of the end. In the sporadic lucid moments when the fog cleared, I searched for glimmers of hope, but none came.

I sat in a chair in the corner of the room and stared out the window at a brick wall – a stark reminder of my days locked in the basement with Imran. My life had been for nothing. Even my children were suffering from my mistakes. I had no strength to move, so I just sat until it got dark.

Noises outside suggested people were going out for the evening. Too tired to make any attempt to find food, I climbed into bed with my clothes on and fell into an exhausted slumber. Waking in the night, I heard party revellers returning. I could just make out the lower legs of passers-by who walked past my window. I felt vulnerable and scared. Everyone out there had someone to love and share life with except for me. Finding it hard to get back to sleep, I switched on the TV. All I could find that gave me any peace was a channel with a woman doing yoga. Everything else was noisy and hard to focus on. I was mesmerised by the yoga exercises and music playing in the background. I decided to do some yoga to keep my mind from wandering.

The next day, I ventured out early and found I was close to the beach. Coogee was already alive, although it was only seven in the morning. There were groups of swimmers training as lifeguards, and people jogging along the beach or doing yoga further up on the cliff that surrounded the coastline.

It was August and felt like a warm autumn day in England. I suddenly felt homesick wondering what the children were doing. I walked onto the cliff along a footpath and along the coastline. It took me away from the throng of bodies and I found silence and solitude on a huge rock that jutted out over the vast ocean below. From where I stood looking down it was at least a hundred feet above the sea. I sat with my legs dangling over the edge. Looking out at the Pacific Ocean, dark, deep, and unfamiliar, I wondered if others before me had contemplated their end there at that point. Looking down at the rocks below I realised this was where it would be, where I would finally find my peace and end it all.

I felt as if I'd been guided there and felt nurtured by the vastness of the beautiful natural scenery around me. I felt I'd already arrived in heaven. What a way to go! Numbness soon washed over me as if the ocean was calling and I lost myself in my thoughts. I had no idea how long I sat there, but several hours had passed when the chill from the rock took over. I had no idea where the rock began and where I ended. I felt melded into the scenery around me and couldn't move. Eventually, I got up to head back to the guesthouse.

It was around lunchtime and holidaymakers and families with children were scattered sparsely across the beach. I wondered what it would have been like if I'd been able to visit here with my own family. I stopped at a small grocery store on the way. As money was tight, I brought enough food to last me a few days and headed once more down to the sea. This time, I walked further up the cliff and past my rock to tire myself out. I spent the day walking with thoughts floating in and out of my mind.

Each day from then on, I woke and found myself getting into a familiar routine. As soon as I woke up, I switched on the TV to watch the yoga lady and do some stretches. Then I walked down to the beach to the stall that sold a green wheatgrass concoction for breakfast. It was strangely tasty and vile at the same time, but it coursed through my body, cleansing my every fibre. After that, I walked along the cliff until I was exhausted and then sat down to meditate. I always faced the ocean, talking to my guardian angel with whom I hadn't properly conversed with since I was a child. It was a comfortable and peaceful existence and I felt strangely safe and cared for. I was being carried and started to sense my angel was getting closer and closer to me day by day.

On the third day, I found a second-hand bookstore. Curiously, I searched the small selection of books in the mind, body, spirit genre and a book jumped out at me – *The Alchemist* by Paulo Coelho. Every day I took my book, found my spot to sit at and, after meditating, poured over it for hours. I felt by the sixth day that my angel was with me, stronger than ever before. I only had one night left at the guesthouse, but I hadn't finished the book and needed to complete it to find closure. It was as if I was working on a synchronistic parallel with the story. Something told me to go to the local grocery store to see if there were any notices for cheap rooms as my guesthouse accommodation was about to expire. I found one and phoned a woman who asked me to come up and see her straight away.

The upstairs flat door of the modern apartment block was opened by a woman who looked not only drunk, but also unkempt as if she'd just adjusted her clothes after sex. She was a very warm and gentle woman, so I tried to see past her appearance and wondered why she intrigued me. She welcomed me in and showed me a room which was tiny, but OK, and ran through details of the tenancy. Not really listening, I suddenly spotted a young man pulling his clothes on, reflected in the hallway mirror. As he walked past, she said, "Oh and that's my other lodger". He simply nodded politely and said hello.

I felt how strongly the impression of their coupling had come across to me as soon as I walked into her apartment. I felt drawn to her energy and felt strongly that she could be trusted, so I didn't judge her. That wasn't the first time I'd got impressions as powerfully as that. As a kid, I had them all the time and they often saved me from getting more seriously hurt by Sue by guiding me to safe places to be protected before trouble started. I realised my receptors were on fully again just like when I was a child.

I paid a deposit to Julia and left after informing her I'd move in the next day. I was almost out of money, but I'd only need enough to survive for a few more days. I then left and decided to make my penultimate walk across the clifftop to wear myself out physically to enable me one last sleep and to prepare for my last day.

That walk was my longest. I walked around three miles along the clifftops until I reached Bondi Beach, which was heaving with life. It was a stark contrast to my solitude on my journey there. Sunbathers and lifeguards were spread its entire length and the ocean was alive with guys and girls alike with surfboards, dotting the ocean with sporadic splashes of their colourful wetsuits. I took it all in and left after a matter of moments. There were too many people, so I headed back to Coogee. On my way back, I took respite at a graveyard and sat for a while and prayed.

Although there'd been no tears for a few days, I found there they came easily. I spoke to my father and told him how sorry I was for letting him down. I told him I was sorry for not being strong enough. I desperately wanted him to hear me to rescue and protect me, but I heard nothing.

I felt rage burn within me, as I found for the first time the words to tell him how he'd let me down. I told him how painful it was to have gone through nearly fifteen years of torture at the hands of his wife when he knew and chose to ignore it. I told him they'd all let me down, the entire family, as they were all too scared of him, but he was the one who'd let me suffer. I fell to the ground with my head in my hands, exhausted and feeling I had nothing left to give. I begged him to tell me why he did nothing.

I cried out to him at the top of my lungs, "Why? What was it all for?"

As I slumped there exhausted, I listened to the wind running over the cliff and through the gravestones and out across the ocean. All I could hear was the lap of the waves below crashing against the cliff. I sat for hours until finally, with nothing left in me. I decided to get it over and done with and got up and made my way back towards my rock. I had no desire then to see anyone ever again. My mind was made up. I would just keep walking go over the edge, finish it there and then. As I rounded the last corner and spotted my final destination, I gathered speed so my momentum would carry me over.

As I got closer, I noticed something different about the rock and squinted to see what it was. Someone had written something in huge bold letters in white chalk across the very spot where I planned to jump. It certainly hadn't been there before. I squinted in the sunlight to see what it said. As I finally got nearer, I read the words *It's not what I gave you. It's what I taught you that counts!*

I stopped instantly in my tracks and stood staring at it for what seemed like an eternity. I'd only ever heard one person say that statement in my entire life and that was my father. I knew he'd not only heard me back at the graveyard, but he'd rescued me. My angels were there with me at that moment, and I felt the rush of tingling through my body. They'd answered my prayers. My father was with me, and he would always be with me to help make everything that was wrong, right.

"Thank you! Thank you! Thank you!" I shouted up to the sky, arms outstretched and choked by tears of profound joy I fell down on my knees on my rock and wept, elated. I'd been rescued. Then I heard a voice say, "You're not done yet, girl, you've got work to do." And I knew in my heart my father was speaking to me.

Chapter 23

At every given moment we are absolutely perfect for
what is required for our journey.

Steve Maraboli

I'd been given life and brought back from the brink of despair. For the first time in months, I felt a feeling of safety and strength. With a huge smile on my face, I got up and started to walk back down the cliff. I headed straight back into town and to the flat I was about to move into.

When I knocked at the door, I was met by the same woman, although she looked completely different to when I'd met her earlier that day. She was dressed immaculately with her hair freshly washed. I beamed at her and asked if I could speak to her in private. She gently put her arm around my shoulder and welcomed me into her home. She led me into her living room, sat me at her table and went into the kitchen. When she returned with two cups of tea, she sat down and said, "Now, Amanda, tell me what's happened?" as if she knew already.

I poured my story out to her from when my marriage started to break down to the moment, I saw the message on the rock. Not once did she judge or question me. She listened and held my hand and passed me tissues when I needed them. She was like an earth angel. Her long blonde hair framed her heart-shaped face and she looked so peaceful. Eventually, when I'd finished talking, she walked over to her bookshelf and came back to me with a small Bible.

"This is for you," she said and placed it in my hand. "You found God, and this will stay with you always!" It was as if she knew I'd been sent to her. She then said, "I want you to listen to this and never forget these words!"

She walked over to her stereo and switched it on. The CD in her system started to play. As soon as the melody started and the words drifted into the room, tears welled in my eyes. I felt the incredible power of the song as it played and the emotion that came from the female country and western singer was overwhelming. I knew there and then, listening to that song, my heart would never lose its way again. Help had always been there for me it had just been me who had closed the door and couldn't hear.

I asked her who the singer was and what album it was on. She smiled and wrote it down for me. "Her name is Lee Ann Womack and the song's title is *I Hope You Dance*," she said smiling at me. She could see how much it had moved me. "Go and get a copy and never let it go," she said, and as I went to ask her for my deposit back, she stopped me before I finished by placing her finger on her lips, gesturing me to say no more. She got up, left the room and when she came back offered me an envelope with my name on it, containing my money. She knew I'd come back, and she was ready for me when I returned.

"Thank you, for understanding. Thank you for being so kind," I said. "Please can I have your address so I can write to you?"

She smiled, gave me her details, and hugged me. As we went back into the hallway she said, "I wish you well, Amanda, you obviously have work to do."

I gasped as that was what I heard my father say to me earlier that day on my rock. She smiled through loving eyes and nodded. "Your life will change now, Amanda, and you should never look back."

I hugged her one more time and felt an amazing feeling of hope and anticipation for the future. I ran back to the guesthouse and picked up the phone and called Michael. I told him I was sorry for what I'd done, and I was coming home.

"Where the hell are you, Amanda? Everyone's been telling me all sorts of stories and I just don't know what to believe."

"I'm in Australia, Michael," I said, keeping it simple.

After a few seconds he finally said, "Well I knew you'd left and gone abroad with another man as Beverly's been to see us and told us everything."

"Really, Michael? I'm not about to defend anything, but I am going to ask you to go back to when you used to tell me how you disliked her as she was a stirrer," I said.

He was hesitant but then said, "I'm glad you're OK. Everyone's assumed you've run off with another man – the family, neighbours, friends, everyone. When people asked, I assumed that's what you'd done. Amanda, I'm glad you've called but you can't possibly come home as my family and everyone around here at the moment are really angry and protective of the children."

I was glad he was putting the children first. I knew I would find a way of proving myself and show everyone I loved my children and would do anything to change who I was to become a better mother.

"That's fine, Michael, I understand. I'm going to show you I can change. Please tell the children I love and miss them desperately and will be with them one day soon. I won't do anything to upset anyone, Michael, least of all the children so I'll do what it takes."

Again, there was a silent pause. He then followed that with, "Your mother's been to the house, and she's convinced by Beverly's story, too."

I'd messed up so many times before and although my mother had abandoned me as a child and lacked maternal instincts, she had never judged me. This time though I thought I'd blown it. "Mike, I'm going to phone Mum and ask if I can stay with her, and then would it be all right if we met up so we can talk?"

I had no idea if my mother would even talk to me after what I'd done. He seemed unsure, so I told him if he thought I was with Terry, he should go to the leisure centre, and they'd confirm he was still there.

The phone went silent for a while, and I realised he understood what this was all about.

"I never trusted that girl! Why would she do something like that?" he said.

"It doesn't matter. It's no one's business but ours."

I then phoned Mum. Her anguished voice and tears of relief were enough to know I had nothing to fear. Mum said she'd get me back to the UK and collect me at the airport and take me back home to hers. I realised that day that although she had let me down through my childhood, she was there for me probably through some kind of guilt, but I was taking it, as she was all I had left in the world.

I'd studied spiritual laws, and I observed my mum had lucid moments of living by them when she 'woke up' which I believed had come from my beloved grandmother, her mother. I was aware that my deep spiritual ancestry was on my mother's side of the family as opposed to the dark side from my father's. Even though it was not the greater influence throughout my childhood as the darker side had been too overwhelming, it had shone through and shown me the light when it counted.

At a stop off in Singapore I went to find the Lee Ann Womack CD and as I had several hours to kill, I found myself walking into a tattoo parlour. I knew there and then what I wanted and had a set of wings in an oriental design with the word "angel" in Chinese letters imprinted within it, etched onto the base of my spine. The wings represented my newfound freedom to fly, and the word "angel" represented my guardians. I knew it would always symbolise the turnaround in my life.

I set off on the last leg of my flight back to Heathrow to find Mum waiting for me with open arms. She held me tight and guided me out to the waiting car. Bob said little on my return, but I felt he was being diplomatic. When we got home, they left me to have some time alone. I sensed they were deeply concerned about my future.

I phoned Mike and asked if I could see the children but as his mother and father had flown over from Cyprus and taken over, he said he couldn't go against them. Mum suggested I go to a solicitor to get access to the children. I agreed. Although Mike and I were speaking it was inevitable I would need help to deal with the children and our marriage. Within a short time I'd initiated divorce proceedings. I was advised to go through a mediator who encouraged Michael and I to try to get back together. I didn't see my children or speak to them for several weeks. I was determined more than ever before to do what was right this time and threw myself into more study and new courses until I could be with them again. I wanted to do anything I could to improve myself to be the best I could for my children.

One day I came home from an evening tarot course. As I walked in the door, Bob said, "What are you doing going to these whacko courses on stuff that's got nothing to do with helping you get your children back and your life in order?"

"Bob, I'm not learning to become a tarot reader, I'm just learning another aspect of what I do." I said, hoping he'd understand.

"Oh for God's sake, Amanda, it's a load of rubbish and a waste of time and quite frankly you should be focusing on getting your family back," he snapped at me.

I felt hurt and unsupported. "I am focusing on getting my children back, Bob, but I'm doing it the way I'm being guided, for the right reasons. It will take time but I'm not losing faith. You have to believe me. I've learned so many lessons from losing Georgina and don't want to cause Mike to do anything rash."

Bob felt I was opting out and making excuses. I guessed he'd had enough of me living with them and was worried I wasn't trying hard enough. This created a rift between Bob and me.

I did become closer to Mum, however, as she saw how I was changing. Before then, I'd been a very angry young woman who pointed the finger constantly towards others to justify why my life was wrong. The woman who returned from Australia had a new philosophical approach to life that enhanced her spiritual understanding. I was able to show Mum how the change would take me forward, and she had faith in me. It was a turning point in our relationship.

Within three months, Mike and I were meeting for regular dates as recommended by the mediation process. He listened attentively to me talk about who I was becoming, and for the first time in our relationship he took the time to honour who I was at a deeper level. After three months we decided to give it another go.

I moved back into the family home just before Christmas in 2002. Millie was three and Anthony was just two. I told them I'd gone away for a while as I wasn't very well, and Grandma had got me well again. Facing the mums at school was the hardest as they talked about me behind my back, but I ignored them.

Shortly after I'd moved in, sifting through the unopened mail, I found an invitation for Anthony to attend a party. I accepted the invitation and took him along. No one spoke to me at that party and the birthday boy's mum, Anastasia, approached me to say I was very brave to come along considering I'd run off and left my children to be with another man.

I smiled at her and just said, "It's not always what it seems Anastasia!"

"Isn't that the truth?" she asked awkwardly.

"D'you think I'd be here with my son if it was?" I said and I held my head high as I watched my son join in the party that day.

I somehow knew then that whatever life threw at me, and however frightened I felt, I would always get guidance from the Guys Upstairs from thereon as long as I trusted and paid attention.

Chapter 24

One of the greatest diseases is to be nobody to anybody.
Mother Teresa

For the first few weeks after moving back home, Michael hardly acknowledged me. I wrote him a letter explaining how isolated, lonely, and unloved I felt in our relationship and that I still loved him. I focused on the children whom I'd missed terribly. Although I'd been away for three months, nothing had really changed other than Millie becoming a little mother figure to her brother.

I tried desperately to be a good wife and mother, but Michael was more determined than ever to be cold and distant. I eventually resigned myself to the fact he just wanted me there to look after the children and didn't really want to rekindle our relationship. Every night when I slept next to my husband, it felt like he despised me. It was heart breaking to feel such rejection. Months rolled on and the neighbours and mothers who'd been supposed friends before still ignored me. I felt like a criminal but whenever I was in public, I proudly held my head high. I hadn't contacted Terry since my return, although I did miss his friendship. One day I bumped into him in the supermarket. I'd lost a lot of weight and had cut all my long hair off. Terry was shocked to see me.

"Good to see you!" I said, scurrying off before he could speak to me, frightened the children might mention our interaction to their father.

I was no longer allowed to exercise as Michael wouldn't allow me to go to the leisure centre and see Terry or my girlfriends at the gym. There were no more group mother meetings for coffee and no more invites to the neighbours' houses for homemade cakes with the children.

One year exactly after I'd left for Australia, Michael and I went to Covent Garden for a night out. The kids were staying the night at Mum's, so we planned to make the most of it. I'd often gone out with him and his friends to clubs before we had the children, but I couldn't deal with his drug taking. In the early days, he'd once taken me to a club and told me to try a tiny bit of ecstasy which I'd never tried before. I was sick within fifteen minutes so knew my body just wouldn't allow me to take it. To my relief, he never suggested it again.

I'd got used to Michael on a downer on Sundays as his body failed to deal with his drug binges the night before. He'd offered me coke before as well and again, feeling the odd one out around his friends, I'd tried it and felt relieved I wasn't ill but hated the downer the following day. It was almost like having the flu and a hangover all in one and I loathed the feeling. It was a way of life for Michael though and I suppose he'd got used to it.

On that August evening in Covent Garden, he told me he had some coke for us. I felt hugely disappointed and hurt he'd resorted to yet another crutch to bolster up his self-esteem as I longed to try and rekindle the passion in our relationship. But I knew I couldn't reach him unless I was on his level. So I went into the toilets as he'd instructed, feeling cheap and dirty. When I reappeared, we only danced for an hour as it didn't give us the effect he'd hoped for, and we left shortly after. In the old days he would spend all night dancing and feeling good, but the drugs no longer affected him in the same way as they had. Over the years, he'd displayed paranoia and mood swings and I knew he was a sometimes-frightened man who needed routine to control his life. The kids were all we had left. I felt sad he couldn't find any way of connecting with me other than when he was on drugs. As he'd been taking drugs daily for over twenty years, I realised it was highly unlikely he'd ever stop. He only ever felt comfortable around people who shared his habit and as I was now moving along a more spiritual path, anything dark or not good for my health, wellbeing, and that of those I loved, went against the grain.

The next morning I woke with a terrible headache which worsened as the day went on. Mum brought the kids back, but I felt so bad I had to go back to bed. Michael wasn't used to having to see to the kid's tea and bedtimes and took umbrage.

On Monday I'd become very sick. Michael had left me to it and each time I woke to be ill, I had to crawl to the bathroom as the pain in my body was increasing. I thought I had flu and a migraine and kept the curtains closed as I couldn't bear the light. Millie was concerned as Mummy was crawling on her hands and knees to the bathroom but Mike insisted they kept away from me in case I had a bug they could catch. By Monday evening Mike was livid and told me regardless of how ill I was I'd have to cope with the children as he wasn't going to miss another day off work. Throughout the night, though, I lay awake as the pain felt so intense, I thought my head would explode. When I'd crawled back to bed from the bathroom yet again in the early hours of Tuesday morning, Millie came in to see me and tried to open the curtains.

It was unbearable, but for the first time in days I had light in the room. Millie asked me what the rash was on my arms and as I eventually managed to swing my legs over the bed into a sitting position, I pulled down my pyjama bottoms to find my legs covered in a rash too. By now my joints felt like they were being smashed by hammers, especially my right ankle, and Millie looked at me anxiously. I could hear Michael shouting to get Millie back into the kitchen to eat her breakfast so he could go to work, so I ushered her in to him and told her to ask Daddy to take me to hospital. I didn't startle her as I didn't want to frighten her, but we both knew I was very sick. Michael told her I'd be OK and to get on with her breakfast. Then he promptly went out the back door and shut it firmly behind him. I could hear everything in that tiny chalet and I felt trapped, vulnerable, and scared. I prayed to my angels for help. I couldn't even look after myself, let alone a two and a four-year-old.

Millie came toddling in with the house phone though as soon as Mike was in the garden and the door had shut behind him. "Mummy, quick. Call an ambulance!" she said with an obvious fear in her voice.

The ambulance was there within minutes. The doorbell rang and Millie answered it. Michael was still out in the garden. Two crew members came in to see me in the bedroom and Michael arrived in the hall as I was being carried out of the house. He thought it was just a drama to stop him from working, and he wasn't happy to have to stay home and look after the children for another day. I could hear the crew telling him I was very sick and needed to get to hospital urgently and he'd have to stay and look after the children, but he protested.

I was sick constantly in the ambulance and the pain I felt throughout my body was frightening. I was wheeled rapidly into A & E and felt myself losing all sense of reality. There were lots of voices and the sound of trolley wheels and rushing of people getting equipment. I could hear urgency all around me. Needles were thrust into my veins on each wrist. I heard voices telling me I was very sick and telling me what they were doing but felt as if I was in a glass case. My head felt as if it was held in a vice and the pain was so bad, I wanted to scream.

"Amanda, you're very sick and we're administering antibiotics to help you. You've got meningococcal septicaemia and we need to do everything we can to help you."

I wanted so much to sleep but the pain gripped me so badly it was like I was dying. I was vomiting constantly, and the anti-sickness drugs didn't have any effect. I begged them to take the pain away. I rolled around on the bed in agony until I was eventually sedated. I was aware everyone around me was there, but the volume seemed to have been turned down. I didn't understand much of what I heard as it was all technical jargon until a doctor said, "You'd better call her husband and get him here now. If she'd come in an hour later …"

As I calmed into the madness, I realised I might not make it. It was at that point I realised I couldn't possibly leave my children to be raised by their father. I knew I had to fight for their sake. I prayed to my angels to help me so I could stay with my children, and I heard above all the noise around me, a voice say, "Place your hands on your stomach. You can heal yourself, Amanda! You know you can do this."

I then mustered every ounce of energy I had left in me to send healing to my rapidly deteriorating body.

Chapter 25

We must be willing to let go of the life we planned so as
to have the life that is waiting for us.

Joseph Campbell

I drifted in and out of consciousness. Then I heard someone say, "Amanda, we're just putting another needle in you, sweetheart."

I couldn't move. At one point I heard someone say, "Is her husband here yet?" and all I could think was, *I want my mum.*

I remember Michael was there at one point as I heard voices telling him how sick I was. The doctors and nurses worked through the night monitoring me constantly, but I was beyond sleep. The only respite I had was when my angels came to visit me and then I had stillness and peace. During that first night I felt death would be the only escape, but I knew I had to stay for my children's sake. I couldn't leave my children to be raised by a man who put drugs first.

The next day they transferred me to an isolation unit. I heard people entering my room every so often discussing me, but I was still unable to move. The pain was still acute and the sickness constant. I was beyond exhaustion. Michael arrived at one point, but I don't remember which day it was as each merged into the other. When he spoke to me, he seemed angry, saying he and the children had to be immunised because of what I'd contracted, and I was inconveniencing him.

Mum arrived at some point after I'd been admitted. I could hear her talking to another woman in the room, discussing my health. The other woman said she was a neurologist who was looking after me and she was concerned about my outcome. She told Mum she had no idea about my long-term health, even if I got through. I heard Michael arrive too and Mum tell him that she and Bob were due to go on holiday the next day. She asked if she should cancel.

Michael said, "No, Val, don't worry. I'll take care of her. I'm sure she'll be right as rain in no time. Anyway, what can you do here? Just go and enjoy your holiday and don't worry. You can see her when you get back."

I desperately wanted Mum there but couldn't speak. I was frightened Michael was getting Mum out of the equation so she wouldn't discover what had really happened to me. Mum blew a kiss at me and left. I was desperately trying to communicate with her. I tried to ask her to stay but she couldn't understand me. I was screaming inside for her to help me.

Each day was much the same and I was visited at one point by a health representative who'd put an alert out, which was a natural procedure when there was an outbreak of anything as serious as I'd contracted, in case of an epidemic. Each time Michael came to visit me he was increasingly anxious. I realised Michael was concerned the cocaine he'd given me had caused my illness. I'd become seriously unwell only hours after snorting what he'd given me. I knew then that was why he was hovering at the hospital to speak to the staff, always ready to speak to the doctors on my behalf, but not to look after me. I realised he was concerned about his own skin and didn't care if I died or not.

He kept threatening to take the kids to Cyprus for his parents to look after as he had to go to work and was losing money. I understood but begged him to hold on and said I'd be home soon to look after them. The only way I could stop him from taking my children out of the country was to get well as soon as I could and get back home to look after them myself.

I looked at why I'd attracted the illness metaphysically and realised it was to do with core issues. It also related to overwhelming feelings of absolute hopelessness. That made complete sense to me. Having the entire foundations in a relationship shaken, feelings of futility with my husband and no support for my purpose in life had sent me crashing down. I sought inner guidance. I knew I had to face up to what was going on with my relationship as I'd compromised my health and well-being, and that of the children, by going back to Michael. I'd had a wakeup call. I vowed from that moment that I'd heal myself of that debilitating disease and make it my service to others to help those who needed to heal themselves.

As the days passed, I was still developing complications, but I was improving. When the grip of the head pain finally left, I realised I was left with continuous tinnitus. I kept motivated. At least the sickness had stopped. The aftereffects of the drugs were kicking in as my body was trying to get rid of them. Dignity had left me at the hospital entrance on arrival and I was in awe of how the nurses worked so compassionately and with such dedication to help me. I built up a great rapport with the nurses as they were shocked at my rapid recovery. Even the doctors and specialists were shocked. They brought students along to see me daily.

I had no hesitation in telling the staff I was self-healing, but they looked at me blankly. I was used to that reaction. I'd learned early on to only discuss such matters with those open enough to understand, but I was so in awe of my progress, I wanted to share my understanding of what was happening.

The nurses often came in to see me and as we started chatting, they asked me about their own lives. Information flowed into my mind which I passed on. Word spread, and more of them came to ask me questions. I just seemed to know the answers.

At night I prayed to my angels: *Please tell me what's happening to me? I know it's obvious to everyone else I'm healing faster than they've experienced but I need to know what's ahead for me now.*

They responded: *Amanda, you've gone through a great change, a near death experience and from now on your life will never go back to how it was before.*

Finally I was OK to go home to continue my recovery. The blood specialist said my blood had gone back to almost normal, but any deterioration in my health and I was to go straight back to hospital. Likewise, the bone specialist said I was lucky as I could have lost my right foot, but I would have to deal with the joint pains for some time to come. The kidney specialist said my kidneys were clear, but he had no idea how my organs would hold out long term.

Finally, the neurologist told me although my head pain had subsided, I was likely to suffer for many months, maybe years, as each menstrual cycle would create secondary illnesses such as chronic hormone imbalances. As far as the meningitis was concerned, she told me there were no guarantees it wouldn't return, or I wouldn't develop other complications. I put my positive, determined hat on and aided by crutches, finally walked out of the hospital to go home to be with my children.

I knew then that everything would change, as I left that hospital a survivor and no longer a victim.

Chapter 26

Only the wounded healer is able to heal. As long as we
think spiritual leaders need to be perfect, we live in
poverty. I have a perfect teacher inside; there is no
perfect teacher outside.

Angel Williams

For the first few weeks, Mum helped with shopping and the children. She pulled out all the stops to help me with the school runs and chores. She drove me to appointments and ran the kids to school. Soon enough, I was walking slowly to the school gate with the children, albeit on crutches. The women who'd once gossiped and ignored me stared at me, although some did offer to help me with the children. I took no chances and politely declined most offers of help. The staff at the school were extremely supportive as they'd been involved with the whole situation from the onset. Michael spent his time working and avoiding me as if I'd caught the plague.

I slept most of the time, as I was constantly exhausted. The joint pain was easing and eventually I left the crutches at home. I was still very weak but was determined to overcome everything that had invaded my body, including the antibiotics. I ate as healthily as I could, mindful more than ever of my eating habits, and started to walk further and further each day to get fit, but each month I had extreme colds or flu or fell prey to other viruses. I was just about capable of looking after my children, but exhaustion led me to sleep as much as I could.

Eventually, I told Mike I was going back to the gym to exercise as my doctor had recommended although Mike said no at first. I felt different. I felt stronger in my mind and more determined than before as I realised I had so much to live for. The recollection of the angel who had visited me reminded me I was here for a reason. I was determined to find out what it was.

My recovery was slow but steady. After eighteen months, I was no longer in pain. I had become fitter and stronger than before the illness and life had changed drastically. In the early months, I felt inspired to start a business from home and started to collect second hand designer clothes for re-sale. I decorated the new upstairs loft room with vibrant, sparkling purple curtains and fabrics to match. The room was soon full of rails of gorgeous, affordable second-hand clothes. I also started to sell a range of jewellery and accessories by local designers. The more I worked at it the more successful it became.

I hadn't felt as motivated or enthusiastic about life in years. My little boutique created a bridge for many of the mums at school to cross and soon my doors were open to them all. They often came alone, frightened to let others know they were there as they'd once been against me, and it seemed now I had something they wanted. Many of them I thought were intrigued at how I'd gone through so much and come so far; the clothes were just an excuse to observe me. I never divulged who came to my little shop. More often than not, women would sit and chat and ask how I managed to become so fit and healthy in such a short space of time. I indulged them by giving them a little of my spiritual understanding to take away for themselves to work on to help change their lives for the better.

They always ended up confiding in me about some issue or problem they were dealing with, and I offered enough to help them help themselves and no more. They'd often come back, excited, and enthusiastic, to tell me how my advice had worked and how they'd not only moved on but had also started to take control of their lives. It felt so rewarding, but it was also becoming the mainstay of what I was trying to achieve. After a while, people began to turn up at my doorstep asking me to help with all sorts of issues from health to relationships. I never turned anyone away.

Eventually people were asking for much more and realising my little Aladdin's cave had a far greater treasure – the ability to help people help themselves – I closed down the shop and transformed it into a treatment room. I'd completed so many courses and studied so much about holistic healing, but I'd never thought I'd use it to help others. Somehow, I now felt ready. The timing was perfect.

My little shop had windows overlooking my beautiful garden, which I'd transformed. It was all I needed to create a healing space. Word spread, and more and more ladies booked to see me to experience my healing room. Crystals that were powerful and colourful, adding contrast to the room fascinated me. I loved working with aromatherapy oils infusing the space with smells to set the ambience. I was also interested in Bach flower remedies, which I used intuitively with clients needing assistance on their journey.

My desk was set up at the far end of my room. Above were shelves in descending sizes going up towards the roof, which made the room look like we were in a pyramid. I was fascinated with the healing properties of pyramids. When the room was finally finished with a soft cream carpet, cream sofa for clients, massage table and various additional spiritual ornaments such as angels and Buddhas I'd added to assist the energy of the room, it felt as if it had been initiated by a greater force. I marvelled at how I'd reached that place in time after so many years of pain and suffering.

Most of my first clients had fertility issues and health problems relating to the reproductive cycle including menopause, something I felt a connection with. Then it developed into so many different areas where healing was needed. As my confidence grew, more and more women came to see me. They came to me with relationship issues, financial struggles, health related issues, often chronic or long term, and self-worth issues. They came to see me when they'd tried everything, and I was the last port of call.

I had a way of working that was unique to me and didn't come from anything I'd learned. It just evolved and came to be a *knowing*!

The healing process was always the same. Ladies came to see me for three sessions over a period of a month and each went through a transformation process. During the first session (a consultation followed by healing), the issue was brought up. Often, they'd come to see me about something they thought was the problem and deeper issues would come to light, sometimes several. Ladies were generally surprised by this, but I grew to expect it.

There were often tears through relief at having started a healing process and, more often than not, a confidence and hope built within my clients that change would occur regardless of what they had to face. I felt incredibly humbled by the process and was honoured to share these women's experiences. I was simply there to assist by asking the right questions and they found the answers.

My philosophy was built on what I'd learned, what I'd experienced through my own personal crisis and how I'd seen it over and over again with every lady who came to see me. I believe each and every one of us knows deep down the answer to every issue we have to deal with. I learnt in the early days that I was simply there to facilitate the process.

On their second visit, clients talked about what had happened to them since their last session. They had physical, mental, emotional, or spiritual reactions and sometimes all of them. Whatever the issue, they had the reaction necessary to start to create the shift. Something would happen to get them to address the issue at hand. This offered them hope as they could clearly relate to what was happening. I described the process like the opening of a bottle of champagne. As soon as the cork is released, the bubbles or negative programs are forced to the surface.

It wasn't a pleasant experience for everyone, but it was always for their highest good and produced a catalyst from which they could work. After the second session it gave them more motivation and was like pouring the champagne into a glass and observing the other bubbles gently floating to the surface. During the second phase, the release of smaller bubbles was comparable to the rest of the stuff that would come to the surface, which was usually related to the client's secondary conditions. By the third session, marked improvement occurred. Answers to problems and ways forward were evident and each client knew how to move forward on their path or had a new focus. And so it continued.

In those early days, I knew every lady who came to see me was building my awareness of my own capabilities and the capabilities I knew was in each and every one of us. The process was the same for everyone and I marvelled at how humbled I'd become to the intricacy and depth of our ability to find solutions in all ways.

Hope was a beacon of light carrying me forward.

Chapter 27

*The secret of change is to focus all of your
energy, not on fighting the old but on building
the new.*

Socrates

Sunday 16 May 2004. Breakfast that morning was pretty much the same as always. As we'd lived in a state of disrepair since moving in six years ago, we made do with bowls on our laps in the living room. Michael had his breakfast in the kitchen alone with the door shut. His breakfast was a concoction of cannabis and nicotine. I wondered what the magic had been between us when we'd met.

That Sunday morning marked the beginning of the end, not only to our seven-year relationship and failed marriage, but also to the person who I'd been. Most mornings I was tolerant of his disappearance into the void as I called it. But that morning, something inside me came alive. Everyone around me seemed to be addicted to something. Until then, I'd covered up for people, ignored it and accepted how it affected me, but I'd had enough. As soon as the kitchen door opened, I protested, "Michael I just don't think I can face your sister and her family in my house today. Can we go see them another time?"

"Why? What's wrong with my family?" he said defensively.

"Nothing, Michael, I like your family, you know that, and I respect them very much, but sometimes your sister is so angry, and I just get unnerved by it, especially in my own home."

I couldn't face his sister with her anger issues and addictive state (OCD and anorexia) that day. The children ran to their bedrooms to comfort each other as they anticipated another argument, and Michael followed them, knowing I wouldn't want to continue this with them in such close proximity. A cheap shot, but one he often took advantage of. Almost in a dream state, and as if I was being carried by a higher force, I walked into the kitchen, picked up the phone and Michael's drug stash and went straight out to the garage. Once I'd hidden his stash at the back of the garage, I called the police. Something seemed to take over. I was shaking as I experienced a dichotomy of emotions. I was petrified of his reaction on the one hand, but on the other hand, I felt completely rational and calm as I knew everything was going to be all right. When I heard the doorbell, I emerged from my shelter and retreated back into the house to face the music, still in my dressing gown and slippers.

The police told Michael I had asked him to leave the property as I was no longer going to tolerate his drug habit. He was surprisingly submissive and accepted. He packed a small bag and was gone within moments, stopping to quietly say goodbye to the children who were equally calm. I asked the police to remove his drugs from the property, but to my amazement they said there was no point as he would only go to his dealer and get more. They seemed only interested in the supplier rather than the devastation this drug had caused within my family. It was a Sunday, so Michael left without anyone seeing him go and the children went off to play in their bedrooms as if nothing had happened. I couldn't quite put my finger on it, but the house felt so different. I didn't feel fear, anger, sadness, or anguish; in fact I didn't even seem to be thinking of anything at all. I just felt so peaceful for the first time, and I just let myself be with that feeling, rather than analyse it!

That evening, the children went to bed. I'd explained to them gently Daddy had gone to stay with his family, and everything was going to start getting better. They seemed accepting and went off to sleep in a relatively short time. Later that evening, I sat down in the living room in the seat my husband usually occupied. I felt slightly elated. It seemed odd under the circumstances, but I felt pleasure in being able to choose my own seat and use the remote control to decide on my own TV viewing, and then a wave of awareness swept over me as I realised I was feeling the freedom I'd yearned for.

I took out some crystals from my dressing gown pocket and placed them on the table next to me. I'd been carrying them around with me in my pocket all day, more for reassurance than anything. As I placed the last crystal on the table, I counted them. There were thirteen in various colours and sizes. For some reason, with no real understanding why, I started to form a circle with them and took a candle and placed it in the middle. It just seemed a natural thing to do. As I lit it, I became aware of the television becoming quieter. I looked over to the television and it looked as if all the furniture in front of me was moving further away. I fought my conscious mind to understand what was going on. Everything was happening in slow motion. I could feel my heart speed up and my mind racing. I felt then like I was in a cinema watching a movie. It was being played out on a huge film strip, the type you find from an old-fashioned camera, with perforations at the top and bottom. On the left and right side of my peripheral vision were two spools which the film strip seemed to be wound around, and as the spools turned, the film was playing out from left to right. It was bizarre; like watching a movie in the style of reading a book.

And then, the voices began!

Amanda, it is now time for you to remember what you chose to come to earth to achieve and why.

I couldn't comprehend where the voice was coming from and was unsure of my sanity as it certainly wasn't coming from the television. I was relaxed and calm, although my heart rate had risen slightly as I noticed the sudden change in the room. I realised then it could only have come from another realm. As I'd never heard a voice like that before, I still questioned it. *Perhaps it's inevitable, as my husband's just left and I'm suffering some form of delusion.*

Maybe I was emotionally wrecked and desperately searching for solutions as to how to look after my children! But no, that couldn't be it as I hadn't even been focusing on that. So maybe I'd lost my mind and was suffering with some sort of seizure. But again no because I felt so calm and rational!

The pictures kept moving and my mind still tried to justify what was going on and kept questioning what was playing out before me. It didn't make sense. I wasn't drinking, nor taking any medication. I wasn't even tired or suffering from lack of sleep. I certainly wasn't stressed or overburdened with my new situation. So what was causing it? The more I searched and tried to blot out what was happening, the louder the sound became and more formed the pictures became until I finally decided I could do nothing but pay attention. I gave in and decided I would make sense of it afterwards!

The pictures came thick and fast then, and I listened attentively to the commentary that ran alongside it. I was watching myself in the movie, although amazingly, the person who I was observing was nothing like me. I seemed to look younger, though I was distinctly aware I was older in years and then, as it started to unfold, I realised I was being shown what I'd be doing in the future. I was shown myself meeting loads of people. I didn't recognise anyone but could clearly see I had a rapport with those people as I seemed to have a confidence that was uncharacteristic to who I really was. I saw people who worked in the media who had various roles, saw celebrities and people in authority, right up to people in government. I saw myself meeting them through the work I was involved in and how I was helping them. I smirked, laughing to myself at such a ridiculous scenario. I saw myself on television in a programme and how then things opened for me as I gained credibility with the public.

I also saw myself standing in front of an audience speaking and then other audiences and locations, and I thought to myself it looked like I'd been doing that for some time and was comfortable and confident in what I was doing. It was so out of character, and I couldn't possibly see how it could be me. I was such a withdrawn person, happier with watching endless soaps on TV and staying at home, looking after the kids. I knew I certainly had no ambition to do what I was being shown. It seemed ridiculous. I then saw me signing a book I'd written at a book launch, and it being linked with many causes I was helping to raise awareness about. I saw myself travelling all over the world as an ambassador for a cause. I saw myself meet people from all over the world bringing home artefacts from various locations where I'd met people from all walks of life. It was bizarre.

Sitting there in my M & S dressing gown and slippers in my little chalet with no money, a broken relationship and two children to raise alone, it seemed beyond absurd. Even if there was a glimmer of hope the person, I was seeing was me, these were situations I simply wouldn't have the confidence to achieve.

I then saw myself at a beautiful place in the countryside with horses, fields, and tranquillity all around me. I was aware I lived abroad too, but not clear where. I saw myself working in America and then saw myself walking down the red carpet with family members and a man who I could only see from the neck downwards. *Who's that?* I wondered. I was on his arm, so he seemed to be my partner.

I saw myself living a very rewarding existence with a huge array of good friends and associates who helped me to achieve all I was involved in. I seemed to be physically fit and healthy, wealthy, confident and successful. The more I saw and the more I questioned, the more I wondered what it was all about. I was shown this was an incredibly significant time in human evolution and I'd come to earth to help with the process of waking people up! I was shown that the earth was running out of time with what humanity was currently doing to it with its wars, raping natural landscape and dumping endless waste. It was a cycle in time that was coming about to radically shift the earth because of the over saturation point that we'd reached. I was shown I was to help wake people up in order to help them take responsibility. The way it would come about, would be at a time when people were aware of my connection to Source and that of others like me!

Then it got a bit scary!

My heart started to beat faster as I knew I didn't want that responsibility and who the bloody hell would listen to me anyway? Who the hell was I and how on earth was I, Ms Nobody, going to help make changes on the planet? It was laughable, but I somehow knew what I was being shown was very serious.

I started to get irritated as I realised at some level, I had started to get a spark of hope at the prospect of being part of some greater plan. I'd read enough spiritual material to realise something was happening on a large scale and it was plausible – if it had been happening to someone credible. I had no credibility whatsoever. I felt duped at that point as if I were having a carrot dangled in front of me. It was an unfair way of showing me what was to come if it was some kind of mind trick. I resigned myself to the thought it was just my mind playing tricks on me, and deep down I was desperate, even if I had no awareness of it consciously. The more irritated I got, the more insistently the images and messages came to me. It was when I was finally shown the effects of what would happen if nuclear arms were deployed that I started to let go. I saw that all communication with the spiritual existence here on earth would be cut off indefinitely, and that would change humanity forever and therefore the planet.

This is a race against time now Amanda, to move as much of the human population as possible into a place where they can take responsibility for their energy. This is a huge time of spiritual initiation to raise consciousness and we need this to change the way humans interact with the world. Once people are able to make decisions for

*themselves, and realise their power, they can ultimately change the
vibration of the planet and start turning the cartwheel of destruction in
the opposite direction to generate enough positive energy to turn the
planet around. The planet is paying the price for human error and greed,
and we need that to stop if we're going to allow life to continue on Earth.
Soon you will have extreme weather changes, land mass changes and
population shifts. You will become more and more aware of the negative
power that resides on earth and how it's locked many of you in isolation
and despair and that has created deep anger in people. That emotion
however will create the energy needed to drive people to search for
answers. You are there now on Earth to help with answers.*

Feeling sick and anxious by what I'd heard I didn't dare think
any thoughts, too frightened to find out more. Then I was shown
alien intervention and how at last history would have to be
rewritten to incorporate what other planetary beings would
come to show us. I was shown the war that existed in the
universe was a reflection of what was going on here on Earth and
the only way to recognise who was on our side was to
understand what was going on within us. We as humans had the
key to unlocking the mysteries of our ancestry and at last realise
our potential. Again, I was shown I was key to helping introduce
humanity to what was going on out there in the universe. I had
to ask and said out loud, "Why me?"

It was then the spools suddenly stopped turning. I thought at
first I'd blown it and angered the voice. However, the spools then
started to turn the other way, slowly at first and then they sped
up to a fast rewind until eventually they settled on a picture I
recognised! There before me was my mum and dad. Looking the
way they were gazing at each other, they'd just met. I was told it
all started with them being brought together to produce me. I
was then shown the very quick pregnancy and them getting
married and me being born and told this was all predestined and
these two individuals, because of their unique qualities, had been
chosen to help me with my mission.

I felt a rising anger and disbelief start to wash over me. I was
then shown why I was taken from my mother to live with my
father and learn so many harsh lessons to prepare me for my task.
I felt angry and used, but before I could ask what the point to my
mother's existence was, I had the answer and was shown how
she would inspire me to persevere when all felt lost. I was shown
how it was through observing my mother's addiction to alcohol,
I would find my own source of strength so I would learn my

lessons to conquer challenges and therefore help others overcome theirs. I felt terribly sad for the experiences my parents and I had had to undergo. It seemed so cold and calculating, and yet so intricately devised and actioned if it was to help me achieve some kind of mission.

Everything started to make so much sense.

I was shown myself as a three-year-old and remembered those bizarre repetitive dreams I had of me standing in front of millions of people when I was a child. Was that me being shown what I would be doing in the future?

Yes, that's correct, Amanda. You were being shown how you connect with spirit through your dream state.

I laughed aloud as I realised to me it had all seemed so perfectly natural back then. It was as if I'd been in some sort of training. And so it went on. My childhood merged into my teenage years and the rebellious stage of my existence, as I showed the world my anger towards my upbringing. That continued until I met my first husband. I realised with great sadness what was to come. I was shown my naivety towards dishonesty and corruption and the lessons I had chosen to learn there, the end being when my first husband disappeared with my daughter Georgina, just before her fourth birthday. At that point, feeling choked I pleaded for a pause! Tears and overpowering emotion flooded from the depths of me as I was taken back to the pain that had never eased but was buried within me. I could accept what I'd endured as a child, but to lose my own child for the sake of saving the planet, that was a little hard to comprehend and too absurd and cruel to rationalise!

The film slowly started to reveal the reasons why, and gently eased me forward to understand the bigger picture! I could see it, but couldn't accept it, as I never thought anything could possibly justify the mammoth loss I'd endured. I was shown the patterns, the repeated cycles that played out in family roles and that were passed on through generations. I realised I had to live it to understand it. To ultimately do something about it was what my life had been about! I flitted through the five-year search for my daughter, the stalker who turned our life upside down and the subsequent death of my grandmother – all too much for anyone to endure in one lifetime, let alone all at once at such a young age. My heart ached and sadness gripped me like it was happening all over again. I sat patiently waiting for an end. We moved onto meeting my second husband and how he'd eventually help me to awaken. I was shown the reasons for my two children Millie and Anthony and how they would drive me forward to keep me focused on my mission.

I was then shown that for each of the light workers on the planet who were sent to bring light to people and situations, there were at least three substitutes to enable the process to be guaranteed. I was shown it had all been planned by the creator force to help humanity, however, because of the human condition of emotion and having free will to choose, it was not guaranteed for some. Therefore, they had to put in place some people who would have no choice but to choose the mission.

"So what you're telling me is I have substitutes and if I don't choose to do this, someone else will?" I asked aloud.

No, came the reply.

"What do you mean, *no?*" I asked, confused.

There are no substitutes for some of you Amanda, as you are an activator for other light workers!

"What does that mean?" I said, getting irritated and inpatient again.

You have chosen this mission to be fully awoken at this point to awaken others. Your role will be diverse. You've already started your training and will continue as you follow this path. You will be given all information on a need-to-know basis, and patience and trust are your only allies in this process.

"You've got to be kidding! How the bloody hell am I going to do this when I've got my children and a home to support? I've got no money or anyone to help me look after them, so how on earth do you expect me to do all of this. And what's the need-to-know basis about anyway? We're not in a James Bond movie, you know!"

I wanted a break. I wanted to take the kids to school, watch daytime TV and forget the world existed, not save the bloody planet!

Everything is already worked out for you and all you have to do is follow your guidance!

I shook my head in disbelief and sat for a moment in contemplation. The film started moving again. I watched, numb from not knowing if I was about to explode or lose my mind for good. I saw the struggle I'd gone through with my husband over the years to convince him to give up his addiction and the more I tried, the more I seemed to attract addictions in others around me. Then I was shown the small steps I'd taken towards my spiritual awakening and why. I remembered I'd felt such a compulsion to explore healing, that nothing could stop me. The voice told me it was channelled to me to enable me to start working with the process.

"But what about when I left my family and wanted to end it all?" I barked, fuming. I felt tricked.

It was a time of growth for you. A time to allow you to realise who you were and how you fitted into the greater scheme of humanity. As with all these processes, it's necessary to be broken to then be built anew!

It made sense. I couldn't deny it. But it did cross my mind it could have all gone horribly wrong if I hadn't seen that message that day on the clifftop! I shuddered with the realisation of how close I'd been to leaving this world.

"So what you're saying is I have this mission to accomplish and you're going to help me with everything I need to achieve it, yes?"

That's correct!

At that point I felt a little silly. It was ridiculous talking to someone I didn't know, so I asked the obvious question. "Who are you?"

This you will come to understand whilst you're in training, Amanda. From now on, all you need to be assured of is that we work for the highest good of all and our intention is to raise human consciousness to help with the crisis that's now happening with your species and that of your planet.

"You said *we*!"

Yes, you could say we're your entourage of helpers guided to assist you with your mission. "So, there's more than one of you?"

Yes! That's correct.

"What do I call you then?"

I was growing a little impatient by the banter by then, and to say the least, a little cocky as I still couldn't see how it was going to put food on the table for my children or pay my mortgage!

Use your mind to connect with us and we are there. You don't have to refer to us in the way you communicate to others on Earth.

"So no names, then, is that what you're saying?" I asked, smirking, remembering I'd been told it was on a need-to-know basis.

Names separate us and we are not separate, we are one, with you and all of humanity. You however have been chosen to communicate on our behalf.

Another wave of fear coursed through my stomach. "Great!" I said "Timing, eh? So just when I need it least, I get a chance to be in a James Bond movie and you guys have chosen the worst time ever when I'm feeling more like an inmate from Prisoner Cell Block H!" I sighed, thinking the whole thing had gone too far. I felt helpless and weak and thought they'd perhaps got the wrong person. Considering I was sitting there in my dressing gown, feeling there was little hope for me, how could I be someone who could create change? I had no idea what I was going to do about my future let alone consider some ridiculous offer from God knows who I was talking to and couldn't see.

The film started moving again. I saw my return to England from Australia and moving to Mum's to regroup and rebuild my life once more. I saw the struggle I'd endured to face the criticism of all who felt I'd abandoned my children and had run off with another man. I could see I was being shown how people were judgemental and how I'd let that affect me. The growth that came from that was slow but gradual, but I went back to my husband as I felt I had no choice. I felt the sadness as it seemed the only way to be with my children. At that time, I was shown, I did have choice, but I took the easy option, which was the wrong path.

"Easy option?" I said feeling genuine anger. "How could nearly dying of meningitis have been the easy option?"

Because humans struggle when it's not necessary.

"No, I'm sorry," I said incredulously. "I'm not buying that!"

You chose it all, Amanda! The voice held firm.

"You mean, everything that's happened to me?"

Yes, and all to help you understand the compassion necessary to fulfil your task here on Earth."

"Yeah, yeah, yeah," I said, shaking my head. I knew it would take some convincing to get me to fully comprehend I'd actually chosen the life I'd had so far. "This life has been hell. Are you telling me this is what I've got to keep going through for the sake of my mission?"

No, of course not. This now is your chance to fulfil your dreams and live the life you desire.

"But how's that gonna work, if I've got this mission to carry out!" I asked incredulously.

It's already been worked out for you, Amanda. You have to trust that it's for the highest good of all. You will receive abundance, love, joy, health and happiness, and all that you dream of because it's your birth right.

I lowered my head and thought about it. What choice did I actually have? I could stay in the hell hole of a life I'd tolerated so far or give it a shot. I was in a Catch 22 situation. In some ways it made sense to have to force me to go down this path as I really had no alternative.

"So how do I know you're the good guys then and this thing's gonna work?" I blurted out. After all, I wanted some guarantees. I wasn't just about to throw myself into something that had been shown to me in a matter of moments without some reassurance.

As said before Amanda, trust is your ally, and you will find in time that the results speak for themselves.

Then the film moved again, and I was taken to when Michael had left that morning. I was shown that the guidance I'd received was from the highest of the divine, from the Guys Upstairs which was how I referred to them since childhood, having innocently thought they lived in my father's attic room. I was shown it was timed necessary for Michael to be removed so I could begin my journey.

"So are you saying Michael had to leave this morning to allow this mission to begin?"

Yes Amanda. You are correct. That time has now come!

I sat and stared at my surroundings and all I could feel was hope. For the first time in my life I allowed myself to dream regardless of the dire situation I was in.

Chapter 28

The real voyage of discovery consists not in seeking
new landscapes but in having new eyes.

Marcel Proust

The next day when I woke, I wondered if it had all been a
dream, but I felt different and empowered by my experience.
Over the next few weeks, I tried to find strength to cope with
being a single mum. Asking for help from the authorities it just
made me feel like I was a victim and a failure.

I'd initiated divorce proceedings with a new solicitor who
happened to mention his wife's spiritual awareness. I felt I was
very lucky to have someone who understood my inner needs,
and he guided me conscientiously through the next few weeks
without making the process negative in any way. I was in awe
that the universe had found me someone who could help me on
my level, even though they represented the legal system. I was
impressed and felt a spark of hope that The Guys Upstairs were
honouring their commitment.

One day I rushed to an appointment at my dentist. I had an
appointment with Amanda Morley, a hygienist, and that day
when I met her, I had no idea she was also a witch, astrologer,
and psychologist. I arrived feeling very stressed from rushing
around. I excused myself for my emotional state and she calmly
and kindly asked me to lie back on the couch. Then she said, "I
think you need to come and see me at home. I think I know what
you need!"

That's when she told me she was an astrologer and I felt so
relieved I'd been guided to her as I knew instinctively, she would
have insight as to what I needed to do to move forward. She had
a knowing and said, "Amanda, you're simply out of sorts and all
over the place at the moment."

When I arrived for the appointment at her home, she greeted
me like an old friend and felt strangely familiar to me. She made
me tea and soon I was sitting in her living room with diagrams

and charts spread out in front of me as she explained my astrological birth chart and forecast.

"You'll be working in television, in the public eye, teaching classes and working as a leader, showing people how to find themselves. You'll be very mindful of Earth's current state and incorporating compassion for the earth and humanity into your teachings," she said matter-of-factly.

That was exactly what I'd been told by The Guys Upstairs. I still didn't know how it could possibly happen, especially as I had a phobia about speaking in a group dynamic, let alone to an audience. She went on to reiterate how I was going through a transformation and my life would change forever. I left feeling excited and scared at the same time by what she'd told me, yet also hopeful.

I'd been seeing more and more clients since Michael had left and was starting to experience strange insights with some of them. In a few cases, women had told me things that didn't seem to relate to them. *Well, certainly not in this lifetime,* I thought.

I was doing the ironing one morning and watching the TV when Andrea Foulkes, "ITV's Regression Expert" appeared on the *This Morning* programme. I watched with fascination as she regressed people and claimed to heal them by cutting their residues from past lives to allow them to heal issues in this lifetime. As I waited to find details on how to get in touch with her, I held my pen poised at the ready. I had to go and see her for answers about what was going on with myself and about questions I had regarding my clients. When I'd got the details, I called and made an appointment.

When I arrived at her Chelsea home, a bouncy, giggly tall blonde woman, more stunningly beautiful in the flesh than on television, greeted me. She waved me indoors, took me into her living room and ushered me to sit on a large grey sofa filled to bursting with cushions galore. The room was sparsely but tastefully decorated with antique furniture and sprinkled with candles and subtle lights, which gave the room a subdued and relaxed feel. This was the room where they'd filmed her on TV, although it had looked much brighter and warmer – that I guessed was the magic of television. She excitedly told me all about herself and how she'd helped people with many different problems, and I listened in awe.

Wow. She's beautiful, intelligent, rich and lives in Chelsea with no kids. She must have the time of her life!

Feeling inadequate sitting in front of her, I tried to quiet my thinking mind, but something was nagging at me, telling me things weren't what I thought. She started to explain how regression worked. "So, Amanda, we're all different as humans and all react differently to regression, but most have good results. I just want you to relax as much as possible and be guided by my voice."

I tried to relax and decided to let her work her magic. She asked me to get comfortable and then said, "Firstly I will relax your body and mind and will take you through a deepener which is a hypnotic meditation to make you feel very relaxed whilst you're still aware."

Sitting comfortably on the sofa, propped up with umpteen cushions, I was lulled into a deep state of relaxation and followed her instructions. She asked me to visualise myself going through doors and as I stepped through each door, I saw unfamiliar images. Through one door, I saw myself as a soldier in the First World War. I was a man and it seemed vivid and weird, but I could relate to it somehow and knew it was me. I went through another door and was a Samurai warrior. I went through several doors and each time I seemed to be mostly men! Although I was also a poor prostitute in another lifetime during the Victorian era, used and abused and left to die alone. That was a very emotional experience which Andrea dealt with by cutting cords and allowing healing to release me from the residues from that lifetime.

Lastly, I had a bizarre image of a dog. A big shaggy dog with a red collar on and a gold tag. It was during the fifteenth century and my logical mind told me they didn't have dog collars during that era. The more I focused on it, the more I realised it couldn't be so and then I started laughing. In fact, I couldn't stop laughing until I was brought out of my regression and back into the room. Andrea explained she'd cut cords from the previous existences which would create the healing process and it was inevitable I was used and abused in many lifetimes. In fact, in many of my past lifetimes, I'd had to fight or struggle to survive which she said certainly made sense in terms of why I had struggled so much in my current life.

She said, "You'll go through quite a change during the next few weeks."

She never did explain about the shaggy dog, but I noticed that on my notes I saw her write in big bold letters *LIGHT WORKER*.

When I said, "Why have you written *light worker* on my notes?" she told me, "You have to research it, Amanda. Please be prepared for me to contact you in a few weeks as you are someone I come across once in a blue moon. Trust me. We've been brought together and believe we'll be working together in the near future."

I went away from hers that day intrigued, waiting to hear from her and find out why I'd been guided to her. I certainly went through a change over the next three weeks as I started to look at myself differently. It was as though I'd had some sort of personality transplant. I had an awareness which was immense and sensed things I'd never identified with before.

I started to get psychic information constantly and everything I saw from that day came to me as if I had been trained for years to intuitively tune into my environment. Things, places, and people spoke to me in a different way as I seemed to work on a deeper level than my everyday senses and my appetite for insight and information was insatiable. Gone was the little timid, frightened, reclusive, insecure, and lonely girl, and in her place was a strong, committed, brave, explorative, compassionate woman. My focus was on making life for myself, and those around me, the best it could possibly be for the highest good of all. Day and night, my focus was on spiritual matters and everything that related to making a better and brighter life for me, my children, and those who asked me for help. I was attracting good fortune and luck and no longer felt the fear of insecurity. Even though I had no idea what lay ahead, I had a knowing all would be well.

One day I woke knowing I had to look for a medium, but not any old medium. That's how I found Tom who'd been recommended to me. I met him for the first time weeks after Mike had left, and as I walked into his room, he remarked, "Good God, look who you've brought with you!"

I looked around, expecting to see other people walking in with me until he proceeded to tell me I had an army behind me of angels, relatives, helpers, masters, aliens – you name it, they were there.

"You looked like Boadicea as you walked in then," he stated, beaming at me as he offered me a seat.

Immediately I felt a glimmer of recognition of dreams I'd had as a child. When I was very young, I had a reoccurring dream of me leading an army as a warrior woman. It was only when I was doing some research one day for Millie's school project that I found Boadicea had been linked to Anglesey, East Anglia, and St Albans – all places I'd lived in this lifetime. Shivering and shrugging off the reminder of what I'd seen, I sat sceptically at Tom's table and listened without giving anything away about what I'd already been told by The Guys Upstairs. He told me I'd recently left my husband and gone through a one hundred and eighty degree turnaround as a person. He said I'd been replaced as I'd been ill and had a near death experience, and during that process I'd made a pact to leave my body to be replaced with another soul. It was not only eye-opening and shocking; it was also beyond my ability to register what he was on about.

"We call it a walk-in Amanda. It's when souls swap to allow a mission to be accomplished," he said.

I thought it sounded absurd, but it accounted for the radical difference in whom I was becoming. I felt a strange sense he knew my soul better than I did, but my mind told me he was barmy! Still, I let him carry on. He explained it was destined to have been this way as my numbers (numerology) spelled out that I'd chosen to come to Earth at this particular time in our evolutionary history to help with the colossal task of raising awareness and the consciousness to increase the vibration of humans on earth to help save the planet.

"Amanda, there are millions of light workers doing the same thing at the moment, but you are one of the way showers, one of those who can't be replaced."

I almost went white with shock at how he could possibly know what I'd been told only a few weeks before. It certainly all backed up what I'd been told by The Guys Upstairs, Amanda the astrologer, and Andrea the regressionist. I asked what he meant, and he said I was to help activate light workers. I listened patiently as he spoke about things he couldn't possibly have known about. He also told me what I'd be doing in the future and what he said corresponded with other information. At the end of the reading, he told me he'd been written about in a TV series called *Spooks*. He said he'd been used as one of the characters because of what he did. I was shocked when he told me he used to work for the MOD on UFO research and had become a medium later on when he'd realised he had the ability.

Tom, like Andrea, said he'd be in touch with me as we were meant to stay in touch with each other. I was astounded these people wanted to get to know me and for over a year Tom and I sat together for many an evening discussing and exchanging insights into spiritual, earthly, and universal matters. Tom put me in touch with Derek, the crystal man. He told me I couldn't miss him as he looked like Barry Gibb from the Bee Gees but was dressed from head to foot in tie-dyed clothing.

He was spot on. When I spotted Derek, he was surrounded at his stall by people ten deep. People flocked to see him and to buy his crystals at St Albans market on a Saturday. The stall was heaving with people of all ages. Many were obviously regulars, but others looked like they'd come from another planet. Oddly, some didn't seem human, and they certainly prickled when they saw me. I had no idea why. I was so naïve. Derek seemed to recognise me, even though we'd not met before, from the moment I walked up to him. He spoke to me as if we were old pals.

I asked him one day if we could meet away from the stall as people were very protective of him, trying to monopolise him constantly. I found it difficult to talk privately but needed to speak to him. People seemed transfixed by their insatiable need to have the most powerful crystals he had to offer, and it was evident how much people drained him. His crystals were cheaper by far than those from any other supplier and were far more powerful than anyone else's crystals. Most of them came directly from Namibia and other amazing places he'd visited.

He told me he was a new soul on this earth and didn't like humans but had been sent as the "keeper of the crystals" to distribute to light workers to help save the earth. I had to remain grounded as much as possible with all the diverse and wonderful people I was meeting, and especially when it came to Derek. As he was very nervous and never met anyone out of his comfort zone, we met on a hillside in the middle of the countryside at sunset. It seemed very cloak and dagger, but he said he didn't want to be overheard. Somehow, I wasn't surprised or unnerved by his bizarre request.

I was so keen to get more confirmation of what I was experiencing that I would have met him anywhere. I was fascinated by his understanding, and the more people who clarified my recent changes and subsequent insights, the more I needed to understand why, so I was open to anything. Being a Capricorn stood me in good stead he told me. Being the most sceptical of all the star signs, it would ensure I kept searching for facts and answers to prove beyond a shadow of a doubt what I was going through and what I would be doing in the future. Derek became an ally and friend, and I frequented his stall often to listen to him channel information to me that only I understood, and to buy crystals which eventually amounted to thousands in my ever increasing collection.

I was going in at the deep end with my new spiritual awakening and nothing could stop me. I even dealt with the weird people who sought me out and followed me trying to in some way poach information from me or take my power!

Andrea Foulkes contacted me four weeks after my husband had left and by then I was connecting with so many people who were helping me on my journey. She told me she'd been woken at midnight the night before and shown she must work with me as I was at the centre of all things in relation to the massive work going on with the light workers. Ego stepped in big time as I felt I had something others didn't. It had been creeping in steadily as I started to feel special and chosen, but in time I was shown how destructive the ego could become, so reining it in became part of my training. At first, however, I had to experience it, to find its destructive source so I could teach others.

Andrea asked if she could be my client. I had no idea what she wanted so agreed to meet with her for breakfast in Chelsea. I felt special and honoured she'd chosen me but wasn't expecting her to readily pour out her beliefs as to why we'd been brought together. We found a table in the garden of the café, away from listening ears and she said almost immediately, "Amanda, the reason I've called you is because I'd like you to help reorganise my administration and client database. I'm building a bit of a spiritual empire but need help with it. And in that, you'd be learning how to build your own when you're ready."

She knew I had clients, but she wanted me to specifically focus on her to help her go through spiritual changes herself. "I feel you've been guided to help me, Amanda, and in return you'll learn to create what you need for the future."

I was honoured.

She showed me the channelling she'd received to show I was to help her, and I immediately agreed to work for her. Proudly, I told the kids Mummy had got a job and I organised a child minder. Working regularly was a big leap for me. I had to change my dress code, as I needed to up my look! I certainly couldn't work for this beautiful creature in jeans and a sweatshirt, so I got a loan to buy myself some appropriate clothes.

I put Andrea on a pedestal and was keen to learn all I could from her. One morning we met for coffee to go over all the details of how I'd work for her, and I showed her some crystals a man had given me. She asked who he was and as my ego was soaring, I told her he'd travelled to meet me as he'd heard all about me through the network and wanted me to have the crystals to help me on my journey. I'd been so wrapped up in my pat on the back I'd accepted them without question. She immediately told me to leave them on a wall and walk away. I did, surprised by her reaction and as we got to our destination within minutes, my phone rang, and it was the man who'd given me the crystals. Shocked and a little frightened, I showed Andrea who was calling me, and she encouraged me to answer. I tried to remain neutral as he seemed flustered. He asked me straight away how my crystals were. I looked at Andrea and told him they were fine. He asked if I still had them on me. Instantly, my stomach went into butterfly mode, and I had an incredible adrenalin rush as I knew something wasn't right. "Of course," I lied.

"It's just they feel pretty hot to me, and you know I'm very in tune with my crystals! Just wanted to make sure everything was all right, that's all!" he said.

I looked out of the coffee shop window and could see the wall clearly across the road where I'd left the crystals. It was a beautiful sunny day, and the sun was streaming down on that wall. That was my first lesson in learning about ego and fear. "Don't worry, I'm taking great care of them. I have to go now as I'm with a friend," I said, and I put the phone down.

Andrea said, "I suggest you change your phone number. One lesson you need to learn quickly, Amanda, is that darker forces will try to stop you with your mission. He was using the crystals to remote view you and track where you go and what you say."

I learned very quickly how ego could take a person down a dark path and attract lower energy people and situations – it was to become my biggest lesson. Over the next six months my life became a roller coaster of expanding awareness further, and sometimes I was stunned at how accurate information was as confirmation came about to prove I'd chosen well in following my source of insight. I kept my head down as I started to recognise the darker characters who tried to befriend me, but I equally recognised instantly my allies and life had become not only a wonderful challenge workwise, but also refreshingly rewarding with having so many good people in my life, showing me the way, protecting me and guiding me through the obstacle course of challenges I would face. It was the first time I'd found real friendships and credible associates to help me on my journey in life.

I laughed about how life had changed so radically and related it to living in a real-life James Bond movie. I was on a mission, seemed to have allies pop up whenever I needed them to help me discover the next clue on my journey and all insight seemed to arrive on a need-to-know basis. I only ever got what I needed and was no longer bombarded with the many choices I used to have from all the different voices in my head. From that time on, my inner voice was well and truly tuned in and turned up, and all the other voices were turned down to an insignificant whisper.

I had become Andrea's confidante and friend and felt honoured to have the pleasure of working with her and helping her on her journey. I realised she kept herself private and had very few friends as she focused totally on her career and life path and was very dedicated. She socialised very little and was single until the day we had a course she'd organised at Regent's College. We'd sent out at least two thousand emails to ex-clients and enquirers, but on the day fewer than forty people turned up. She was OK with that, saying the right people were there and that's what counted. I was beginning to learn how to accept whatever life dished out, it was right at that time.

The course was an odd mix of Andrea groupies, a few who looked not of this planet, and some regular clients of hers who turned up out of loyalty. Two of us helped to set up the event, and on the day, all went well until during a meditation a girl fell to the floor clutching her chest. Andrea froze until I gestured to her to continue as everyone had their eyes closed. I quietly went over to the lady on the floor, gently helped her up to her chair and when she was ready, I took her outside. I gave her a cup of tea and a sweet biscuit and listened to her tell me every time she'd visited Andrea, she heard the bells ring three times and on that particular occasion, Andrea had rung the bells five times which had shocked her system.

Andrea had always told me she only saw clients once – twice at the most if there was more work to do, but this lady had been several times. To me, this was a danger some people faced, getting addicted to therapy, and it was clear this young lady was hooked on seeing Andrea in an attempt to rid herself of her demons. Eventually I got an email from the girl to say she'd gone back to live with her parents for a while and was getting some loving guidance and security. It was a long way off from the isolation she'd felt living alone in London and clinging to anyone who'd help. Apart from that, she said she was spending a small fortune on finding ways to heal herself, which she needn't have done. I felt glad she'd found her own way.

She wasn't the first spiritual junkie I'd met. I encountered many people who were addicted to finding solace in spirituality, but disturbingly hiding behind it. They went to see many different holistic therapists, healers, mediums and so forth, but never took any action to change their lives. I was determined to find a way to help people to get on and take action, to create the balance they needed.

On that occasion at Regent's College, a fireman had turned up for the course and when it came to a close, he chatted Andrea up for a date. The relationship started up with her hoping that as he was a grounded kind of guy, he didn't just want her because she was on television. At first, it went wonderfully well until one day he invited her to a work do in the hope he could show her off. She ran a mile. He was shocked she'd ended it. I think he'd genuinely cared about her, but it was as if she just couldn't let anyone get too close. I watched her cry like a teenager for two days until she got him out of her system. I felt for her and wished she would break down the barrier between us, but ironically, I realised she was teaching me about opening up my own heart and fully trusting. After that she became more needful of my time, asking me to stay late after work, go out with her and take her to places I liked to go to, and it seemed she was on one level wanting to become close friends and, on another level, wanted me to help her go through some kind of healing herself. I never felt we would get close, as she always held back as soon as she felt vulnerable.

When I was at home, I seemed to spend most of the time on the phone to her as she liked to be alone less and less. I started to see a side of her unravel which was vulnerable, lonely, and searching and even though she needed me and spent most of her time with me, she equally kept a safe distance as she felt in control that way. Andrea had explained to me she'd asked a friend she'd known called Arielle to get her a job on *This Morning* modelling as Arielle happened to work on the programme. The day Andrea worked on the programme as a model she was sitting in the green room when she met a gentleman called Dr Keith Hearne. Keith was about to perform a live regression on TV. A psychologist and parapsychologist, and one of Britain's leading hypnotherapists, he was a spokesperson for the media on conditions of the mind, especially the sleep state. Having developed the Dream Machine in the Science Museum, he became expert on the subject of lucid dreaming. An incredibly gifted man, he was also a composer.

After meeting Keith, Andrea had a knowing that she wanted to learn about regression as it offered her a new path – she felt it was her calling. She'd sent numerous show reels off for various areas of work on TV, including work as a stand-up comedian, but she'd not had a glimmer of anything. Her senses were ringing as Keith spoke about his passion for regression work and she managed to persuade him to meet her after the show. Keith went on to perform the live regression, which immediately fascinated the general public as something new and unique. Andrea watched avidly from the monitor in the green room. They met afterwards and Keith went to her home two weeks later to teach her. Usually, he taught regression to qualified hypnotherapists.

Andrea applied to the head of the programme at the *This Morning* to inform them she was one of Keith's protégés and she could do a regular slot on their programme. Andrea was far more charming and appealing to the public than Keith so, to keep it fresh, they got her a slot on the programme as ITV's regression expert! Andrea had opened up to me and confided in me about so much, especially her spiritual understanding. Ultimately, I wondered why she was with me and what she'd seen and not told me. Even though I felt she wanted my friendship, I still felt her holding back and wanted to get to understand why. Breaking up with her latest boyfriend had obviously touched some raw nerves. I felt for her lonely and sculptured life as I realised she'd developed a persona that fitted into the world she wanted to create. As I headed home on the train, I relived all she'd told me and realised we were very different. When I next went into work, she seemed embarrassed and perplexed by the fact she'd let her guard down. She reverted to being like she was just my client again, and I felt the relationship couldn't continue with such uncertainty. The more I worked for her, the more I realised how I wanted to connect with my own clients, and my time working with her helped me to plumb the depths of who I was to give my all to each and every one of them. Working with someone who was focused on the media gave me insight into how I didn't want to do things, and I realised I was just there to observe.

I was fortunate enough to have met some very honest and compassionate people through the Spiritual Church, which had been a huge comfort and point of focus to me when I needed it back when I had lost Georgina. When things had started going wrong with Michael, I'd sought a healing practitioner through the church who happened to be a medium. Seeing her on a few occasions had given me solace, faith and understanding. It had given me such strength knowing there were some very gifted individuals who lived very humble lives and dedicated themselves to helping others.

Andrea was also working to help people, but I started to feel conflict with her work as it was portrayed so egotistically through the media. I was beginning to question what I was achieving by working with her when I was building a good client base myself and working at a different conscious level. One evening I was making the usual calls to her email requests for appointments. By then the emails were dwindling as her appearances on TV were becoming fewer. A man called Chris (most clients of Andrea's were women) told me it was his partner who wanted him to have the regression as she felt their relationship failure was down to his past life issues. I told him it should be his choice as it was not encouraged to book clients who were coaxed by loved ones. He told me he was OK about it and he'd do it for her sake, but he wanted to talk and started to open up about spiritual matters. He talked about his fascination with the ocean and how it made him question there was more to life than he perceived.

Most potential clients of Andrea's called and got to the point, sometimes starting to outline why they wanted the session, but each time I'd gently tell them to keep that to themselves as it was between themselves and Andrea. Chris was different however, and I instantly felt drawn to his strength of character and openness and listened politely. I remained professional and tried to steer us back to making the appointment. He was very charming and managed to steer back to what he wanted to talk about. It was as if he didn't want the conversation to end. Eventually he started to insist he needed to see me and not Andrea. That's when I had to put my foot down.

Andrea had started to become quite forthright and prickly towards me of late, and I sensed she felt I was gaining my own power. I wondered if she felt vulnerable as she'd confessed to me her innermost fears and how she'd come to do what she did. She'd warned me once not to poach her clients which I felt hurt by. Firstly, I'd never contemplated it, as all my clients had come to me directly and secondly it would only create bad karma and not serve me in the long run – she above all knew that. The fact she had to say it made me sad as she obviously was starting to lose her power in other ways, and as she trusted no one I realised I was at the end of my contract with her to help and had to move on for the highest good of both of us. I'd always felt everyone that's guided to you is for a reason so therefore it could never benefit you to try to be competitive or steal from others. Ultimately, it would only harm you.

Andrea was running out of TV work, and I felt I was perhaps adding to her worries as I was becoming more aware and confident and looking forward to what was to come. She had no idea at that time where her path was heading. Naturally, I understood her anguish, but I had a different philosophy as I was aiming always to help the greater good and it was conflicting with the work I was doing with her then. I felt it was time for us to both move on. Everything happened for a reason, so I knew at that stage in my life we were all taken care of as long as we recognised the signs to help us.

Then one evening Chris called me again and we ended up talking for some time. I was intrigued by his spiritual understanding. It made a refreshing change to speak to someone so attuned to a higher awareness, as most of Andrea's clients were just starting to open up on their spiritual journey. Chris seemed so much more advanced. I hadn't noticed the time go by until I politely I made my excuses to end the conversation, but he seemed reluctant to go. I answered the questions Chris had asked, but he wanted more. In fact, he insisted we speak again. Putting my professional head on and being cautious, I said it would be OK to make an appointment for him, but I couldn't talk to him again and however much I'd enjoyed our chat, I would be passing him on to Andrea. He wouldn't let me put the phone down and said, "Please, Amanda, can we speak again? I feel I can relate to you so much and want to know more. Perhaps it was you I was meant to meet and not Andrea."

I was nervous as it was crossing the line. Concerned he may have got the wrong idea, I said, "Sometimes I do have to answer client's questions and people want to chat as they're excited by what they're experiencing, but I certainly can't allow this to continue as you are potentially one of Andrea's clients. It would be wholly unprofessional to strike up a relationship, albeit friendship, as it's unethical."

I hoped he'd get the point.

"Amanda, I know it's much more than that. I've never been able to speak to anyone before about things I believe in and all I know now that I've spoken to you about, is that I have to find out more."

I sensed the need in him and was wary, but gently said to him, "Regardless of that Chris, we've probably opened things up more for you by having this chat but that's something you will have to investigate further and follow your inquisitiveness elsewhere."

I managed to make an appointment for him with Andrea and when I called her to tell her what bookings I'd made, I told her about my conversations with Chris. She flew off the handle, accusing me of doing exactly what she suspected. "I've told you, Amanda, you must never take my clients. I did warn you!"

"Andrea, you know full well I don't need to poach your clients. I think we'll leave it at that, though."

She didn't apologise and I didn't expect her to.

When I phoned Chris to confirm I'd booked an appointment for him with Andrea, I told him in no uncertain terms I would have no further communication with him and hoped he would honour that. Andrea mentioned it again as she was obviously stirred by our connection.

"I understand this can happen, Amanda. He probably thought he was attracted to you, but he's contacted me, so he needs to come and see what all this is about."

I still felt hurt as she'd reacted angrily towards me, although I'd been wholeheartedly loyal and committed to her and done my utmost to show Chris, I was just the booking agent. I wondered if she would open up this time as she either confided in me or closed up and protected herself. It was one way or the other and I never knew where I was with her. She started to tell me I should never discuss her as my client in an attempt to use her credibility to boost my own clientele. That was when she crossed the line. I'd seen her as a friend as well as my client. All my clients had come to me without knowing I worked for Andrea. In fact, I'd protected her just as she'd asked, and I was starting to feel the relationship was no longer serving either of us.

I was even more surprised and a little perplexed when Chris called the next evening and asked to meet me. Although I explained it wouldn't serve any of us, he wouldn't let go and deep down I was starting to feel I didn't want him to. He was very honest with me, explaining he was with a partner, even though they had difficulties, and he had a young daughter, too. He wasn't looking for anyone to fill a void; it was strictly a meeting of minds. But again, I turned his offer down. He then started calling during the day and even though our conversations were brief, he managed to make me laugh and I started to look forward to our brief interactions, but I was adamant I wouldn't have anything to do with him every time we spoke.

Soon Andrea was due to see Chris for his appointment and started to discuss him. She was intrigued as to why he'd want to make contact with me. She often asked me what it was I was going to do in the future, which was so important as she said she knew I had an important role to play in helping others. I sensed she was holding onto me for that reason alone. I started to feel she was with me only because she wanted to be involved, but lately she was showing insecurity and pressing for information. I told her I hadn't got a clue what I was to do. I started to feel vulnerable as she was putting pressure on me. She didn't mean to, but I guess time was running out for her in some ways as client bookings were thin on the ground.

Chris went for his regression and immediately after his appointment, she called me to say she was shocked. She said he was a tall, dark-haired, dark-eyed Italian Adonis, built like a middle-weight boxer, and was a director of a company employing over eighty staff. She seemed very impressed.

"He's in the alarm business and his company's doing well and evidently, so is he. So I can understand his intrigue in you as when I regressed him, he told me he'd been connected to you in a past life as he saw you both together."

"What do you mean? He's never even met me?"

"You'll have no chance with him as he's deeply dedicated to protecting his relationship with his daughter and therefore isn't interested in destabilising his already vulnerable relationship with his partner. It's clear he's spent lifetimes before with you, so I guess he's intrigued why he's connected with you now. He certainly wasn't interested in me, though he was *gorgeous*," she added.

I was relieved as I felt she was telling me he'd not accepted her advances. She shook it off by saying he was dedicated to his partner. I wished she hadn't told me as it made me more intrigued as to why he was so determined to meet me. Chris called me almost immediately after I'd spoken to Andrea. He gave me his version of events and said he was disappointed with the regression session as he'd expected more. Not only that, he wasn't wholly convinced she was genuine, or it had worked, but he did recall seeing us together in past lives and also seeing millions of stars. He seemed confused by it all and I just listened.

Andrea had explained to him he and I had come from the beginning of time as star children. He said she was too airy-fairy for him, and he hadn't got what he was looking for, which made him even more insistent and determined to see me more than ever. Though I wanted so much to understand my own feelings of connection with him, I held firm and said no. That went on for several weeks until eventually Andrea told me out of the blue, she wanted me to go to Egypt with her and Chris as she felt we'd find revelations there about our past life connections. She was sure she knew him from a past life, too, so as a compromise she allowed us to meet on the proviso we'd both agree to go to Egypt with her. It was a bizarre turnaround, but also exciting for me as I'd never been to Egypt and had no idea what to expect. Chris was elated when I told him me we could meet at last and I planned our first interaction at eight o'clock on a winter's evening. We met under the clock tower in the square in St Albans in Hertfordshire.

As he turned the corner and walked towards me, I knew him instantly and felt not only an instant attraction, but also a deep connection to him. I kept my cool. I was dressed elegantly in a long black fur lined coat, black boots, and a long conservative black skirt and a simple but exquisite ruched white blouse. I realised we mirrored each other completely. He, too, was wearing a long black coat and a black tasteful and expensively cut pin-striped suit with black boots and a simple white shirt. As we got close, we stared into each other's eyes. The recognition was incredible. It was as if I'd known him all my life and the feelings I'd only ever had for Graham, my first love came cascading into my heart and soul as that breath-taking creature stood before me.

My first thought was, *Why didn't he fancy Andrea*? But my answer came to me the instant our eyes locked as it was far deeper. I knew we'd shared lifetimes together. His deep brown eyes bore into mine and I almost lost my balance as I became entranced by him. He smelt divine and his strength and power felt awesome. I felt protected and safe in his presence. We smiled at each other in silence and kissed each other on the cheek and I guided him to a little old pub which we walked to through the park. We linked arms and chatted like old friends and couldn't stop gazing at each other, but I remained mindful Andrea had insisted she be part of our trio. It was as if Chris needed to meet me to find his destiny. I wondered what it was I needed. We found a cosy corner in the pub and sat and talked in depth until it closed and when I got up to leave, he insisted we spend more time getting to know each other. I said, "Andrea's proposed we all go to Egypt so I guess we'll find out what this is all about soon enough."

He smiled and seemed happy as if he'd got what he set out to achieve. "So when are we off then?" he asked, keenly.

"I have no idea. I guess Andrea will let us know." I replied, feeling excited that something was stirring in me.

After that first meeting, Chris and I spoke daily or met for dinners, lunches, or coffees – whatever we could manage. I was aware that chemistry was weaving its magic between us. Andrea chose three days for us to travel to Egypt at an auspicious time. It was January 2005 and had been almost a year since Michael and I had separated. Adventure was entering my life for the first time ever and I was relishing it. We all booked our own flights and hotels, all staying within the same area. Chris and I planned it this way to stop any boundaries being crossed. I was finding it increasingly difficult not to show how I felt about him, and it was obvious he was finding it equally hard too.

Chapter 29

"You can never cross the ocean until you have the courage to lose sight of the shore."

Christopher Columbus

It was only when Chris and I turned up at the same check-in desk we realised we were on the same flight. I got a text from Andrea while we stood there that said she was going to miss her flight. She'd got up too late and missed her alarm and would try and make the next flight and meet us in Egypt. We left without her. I was relieved to have Chris all to myself. We were both in awe of what was to happen on our adventure, and it was obvious our mounting excitement was not only for the exploration that lay ahead, but also for the time we'd share together.

Chris kept talking about all the hopes he had of how we'd known each other in previous lifetimes coming to light whilst on our visit to Egypt. He was like a kid with a new toy and wanted to get on immediately with our adventure. He'd often told me he'd had repeated dreams where he was a diver and had rescued a sunken treasure and given it back to the people rather than the greedy seekers who wanted the treasure for themselves. In the water, he was a different man. He'd often told me how he felt calm, at peace and relaxed in himself while diving. In all the years he'd dived he'd been fascinated by the sport and the ocean, but out of the water, he was a ruthless, competitive businessman, constantly on the go and seeking the peace he craved. It was like he was two men, hence why he sought answers.

We spoke in depth about what Egypt would perhaps reveal to him and I said, "Chris, as those dreams constantly plague you, perhaps that's what Andrea's getting at as to coming here. Perhaps you'll find out why you're here at this time on Earth like I'm discovering. It certainly seems like you're waking up to something."

We spoke often about spiritual matters and I said as I'd explained to him before, "Many light workers had the same feeling as it's woven into their DNA to wake up when the time is right. It's to help them fulfil what they've chosen to come to earth to achieve in this lifetime."

I'd begun to understand the world was a vastly complex and clever system of reproduction and connection on a unified level which allowed Earth, the animal and human kingdoms to connect and create balance and harmony. I'd explained to Chris before how Mother Earth is perfect and only out of balance through past human intervention. The animal kingdom was out of balance, too, to some degree, but it was down to humans to help realign balance. So many humans take so much for granted and miss what's going on at a deeper level. I'd read a quote once which simply stated, "Everything we see around us is only one per cent of what's going on. Ninety-nine per cent is behind a veil!" That became more evident the more I researched it. The more I put faith into that statement, the more it opened my eyes and the more the statement became true. Chris was at the waking up stage that I understood many light workers went through. Many are woken slowly in readiness to learn and act towards their predestined goals. I'd had a full awakening in one hit, and it felt like I'd been completely rewired.

When we finally arrived, we went separately by taxi to our respective hotels in Cairo. Chris was staying at the Marriott near the Great Pyramid while I was in a low budget affair, a beautiful but very old hotel which needed updating situated right on the outskirts of town. Chris asked me to get a taxi to his hotel as soon as I was unpacked. After I arrived at my hotel, I checked in and was shown to my chalet, which was situated in a beautiful mature garden. I showered and changed and headed to Chris's hotel. I walked into the lobby of the Marriott and saw him instantly in the lounge area and headed towards him. As I sat down next to him, he motioned for a waiter to bring more coffee. He explained he'd already been on the case and put the wheels in motion. I wasn't surprised to discover he'd demanded the concierge put him in touch with someone who'd take us off the tourist trail and to places no-one else visited. I felt attracted to that beautiful and strong-minded man who just grabbed life by the horns, but I wondered if he would ever be able to handle what he might discover if he let the answers come to him naturally. More importantly, I didn't know if he would be able to slow his pace down enough. We drank our coffee and chatted, and Chris said, "Right, so I guess we just wait here until that guy comes back and tells us where we're going to visit." He was proud he'd initiated the search.

"Chris, perhaps we need to just take time out and see what's planned for us. It's not about rushing into it; it's more about understanding how to see the links as everything's already been planned for us. All we must do is follow each link on our path, but we'll only get there if we're in balance."

He laughed at my theory and told me he'd get what he wanted, when he wanted it as he had money to grease the wheels and that's what these people needed. I was concerned at that stage as to whether he'd get it or not. Every light worker had their chance and if he blew it, someone else would take his place. Light workers come in all shapes and forms – teachers, nurses, politicians, cleaners – there were light workers everywhere on Earth, waking up and sharing information, insight, and a higher awareness to create a ripple effect to spread to others. With eight billion people on the planet, many were waking at different stages in different ways to provide a framework of higher consciousness. My heart longed for him to see but I was anxious he wouldn't get it. Ultimately, the aim of our mission, and of every other light worker, was to save our planet and all who reside on her. I knew whether Chris woke up or not, whether I wanted him to share the journey with me or not (because all humans are created with free will), he alone had to make the choice whether to listen to his heart or his mind. As we finished our coffees, a small Egyptian man in a suit that was far too big for him arrived at our table. He introduced himself.

"Hello, Miss Amanda, my name is Mahmoud. Mr Chris has requested I take you to a man who will help you on your journey here in Egypt." He bowed and grinned at me with the gentlest face and a sincere smile. I instantly liked him.

Chris smiled with a satisfied nod and gestured that we go with him. At that time, all cars going in and out of the hotel were being searched by security for bombs as a number of attacks had been targeted on tourist destinations during that time by the jihadists protesting against the Egyptian army. I didn't feel unnerved as I felt immortal. I felt that if I had a mission to accomplish, I'd have to live to carry it out. As we waited to have Mahmoud's car checked, he chatted with enthusiasm about his country, his family and love of his life. He was a taxi driver but worked for many important people, shepherding them from place to place beyond the tourist trail to places not everyone got to see. I sensed Chris didn't trust him as he went quiet, and I knew from the short time I'd known him he was working things out in his mind.

Chris didn't divulge any personal details about us, but somehow, I couldn't help liking Mahmoud. I found him genuine, warm, and open. He said, "Please, it would be my utmost honour to invite you both to my humble home. My family will prepare a meal for you. They would be delighted to meet you."

Chris declined gently. "That's very kind of you, Mahmoud, but we're only here for three days and have much to do."

Mahmoud didn't take no for an answer. He spoke to us as if we were old friends, and talked continuously about all the buildings we were passing. He drove manically through the overcrowded streets that were filled with cars, trucks, and bikes, with no order whatsoever. Chris and I were tense as the car was manoeuvred this way and that to avoid blows with other vehicles, and at long last after twenty minutes or so of moving not very far at all, we arrived outside a plain building that had a few people milling about outside. As we pulled up, they moved swiftly to the car to let us out and several men greeted us in Arabic bowing and gesturing for us to follow them into someone's home. When we got inside, the pungent smell was incredible. Jasmine, rose, lavender and geranium and combinations I couldn't put my finger on. The smell was delicious and very seductive.

As we were ushered into a large room, we were greeted by a man who asked us to sit. The room was large enough for four beautifully ornate benches set in a square with exquisitely coloured throws and cushions adorning them. In the centre was a large low wooden table with incense and candles burning and there was a large oval chair positioned in one corner of the room. Surrounding us were screens and behind them you could just make out women who were busily preparing food and chatting. The man who seated us offered us tea and Mahmoud told us we'd be meeting a Bedouin priest who would join us shortly. Chris and I weren't expecting this as Mahmoud hadn't mentioned who we'd be meeting apart from it being a man who would help us to find what we were looking for in Egypt.

I sensed Chris was getting nervous. Being a man who was always in control, it was clear he was out of his comfort zone. He started cracking a few jokes to relieve his tension saying, "This looks like it's going to be expensive. I guess they do this to all the tourists and then flog them those oils over there." He pointed towards a huge ornate sideboard filled with beautiful differently sized and shaped bottles.

I trusted Mahmoud and felt very at home in that room and was relaxed, knowing we'd been brought to the right place to see the right people. Our tea arrived and tasted better than I'd expected. It seemed to be infused with herbs and was very sweet.

Chris didn't like his. "God, what's in this? They call that tea."

I became a little embarrassed by his comments and hoped no one heard him as I didn't want them to think we were disrespecting their hospitality. As we started to look around the room, we noticed hundreds more ornately made glass bottles in all colours and sizes and Chris said, "This must be a perfume shop. What's a priest doing in a perfume shop?"

Before I could answer, a man walked in, draped in fine robes with his hands gently clasped and uttered, "In actual fact, they're bottles of our finest oils, Chris."

Chris looked embarrassed and the man said, "Good day to you both. My name is Abraham. I believe Mahmoud has brought you here to help you on your journey." He walked slowly to the chair, smiling. An entourage of men followed him, all sitting around him, gazing at him as if he were a god and Chris and I looked at each other as we both felt the magnitude of the man's power.

"It's been a long time, but now you're here," the priest said, looking directly at me.

Putting my hand on my chest, I looked at Chris and then back at the priest as I wondered if he was directing his comment straight at me and wondered if I'd insulted him by being late.

"Yes, you, Amanda!" He smiled. "Do you know how long we've waited for this day?"

Confused, I looked to Chris for reassurance, but he just looked back at me equally puzzled.

"Look," said Chris as he shifted awkwardly in his seat. I was uncomfortable, too. "We were told we were coming to see someone who was going to take us to places and see things the tourists don't get to see. Is that right?" Chris asked.

"Yes, you're quite right, Chris! But all in good time," said the priest.

Chris was getting irritated, and I was concerned he'd blow it. I knew Chris wasn't a patient man as he'd always got what he wanted, when he wanted.

"OK, so what's the plan then?" Chris said.

I cringed. The priest however seemed quite unperturbed by Chris's impatience and continued to smile. His gaze remained on me and started to make me feel a little uncomfortable. "I will tell you this! I have healing powers and my energy is this." He gestured as if to create a large ball of energy that surrounded his body. "But you, your energy fills this room!"

I didn't quite know what to say and was starting to feel unnerved.

Chris butted in. "So what are you trying to say? We've been waiting for you and it's an honour to be in your presence but I'm not quite getting this?"

Abraham said nothing but just continued to smile as if he was transfixed by something. I sat open-mouthed while Chris fidgeted in his seat. "So, OK, you've found her! What is it you can do for us so we can get to see some real stuff then?"

"All in good time Chris! Firstly, we'll have to anoint you both in oils to prepare you for your visit!"

"What visit and what oils?" Chris asked with strangled annoyance.

I tried to catch his eye to make him realise he was starting to sound impatient, rude and above all disrespectful. He ignored me, sitting so far forward on his seat I thought he might fall off.

"You both come back here tomorrow at midday. Mahmoud will collect you. You will both go through what we call a cleansing and purifying process where I will massage you with special oils," Abraham stated.

"Massage sounds good," piped in Chris, smirking.

The priest chose to ignore the interruption and continued. "Then you will be taken to the Great Pyramid where you will be taken up into the king's chamber. You will be shown tombs that are closed to the public. Mahmoud knows what to do."

Chris and I both looked at Mahmoud politely sipping his tea from a dainty cup and saucer with a beaming smile on his face.

Chris asked, "So what are we going to get to see and is it going to help answer the questions we came here for?"

The priest gently reminded him, "Just be patient, Chris."

The priest told us we would dine with him and his family in the evening after our trip, and he gently rose out of his chair, bid us farewell and left the room, his entourage, including Mahmoud, in tow. Chris and I were left alone for some time and waited for Mahmoud to return. Chris turned to me and said in a loud whisper, "You know what this is about don't you? He's gonna flog us some of his oils – that was just his sales pitch!"

I was disappointed at Chris's comments and felt he was perhaps too sceptical to open up and trust. I felt like Chris had slapped me round the face as Abraham's words had lifted me so much and given me such hope. I thought I was about to find out my mission, but Chris seemed irritated by the whole thing, and I felt like he'd rained on my parade and blown our chance to find something of value in Egypt. Sighing, I got up to go and look at the perfume bottles and then Mahmoud walked in. I turned around to face him.

"I knew this was a special day," he said, beaming. His eyes were like dark stars shining at us.

Embarrassed, the saga was continuing, I asked him, "Can we go back to our hotel now, Mahmoud?"

"Of course, Miss Amanda," he said, and he bowed as I walked past him.

I simply smiled at Mahmoud but felt uncomfortable as I didn't want to goad Chris in any way. I politely talked in the car on the frantic journey back to Chris's hotel as we weaved dangerously in and out of cars coming from every direction just like our journey earlier. I was very tired and asked Chris if he minded if I went back to my own hotel to sleep. We agreed to meet later that evening at his hotel and have dinner. I slept all afternoon. Eventually, I showered and changed and got a taxi back to Chris's hotel. Dinner was relaxed and fun as Chris was in his comfort zone again and on form. He certainly wasn't the Chris I'd seen that afternoon, although he did make several jabs at our visit to the priest that afternoon.

"You're not really buying that bullshit are you, Amanda?" he said. "I bet it's just some tourist scam they use on those they think are stupid enough to part with their money. We'll see what they offer us tomorrow. But I'm not buying any of their bloody perfumes or oils, that's for sure."

I just nodded in agreement and didn't dare show my disappointment. We went back to my hotel after dinner to see the entertainment they were laying on that evening. The cocktail lounge had come alive with diners dressed in full evening wear, a pianist playing, a male singer belting out provocative heady Egyptian songs and waiters rushing to and fro attending to the guests. As we walked in, we saw a man sitting directly in the middle of the lounge with several beautiful ladies. He stopped talking and made a point of watching us. We were sitting near his table and as we ordered drinks and sat back, we started to both relax and listen to the music. I became lost in Chris's hypnotic banter as he started to talk about how he felt we had one chance at finding our soul connection and how I made him feel alive. It was a very romantic setting, and the music was heady and sensual. Chris looked like James Bond in his suit and the conversation was starting to draw us both closer to each other. He talked for the first time about us potentially having a relationship, which shocked and excited me all at once. He'd told me repeatedly in the past he'd not been having a romantic relationship with his partner for a few years, but as she suffered from OCD, depression and other conditions, as he was a loyal man, he had no intention of cheating on her. I totally respected that.

That night was extremely difficult as it was obvious how we both felt. The wine was flowing, the music haunting and hypnotic and the conversation had drifted on to us. As he stared at me with his deep brown eyes with the darkest lashes, I knew Chris could feel how attracted I was to him. Our eyes locked and although the room was full of people, noise and movement, our gaze locked us in a private dance of two souls entwined in an energetic moment of sensual and heightened desire. My breathing was shallow, and my heart pounded as he took my hand. I thought I'd melt from the heat of his stare. And then at that moment a man arrived at our table which brought us both abruptly back into the room as if we'd been caught in bed together, totally naked.

Feeling vulnerable and exposed, I coughed and politely apologised. "I'm so sorry, I didn't hear what you said." I had no idea how long he'd been trying to get our attention.

"I'm so sorry to intrude. My name is Abraham! Welcome to Egypt! I saw you earlier at the Marriott with Mahmoud and took the liberty of asking who you were. I hope you don't mind. I'm a businessman dealing with exporting oils. Please, do join us for a drink!"

Chris looked at him curiously and nodded in agreement. I sighed feeling the man had intruded upon an intimate moment we would never get back. We watched Abraham walk back to his table as we gathered our things to join him, and as we got up to walk over and join him and his entourage of female guests, Chris whispered, "Are they all called bloody Abraham here?"

It was only the second person we'd met with that name, but Chris's humour revealed his cynicism and I laughed to appease him. We sat down as more chairs were placed strategically for us to sit close to Abraham, and Chris immediately got straight into talking about business, hoping somehow there'd be money in it for him or some link to help us on our mission. I caught Abraham looking at me in a strange way several times. The conversation was very much focused on finding out what our relationship was, and Chris forthrightly said, "Oh, we're just great friends looking at exploring a few adventures together."

Abraham however, kept digging deeper. It seemed to unnerve Chris as he wasn't comfortable discussing personal stuff in front of strangers. He kept his voice level and steered the conversation back to business. Drink continued to flow and although Chris seemed pretty together, he was getting more and more relaxed and off guard. Again, Abraham questioned our relationship. "So, you two are looking to find your connection together then, are you?"

I decided to make it clear Chris and I were just good friends and said, "Abraham, I'm simply a working single mother with no interest in having relations with any men at this time. Chris and I are out here to meet a colleague and explore historical and spiritual avenues to help us with our journeys back home."

I felt Abraham was digging for a reason and felt uncomfortable. Abraham and Chris stared at me, both grinning. I found it slightly intimidating and frustrating. From then on, Abraham dropped the subject and we continued to enjoy the music and drink (or rather Chris did) and eventually, feeling tired and apprehensive about the next day, I decided to excuse myself and retire for the evening. Abraham stood up and kissed my hand to wish me good night. He looked up at me with my hand in his with a penetrating stare, as if to tell me he was satisfied with the evening's outcome.

"Thank you for your generosity this evening and it was lovely to meet you and your friends," I said.

The women hadn't spoken to me once and had chatted amongst themselves all evening. I assumed they didn't speak English. They nodded politely and said something in Arabic which I acknowledged by nodding. Chris tried to follow suit but was struggling to get up and follow me. He likewise shook hands and thanked everyone at the table and said he had to get back to his hotel. He offered to walk me to my apartment which was some distance away, but I thanked him and said, "I'll manage just fine."

"You're a woman walking back in the dark alone and it's quite a walk to where you're staying, surely."

I insisted I would be fine to walk back alone as I didn't want Abraham to get the wrong idea. "Chris, I'll walk with you to the reception area to get a taxi back to your hotel and then I'll walk back to my room."

Chris seemed to get what I was saying and equally, Abraham appeared placated by my insisting I got Chris back to his hotel. Chris and I then headed for the reception.

"What the hell was that all about?" Chris blurted as soon as we were out of sight. "Anyone would think he was your father the way he carried on! Thought it might have been a bit of business, but he threw me completely in there. What the hell was his game?"

"I have no idea!" I replied, but a familiar feeling washed over me as I remembered where I'd seen him before.

He'd been sitting at the table next to Chris at the Marriott when I'd arrived that morning. Perhaps he'd overheard our conversation. Even so, I had no idea what he was up to and why the focus was on me. I chose not to share my thoughts with Chris and instead told him I was going to my room.

"Not bloody likely!" he said laughing. "You think I'm gonna let you walk back alone with Mr Chancer lurking about! I'll walk you to your room and then I'll come back and get a taxi."

When we were safely out of sight of Abraham and his guests, I turned and started to walk in the direction of my chalet. Chris and I slowed down as we entered the garden and walked unhurriedly. It took what seemed an eternity to walk back and I felt the tension between us mounting once more and wondered if it was just me who felt it.

"How are you feeling?" Chris said. I didn't know how broad his question was, so I simply replied, "Tired but excited about what's to come." I realised as soon as I said it that it had deeper connotations.

"How beautiful these gardens are," said Chris. "I guess you've got the traditional Egypt here as my hotel's geared more for business class."

Every now and then our arms brushed against each other, and electric shocks ran through my body making the ache rage within me. I didn't want the moment to end. I knew in my heart

I was head over heels in love. More than that, I'd loved him for lifetimes. My heart was beating so hard I thought Chris might hear it and as we rounded the last corner just before my apartment, I felt tears well up as I realised we'd never have this time again. We'd fallen silent lost in our own thoughts, both battling to fight the urgency of the moment and as we finally reached my door, we turned to each other. Bathed only in a dull streetlight that was positioned yards away, we looked into each other's eyes.

There was no awkwardness, no fear. It was just us in that moment and we stood there looking deep into each other's eyes until finally the urge was too great and we gave in to our hearts. Chris pulled me into his arms and our lips met, urgently at first as we let the passion take us, and then we slowed our kiss to a deep sensual exploration as sensations coursed through us like magical explosions. We stood for what seemed like hours, gently caressing, and kissing and holding each other, not once stopping for breath, too frightened to let it end in case we never had the chance again.

Finally, we pulled away and stared at one another until Chris whispered, "Can we go inside?" He was breathing deeply, and I desperately wanted him to make love to me, but I knew in my heart we would regret it if we did. I couldn't go through with it.

Without letting him see the tears beginning to well up in my eyes, I looked down and whispered, "Chris, you know we can't no matter how much we want to!" With that he drew me back into his arms and kissed me more deeply than I'd ever been kissed before.

Eventually he walked away. I watched until he was out of sight before going into my room. His smell was all over me as if he was still there and I was still in his arms. I stood for a while trying to put into perspective what had just happened and realised I couldn't. Getting ready for bed, still numb from the sensations I could still feel his touch coursing through my body. That night I cried myself to sleep. I just knew somehow we were meant to meet but never be together. I felt cheated and sad as he'd woken something in me, I hadn't felt since my first love and I knew I might never feel again with anyone else.

The next day I felt heavy and exhausted. I arrived at the Marriott at midday and walked into the coffee lounge expecting Chris to be there waiting for me as planned. After looking around, I realised he was nowhere to be seen. I went to the reception and asked if Chris had left a message for me. The man behind the desk said, "Ah! Miss Amanda, we're terribly sorry, but Mr Chris is not well at all! He's in his room and asked for you to go up when you arrived!"

"Not well?" I said, shocked at this revelation.

"I'm afraid he's been very sick throughout the night and the doctor has just left him," he said, looking concerned.

I found Chris's room and knocked at his door which was on the latch. Before I'd opened it halfway, the smell hit me. I could see Chris curled in a ball on his bed. It looked as if the bedcovers had been involved in a fight and from the doorway, I heard Chris groan from under a pillow. "I'm sorry about the smell but I'm so sick, hon!" he croaked. I could see the room was a complete mess when I entered, with clothes and towels strewn everywhere.

I walked in and sat gently on the bed next to him and asked what had happened. I touched his forehead which was burning, but he winced, complaining everything hurt.

"I don't know!" he said, "I was fine when I left you but as soon as I got into my room last night, I started to feel sick and ever since then I've not been able to get off the toilet!"

He looked dreadful. "What did the doctor say?" I asked.

"Well, he doesn't think it's food poisoning so says it must be a virus and has given me some tablets, but I know I won't keep them down."

"Oh Chris, you poor thing. Look, I'll go down and speak to Mahmoud and cancel the trip today and come up and look after you."

"No," he said quickly. "We've come all this way to do this, and we've only got today to do it. You go and come up and see me when you get back and tell me everything that happens."

"I can't do this without you!" I said, disappointed and a little scared at the idea of going into the unknown with strangers in a foreign country.

"Look, it's bloody obvious Abraham doesn't want me there today, so this is just what they want. It's you that's the chosen one, so go and see them."

"That's not very nice, Chris."

"I wouldn't put it past them to have put some Egyptian curse on me to stop me going today."

"Now that's just ridiculous and childish."

"Well, it's what they used to do – the mummy's curse and all that. What's to say they didn't want me to go, and I was just the scapegoat to get you here? Funny Andrea never made it either, wasn't it?"

"Well, she missed the plane before we even met them," I said, startled.

"That wouldn't stop them, and you know it. That's the whole point of being here because you and I know there's something huge going on that works all of this and there's some agenda going on – and you have to find out what it is."

I looked at him in silence.

"Anyway," he said, a little calmer. "We have to find out how we knew each other in a past life to help us now." He made an attempt to turn in bed to look at me.

"Well, perhaps you should focus more on what's going on in this lifetime and do something about it rather than seek answers to stuff that's gone on before," I said and then walked around the bed. I kissed him on the forehead, asked if he needed anything before, I left, and went to walk away.

He grabbed my hand as I tried to turn. "Amanda?" he said, lifting his head for the first time off the pillow. He looked at me for a long moment while I waited for his response and then he slumped down sighing. "Nothing," he said shaking his head.

I left the room.

As I got down to the ground floor and reached the lobby, I saw Mahmoud, smiling from ear to ear and waiting for me. As we exchanged greetings, he said he was sorry to hear about Mr Chris.

"How did you know?" I asked suspiciously.

"They told me at reception."

I apologised and told him I was ready to go, but I didn't feel ready at all. In fact, I was petrified, but for some reason, something told me to trust, and so I did. And so we set off to prepare me for my apparent awaited return to Egypt. I wondered if Chris was denying what we had between us. How would I ever know? But I knew for sure that I was the strong one out of the two of us.

Chapter 30

I love you not only for what you are, but for what I am
when I am with you. I love you not only for what you
have made of yourself, but for what you are making of
me. I love you for the part of me that you bring out.

Roy Croft

Mahmoud had a way of putting me at ease. He was slight in build but huge in light, laughter, and energy. While we were in the taxi, he chatted enthusiastically about our day together. He seemed genuinely concerned about Chris and reassured me he'd take extra special care of me. I started to relax as we got nearer to Abraham's, feeling perhaps I could do this after all. When we arrived, I saw familiar faces from the day before and Mahmoud jumped out of the car to open my door and guided me into the building.

I felt a pang of disappointment that Chris wasn't there to share the journey with me, but followed Mahmoud into the same room I'd sat before with Chris and took the same seat as he gestured, I wait for Abraham to arrive. I sat thinking about whether Chris and I would ever have the chance to be together until my thoughts were interrupted when Abraham walked in.

This time he was alone and that's when I noticed the room was silent. He greeted me warmly and said he was sorry Chris was unwell and unable to be with us, but I got the distinct impression he wasn't surprised. I pushed it to the back of my mind as he told me what our plans were for the day.

"So Amanda, we will continue without Chris, and you will be anointed with the oils as a ritual of cleansing and purification before Mahmoud will take you on your journey."

"OK, I understand the process, but can you please tell me how much it's going to cost?"

Almost immediately he reeled back saying, "Amanda, I wouldn't dream of asking for money. This is certainly not about money and it's an honour to assist you on your journey today. Please accept this as a gift."

Abraham smiled to reassure me I'd be taken care of. "Don't look so worried. Why don't you go behind the screen and undress to prepare for your massage?" He saw the concern in my eyes and gently smiled at me. "It's OK, Amanda. It is simply a cleansing and blessing ceremony. I will just be anointing your body with oils to prepare you to go into the Great Pyramid."

Chris's voice came screaming back into my head. *Anointing eh, and what else?*

I went around the screen and got undressed. "All my clothes off?" I asked over my shoulder.

"Yes, all!"

I felt uncomfortable at the thought of being totally naked in front of a stranger, but Chris's face kept appearing in my mind and I knew it was his negativity feeding me, so I chose to trust my instincts. I slowly undressed and drew on faith that I was being looked after by The Guys Upstairs.

As I lay on the table with the sheet firmly pulled up to my chin, covering as much of my body as possible, I kept seeing Mahmoud in my mind. I thought nothing untoward could possibly happen to me as too many people were involved with encouraging my initiation. Abraham wouldn't want to risk his credibility. I also thought of Chris back at the hotel. Even though he was ill, I knew he wouldn't allow any harm to come to me. He wouldn't have let me go alone knowing what I was to face – or would he? That I was less sure of.

I had my eyes screwed tightly shut. Eventually, I heard Abraham appear quietly and the chinking of delicate glass on metal trays. He started to mumble in Arabic and began to massage my head and face. I had a momentary feeling of reassurance it was going to be all right, followed by a deeper and overwhelming sense of relaxation, which I tried to resist but couldn't. Abraham massaged my entire body, and I mean my entire body, and it felt very natural, although I'd never experienced a massage like it. When he'd finally finished, the smell of the oils was incredibly intoxicating. I felt as if they'd been absorbed into every part of my being. He left me to dress and told me to sit back in the main room when I was ready. When I appeared, he was waiting for me and so was freshly poured tea.

"You are now ready, Amanda," he said. "Mahmoud knows what to do and we've arranged for you to visit the Great Pyramid and some of the tombs today which are strictly forbidden for public access. Drink your tea and rest a while and enjoy! I hope you find what you came here for!"

And with that he got up, bowed, and graciously left the room. I sat in quiet contemplation going over the experience I'd just had. It wasn't my nakedness that concerned me, it was the sensations I'd experienced whilst having the massage. I was tingling in several areas of my body, but the weirdest sensation was a shooting of energy, rushing up and down my arms and legs. I sat drinking my tea, but by the time I'd finished the feeling had subsided. In its place, I had a feeling of calm relaxation and incredible openness along with readiness for what was to come. Mahmoud came into the room just as I was finishing my tea and his sparkling eyes and eager grin made him look like an innocent child full of adventurous spirit. His over-sized suit looked odd as he seemed so childlike, but he said to me in a sure adult way, "You've gone through a kundalini awakening to stir up all your body's energy centres so you can fully participate in this whole experience on a deep spiritual level."

I certainly felt dynamically alive. When I was ready, he ushered me to his car and drove me directly to the Great Pyramid. The first time I saw it I was shocked to see we were on the periphery of Cairo. From the dusty, dirty, hectic, bustling streets full of noise and commotion we drove up a slight incline and parked. There, bearing down on us, was the Great Pyramid itself. As we got out of the car and walked towards a man in a kiosk, I saw Mahmoud pay and talk quietly into his ear, so as not to let the other men who were hanging around smoking and talking near him, hear. They were all staring at me – not unexpectedly, as I was a British female alone with an Egyptian guide.

I felt safe with Mahmoud and had a surge of confidence within me since the cleansing earlier. I felt more in awe of my surroundings. First, he took me to the foot of the Great Pyramid, which had a power beyond what I'd ever experienced and was swarming with tourists taking photographs and walking around and marvelling at it. Mahmoud walked me round the perimeter of the pyramid and batted off the many locals who approached me. They bowed and let us pass. As we circled the Great Pyramid, he pointed to the other two pyramids which he claimed were not significant to my journey. At one point, he asked me to stand and wait for him whilst he walked towards a crowd of people milling about around the base of the pyramid and approached a man and whispered into his ear. The man turned and looked at me and nodded. Mahmoud then walked towards me and beckoned for me to go to him and as I approached, he said, "It's all taken care of. Come with me!"

We headed for the entrance into the pyramid itself which wasn't visible at first. We climbed some steps until we got to what seemed like a ledge and found a group of backpackers waiting in a line to go in. We were told to wait and wait we did. Eventually, the doorkeeper beckoned us, saying, "Come!"

Mahmoud eagerly told me, "The Great Pyramid of Giza is the largest, heaviest and oldest, most perfect building ever created." He then encouraged me to walk up the carefully carved stairs, about twenty feet, until we came to an entrance. Mahmoud continued "This was created in 820 CE by a young man named Abdullah Al-Mamun. It isn't the original entrance."

As we entered the shaft we arrived through the well-lit passage and came out to a staircase. Mahmoud encouraged me to start the climb. It was approximately three hundred feet high and the higher we climbed, the less air there was to breathe, or perhaps we were just becoming lighter. I had no idea. We stopped a few times to rest, but I dared not look down. A strange sense of being there before washed over me, but I shook my thoughts away and carried on up the massive climb, not daring to stop as I knew Chris was relying on me to find answers.

We got to a certain point and Mahmoud said, "We've got to the Queen's Chamber, but we need to ascend to the King's Chamber."

I realised eventually no-one was following us, nor had we passed anyone coming down. We were alone. Finally we got to the top and before us was a wall with a very small opening. It was as if a large brick had been taken out to create an entrance, but the thought of passing through it made me fearful with claustrophobia.

"That's the King's Chamber ahead but we have to pass through the antechamber," Mahmoud reassured me, and he scurried through the hole, waving me to follow.

Feeling exhausted and elated, I followed him through the horizontal passage with my eyes closed, praying for protection as I felt giddy with fear. Feeling claustrophobic, I crouched down and crawled through the passage before entering the King's Chamber.

Mahmoud said, "Miss Amanda, the King's Chamber is seventeen feet wide, nineteen feet high and thirty-four feet long. The walls and ceiling are made of red polished granite, made up of nine slabs weighing an astronomical amount."

I hardly listened as I felt the awesome power of the tomb. Once inside I could see the sarcophagus, carved out of a single block of granite which stood alone at one end together with a slab resting to one side and a rock. Mahmoud let me explore then announced, "These are to do with rituals. Two vent holes on the north and south side emit fresh air and keep the room an even sixty-eight degrees throughout the whole year."

I was still only half listening.

"OK," I said with trepidation and followed him up to the tomb laid out at one end of the room.

Standing in the King's Chamber I felt welcome relief at being upright and stable in a tall room with the apex of the pyramid above us. There were several tourists inside, some walking about, some sitting in quiet contemplation, others praying. As I walked around the room, I noted the huge blocks that made up the fabric of the colossal structure. I approached the sarcophagus and felt a strange sensation stirring in my body. A vortex of energy passed through me suddenly and I turned around to see what had caused it. As I looked up, I saw I'd been standing under the apex of the pyramid. I walked away and felt it ease off and when I returned to the same spot, I felt the same sensation build yet again. It made me feel very light-headed and I made my way to a wall and sat down to get my bearings. I leant my back against the cold granite.

As I closed my eyes, I saw images flash into my mind. I saw myself dressed in white with other women. I had very long dark brown hair and very colourful make up in gold and turquoise. We were holding flaming torches and walking towards the pyramid at night. We were chanting something and were engaged in a ceremony, walking slowly but in time with each other to the rhythm of our chants. We were heading into the pyramid.

I came to when Mahmoud said, "Miss Amanda, come with me."

I got up slowly and he led me to the tomb at one end of the room and Mahmoud said, "Let me show you the resting place for the king, Miss Amanda."

He gestured I should lie in it. As I looked around, I was surprised no-one else was in the room. Where had I been when all those people had disappeared? I did what he asked, hesitantly, but when I lay back, the same sensation returned. Furthermore I felt a deep undying love for someone. I could feel deep sadness and regret, but also a feeling of great strength and power. The energy vortex was evident again and the vision of me in white, standing, looking out of a palace window was strong. Fear started to creep in as I wondered if I'd been drugged, but I knew that wasn't possible. I opened my eyes and Mahmoud was staring down at me, tears pouring down his face. I jumped up a little too quickly and felt dizzy. "What's wrong?" I asked Mahmoud, feeling his sorrow.

"It is nothing, Miss Amanda. It is just I am overwhelmed."

"Mahmoud, is it all right if we go now? I'm feeling very strange."

As we started our descent, I realised there wasn't even anyone on the stairs; the pyramid had been emptied of all souls. Eventually we got to the Queen's Chamber. The feelings were not as strong there, but I wanted to get away as the claustrophobia was getting too much. I had the feeling in there of something much colder and was anxious to leave. When we reached the bottom, we turned a corner and Mahmoud opened a locked gate and encouraged me to go down the steps. I took two steps but couldn't go any further. Overwhelming fear hit me, and I looked back up at him for reassurance.

"It's OK, Miss Amanda. No-one is allowed down here but you may go."

"No thank you, Mahmoud. I don't want to."

Something evil seemed to lurk down there and flashes of re-occurring dreams I'd had when I was a child came into my head. I had been in part of a huge ceremony taking place in what looked like a huge cave or building made out of stone. There was a large hole in the centre and an altar. People all around were taking part in a ritual. They were singing and chanting, and I was hanging over the edge of the hole, holding onto the edge for dear life. The hole was huge, circular, and ablaze with a fire as if from the centre of the earth. In my dream either my father or mother was holding one of my hands and I was screaming for them to save me. On each occasion, they tried their hardest to pull me out of the hole but there was always someone there trying to distract them. The other force won, and they lost their grip. I started to fall down into the pit – at that point I'd always wake up.

As Mahmoud and I returned to the entrance of the pyramid and walked out into the blazing sun, the heat and light hit us. People were queuing and as we left the man at the door started to usher them in. We found a quiet place in the shade and drank water. Men on camels sidled up to us and peered down at me quizzically and tourists were scattered all over, some at the base of the pyramid and others dotted around some of the tombs which poked out from the uneven and barren ground.

Mahmoud gestured towards the tomb we were to go to next. A guard sat next to it and Mahmoud spoke to him, gesturing towards the tomb itself. The man got up instantly and unpadlocked the gate for us. The tomb felt lighter and not as intimidating as the pyramid, and as we walked down the steps, we came upon a wall ornately painted with images of pharaohs. I felt compelled to kneel in prayer. As I closed my eyes, I heard Mahmoud start to chant. I joined in. I had no idea how I knew what to do, but it was something I knew very well and the harmonics between us built and built until the whole tomb was filled with electrifying energy sending a pulsing vibration through me combined with a sense of great contentment and joy as we both made the most beautiful sound in harmony together.

We stopped at the same moment and, as silence fell, the chamber echoed our vibration which was still reverberating off the walls and through our bodies. I opened my eyes and somehow the images drawn on the walls felt very familiar to me as if they were family. I felt I missed them and was somehow paying homage to them. As I eventually got up to leave, I bowed to the figures on the wall and Mahmoud did too.

As we walked out into the sun, Mahmoud turned to me, bowed, and said, "Welcome back my queen!" I didn't know if he was going to laugh or cry. "Welcome back to your homeland. We have been waiting for you!"

I stared at him.

"This is your third time here and this time your people are looking to you to do the right thing!"

I couldn't find the words to ask what he meant.

Chapter 31

Love is our true destiny. We do not find the meaning of
life by ourselves alone – we find it with another.

Thomas Merton

Mahmoud dropped me off at Chris's hotel. He thrust a huge chunk of clear quartz crystal into my hands, asked me to keep it with me always and gave me a huge hug before disappearing off out into the fading daylight and overwhelming heat. I stood for a while staring after him, trying to gather my thoughts. I went over to the gentleman behind the desk and, before I could speak, he politely pointed towards the lounge saying, "Mr Chris is feeling much better now, Miss Amanda." I looked where he was pointing and saw Chris quietly reading.

I thanked him and walked towards the lounge, which was filled mostly with businessmen having refreshments. I imagined many of them wouldn't even contemplate visiting the pyramids. I walked towards Chris who was sitting in a corner, obviously still unwell as he sat almost hunched over a paperback on a soft chair. All I could see was a glass of water in front of him on the coffee table. As I approached, he looked up at me. His usual deep brown eyes were murky and sad, his face aged with what he'd been through for the past twelve hours, and his body weakened from his experience. This was not the Chris I knew, and my heart went out to him.

"So you're back then?" he asked with what sounded like resentment. I smiled as I didn't want him to hurt me.

"Yes, Mahmoud's just dropped me off," I said and as I slumped down in the chair opposite, an attentive waiter came over to offer us drinks. I ordered a coffee but could have done with something stronger. Chris shook his head at the waiter and pointed at his untouched glass of water. Then I told him everything, only pausing when the waiter brought over my coffee.

When I'd finished, he quietly asked, "Did you see anything to do with us today?"

That's when it dawned on me that the trip had been to satisfy his curiosity about any connection between us in a past life. I wanted to find out our missions too, but felt if he was only focused on his own emotional needs, it wouldn't serve anyone and he would get nowhere.

"No, Chris. I saw images of myself at the pyramids in some kind of ceremony and then I remembered the dreams I had as a child. I then felt they were to do with something here, but apart from that I had no feelings in connection to you except for—" I broke off, realising I'd gone just a little too far.

"What?" he demanded, as he sat forward on his chair, wincing at the pain.

"Well, it's nothing really, and I think perhaps my mind has gone a little haywire," I replied.

"No, go on!"

"Well, when I first met you, I had a dream about you. I had it again just before I came out to Egypt. The thing is...well, the thing is, I had no idea back then we'd be coming here so it seemed a bit odd at the time."

"Just spit it out, will you?" he said impatiently.

I frowned at him. "It may sound a little bizarre, but I had this dream twice and on both occasions, it seemed so real. I was Cleopatra and you were Mark Antony. In the dream, we were in love and promising to be together forever. There was trouble though and a war was going on around us, and I woke up when we both died."

"Is that it?" he said with obvious disappointment. He smirked at me. A little upset, I shrugged off his rebuff.

"I did see myself today as her again and when Mahmoud referred to me as 'my Queen' she came into my head."

"So you're telling me I'm Mark Antony?" he asked in disbelief.

"No Chris, you were!" I said, feeling trapped into explaining what I'd been shown. I sighed. "The coincidences match up. Your surname sounds almost like Antony, and I named my son Anthony. When I was born, my mother named me after Amanda Barrie, the actress who played Cleopatra. My grandfather was involved in a mission which took him to Alexandria during the Second World War and was stationed in Egypt for four years. Cleopatra lived in Alexandria. Mark Antony gave Cyprus to

Cleopatra and Michael, my second husband, comes from Cyprus."

"If that's the case then, why are we together and what did Mahmoud mean about doing the right thing this time? I don't understand it. Where do we go from here?" he asked me.

Mahmoud came into my mind and his light felt so refreshing, his energy so alive and loving. Chris had been showing a much darker and sceptical side to himself which I realised I needed to see for some reason. I felt his selfishness poisoned my deep connection to him and I observed what was going on from a higher perspective.

"I need to go back to my room," Chris said.

I nodded and said I'd look in on him later.

"I'll call you on the mobile," he shouted over his shoulder as he left the lounge.

Once he'd gone, I sat a while and tried to work out what I was supposed to understand due to what I'd experienced in Egypt. So many people had said I was about to embark on something that would help others. I'd received information from people telling me it was linked to past lives and the one person I wanted to honour and adore was displaying disdain for what I'd gone through.

As the sun shone through the window, I let the rays warm my body and drifted into a daydream. An image of Chris and I came into my mind. I was dressed in white and in a room that was exquisitely dressed in colourful silks and gold. The smell of oils stung my nose, and I noticed cushions and ornate furniture, fruits in bowls and beautiful curtains that hung like waterfalls. As Chris walked in (Mark Antony,) I ushered several ladies (also dressed in white) out of the room. Chris had arrived in a rage and accused me of playing games with him. I just smiled at him.

"Mark Antony, I have always pledged allegiance to you, and it is you that needs to look at your motivations towards our union. It is I that give unconditionally, and you who seeks a power that will ultimately destroy everything you yearn for."

I was amused by his reaction. I had an awareness he certainly couldn't tap into and he was not happy about that power I had over him. Not only did I have great wealth, he could not resist me. I had a sexual power over him that he was entranced by but was also aggrieved by as it made him feel weak.

He said, "I want you Cleopatra, but your power is hypnotic, and I have no defence."

"You need no army with me Mark Antony, only trust."

When he finally calmed down, I seduced him by showing him how opening to me it reminded him of a power beyond what he'd known before he'd met me. Then instantly the image disappeared, and a voice said, *This is why he resents you. Egypt has brought back many fears, and this is why he's fallen so sick. All will be well, but you must understand he can't see like you do!*

I threw open my eyes and looked around me to see if I'd spoken aloud or if someone in the room was talking to me. The room hadn't changed. People were still drinking their coffees, oblivious to me in the corner, so I guessed it must have all happened in my head. I accepted what I'd seen, said my thank you to The Guys Upstairs and headed back to my hotel.

Later that evening, Chris called me. "I'm so sorry, Amanda for leaving so abruptly earlier, but I felt unwell again and had to get back to my room quickly. I do feel better though and after another night's sleep I'll probably be OK to do something on our last day together."

But I knew he'd missed the boat. I wished him a good night and soon after the call, drifted into a deep sleep. During the night, I saw myself once again distressed, crying over Mark Antony who was lying in my arms, clenching his stomach in pain. He was dying. I was frightened of losing him, as I knew I would die too. He faded away in my arms, I screamed out his name, and then I woke feeling utterly bereft at my loss. The room was dark and silent, but the dream rang out in my ears as my screams echoed within me. My heart was pumping madly, and my panic-stricken body was ready to leap out of bed. The dream had been so real. My first reaction was to call Chris to see if he was OK, but it was midnight, and I knew I wouldn't be thanked if I woke him. I tried to go back to sleep but the images seemed so tangible. After reading and listening to music, I finally fell into a dreamless sleep.

The next day I went to the Marriott and waited for Chris in the lounge. When he appeared, he still looked awful. "Do you fancy going to see the Sphinx today?" he asked.

"OK."

"I'm still feeling rough but want to do something today. I had a bad night last night though. I dreamed I was dying and kept waking up."

I tried to gently prompt him to tell me what he'd dreamed but he was reluctant to share his dream with me, shrugging his shoulders and saying, "It just wasn't pleasant."

We were due to fly back later that day, so I knew we'd have to get a move on to do any sightseeing. At that point, I got my first text from Andrea. *Hi guys, sorry not to have been in touch. Having a whale of a time. Met a nice man called Abraham at my hotel who's into oils and he's been showing me round. Ended up in Sharm El Sheikh so staying a few extra days. See you when I get back. Andrea.*

I read it out to Chris who laughed out loud. "Oh my God, he's got his clutches into her now, eh? Well they deserve each other."

I asked him why he was so bitter about Abraham, and he said, "Well he's obviously an opportunist, trawling the hotels for potentially wealthy tourists. He's probably paying the hotel staff for information. How the bloody hell did he manage to find Andrea?"

I texted back. *Hi Andrea, have you managed to see any of the sights in Cairo?* But she was obviously struck more with the supposed wealthy businessman and replied, *I'm getting to see much more than I bargained for.*

I told Chris it could be any Abraham. Chris said, "You may think my intuition is limited, Amanda, but I know damn well that it's the guy we met at your hotel, and you know it too."

I didn't reply but I felt the same. In the taxi on our way to the Sphinx, I couldn't help but feel that both Andrea and Chris had been diverted whilst I had been shown so much. When we arrived, Mahmoud showed us where to walk for the best view. As we started to walk towards the huge statue, a man dressed in traditional robes ran towards me, unnerving me at first until I saw Mahmoud walk towards us. The man was saying something I did not understand and trying to give me something.

"Don't worry, Miss Amanda. He's trying to give you a turquoise scarab beetle. It's for protection. Please take it. He wants you to have it."

I thanked the man and Mahmoud for his intervention.

"Keep it with you as you'll need it," Mahmoud said.

We walked down towards the Sphinx with the man and Mahmoud behind us, chatting in Arabic. When we arrived, the crowd was five people deep and we struggled to get up close. Chris looked as if it didn't bother him at all to be standing in front of one of the Seven Wonders of the World. I felt disappointed by his lack of enthusiasm. The Sphinx looked far smaller than I remembered it appearing on TV, but when I managed to get a good focal point and relax, I had sudden images flash in my mind of it standing over me, lit up at night with torches, and again I saw a ceremony taking place. The Sphinx in my vision was more defined than it was in person that day. Its carved features stood out more in the image in my mind and it looked more ominous than it did in front of me at that moment there with Chris. After our visit, we went back to the hotel. Chris was disappointed nothing had come to him and no one had approached him.

He hardly spoke and was lost in thought. This quashed my feelings towards him, so I found it easier to get through the day knowing we were soon to depart for home. It wasn't until we got to the airport that he finally asked if he could rest his head on me and that was when all the familiar feelings came flooding back.

"I'm sorry, Amanda," he said, with his head resting on my shoulder as if to hide his face and his true feelings. "I've just felt so bad these past few days and still do. I don't know what's happening to me. I honestly thought I was going to die. I've never been that ill and, apart from that, we never even got to see what we came here for either. Perhaps we'll find the answers somewhere else. I hope to God we do."

I felt he was being totally open and honest with me. I knew it was a big thing to let his guard down. Chris slept on me most of the way home. I watched over him as tears poured down my face and I recalled the strong feelings I'd had in my dream of him dying in my arms. When we finally got to the UK, I felt a wrench as he left me and I went home, the only comfort being the thought of seeing my beautiful children. That night when I got home and after speaking to them on the phone and Mum too (who'd had them whilst I was away), I rushed to get the computer fired up.

Once on the internet, I started to do some research into Antony and Cleopatra. My stomach lurched as if I'd been struck by a thunderbolt when I read about how Antony had gone to Cleopatra and died in her arms from trying to do the honourable thing and that he'd fallen on his sword to commit suicide. Cleopatra had committed suicide shortly after. There were so many coincidences. I knew I had to find answers.

Chapter 32

Everything that happens to you is a reflection of what you believe about yourself. We cannot outperform our level of self-esteem. We cannot draw to ourselves more than we think we are worth.

Iyanla Vanzant

The next morning I drove over to see Mum and the children. When I arrived, the kids screamed with delight, jumping up and down, which made my heart melt. We had cuddles galore and I held onto them both tightly.

Mum was looking tired and said she missed Grandma, who'd now been dead almost nine years. To soothe her I said I'd do a reading and see if Grandma had a message for her. Sure enough, the reading had a poignant and reassuring message for both Mum and I, although it brought a tear to our eyes. As I finished the reading and switched my mobile phone back on, I got a text message from a number I didn't recognise. At first, I couldn't make head nor tail of the message. *Searching for answers with Chris recently is a dangerous path to travel. Be warned. We are watching you and see everything. Archangel Michael won't save you!* A wave of nausea flooded my stomach. More worryingly, the reading I'd given to Mum only moments before had included a message that Archangel Michael would protect us. Open-mouthed, I showed Mum.

I shook my head in disbelief and said, "All I can do is call to see who it's from." I instantly phoned the number logged in my phone. Of course, there was no reply. The text implied this person had witnessed the reading that had just taken place and also knew of my trip to Egypt with Chris. Someone had to be watching me. Mum and I were in the kitchen at her house and the curtains were closed. I felt mounting fear. The only person I knew who could help me was Tom, so I called him and explained what had happened. He was calm but firm and told me to go home, pack a small bag and leave the area. I asked him why and he simply replied, "You're getting a warning!"

"A warning about what?" I asked, scared.

"You need to get away and work out what they're telling you."

I was starting to get agitated by then and so was Mum who was standing next to me and could see how concerned I was.

"Just go home, pack a bag and leave and get to a hotel somewhere and call me from there!" Tom said.

When I told Mum what Tom had said to me, she hugged me looking extremely worried. She kept looking at the text message on my phone and said, "But, Amanda, I don't understand how someone has seen what was going on in our kitchen tonight. And why are you being warned about Egypt and Chris? I don't know what the hell is going on, but you need to go."

It was the school holidays, and the children were happy enough staying with Grandma and Grandpa. "The children are fine with us so why disturb them?" Mum said.

I hugged my children longer than usual before I left. They ran off squealing with delight at the thought of staying extra sleeps at their grandparents. Deep inside, my fear returned. Fear I might never see them again and fear of going off alone into the unknown.

"You keep in contact with me this time, Amanda, and tell me what's going on, sweetheart," Mum said. I hugged her and left.

I went home immediately, packed a bag, and got out as soon as I could. It felt cold and ominous in my house, and I didn't want to hang about to find out why. I ended up at the hotel I'd stayed at before I ended up in Australia. I was tired as it was about two in the morning. I phoned Tom as soon as I arrived, and he answered straight away. He said I was being watched and needed to take the challenge on and show no fear.

"Who the bloody hell's watching me?" I asked, petrified.

"The dark side of course, Amanda! You don't think they're going to let you get on with your mission without trying to stop you, do you?"

He told me to stay calm as I had to stay tuned in to receive my guidance from The Guys Upstairs and I should simply feel where I needed to go.

"I have no idea what to do, but I feel I have to go to Glastonbury for some reason."

"Amanda, just sleep as you'll need all your strength to go through the next part of your journey."

I found it hard to sleep that night as I felt vulnerable, scared, and fearful of the unknown. I left early the next day and drove down to Glastonbury and, immediately on arrival, I went to see Chris who owned one of the crystal shops and we talked about my experience.

I had struck up a connection with Chris whenever visiting Glastonbury before. He seemed to be the anchor of light that was holding that community grounded, as there was such an array of light and darkness among the people. He'd welcomed me like an old friend each time I visited and, on this occasion, his eyes lit up and said he had a feeling I would return. I told him I felt a deep sadness. Chris explained a deep grieving process was taking place with everyone as someone very well known in the area had gone on a spiritual quest recently and had only made it to the third day before committing suicide. The town certainly felt very sombre, and I felt that was perhaps what I was feeling, but I didn't understand the connection immediately.

"Amanda, you've obviously been sent down here to take over that obligation and take on the spiritual quest yourself."

I had no idea what he was on about and was feeling overwhelmed and panicked by the thought of my spiritual duties. I knew though if he was right, I'd get confirmation from The Guys Upstairs, so I chose to be open to what he was saying. Instantly I felt The Guys urging me to pay attention to Chris.

"OK, so where do I start and what do I do?" I asked.

"Well, firstly I suggest you find somewhere to stay as this will take time."

I realised whatever was going on, would certainly not be revealed, or resolved overnight. I did a bit of asking around and found a room in a nice house just on the outskirts of town. As I was unpacking, I started to get a very strong feeling about an author of a book Tom had once recommended to me. His name was Palden Jenkins, and his book was called *The Only Planet of Choice*. It comprised a series of channellings transcribed by Palden. Tom had told me it would give me an understanding of who or what was communicating with me. Although the book was extremely radical, it fitted in with what I was getting. The channel was a woman called Phyllis V Schlemmer and the transcripts had been transmitted over a period of over twenty years. I was struck by the fact three people involved in the book were members of a research group Tom had looked into when he was working for the MOD. They'd worked with Phyllis on the book and included Star Trek's creator Gene Roddenberry, former British racing driver Sir John Whitmore and British Olympic hurdler David Hemery.

I knew Palden was the first person I had to find. I went into Glastonbury and located a copy of his book. There in black and white was his address. Incredibly, he lived in Glastonbury. Finding his house was easier than I thought it would be. Knocking on his door, I started to worry he would think I was a spiritual junkie who had lost her way, but the woman who answered, warmly invited me into their home. The house seemed to be in chaos but when I looked deeper, I realised it was an incredibly rustic and natural living space, which was obviously well-loved and lived in. Two children sat in the kitchen eating and drawing and the lady asked me to wait whilst she fetched Palden.

When he arrived to greet me, he looked at me questioningly. I simply said, "Hello, Palden. My name's Amanda and I know this may sound strange, but I knew I had to come and find you."

He nodded, looking at me intensely and said, "Fine. Why don't you follow me to my study?"

His study was at the top of the house, and we climbed the narrow stairs. Everywhere I looked there were piles of books, toys, and boxes. His study was even more over-filled with books and papers everywhere. He asked me to sit down and sat himself at his desk, swivelling his chair to face me.

"So, what is it you've come to see me about?" he asked.

I told him how I'd ended up in Glastonbury.

"I don't quite know what it is you've come to find out from me or how to help you. Perhaps you need to find another source."

I felt disappointed and sighed, saying inwardly, *Thanks Guys!*" feeling they'd led me on a wild goose chase. I thanked Palden and got up to go. As I was walking towards the door, he asked me, "So who sent you down to Glastonbury then."

"The Guys Upstairs of course."

That's when he stopped me. He told me to come back in and sit down.

"Amanda, that was the answer I needed to hear to know you passed the test. I apologise, but in my line of work I have to be careful."

It was refreshing to talk to someone who didn't think I was a complete nutcase and understood why I was there. He told me apart from being an author, editor and humanitarian involved in many projects, he was also involved in international relations and spiritual-political issues. He went on to say his current project was in relation to Atlantis and the Bermuda Triangle, which he was involved with on behalf of governments. He gave me a brief outline but didn't go into detail.

"So do you know what role I've got to play with regard to my mission?" I asked.

"You know perfectly well by now it's on a need-to-know basis," he said.

"I've got children to think of though, Palden. I need to know what I'm doing so I can plan for them!"

"You've been told already all that's been taken care of. You therefore have to trust implicitly and follow your guidance. It's all about building trust and most importantly, patience."

I nodded and looked down as I resigned myself to the fact I was only ever going to get my information through The Guys.

Palden then said, "You're down here now on a spiritual quest. This is your first step and you and you alone have to work out the clues to get to where you need to be."

When I finally left, I stood outside his house on the pavement and shrugged my shoulders. I knew I could be in Glastonbury for some time and felt rising panic as I thought about my children. Immediately, I felt The Guys kick in and say, *Just relax Amanda, and get on with the job in hand as it will all work out perfectly if you follow your guidance.*

"So what's the alternative then if I fail?"

There are no alternatives, Amanda."

No pressure then, I thought.

I called Mum. At first, she was OK about it, but she was concerned. I had to reassure her. The children were fine when I spoke to them and loved the fact they had more time at Grandma's, so I knew all was well with them, just like The Guys had assured me it would be. I went back to my room feeling completely exhausted and fell asleep on the bed fully clothed. I woke up when I heard my mobile ringing. It was Chris saying he needed to see me.

"Chris, I'm away for a few days down in Glastonbury doing some research. Can't this wait until I get back?"

"I'll come down to see you there then."

"But I'm working and need to stay focused."

"Well that's perfect then. I'll just come down for the day and it'll give us a chance to find out for sure what our connection is. I promise I'll go once I've seen you and let you get on with your work."

I sighed and agreed feeling actually it would be nice to see him as I felt so alone. One day out wouldn't do any harm. The next morning we met at nine on the outskirts of Glastonbury. There was an incredibly thick mist hanging like a cloak over the place. Chris told me he couldn't get it out of his head and needed to find resolution to our connection. Sitting in his car looking into his eyes, I felt what I'd felt the night outside my chalet in Egypt and so wanted him to kiss me, but I held my emotions in check.

"So come on then, Amanda. Where shall we start? It's got to be here we'll find something considering it's supposed to be spiritual and all that. Why don't we start at the Abbey?"

It was as good a place as any. I'd never visited the Abbey myself, anyhow. When we arrived, we were the only people there. Chris started to behave oddly shortly after we'd entered the ruins. He took my hand and insisted I went and sat down with him on a bench. As we sat, he pulled me to him urgently and said, "Amanda, I can't hold back anymore. You have no idea how much I want you. You're constantly in my head and I need to deal with this."

"Chris, this is a religious site. What are you doing?" I said feeling awkward, trying to peel away from his arms.

"I can't help it anymore, I can't get you from under my skin," he said, and with that he drew me in and kissed me deeply. My head began to spin, and he pulled me onto his lap so I was facing him, and he could kiss me more deeply. I felt myself melt into his soul as I opened up and let him feel how I felt too. Eventually when I pulled away from him, I stood up and said, "Chris, we have to be sensible. You still have a partner even if you're not with her emotionally. And besides, we have to get on if we're going to find anything that will help us."

He nodded and as he stood up, he looked at me excitedly and said in a very sure voice, "It's here! This is where we've been before. I can feel it, Amanda."

In that instant I could feel something deep inside pull me to him. Holding hands we walked around looking at the plaques until eventually we came to one that read, *Site of King Arthur's tomb*. We stood with our mouths open.

"Do you suppose I was Arthur, and you were Guinevere?" asked Chris.

I suggested we did some research. Going back into the bookshop, now full of tourists, we leafed through the numerous books on the subject to find answers and bought one. Over lunch, Chris talked enthusiastically about the feasibility of us having been Arthur and Guinevere in a previous existence. We looked through the book and eagerly trawled through the history. Chris certainly had the capabilities of a leader in his own right in this lifetime so it could be a possibility, but Guinevere had an affair with Lancelot, and when I pointed that out, Chris responded immediately.

"Perhaps that explains why I feel so insecure with you even though I want you so much," he said.

I was confused. I'd thought Cleopatra and Mark Antony were who Chris and I had been in a past life. Now Chris was urging us to explore Arthur and Guinevere. It was just at that point that Chris found a mention of how many people had felt Arthur and Guinevere were souls reincarnated from Antony and Cleopatra that it dawned on us we could be souls from many lifetimes. The book suggested Arthur was tested with Guinevere, because in their previous incarnation, they'd been twin souls and he couldn't get over her betrayal with Lancelot.

We did some more research on the internet and found information that suggested each of us has a divine other, a twin flame who has either the feminine or masculine polarity. The soul memory is so powerful it can make us feel lonely and driven to find that original flawless love, the twin flame. As we trawled through as much information as we could find, we discovered that twin flames were comparable to no other love such as Cleopatra and Mark Antony and Samson and Delilah. Chris highlighted some text he found that suggested darkness runs rampant on earth, working to sabotage twin flames and keep them apart. As they don't have enough self-mastery to maintain a healthy relationship, they seek the next best thing which is a soul mate.

Chris and I looked at each other wondering if that was why we found it so difficult to be together yet so connected. Soul mates, we found out, make happy marriages as they're working on similar soul initiations, life lessons and projects in this life. I was shocked to read soul mates have been friends for lifetimes and need each other to satisfy or complete a mission. I so wanted

Chris to be my soul mate, but I knew without any doubt that he was my twin flame.

Chris and I looked at each other. "We have to have a reading this afternoon and find out what's going to happen to us once and for all," he blurted.

So off we went in search of a medium. We started out by walking down the high street looking for what we felt would draw us to the right person. We came across a board outside a house advertising a woman who did tarot readings, and we just knew she was the one for us. Her house was very gothic looking and dimly lit with large candelabras, dark velvet fabrics draped here and there, and large paintings and ornaments of dragons and lions. We walked up three flights of stairs until we reached a largish room lit by candles. The room contained several comfy armchairs scattered sporadically, and she guided us to sit in front of a large circular table which was filled with crystals and dragons, cards, and other spiritual symbolic talismans. Chris asked if the reading would be taped.

"Of course!" she replied. "So you are twin flames looking to find your connection to each other and why you've been brought together in this lifetime. Chris, you've come into Amanda's life to help her with her mission. You are here to help her on her journey. Amanda, I see many helpers who will assist you along the way. Chris will of course help you the most, but he is simply to assist and even though you have a deep connection with each other, you are not meant to be together as lovers in this lifetime."

We were astounded by her revelations as she continued. "Even though you've found each other you will eventually understand why you cannot be together in partnership. Amanda, it is an incredibly busy time for you, and although you have much work to do, you will meet men along the way who will help you, but they will likewise not stay with you. You have to achieve your mission and as you draw nearer to when that happens, you will eventually meet your soul companion. Then you will be rewarded. This will not be for many years as there is much work ahead. Both of you have come together to awaken that deep love that eventually you will be able to feel when the time is right for your true companions."

Chris hung his head and I felt like I'd loved and lost all over again. Dispirited, we went to have something to eat before he left, but the mood was very sombre. I wished we hadn't gone to see the medium. I had to resign myself to our kiss at the Abbey that afternoon probably being our last. Chris left after we'd held each other for what seemed like an eternity, and he then simply got into his car and drove away. I felt angry at the universe for toying with me, but I knew deep down The Guys Upstairs would not put me through situations needlessly. I knew I had to find out for myself why I'd learned to love and then had to let go yet again.

The next day, I woke feeling very low. Even though I had no plans as to where I was heading that day, I had a vision of the Tor come into my head and felt relieved as it was remote, and I didn't want to see anyone if I could help it. After breakfast, I set off with refreshments in case I'd be there for some time. I'd read in a guidebook that people were drawn to the Tor from far and wide, and when I got to the bottom I could see why. It just invited you to climb to the top.

It was a conical shaped hill that rose about five hundred feet. I started to follow what seemed to be a series of paths that climbed upward like a huge maze, with occasional plateaus. It took almost three hours until I finally reached the top, and during that journey I went through some huge soul searching. I looked out across the Somerset countryside. It was a foggy day, so visibility was minimal. I sat and ate while contemplating how my life was changing so radically. I'd read in the guidebook that on a good day from the top of the Tor you could see the Mendip Hills together with the city of Wells and its cathedral. To the west you could see the island of Steep Holm in the Bristol Channel. Brent Knoll could be seen facing the northwest and the Polden and Quantock Hills to the southwest. The Black Mountains of Wales could be seen in the far distance, the Hood Monument and Dorset to the south and to the east Alfred's Tower on the borders of Wiltshire and Cley Hill, famous for UFO sightings. Eventually, as the weather changed, and the wind got up and the rain started coming down, I ventured down the paths that brought me back to the gate where I'd started six and a half hours previously. I walked into town and went to find a book that would give me some more information on the Tor so I could gain more insight into my journey.

Apparently, there was little evidence regarding who had made the series of paths I'd walked, let alone when they were created, but the consensus was they were made as an initiation path for druids to complete their apprenticeship. According to myth, the labyrinth represents the inner labyrinth made up by the waterways within the Tor, which again was part of the druid initiation. In another book, I found there were seven paths in total relating to the seven levels as they ascended the hill. Each level related to a chakra (wheels of energy in the human aura), which in turn allowed the initiate to go through the full spectrum of energy centre initiations within the body to achieve fulfilment. When I came out of the labyrinth on the Tor, I certainly felt something profound had shifted in me.

That night I spoke to Mum as it dawned on me how long my quest would take. She was concerned when I told her I thought the process would take seven days.

"Mum, I know it sounds bizarre, but today I discovered something which makes me think the quest I'm on is all about the chakras and therefore I'm probably going to be here to deal with each one daily. I haven't quite worked it out yet, but I feel it."

She had no idea what I was on about and started to say she was worried about the whole thing. "Amanda, you said before that guy down in Glastonbury killed himself doing a quest. How are you going to achieve it if he didn't and was some guru?"

"Mum, I have no idea what I have to do or how I'm going to do it, but I can't come home until I've achieved it for the sake of the children more than anything. I have to protect us all and I don't know any other way of doing this. Tom and others here have told me I'll do this, so please just trust me I'll get through and come home soon."

"OK, darling, but please be careful for God's sake. You seem to be getting so involved in all this stuff these days and I'm worried about you. I know I should trust, but I don't see it like you do."

"Mum, please don't worry, just please make sure the children don't feel your concern as they think they're having a lovely holiday with you and that's all they need to know."

When I came off the phone, I burst into tears. I missed my children terribly and my mum too. She was no longer just my mum; she was becoming the only real friend I had and for the first time in my life, I felt although we weren't as close as I wished we could be, she was the only person close enough to me that 'got me'. I went back to my room, exhausted, and prayed to The Guys Upstairs they wouldn't let me down. I was completely spent and knew instinctively the quest definitely related to the chakras of the body, but I didn't know how and why. All I knew was the Tor had brought it to light. That night I slept like I'd never slept before.

On the fourth day of my journey I felt the urge to visit the Glastonbury Thorn on Wearyall Hill. The bookshop had become my source of knowledge and as I'd bought many books there that week, they were happy to let me research from others. I read about the legend of Jesus as a young boy and his travels with his Uncle Joseph of Arimathea. At that time, Glastonbury was an island and the Mendip Hills that surrounded the island were rich with tin. Joseph was a wealthy tin merchant and had visited the area many times. After the crucifixion, Joseph went to Glastonbury with twelve companions including Mary, mother of Jesus, her sister Martha and Mary Magdalene. Joseph arrived, tired after his journey and drove his staff into the ground on Wearyall Hill. According to the legend, it then took root and flourished into a thorn bush. The thorn bush is only usually seen in the Middle East and it's unusual as it flowers twice a year, in spring and again in winter – or at Easter and Christmas. Joseph also buried the cup there that had held the blood of Christ. The hill was renamed Chalice Hill.

As I walked up onto the hill, I felt an incredible feeling of peace and contentment wash over me. It was so different from my arduous six hour plus walk the day before. I sat and contemplated the dynamic change in my life and the extraordinary journey I was on. Sitting alone on that hill I realised how incredibly lucky I was to be alive. Not only to be alive, but for the first time in my life to have the capacity to fully interact in the world. I knew not all people would ever fully understand the depths of their ability as a human being to experience the magnitude of what this existence can offer as I'd discovered. I wondered if it would happen in my lifetime to see that all would discover what was going on at a deeper level. If it did, we would certainly have the ability to all live in complete harmony with the world. There was still such a long way to go but I knew I was just a small part of a bigger plan to open people's hearts and for them to feel their own power just like I had begun to.

It's in your heart, Amanda. It always has been. I heard the voice say. I turned around thinking someone was there or the wind was playing tricks on me. Silently I prayed and asked for guidance.

287

It was beginning to get drizzly and cold, so I got up and turned back. I felt humbled and honoured at having the ability to feel so much more and I thanked The Guys Upstairs for saving me. For the first time in my life I had a sense of purpose. With that power, I could achieve so much for the greater good of all. Feeling fully open and alive, I walked back slowly to where I was staying. It was as if someone had changed my television set from an old box TV to a huge plasma screen with 3D. Everything around me became more emphasised and beautiful. The trees, the sky, the colours, the sound of the birds … everything became more heightened in my senses. Something profound was waking inside me.

On the fifth day, I found myself wandering until I came upon a temple that had been created in the honour of the healing springs. I rifled through some brochures I had in my bag and realised there were two different springs there. One was red with iron and the other white with calcite. They both rose from the caverns beneath Glastonbury Tor and were only a few feet from each other. According to the brochure, each one contained healing energy.

I went into the Victorian built Well House. It was certainly a stark contrast to the day before in the beautiful natural surroundings on Chalice Hill. The cavern was dimly lit, and I felt claustrophobic. Inside, there were three domed vaults about fifteen or so foot high, with beautiful, bowed floors. With the sound of the continuous flowing water, it felt like I was going through a cleansing and purifying process. A series of pools built according to the principles of sacred geometry lay within with shrines to honour the ancient energies. According to the brochure, a ley line known as the Michael Ley line ran through the area, which enhanced the power more so. I wondered if it was connected to Archangel Michael. That day I lost myself in a series of meditations and prayer allowing my body to release and let go of what it no longer needed. I felt myself cleanse as if the water was flowing right through me. I was coming out of the darkness and could feel hope in its place.

By the sixth day, the fear had long gone, and my body and energy were slowing down to embrace my healing process. I headed for St Margaret's Chapel on Magdalene Street, wondering what was in store for me. All I knew was that it was once a former medieval complex outside the Abbey and served initially as a hospital, run by monks who looked after the sick.

288

Later, it became an alms house and again the monks would then look after the old and those too old to work. It had been built in 1444 and was still used by Christians, Sufis, people who meditated there and those who followed the traditions linking to the Magdalene. The Chapel and the garden itself were an incredible experience of peace and harmony. I went there with no preconception of what to expect, but the feeling of Mary Magdalene was so strong, I couldn't help but embrace my own feminine power. I meditated for some time that day and felt so at home, I didn't want to leave.

During a meditation, I had a bizarre connection come to me. I saw the names of my siblings Maria and Sarah my sisters and my brother Christopher. Then I saw the names of Mary Magdalene, Jesus and Sarah, their daughter. I had a strong sense the message implied the connection was showing my link to the powerful message behind the Bible. I left feeling I could draw upon that experience, even when I was back in my everyday world.

On my last day, I was guided to go to the Chalice Well. From what I'd read it was one of Britain's most holy of wells. Many legends were attached to its endlessly flowing waters, and I wondered what it would tell me that day. According to what I'd read, the waters represented the blood of Christ. This all stemmed from when Joseph of Arimathea buried the cup used at the Last Supper. For some though the water was the quintessence of life, the gift from Mother Earth, the continuous spring which represented the life force energy we all can tap into. I walked into the beautiful tranquil garden and when I arrived at the well itself, I instantly saw the message. It was as clear as the message written on the rock at Coogee in Australia.

The symbol on the well was a *vesica piscis*, a profound geometric shape from ancient times. I'd learned previously that the symbol represented two interlocking rings much like the shape of two of the Olympic rings, which formed three regions and held a deep symbolic message.

The symbol to me meant the interlocking stages of humanity evolving. The first region represented people who were asleep. These were what I jokingly classed as those who go to work, come home, and think EastEnders is a documentary. It was how I described those who lived a life without spiritual challenges and neither understood nor wanted to believe anything else occurred in the universe unless they could rationalise it for fact.

This circle of people were closed to any desire to be inquisitive about things they couldn't see or explain.

The second region which forms in the middle of the two rings relates to those who do the same but are waking up and becoming inquisitive. Understandably, they are drifting back to sleep and waking sporadically to allow their awakening process to take place.

The last region in the second circle represents those who are fully wide awake. Those people cannot possibly interact with those who are constantly asleep. So the universe derived a plan to allow each region to influence the region below to help open up and initiate the awakening for each individual.

It was just like in Australia. I'd been at Chalice Well for only a few minutes when I realised what my higher plan was. I'd passed the test. I'd spent seven days in Glastonbury and realised every day was working on each of my energy centres or chakras to acclimatise me for my mission.

In a flash, I could see my arrival in Glastonbury had been based on fear, family, security, and money – all related to the base chakra and toward building trust. The day Chris had arrived it highlighted our past life connections. The sacral chakra relates to intimate relationships and past lives. I walked the labyrinth on the third day at the Tor. This was an inward journey of discovery relating to the solar plexus chakra, or the energy centre that relates to the inner self and core strength. On the fourth day on Chalice Hill I discovered my power was through my connection through the heart chakra as was those who helped to create change. My surname being Hart was shown to me to clarify this. On the fifth day at the Well House, the cleansing process was symbolised by the water. The throat chakra is the gateway to healing and I'd gone through that purifying process to make way for the new. On the sixth day at St Margaret's Chapel my third eye chakra allowed me to see more clearly through meditation and highlighted how my inner senses had been tweaked. Finally, the visit to Chalice Well spoke volumes. Seeing the symbol was the last piece in the jigsaw that confirmed what I'd been told to do with regard to my mission from Source through to my Crown Chakra – to help initiate light workers ready to take on their role to help others. I knew I'd successfully completed the quest and went straight back to my room, packed, settled up with the owners and drove home later that day knowing the dark side had taken a step back. I'd discovered a strength I didn't know existed and all my senses were singing and dancing.

I was spiritually rocking and rolling!

Chapter 33

A man travels the world in search of what he needs and
returns home to find it.

George Moore

The more I learned, the more I needed to learn. A spiritual master based in Luton had heard about my quest via Chris from the crystal shop and he phoned me to say I needed to contact a woman in Glastonbury.

"I've just got back from there!" I said.

"Amanda, the journey is never about straight lines. There are twists and turns. Go with it! You must contact Isis and go back to Egypt."

"But I've just come back from there, too!"

"This time, you will learn why you went there in the first place."

I sighed deeply. How on earth could I go again? I had no money and no way of getting help with the children. I'd learned enough to know if something was meant to be, heaven and earth would move to provide solutions. I found and contacted Isis (as a sceptical Capricorn, I knew she hadn't been born with that name) and after a long talk, I arranged to see her.

The instant we met, I knew I had to trust her. After a bizarre introduction and initiation, I booked to travel with her and a party of forty people to Egypt for two weeks leading up to the spring equinox and also agreed to do the Flower of Life workshop in preparation. Mum said she'd help in any way she could which was bizarre but welcoming as she seemed more ready to look after my children than she had me as a child, but I didn't question her intentions and trusted it was all part of the plan. I spoke to Chris, and he surprised me by saying without hesitation, "I'll pay for your flights."

I was dumbfounded by how much assistance I was receiving and counted my blessings, trying not to question any of it.

A young friend of mine offered to help with the children. Sarah needed to move out of her home, so it was the perfect solution. She didn't want money but needed a new focus in life. It made perfect sense for me to teach her what I was learning in exchange for her help. All was flowing in readiness.

So, when I visited Isis at her retreat at Shambhala in Glastonbury, she asked if I knew in my heart I had to be with her during the spring equinox.

"I need to gather the great initiates who are ready to follow again the ancient pathway of the Great River of Light. Those who walked the path before have an opportunity to do it again, a quarter of a million years later. You might have followed the journey many times, Amanda, but this time is the most significant," she said.

"The journey won't be easy," she continued, "as it incorporates visits to many sacred temples along the River Nile. The Nile represents the kundalini serpent energy of Egypt, which is connected to our inner kundalini serpent which ascends to the immortal divine as we travel along its waters. It's connected with your energy centres and travels up your body like a snake along your spine. Travelling the river and waking those energy centres will waken us to our calling in this lifetime."

"So where exactly will we be travelling?" I asked.

"We'll begin at the head of the serpent in Abu Simbel and travel across Lake Nasser to Aswan. Then we'll follow the Nile, past the temples of Kom Ombo, Edfu and Esna, onto Luxor and Karnak, Dendera and Abydos and finally to Cairo where we'll visit the King's Chamber in the Great Pyramid. Once we understand what we are to do on this earth, it will change our lives completely. The Hathors will guide us and highlight everything we need to know on our journey."

"Who are the Hathors?"

"A group of inter-dimensional, intergalactic beings who connect with ancient Egypt through the Temple of the Goddess Hathor."

My world was becoming so bizarre. *But what have I got to lose? I'm open to anything these days.* I thought.

Isis continued to describe the trip, but I didn't understand everything she said. She mentioned us working with Ka and Ba energies to help bring about an immense tuning into solar energy.

"What are Ka and Ba energies?" I asked.

"Ka is our life force energy that leaves our body when we die and Ba is the energy within us that can travel between the worlds of the living and the dead."

I was drawn to the trip and needed to be in Egypt for the spring equinox, although I couldn't rationalise why. When Isis started to go deeper and mentioned the Councils of Light beyond our planet, I wondered if it would help me understand more about The Guys Upstairs. I knew everything would flow and I would find out the reason for my journey in good time. I was getting used to doing things on a need-to-know basis.

Several weeks later I arrived at Heathrow and met my companions. I was instantly drawn to Janet, a therapist from the Midlands, David, a businessman, and Paul, a sound therapist. The four of us gelled immediately. When we arrived in Egypt, we flew to Aswan to stay at the Old Cataract Hotel. It was a majestic hotel caught in a time warp, overlooking the Nile and its islands. I stood on my veranda and watched the boats sail by, feeling as if I were in a movie. That evening I sat on the terrace with my new companions listening to the flute player as we watched the old sailing ships drift gently through the water.

The next morning we were allowed some time to adjust to our new environment. We met in the afternoon for a felucca ride to enjoy the islands. Isis explained we were tuning into Hapi, God of the Nile and Khnum, Lord of the Cool Waters, both ancient deities associated with the annual flooding of the Nile.

"Hapi lived on Elephantine Island and on his journey, he flowed through the underworld, through the heavens and then through Egypt providing sustenance for all. Khnum created the gods and fashioned mankind on a potter's wheel," she explained.

After the most magnificent sunrise the next morning, we began our coach journey to Abu Simbel in the great land of Nubia. Isis explained, "Each temple you visit will release memories of past life experiences or healing that will unlock energies to help assist you in this lifetime. Each temple holds a key from which you will draw knowledge and wisdom into the cells of your being."

I was excited and couldn't wait to start. That afternoon we visited The Great Temple built by Rameses II. As we stood gazing at the four colossal figures outside the entrance, Isis said, "The northern temple is dedicated to Queen Nefertari. She's the Goddess Hathor. She embodied the harmonic of divine love and unconditional acceptance and from that brought forth a unique understanding of consciousness."

The heat was sweltering so it was a welcome relief to go into the temples where it was cool and dark. When I came out, I didn't feel any different to when I went in and was disappointed. I'd thought something radical would happen.

Isis said, "Expect the unexpected, Amanda."

Great, that helps.

We stayed overnight at the Seti Abul Simbel Hotel, gathering for a sunset meditation which was out of this world. I felt incredible energy surge through my body in that amazing setting. The next day we stood in front of the Great Temples of Rameses II at Abu Simbel feeling the warmth of the sun on our faces as it rose across the water of Lake Nasser. Isis led the mediation for us to call upon the Great Creator God of Egypt, Ra, father of the gods, to begin our ceremony of light. We stood in silence as she called upon the gods and as I felt a chill run down my spine there was an energy shift in my body. I was in the presence of something very powerful. Isis then showed us how to chant the Akul, to draw the energy of the Great Ones. "Eventually we ourselves will become the Akul," she said.

It was hypnotic as we harmonised and chanted *Akul, Akul,* over and over again. The sound created an amazingly powerful vibration, and I felt my body tingle. We set off after the meditation and arrived in time for lunch on the cruise boat. Once aboard, we found our cabins and gathered on deck to enjoy the gentle journey down to the Temple of Philae.

"This Temple is dedicated to Isis, known as The Throne. It's a beautiful sacred island in the centre of this tranquil lake," said Isis.

At that moment, a flock of herons flew from the water. I felt as if I were on a film set and someone had shouted, "Cue the birds!"

"Many Egyptians still come to this temple, as the sacred island has become a site of pilgrimage."

On the way there on the boat, one of the group said she felt unwell. I was sitting near her and went to assist. Once we got ashore, she felt better and once I was reassured she was OK, she told me she was a doctor. "You seemed to know just what to do. This is what I've come here for myself. I want to find my own ability to heal and help others on a deeper level," she said.

"I guess what happened earlier was to assure you you'd find the answers," I responded.

On the island, I went into the temple next to one of the party and as we walked through the door she turned to look at me. I knew that she'd been my mother in a past life. She looked at me and nodded. "Yes, Amanda," she said. "I can feel it. My name's, Amanda too," she said. "I guess you felt that instantly like I did."

Feeling a little silly, I nodded.

"It's OK, Amanda. I recognised you. You were my daughter in a previous life."

Feeling light-headed, I excused myself and went in search of Isis. When I found her, I explained what I'd experienced.

"Amanda, the essence of the island is to bond with all of humanity and understand one's path in this lifetime, especially with soul brothers or sisters," she said.

As I looked around, I could see many different groups starting to form. I wondered if the others were bonding with their soul families.

"The Temple of Isis is the most profound to work with as it opens up the relationship with one's self. Isis, the Great Mother Goddess, and maternal spirit, is the Goddess of Magic. She worked with Thoth and together they taught humanity many secrets. She was the wife of Osiris and the mother of Horus. By coming here she helps to attune us again to the love, gentleness, and compassion within us all," Isis said, and then she smiled and left me to my thoughts.

The next day we sailed to Kom Ombo, situated on a hill overlooking the Nile. It was an incredible experience to stand there looking out at the Nile where the feluccas quietly glided over the water. I didn't want to leave. The temple we visited was called The House of the Crocodile and The Castle of the Falcon. Isis told us, "This temple represents our deep unconscious emotions. It's a place of initiation through the watery tunnels beneath our feet which can bring up memories. It's also a healing sanctuary. The energy here brings a deeper awareness of unity between people at the deepest level, and affects our unconscious ability to align with Source, bringing through energy from the star Polaris that we can use in the world for great benefit."

It was all beyond what I knew but I soaked it in like a sponge.

"If you follow me, I'll take you to the Star Gate itself where you can feel the unity and oneness."

"What do you mean? Like the TV series Stargate?" I asked.

"Well what do you think they based it on, Amanda?"

After lunch, we sailed to Edfu. Isis explained, "The Star Gate here is linked to Alcyone, a star cluster, and the energy will help us transcend the limits of time and space. You may have an inter-dimensional experience on your soul's journey, and perhaps experience astral projection and lucid dreams."

I was a little confused but worked out there were different star gates relating to different temples.

Isis went on. "Alcyone, being the primary star in the Pleiades, will help us to significantly enhance our ability to channel from the Council of Light."

I knew even though I was confused, I had to keep an open mind. When we finally arrived at the temple, Isis asked me to touch the back of the throne behind the high altar. She explained I was touching nine emerald crystals that formed a replica of the Pleiades. The Council of Nine could be the nine I'd been introduced to associated with The Guys Upstairs according to my dreams and what Tom had confirmed to me on numerous occasions. I wondered if it was all a huge coincidence, but something deep within me told me it wasn't.

Some of the party were finding it difficult to deal with issues coming up for them, including Janet. Within the first few days of our journey she became seriously unwell. One day, we were all aboard the coach when the hotel asked us to go on ahead without her. I left the coach to see her and immediately alerted one of the helpers to let them know she couldn't travel. The woman simply said to me, "Step out of the drama, Amanda."

I reeled back in shock. I'd only wanted to help Janet. Even though she was extremely ill, she was encouraged to get on the coach, and she came with us. We stopped when necessary, but David, Paul and I became closer to help protect her. I felt intimidated by the helper, but one evening when she caught me alone, she explained I had to toughen up, as I'd be tested greatly by people in the future. It highlighted to me the strength I needed to deal with my journey. Janet was feeling better when we visited the Valley of the Kings on the West Bank of the Nile. It was known as the Place of Power. This was where we went to see the celebration of the transition from one world to the other. The ancient Egyptians saw this as a joyful, blessed and sacred place. "This is what we've lost in our civilisation today. You are here to experience the beauty of trust and faith," said Isis.

The place was extremely positive in energy and whilst walking around in the dust and sand outside, I came across what looked like a carved piece of rock. I showed it to Isis.

"That's a carving of Hathor. You've found this to symbolise that she is working with you to help bring about unconditional love to all," she said.

I felt honoured. After that, we visited the Valley of the Queens nestled in the foothills of the Libyan mountains behind the western cliffs. We'd travelled for hours on the coach for a few days now and it was becoming challenging for those who felt unwell. Isis told us, "This temple is known as Neferu or Biban Harim, the Place of Beauty. It contains over eighty tombs of Egyptian queens and royal children." We only stayed a short while, but it felt much lighter than the other temple visits.

Janet was weary, but she kept on, bless her, staying on the coach when she couldn't make the tour. I was concerned that the leaders of the tour made her continue as I worried she might need a doctor, but so far it was all flowing and I decided to just let go and trust. The next day we went to the Mortuary Temple of Queen Hatshepsut at Dier al-Barari. The temple rose out of a series of terraces and seemed to merge into the cliffs of the Theban mountains. From there we could see the Nile and the green valley of ancient Thebes, now known as Luxor. We were cramming in one temple after another with endless driving in between, but we were having such a laugh on the coach it seemed to fly by. Later, we went to Dendera and visited the Temple of Hathor, the Lady of Heaven and the goddess of joy, motherhood, and love.

Isis said, "You have to focus on her more than anything as it will become symbolic to some of you later on."

I wondered if she was referring to me as I realised my future was becoming focused on children, families, and feminine energy more than anything. As I went from one visit to the next, a process within me was opening me up to remind me of my task. We then visited the Sanctuary of Amun where the power felt alive in the ancient stones. The temple was truly amazing, and Isis told us it had once been surrounded by myrrh trees, beautiful gardens, and a grand sphinx-lined walkway. It was incredible enough without all that and I wondered how amazing it must have been to see its true splendour.

The following day we visited the Great Temple of Karnak, dedicated to the Great Egyptian deity Amun, who Isis told us represented the warrior within. I felt an awesome presence, and wondered if I was starting to imagine it but something seemed to be intensifying in me. As we looked up at the huge, tall pillars, Isis said, "We connect here through the star gate to the star Sirius. This will create a shift in our vibration, and we'll move forward from the known to the unknown. Sirius demands you become a seeker!"

I felt readier than ever, but my ego as ever was tripping me up and I was in conflict with Paul as he was making unwanted advances towards me. I was disappointed as I'd trusted his friendship and felt he was showing weakness. I had to be firm with him and told him it was out of the question as it would upset the equilibrium of the dynamic between us all. Besides, I didn't feel anything for him in that way.

I went to Isis for help as he was becoming persistent. She said, "Amanda, we've all been together before, and you will need to deal with this in the best way possible to find the best solution."

I thanked her and realised I had to dig deep and deal with it.

The following day we visited the Temple of the Sun Goddess Sekhmet and Ptah. Isis told us "Ptah is one of the creator gods of Egypt and by speaking the names of all things, Ptah causes them to be. Sekhmet represents the scorching burning heat of the sun and can be a fierce goddess of war. She is also a great healer and wife of Ptah."

After another meditation I felt as if I was leaving my body. Isis afterwards referred to the meditation as having been a ceremony to raise the *sekhem*, our healing system. She said, "You will draw on this in the future as it is a powerful tool for transformation that accelerates your personal development and helps you all to achieve your full potential."

I asked some of the others in the group how they were feeling, and they said they could feel the energy building. At least I wasn't going loopy. Something was definitely happening. As the days rolled on, my eyes opened more deeply to the people around me. My fellow companions were an eclectic mix of accountants, doctors, lawyers, mothers, teachers, and seekers. The group opened me to a greater understanding that we were a small percentage of those who questioned the greater scheme of things taking place within the universe. Each person was a credible seeker, each looking for their own answers.

That night we moved to the Temple of Luxor, known as the Harem of Amun. Isis told us, "The star gate here is linked to

Alderberan. This star provides a blessing of comfort for those who grieve through loss. From this, a greater understanding can come bringing a sense of peace and calm. This then connects us to all, past and present. Deep compassionate love and inner strength can come through Alderberan."

By the ninth day, we were weary from the gruelling travelling and intake of information together with the constant challenges we were all facing on mental, emotional, spiritual, and physical levels. None of us were capable of avoiding the metaphysical challenges we faced individually, but we all supported one another. We had an early start and set off to the temples of Abydos and Dendera. The Abydos pilgrimage was to give us a true initiation into the underworld. This temple of knowledge was built by Seti I in the image of Osiris, Lord of the Underworld and linked through a star gate to El Nath.

Outside the temple Isis told us, "Once you enter the temple, you will realise we are not here to celebrate Osiris but to be associated with his fate, to resonate at his trials, to experience his anguish and to be comforted by his regained serenity. This temple above all is the initiator temple which prepares initiates for their life's journey."

Once inside we had another meditation which Isis referred to as an activation ceremony into the underworld. I didn't like the experience as much as the other meditations and came out feeling I needed air and light. Isis assured me it was normal, and it was helping me to see the difference between dark and light so I always found my way on my path. "Amanda, you need to experience the darkness to know how to move into the light," she explained.

People were finding greater and greater issues rising within themselves and Isis had to deal with one to ones in the evenings to help people go through their stuff. On one occasion, a girl took umbrage to me. When Isis summoned us both to see her, she said, "Amanda, you stabbed Sarah in the back in a past life. You were both fighting for survival. You won but the issue has come out now as you are here to learn from this experience. Sarah, you need to forgive Amanda and learn to let go instead of harbouring pain from the past. Amanda, you need to understand there are other ways to win fights. You will use unconditional love as your power, and will no longer need weapons as you are protected always." She did some kind of healing on us although she'd told us to close our eyes, so we had no idea exactly what she did. Strangely, we found after that we got on like a house on fire.

Each day was crammed with visits, initiations, and meditations. It was as if we were being fast tracked and each one of us could feel awareness building incredibly within our individual selves and as a group dynamic. After lunch we visited the Temple of Dendera, dedicated to Hathor, goddess of love and music. We were shown a picture of her, a beautiful woman wearing a crown of cow horns and holding a sun disc. We were told that within the walls of the temple were two birth houses, which contained the Star Gate connected to Venus and Sirius. We visited the sacred lake of Cleopatra, and I left the group for a while to sit by the lake in quiet contemplation. I asked The Guys to let me find peace with my past, including lifetimes that had created issues in this lifetime. I left the lake feeling lighter.

After wandering around at our leisure we all met back up to go up to the Rooftop Temple which had an amazing astronomical ceiling. Isis explained, "The ceiling represents the vault of heaven. The thirty-six spirits around the perimeter symbolise the three hundred and sixty days of the Egyptian year and the constellations inside the circle include the signs of the zodiac." I wondered if it was one of the first recordings of the signs of the zodiac.

When we got to the rooftop, we found the view out of this world. I could imagine the priestesses and priests walking on the sacred stones, moving to the sacred dances. Isis said that in olden times a statue of Hathor stood at the entrance of every temple on the Nile, symbolising the divine feminine principle, compassion, and love and everything that comes from it. "Hathor teaches us if you want love, you must become it first and become the living bridge others can follow."

Later we had the privilege of exploring the Kundalini Crypts which were beneath the floor as we neared the high altar in the Hypostyle Hall. Isis said, "Many memories will come up for you from moving into the underground tunnels," and asked us to chant the Akul again as we'd been taught.

The harmonics resonated throughout the temple. I could feel it flow throughout my body and felt a tingling sensation for a long time afterwards. Before we left, we were shown the extraordinary hieroglyph of a modern-day helicopter on the wall amongst all the other hieroglyphs. I stood there with my mouth open. There was so much to take in; I was in another world.

Thankfully, the next day we had some leisure time. We made the most of shopping and taking in our surroundings. Janet was now stronger, David was a perfect gentleman and looked after us girls like a protective father and Paul, bless him, was still trying his hardest to win my affections. Although he was a lovely guy, my heart was with Chris.

That evening we went to the opera in the majestic Temple of Karnak and listened to Verdi's Aida. Sitting outside under the stars was an unforgettable experience. Late that evening we flew to Cairo and arrived to stay at the Giza Plateau, the beautiful royal palace that overlooks the Great Pyramid.

That next morning I woke and after an early breakfast, went to sit in the beautiful gardens. Isis had said the night before, "Staying in the inner ring of the power of the Great Pyramid may well be very intense for you. It can bring up anything within that needs healing, so pay attention to what's necessary to deal with it."

I sat in quiet meditation to see what came up for me. I felt ready. I sensed some of the group moving into the garden and quietly thanked my Guys for their help and asked if they could remove anything I feared. I sat a moment longer with my eyes closed and felt my stomach flutter. It was then I had my first experience of psychic surgery. In my mind, I saw ropes coming out of my stomach and a pair of hands pulling and heaving on them. When they stopped, the ropes were cut with a huge pair of scissors. A knot was tied in the rope and the knot pushed deep back into my stomach. Then I saw a large needle and thread come down and sew me up. I felt at peace and more accepting. I also had a knowing I had to complete my mission, or I'd never find complete, unconditional love with a partner. In some ways it felt like the dangling of a carrot, but equally I knew it was the way to get me to complete my goal.

The day before we were to visit the Great Pyramid, we visited the Temple of Saqqara with Abd'El Hakim Awyan, an archaeologist, and the Holy Man of Egypt, where we recreated some of the wonders of ancient times through healing energies, psychic perception, and vision. I was partnered with Amanda and that was the first time I experienced morphing. It frightened me at first. We were sitting a couple of feet apart, staring into each other's eyes, when I suddenly saw her physically change into another person, then another and then another. Amanda realised what I was going through and told me to relax. Person after person flashed before me, old, young, women and men alike. It was an amazing and bizarre experience.

Isis came over to me and said, "You've just witnessed some of Amanda's past life experiences. Your awareness has heightened, and you will see so much more now."

She told me to practice the technique in the mirror, which I did later that day. I saw myself morph into different people. I was excited my senses were heightening.

We then visited the Step Pyramid of King Djoser built by Imhotep, the High Priest of Ptah who was the first architect to build in stone. Patron of medicine, philosopher, and writer, he was later deified. This was where the star gate connecting to the star Arcturus was located. Close by were the Healing Chambers situated over running water. The Healer Priests, Isis told us, could use the Arcturus connection to amplify and strengthen the subtle bodies of their patients, which is the key to all healing. I was more interested in this than anything, as I could relate to this with my own healing and that of my clients to date.

Isis said, "The Healer Priests would focus and connect with singular intention so a perfect diagnosis could be made. Deep healing resulted and many life lessons were revealed."

At our regular sunset gathering and meditation, which by then was becoming deeper and deeper for me, we all sat transfixed by the moment and Isis said, "The great god creators Thoth and Maat will greet us at the Great Pyramid tomorrow. Thoth, The Great Treasurer, will be fully present. He was self-conceived at the beginning of time and is the treasurer of the Earth and the counter of the stars, the keeper and recorder of all knowledge and the architect of the Great Pyramid. His wife Maat, known as The Goddess of Truth, was the daughter of Ra, the Sun God. In the Hall of Maat in the afterlife, it is she who weighs your heart against a feather. Pure joy is all you need!"

On the last day, we completed the work of the activation of the kundalini energy of Egypt at our final destination. Our hearts, we were told, would quicken in anticipation as we found our way to the entrance of the Great Pyramid itself. We then had to ask the Guardians permission to go forward into the darkness. Enroute, on the short coach trip from the hotel, a strange woman who I'd not conversed with much on the trip made herself known to me. She asked me to regress her, saying I knew how. I was a little shocked by the request, but said, "Yes why not."

Amazingly I immediately saw her in another life. "Wow, I see you as a Nordic Goddess. I can see you standing tall and lording it over your people wielding great power, but it seems to be on a negative level as your people are frightened of you."

I didn't like what I saw, nor what I felt. She was cold, controlling and frightening in her past life. When I told her diplomatically what I could see, she smiled at me strangely. When we arrived at the Great Pyramid, I pushed it aside and focused on the job in hand. We left the coach and forty of us, all dressed from head to foot in white, lined in pairs, headed towards the entrance. It had begun.

Isis asked us to pause as she asked the gods permission to enter, and when she was ready, she beckoned us onward towards the opening in the pyramid. As we entered, we bowed our heads and walked through the entrance tunnel of roughhewn rock to the steep incline that led to the Grand Gallery of a thousand steps. We'd rehearsed what we had to do and began the chant which became incredibly hypnotic as we started to ascend the steps. Having been there before I knew the incline, but many didn't and were nervous to go in, let alone all the way up to the King's Chamber.

The darkness encouraged us to trust each step and rely on the person in front of us to lead us forward. Every breath we took we were fully conscious of, our hands pulling us up the cold metal rails, our feet seeking the next foothold. Our collective breath filled the space. The vastness of our challenge wrapped around us and guided us forward. Our closeness comforted us on that upward journey. We were heading for our thirteenth Ascension Merkabah Initiation. When we got to the last step, we bent down to crawl through the antechamber into the Kings Chamber. Our breathing was deep; many feeling the headiness of that moment in time. I felt at home. We all moved systematically to a place against the wall, and I went to where I'd sat when I'd visited with Chris only two months before. Isis gestured for us all to sit.

There was just one flame alight in the centre of the chamber and all forty of us were cast as ghostly shadows on the walls surrounding us as the flame of the candle flickered. Isis began the chant we'd rehearsed … the great Om, the sound of the universe, and as it started it reverberated throughout the chamber increasing in volume as we all joined in, the acoustics perfect for that occasion. After a few moments, a woman stood up dramatically and moved towards the centre of the chamber, holding high a wand adorned with crystals. She faced Isis and challenged her. At first, we thought it was part of the ceremony and had been rehearsed, but then felt the fear and hatred in the woman. Isis sat firm and didn't flinch, but the chant diminished as we watched, shocked by the interruption, and frightened by the negative reaction.

"Go back and sit down," Isis said firmly but in a calm tone.

"I challenge you," yelled the woman who I realised was the Nordic Goddess I'd spoken to on the way to the pyramid.

"Go back and sit down. You no longer have to fight. I send you love and compassion," Isis said, without batting an eyelid.

The group stared as if a playground fight was about to erupt. The Nordic goddess moved nearer to Isis, but Isis did not flinch. She simply smiled and said, "I send you love, healing and compassion." And with that we could see how genuinely she wanted to help this woman.

The woman took a deep breath and her demeanour changed as if something awoke in her and after exhaling deeply, her body relaxed, she bowed, retreated and sat down. Isis took a moment and then initiated the chant once again. We continued with the Om and eventually stood and moved to different places within the pyramid to meditate before dispersing. Only a few of us remained but I don't remember what happened and how I got there (it was as if I lost moments in time) but when I came to, I was standing under the apex of the Great Pyramid, chanting. I turned and realised I was the last to chant on my own. There were two others standing directly behind me in a line and Isis, who was behind them, said, "You've done exactly what you set out to do. You've now set the harmonics. Well done."

I had no idea what she meant, but as I left the King's Chamber to descend the steps of the pyramid, she turned to me and said, "I knew you'd do it. Tomorrow the three heads of state meet here, and you've helped set the harmonics in preparation."

When we went back to our hotel, one of the guides said, "You have all helped create something great here today. Currently staying here at the hotel are the Israeli, Palestinian and Egyptian heads of state that are to meet tomorrow, the day of the spring equinox, in the Great Pyramid itself."

I wondered if it was all for effect as it was hard to believe we'd been part of a ceremony to prepare these men who were to equally go into the pyramid and pay homage. The guide continued, "There have been three groups in the pyramid today to prepare the harmonics for the spring equinox tomorrow and you, being the last group, have set the dynamics perfectly. Just like the betrayal, death, and resurrection of Jesus, in ancient Egypt the spring equinox was the time of the betrayal and death of Osiris and his resurrection as the god Horus. This time in history is one you'll come to understand as hugely influential, energetically."

I was getting less and less surprised by what I was being told but equally I still let my enquiring mind seek confirmation. On the day of the equinox, we gathered to go and visit the Sphinx. Isis had permission to take us directly to do work between the paws of the mighty beast which was closed to the public. The Great Sphinx, having the body of a lion and the head of a Pharaoh had the most enigmatic gaze as if it held many secrets. Isis said it was the Temple of Wisdom, the ancient place of initiation, known as Abu al-Hol (father of terror). It was terrifying standing beneath the paws of this huge beast as if at any moment you could be swallowed whole.

Isis called us together, "I want us all to stand here at this certain point between the paws of the Sphinx. We need to do this at a certain time to align with a particular star system." We stood there between the mighty paws whilst she said something I didn't quite hear. I was there one minute and the next I was gone. I felt I'd fallen down an elevator shaft deep into the earth. It was the Emerald City I had often dreamed of as a child. I was walking down a path alongside a stream. The place, as in my dream, was beautiful, with people walking along in couples and groups. There were flowers and grass around and the place was rich and abundant with colour and life. It was a place of belonging and safety, a place where harmony was the fabric of life. I hadn't thought of that dream once as an adult, but standing between the paws of the Sphinx I felt as if I'd found that world I craved as a child.

When I opened my eyes there were only a handful of us left. Isis was looking at me and asked what I got. I told her and she smiled. "We've just meditated at the divine doorway by the Destiny Stone. It's allowed our consciousness to drop deep into the earth connecting with the initiation tunnels and the Inner City beneath the Giza Plateau, the home of Osiris."

No! This can't be happening, I thought.

Isis smiled and nodded as if she'd heard every word inside my head.

306

"Amanda, our paradigm has been set and our cosmic work completed for this time. You may not remember the details of this experience, but your heart will never forget your journey. You've delved into new realms, new dimensions and the deepest place of your own heart and soul. You and all here today are the ones we've been waiting for and those who've stood up to be counted as spiritual light workers. You heard the call and responded. Now your work begins."

On the final day, I stood in the garden of the hotel packed and ready to leave, watching the first rays of the sun illuminate the Great Pyramid. My heart opened and I felt the joy I'd always yearned for. I was ready for my great opportunity to serve.

Chapter 34

Man could direct his ways by plain reason, and
support his life by tasteless food, but God has given us
wit, and flavour, and brightness, and laughter to
enliven the days of man's pilgrimage, and to charm his
pained steps over the burning marble.

Sydney Smith

At thirty-eight years of age, I was finally starting to enjoy life. Being in Egypt had opened my eyes to how difficult it was to carry my body around, so I decided to get into shape and focus on eating a healthy diet.

Driving past the leisure centre one day, I turned into the car park and sat with the engine off. I knew if anyone was going to be able to help me get fit and well, it would be Terry. I hadn't seen him since I'd bumped into him in the supermarket several months before, but I knew if he still worked there, it was meant to be. Sure enough, he did. I signed up there and then and was in the gym starting my training with him within a few days.

I still worked for Andrea from home and travelled into Chelsea on a Saturday, but the travelling was becoming an issue with the expansion of my own client base. On one occasion I got three speeding tickets due to rushing to work as I was always running late. It was becoming increasingly difficult to juggle looking after my children, running a home, seeing my own clients and my development work. One Saturday, my car started juddering. I pulled up and saw my front right tyre was going down. I phoned Andrea and told her I needed to get home and sort it. She wasn't happy. I bravely said, "Look, Andrea, don't you think it's perhaps a sign we've come to our expiry date, and you can now do without me, and we both need to move on?" I felt sad but I knew in my heart it was time for us to part.

"If you decide to move on, Amanda, I hope you won't use my credibility to build your clientele for the future."

I was offended. "Andrea, I've given you a hundred and twenty per cent since I've worked for you and hope one day you'll appreciate the reason why we were brought together. You know in your heart my integrity goes beyond what you've had before with others."

I assured her she needn't worry as the universe had a greater plan for both of us and set off home. I was sad to walk away, but she told me she'd write me a wonderful testimony for my business. I knew I'd miss her, but I had to break free. For the first time in my life I was finding my voice and my feet.

I ran my first charity run in May that year and met one of my closest friends, Yvonne. She was a barrister and very bubbly, self-motivated, and driven. Whilst we ran, I explained techniques she could use to focus the power of her mind. She was amazed at how it worked for her and was intrigued by why we'd met. I found most of my friendships were forming in that way. I just kept attracting all the right people at the right time. Deep friendships were forming for the first time in my life.

I was seeing more and more clients, but it came to the point when I could no longer continue as it was evident there was things going on I had no idea about. I contacted Dr Keith Hearne as I needed to know about past lives, and he invited me to attend a course on past life and spirit releasing therapy. He was not only a doctor, but also a media spokesman for his specialised field of expertise and was known for having created the Dream Machine in the Science Museum. Keith was a loveable, cuddly middle-aged man who adored women and red wine, was deeply passionate about his work, and had followed his dream to become a composer. He was a man of many talents.

The course was in Spain and again, I had to find the funds, the time, and the help I needed with the children. It all worked out perfectly. Sarah had moved in and was like a big sister to the children and the money arrived through an influx of clients. I was the last to arrive for the course and worried everyone had already bonded, but Keith assured me no work had started. The group were fantastic. They were down to earth people who specialised as hypnotherapists or therapists who felt they needed to enhance and understand a deeper concept of inner work, just like me.

The night I arrived, we went out to dinner and had a great evening. I met the girl I was sharing my room with, Jane. She was intent on making friends with me, but in a needy way. I sensed a wariness I couldn't put my finger on. I thought she'd been drinking too much as her behaviour was quite loud and outspoken in an attention seeking way. We kept the evening short as we had an early start the next day. When we got into our room, Jane was very nervous and jumpy and was talking to herself about how she was concerned about her possessions. I assumed she was out of her comfort zone sharing with a stranger, so I dismissed it and fell into a deep sleep.

I was up at five in the morning and went down to the beach before anyone else awoke. It felt good to be alone. When I got back for breakfast, Jane immediately asked where I'd been. I simply told her I'd been jogging, and she said she'd come with me next time. We spent long days studying and I kept up a healthy regime of good food and water so I could manage. Having given up alcohol, I found the healthy regime assisted with my training and allowed me to make the most of my study and busy life. As the days went on, Jane's behaviour was not only erratic, it was also irritating. She kept accusing people of stealing her things. She said hurtful things and had outbursts when we were in the middle of intricate work that needed our full attention. On one occasion, when we were regressing one of our class participants, Jane stood up and walked to a bookcase, talking loudly about what book she wanted to read next and how she didn't trust people around her. Keith encouraged her to take some time out and leave the villa, but this was occurring daily. We tried to ignore it, but we felt as if we were walking on eggshells. By the second week, she was really upsetting people, accusing them of being thieves and blaming then for damage she was creating in front of us. No-one dared to tackle her.

Keith pulled me aside one day and said, "Amanda, I don't want to alarm the others, but I'm concerned about Jane. I don't think she's telling us the truth." I felt humbled he'd approached me out of the group, but also concerned as the responsibility to help lay with me too. He continued, "Amanda, I approached you as you're seeing something the other students aren't quite able to see. Have you got any idea what's going on with her?"

I did, and I didn't feel it was my place to say, but it was clear she obviously had a chemical imbalance.

During our daily study periods, we'd had to do a lot of regressing of each other to witness and learn the effects of the healing and understand the whole experience. When Keith regressed each student, he relied on them to voice what they were experiencing under hypnotherapy. Whilst in that deep state, I got pictures in my mind and started to sketch images of people, even though I hadn't sketched since I was at school. The images always matched the characters in the regression. One day, one of the students was regressed but couldn't speak. I drew a Samurai warrior who was sworn to silence, and when I showed the drawing to Keith and explained, he nodded and asked the student if that was the case. The student nodded and Keith looked at me with his mouth open. After the session, he told me whatever had led me to study regression it went beyond what he could do. "You take this to another level!" he said.

Keith spoke to Jane on her own when her behaviour had started to radically affect the group saying, "You have to heal that within you if your intention is to help others."

Jane replied, "Keith, I'm feeling so much better now. That's why I've stopped taking my medication."

"What medication? What's it for?"

"I take medication to help me feel better, but I don't need to take it anymore. I've felt so much better since I've been here."

Keith realised the course was making her feel better but given that she had stopped taking her prescribed medication, he was concerned it would get worse – and it did. It was obvious she was doing the course not to help others, but to help herself. Jane was a loose cannon. Her behaviour was getting more erratic, and she was shouting out in classes, damaging property, and making unfounded accusations. On the tenth day, Jane walked out of a regression and slammed about in the kitchen in an attempt to stop our work. Keith guided us out of the regression and Jane came out of the kitchen throwing bottles of herbs at us. Keith told us to ignore her behaviour and Jane went outside into the garden and headed for the pool. In full view of us sitting in the villa, Jane stripped naked as we watched open-mouthed.

She marched angrily around the pool, grabbed all the cushions off the pool chairs and threw them into the water. Keith told us all to sit tight. Jane started to dance around the pool like some sixties hippy chick and when she'd finished with the cushions, she started to throw empty glasses, together with chairs, loungers, and anything she could lay her hands on. Keith and a couple of the guys ran out to try to calm her, but she was like a rat in a trap. She ran for the garden gate and scarpered into the street. Keith coaxed her back eventually and we had to go through her belongings to find details of a loved one to rescue her. Keith spoke to her husband, and he explained her condition and that he'd been against her doing the course as he felt she wasn't capable, but she'd insisted. He came to collect her.

I was to leave two days after the rest as my flight was booked for a two-week turnaround. Everyone was relieved to leave although they'd all gained so much from Keith. The morning he left me at the villa to travel back with all the other students, he said to me, "Amanda, you know just as much as me you're being tested and need to deal with the negative entities here in the villa. You've learned enough to know these have been attracted by Jane and it's your test now to see how you can deal with the dark forces."

I didn't want to be tested, let alone with the dark side, nor be left alone in the villa whilst they all went home. It had certainly become a dark and frightening place to live even though it was in a beautiful location. Keith assured me I needed the lesson and left me there, saying I'd cope and deal with the challenge at hand. I locked all the doors and windows and went in search for something to keep my mind from fear. All I found was a book Keith had written, *Understanding Dreams*, which he'd left on the coffee table. I ploughed through the book for comfort for the rest of my stay, hoping it would bring me some kind of protection. I managed to get through the time on my own and took ownership of the negative entities at the villa and faced them head on like he'd taught me. It wasn't a pleasant experience, but it taught me to face fear head on. By the time I left, I yearned to be home with my family.

On my return, word started to get round I was now working at a deeper level. A local paper contacted me, and I agreed I would regress someone who was sceptical, thinking it would have more of a profound effect than regressing someone who was open. They sent their reporter Henry Ellis.

Henry told me when he arrived, "I've no interest or belief in anything spiritual and want to try this out being the most sceptical on the team."

Reassuring him I explained, "I will take you into a state of deep hypnosis and then guide you through possible previous lifetimes."

He was intrigued and ready for the challenge as he felt no one could convince him we had past life connections. I certainly had no prior knowledge that deep down he had a true desire to find the root cause of a concern that was repeatedly occurring in his life. He joked to me before we'd begun the session, "I'm always able to get a girlfriend OK, but never manage to keep one long."

After we'd had some photographs taken and were alone, I took him through a visualisation which enabled him to see different colours. Then I guided him through previous incidents that had occurred for him the previous week, gradually working back through his life until eventually we went back to when he was born. When I took him back to a previous life, he instantly said "I can see images of a wooden slide and a deep well, but it's hazy. I'm a girl and I know my name is Sarah. My parents are dead, and I live alone in Arizona in America."

Henry elaborated after the regression, "In my previous life I was a young girl and part of an Amish community in 1848. It feels so real, but I feel I'm making it all up. I have no idea why I thought of Arizona and that year in particular. Perhaps I'd have been more suspicious if I'd gone back to an Egyptian life or that of a wealthy merchant."

I knew what he'd tapped into intrigued him.

He continued, "Whilst you regressed me, your questions were annoying to me, as the answers seemed to be obvious. The images weren't vivid, and I didn't seem to be in a dreamlike state."

I knew he was holding back as he wasn't sure what had happened to him. He left and went back to his office but telephoned me once he'd digested his experience, having written his piece for the local paper. That's when he revealed the whole scenario to me. He'd googled what he'd seen in the regression which linked amazingly with the Amish at that time. Gold and gemstone mining had occurred during that last part of the century in Arizona – which was what he'd seen during his regression. As a young girl, he'd been used from a young age like many children, to collect water to find gold with buckets that eventually made her back stoop. Sarah was young and her spine curved as she developed and became less attractive as a marital prospect in her community, unlike other girls who weren't affected. She eventually died a spinster. I worked with Henry to release residues from that lifetime, and when we eventually discussed this on the phone again some months later, he told me he'd met someone he wanted to settle down with and was engaged and was over the moon. He told me something had happened and radically changed his luck.

After the article went to press, people started to come and see me for regression. I needed to find my own past life connections and decided to dig deeper. That's when Terry told me he wanted to do a pilgrimage from Avebury, the Ridgeway Walk, to Ivinghoe Beacon – an eighty-five mile walk that many endeavoured to accomplish, but few succeeded. He'd tried it twice before with two other personal trainers who'd had to give up. When he mentioned it, I said I'd give it a go, but he laughed at me saying it was only feasible for men who had military training. That simply encouraged me even more to take on the challenge.

"Amanda, if two guys who are fitness personified failed, how on earth do you think you'll do it?"

"I have no idea, but something's telling me I've got to do it."

He simply laughed.

Several weeks later, we began our walk on the chalk hills between Avebury in Wiltshire and Tring in Buckinghamshire. The path is part of a busy Neolithic highway that stretches across the country from Dorset to Norfolk. Terry thought I'd wimp out on the first day or so, considering his fellow walkers had failed by day three. I felt he was prepared to see me try it but equally prepared for me to fail. I had no idea how I'd do it, but failure didn't come into the equation.

We travelled from Hertfordshire by train with our military style backpacks, weighing over forty pounds each, and arrived at Overton Hill at two in the morning. As it was pouring with rain, we needed to find cover. The paths were slippery with mud, so we camped under a bush until dawn. Terry instructed me to get into my sleeping bag and bivvy bag which would protect us out in the elements. The bush protected us to an extent, but the rain was lashing down. The moment I was zipped up, I felt a crawling and writhing on my body and started to squirm. I called out to Terry, "I don't think I can do this! What the hell is crawling on us?"

"Amanda, just try and keep calm. It'll stop soon. I think it's just slugs because of the rain."

I started to feel panic set in. The bivvy bag was surrounding me, and I was concerned about the tiny airway that was my only connection with outside my cocoon. It was stifling in there. The more Terry told me to calm down, the more the crawling and slithering there was. I knew from the torch light outside that slugs were surrounding us en masse. All he could offer was, "Close off your bivvy bag as much as possible."

"I don't think I can cope with this, Terry. They're writhing all over me."

Three hours later I was able to come up for air. There were hundreds of slugs on our bags. I wanted to walk as far and as fast as I could to create distance between me and the creatures tormenting me. We finally ventured forth around first light. Within the first few steps, I felt I was stepping on a significant ancient route. I had the strangest feeling I'd been there before and felt something building in me. A sudden flash of Terry on a horse came into my mind and then it came again, and he was surrounded by other riders. They were riding with urgency and all wearing the same type of clothing, what seemed to be uniform from a medieval era with large crosses on the front of their clothing. They all wore combat helmets and carried swords. Then I saw myself in a long dress with my hair long, down to my waist. As Terry rode up to me, he put his arm down to catch me and I held him as he lifted me effortlessly onto the back of his horse – and then we rode away.

When the vision vanished, I said out loud to Terry, "That was incredible."

"What was?"

"I've just had a vision. I saw you as you rode up to me on a horse and pulled me up on to it and we rode away. I think you were a knight in the Middle Ages. You were riding with other men and there was an urgency about it. It looked as if you were trying to save me from something and take me away. I've got a feeling you were one of the Knights Templar."

He looked at me incredulously. We continued with our walk chatting about his plans for the future. "So I want to set up a health and fitness company of my own ..." he said, but I wasn't really listening. I was trying to fathom out why I'd had that vision and what it meant. We passed Waylands Smithy, a chambered long barrow. This held a much darker energy, and we didn't stay there for long. Then as we approached Silbury Hill, again I had a knowing that there'd been a lot of UFO activity around the area. It wasn't a dark energy, but I could feel it had an incredible power there. We walked on to Liddington Hill fort and had lunch. Terry made us tea and supplied us with army rations, which were surprisingly delicious after a hard morning's walk on little sleep.

The days that lay ahead were an average of twenty miles a day on foot and the nights were spent foraging for firewood, making the most of our supplies of food and finding warm shelter. Terry was very knowledgeable about sleeping outdoors and I enjoyed the total shut off from the outside world. My feet however were starting to become a problem from day three with incredible burning and swelling, blistering, and bleeding, and every step I took from then on was like treading on glass. Terry bound my feet as much as possible, but his were as bad as mine so I was determined not to wimp out. The weather was against us as it rained constantly and as we were walking uphill, it was harder with our backpacks on, especially when we were wet through, but we carried on regardless. Eventually, we left the Wessex Downs and started our descent onto the landscape of the Thames Valley, a mixture of ancient deciduous woodlands, rich farmland, and idyllic well-kept country villages. That's when we arrived at Goring and stopped at a beautiful hotel.

As soon as I walked into the hotel, I felt drawn to it. Although we were dishevelled and not appropriately dressed, I begged Terry to stop. "Terry, can't we just stop and have a civilised cup of coffee. It won't take away what we're doing as we'll still be roughing it, but look, we can sit out by the river in the garden there." I said, pointing over the bridge at the tables and chairs by the edge of the water. We went out to sit by the riverside in their courtyard garden and it was there that I saw a strange but profound vision of me at my own wedding celebration. Something told me I would be getting married again but this time it was somehow connected to that river. No sooner had the vision arrived, it was snatched away with Terry interrupting me with his plans for how we would continue our walk that day.

As we looked downstream, we could see that the river merged into a canal and to our left people were enjoying boat cruises. It felt like heaven after our gruelling walk. After an hour that I had to plead for, we left Goring and followed the riverside banks up the River Thames and onto the chalky Chiltern Hills. My feet were beyond pain. Every step was like walking on broken glass and I tried to numb the experience by using visualisation to anaesthetise the excruciating agony.

We walked along a roller coaster path of deciduous woodland and wide chalk downs along the Chiltern Ridge to our final destination. By the fourth day, Terry and I were hardly speaking to each other, each going through our own hell and neither of us wanting to give up. Sleeping rough and eating army rations was losing its appeal, but I was determined to see it through even if I wore my feet down to the bones. I could feel so much negativity coming up for both of us at so many levels and no wonder –the path had been the main route for the Saxons and Vikings during their advances into Wessex during the Dark Ages. We eventually got to Ivinghoe Beacon and painstakingly climbed the last few hundred yards to the summit. When we arrived, we found a spot to sit and, exhausted, we sat in silence and took in the incredible view that stretched as far as the Midlands.

My visions suddenly appeared again. This time it was clear to me Terry was actually Lancelot and I was Guinevere. I lost myself in the vision and watched it play out in my mind. I felt for him as he fought for me against Arthur. In my previous existence, I'd betrayed Arthur for Lancelot. This explained why Chris felt he couldn't trust me. The man I wanted to be with was Chris, but I'd realised some past life battle was influencing us and it was down to us to resolve the residue that had passed over into this lifetime. We'd all been brought together in this life to resolve the issues of the past, so we could all be set free. I knew I could cut the cords from the past, but I wondered if Chris was able to. I wasn't going to starve myself of male company for the sake of my mission. Chris might never set himself free from his chains, so now Terry had come into my life, perhaps it was meant to be explored further with him. I felt he was the one I should trust at that time. Something had shifted in me and for the first time in my life I started to value myself.

Chapter 35

All I have seen teaches me to trust the creator for all I
have not seen.

Ralph Waldo Emerson

I was flattered a man eight years my junior found me attractive. Terry always wanted to take up challenges and as I'd skydived, he decided to organise a group to do a tandem skydive. I went along, but it didn't feel the same. The addiction and buzz of years before was no longer there. I'd moved on.

I came across an internet-based radio show called *My Spirit Radio* and started to listen to it whilst working. One day they put out a request for people who had walked a pilgrimage to write about it so it could be read on air. I sent a piece to the producers and Suzanne Corbie got in touch with me shortly afterwards. She said whilst it was a great piece, someone had sent in a story of her walk on the Camino, a journey across rough terrain with wild dogs along the north coast of France and Spain. There was really no competition. A few weeks later, she contacted me again and said when they aired the piece on the Camino it hadn't done as well as they'd hoped and on reflection mine would have been ideal. She also said she'd send me an application for a television show coming up on Channel 5. Later that morning it arrived. It was to audition for a programme hosted by Trisha Goddard called *Britain's Psychic Challenge*. I was petrified of talking in front of other people, especially groups, let alone exposing myself on national television. Also, I had no formal training as a psychic, so I wondered what on earth had possessed The Guys Upstairs to put me up for something as trivial as a reality TV show. The message came loud and clear. *Don't analyse, Amanda. Apply for the audition and trust us. You'll see as you go through each stage that we're helping you for a reason.*

A picture flashed in my mind to remind me of the vision I'd had of myself on television the previous year, so I pretended I was simply applying on behalf of a friend and dealt with myself like I dealt with all my clients. That bypassed the fear. I received a call from Townhouse TV asking if I was willing to go for an audition and, without thinking about it, I said yes. When I came off the phone, I panicked and shouted at The Guys asking what on earth I was going to do to overcome my fears.

Just trust the process, Amanda! came the calm reply.

"Trust the process?" I almost bellowed at them "You don't realise how terrifying this is for me. How on earth am I going to do this?"

Remember, Amanda, there are things at many levels that are going on for the greater good. You'll be assisted as always, every step of the way. Just ask and we'll be there for you.

And that was it. I asked for guidance and was reminded yet again of my mission. The only purpose I could see for going on the programme was to advocate we all had the ability to tune in. I'd learned enough to know we all had inner senses; it was just a case of waking them up. Two days later, I arrived at the London studios. I was petrified, hadn't eaten and had a rotten headache. Not a good start. I was shown to a room full of people and the director gave me his watch and asked me to tell him something about his life. Nothing came and even when I asked The Guys, I couldn't hear them. At that moment, a woman walked in. I felt I'd blown it but I'd seen her before in the reception and felt her striking energy, so when she sat in front of me and smiled it was as if I'd known her before. The way she looked at me, it was evident she felt it too. She introduced herself as Deborah Borgen and told me she was the mediator for the show, auditioning the psychics and setting up the challenges. I felt she was an ally and immediately warmed to her, though I felt huge amounts of negativity from the crew. She set me several challenges and at the end of it she smiled and said she'd be in touch.

I had no idea if I'd passed or failed, but I knew from her expression she was happy. I hadn't even reached home when I got the phone call to say I'd passed the audition and was invited with seven other contestants to take part in the pilot show. I could have screamed with delight, but I was on the train and couldn't wait to get home. My children were too young to understand. Chris would have been unnerved by the news. My family would have been concerned, so I broke the news to Terry who sat rigid when I told him. A light went on when I delivered the news. Up to that point, he'd told me not to tell people at the gym what I did, as he thought it was whacky but when I told him the news, I could appear on TV he was excited and wanted to spread the word. I should have realised then it was all about his ego, but I was so exhilarated The Guys' plan was working and I needed someone to support me, so I ignored what I sensed.

A few weeks later, I was invited to London for the pilot. I was met by a chauffeur who drove me to a hotel in South London and then I was sent to a room to rest. I was told it could be a couple of hours before they needed me and then I'd be taken to a secret location to take part in a challenge with seven other contestants. Those who got through would go onto the pilot show. I paced the room until someone knocked on the door. A young girl was waiting to tell me I'd be driven to a secret location. I was extremely nervous, but she cheerfully told me to relax. The chauffeur drove me in silence to a part of London I didn't recognise, and we pulled up at an old lock up. It was around five o'clock in the afternoon and being December, it was dark and cold. We pulled up behind a row of similar looking cars and as we came to a halt, a woman walked up and tapped on the window, which the chauffeur opened. She explained there were a few other contestants in front of me in the other cars waiting to go through the challenge and when it was my turn, she'd give me the go-ahead and tell me where to go. It was like waiting for surgery. The suspense was awful, and I felt sick with a knockout headache but just wanted to get it over and done with. Eventually the woman knocked again to say I was the final contestant of the day. "Can you just make sure you hurry up as the crew are tired and cold and only two people have made it through today," she said matter of factly.

No pressure then.

"Right, so if you just walk towards the end of that building and turn right, someone will meet you there to explain what you need to do!"

I got out of the car and walked towards the end of the building. It was pitch black and freezing cold. As I rounded the corner, I saw the building was just a huge open garage. It was floodlit with people dotted everywhere. There were cameras and cables interweaved through the garage, which was surrounded by cars. A woman walked up to me who I later learned was one of the three sceptics on the show (DCI Jackie Malton, best known for being the inspiration for the character of DCI Jane Tennison in the *Prime Suspect* drama written by Lynda La Plante). She thrust a microphone into my face saying, "And this is Amanda Hart from Hertfordshire. Welcome to the show, Amanda."

The Guys were saying – *It's OK, Amanda, we're with you.*

Jackie went on to tell me I was to find the body of a man in the boot of a car and there were fifty cars in total. The only help I would get was a photograph of the man sealed in an envelope. The instant she gave me the envelope I got the most vivid colour navy blue come to me, so I started to look for a navy-blue car. However, as I scanned and walked around the car park, nothing jumped out at me. I could sense the crew getting fed up before I'd started. Feeling frustrated with The Guys, I screamed to them in my head, "Give me something if you want me to do this, please!" Instantly I saw a yellow registration plate in my mind, with just three letters – CUR. *Great*, I thought, *I have something to go on!* I started again through the cars, searching for a registration number with the letters CUR on it. But even though I went through the whole parking lot, no registration numbers jumped out. I screamed to The Guys in my head again "Come on, what the hell are you playing at?" There was silence and I felt abandoned. "OK, CUR, CUR" I kept repeating in my head. "CUR … the number plate! The number plate … CUR!" and that's when it struck me. "Oh Guys … I've got it … CUR the number plate! See you are the number plate!" At that point I realised it was in code and I had to find a number plate associated with ME! Knowing I was down to seconds rather than minutes, I darted through the cars at a rate of knots. When suddenly I noticed a white car at the entrance to the parking lot. It had my initials on it – AJ (for Amanda Jayne) – and I knew immediately that was the car. I suddenly had a surge of heat searing through my body, which overwhelmed me. Not wanting to chance it, I stopped in front of the car and asked The Guys to confirm it was the right car.

I instantly saw an image of me in a class with Keith Hearne during my hypnotherapy training. I remembered the day well. He had been teaching us about using pendulums, and how they helped huge corporations find oil and precious metals below the earth's surface. He had taught us we could use our own bodies as pendulums if we needed accurate yes or no answers. I had no option but to chance it. I set my body by asking a yes question and found I swayed back and forth. Then I set my body to respond to a no question, which made me sway sideways. Once I had my yes and no set, I asked, "Is this the car with the body in?" My body instantly swayed back and forth. "Yes, this is the one," I said to Jackie.

She moved towards the car with a key in her hand, put it into the lock of the boot and flung it open. There lying in the boot was a man. As he started to climb out, I saw he was dressed from head to foot in navy blue. Everyone clapped and cheered. I heard The Guys loud and clear – *Now you realise your training can come in at any time, especially under pressure. Don't assume the answers, Amanda, with the information you first receive. Always wait to see how things develop.*

That day I learned more under pressure than I could have done in years of meditation. Only three of us had made it onto the pilot show. It was nothing to do with luck, The Guys were orchestrating something so magnificent I just had to sit back and enjoy the ride.

Chapter 36

It is by no means an irrational fancy that, in a future
existence, we shall look upon what we think our present
existence, as a dream.

Edgar Allan Poe

Townhouse TV phoned a few days later to say filming for the
pilot show was due to start. I was met at a hotel near Luton where
I'd be staying for the weekend. We were supposed to make an
early start that next morning, so I tried to get an early night, but
my sense of anticipation was on full alert. I woke the next
morning from a dream of being blind. At first, I was concerned I
would not be able to visualise, but I told myself to ignore it until
it became clear what it meant. Not being able to eat breakfast, I
was relieved to get going when the car arrived to take me to a
secret location.

When I got into the back of the people carrier, I was
introduced to Anna Galliers and Diane Lazarus. I had an instant
feeling of uncertainty about Diane and couldn't understand why.
I tried to brush it aside. We were only a few minutes into our
journey when the passenger in the front, who told us he was
security, handed us each a blindfold (hence why I'd dreamed
about being blind the night before) and told us to put them on. It
was some distance to our destination and when we finally
arrived, we were led one by one into a building.

It was unnerving being guided through corridors and a relief
when we finally arrived at a room. We sat down side by side and
only then were we allowed to remove the blindfolds. We were in
a small kitchen, or perhaps a utility room. There was nothing in
there but cupboards, a table, and a sink. The décor and high
ceilings made it obvious this was an old house. The runner
announced herself as she popped in to see how we were and
asked us to sit down. "You can remove your blindfolds now.
You're here at the location. If you can all stay put here until we
call you for each challenge, then we'll take you out one by one."

Anna, who was sitting in the middle, said, "How long will it take before we're called?"

The young girl just shrugged her shoulders. "I've no idea but there's three challenges each for you today and we're booked to be here until late afternoon."

We sat and waited. The only company we had was the young security guy from the car. I sensed things were not quite what they appeared. I liked Anna and the more we chatted, the more I felt a rapport with her. When I told her she had angels all around her she explained she worked predominantly with angels. I couldn't get past a wall with Diane though. She had her guard up and I was thankful she was sitting on the other side of Anna. We sat there all day, with no food or drink and only left the room one at a time to go to individual challenges or to the toilet. Each time we were blindfolded. With yet another headache from lack of food and air, being kept on tenterhooks all day didn't help. Diane was a star in her own right and she ran through her repertoire of accomplishments in the psychic world. Next to her I felt like a complete novice and didn't realise I was losing my power by having such negative thoughts. I felt I'd failed miserably at the first two challenges and struggled to make connections, but the third was similar to the one I'd had in the car lot. I was taken into the room last and only given ten minutes to accomplish the challenge. I realised the pressure was on and focused. Something clicked into gear for me as I remembered The Guys' advice after the car lot challenge. *Just focus, relax, and see what we give you.*

As a member of the crew took the blindfold off, I found myself sitting next to a four-poster bed in a small bedroom. The dark room was full of crew members, including Deborah. I felt strong again. I was given the envelope and told to work out what was inside in relation to someone who'd stayed in that room. At first, I saw a woman, dressed in old-fashioned underwear. She was in an old Victorian style bedroom standing in front of a mirror whilst behind her a maid was doing up her very tight corset. She kept pulling the corset tighter and as I was explaining this, Deborah nodded, and I knew I was on the right track. Suddenly, I got a picture of a man wearing what I thought to be some kind of shield he'd wear for a game of cricket (around his nether regions). I felt embarrassed and looked at Deborah. I tried to describe what I was seeing but my rational mind kept telling me I was ridiculous. I described it as a protective undergarment a man would wear, and the crew nodded and smiled. Then I saw a picture of Mowgli from the film *The Jungle Book*. He was walking through the jungle, skinny, with dark hair and just wearing his pants. They said I'd got it and started to pack up.

Deborah came over and hugged me. "Well done, Amanda. See what you can do when you relax."

I was thrilled when she told me I was the only one who'd got the challenge. When the envelope was opened a small pair of red boy's pants was inside left by Mick Jagger who'd worn them once when he'd stayed in that very room. It was only when we were allowed to leave that we saw the house for the first time. As I was walked through the splendid corridors adorned with paintings, I realised we were in a historical house and eventually we entered a room full of people who appeared to be part of an audience. The runner explained filming had taken place in that room throughout the day for part of the show. We saw Trisha Goddard who briefly said hello to us. When we got outside, the runner said, "As you can see you've been at Knebworth House in Hertfordshire all day."

I went home knowing I'd done my best, but something played on my mind about the warning The Guys had given me. What did *All is not what it seems* mean? I was on such a high; I chose to push it aside. That was my mistake. I should have paid attention to the undercurrents. I should have listened to The Guys.

Afterwards, back in the hotel, The Guys Upstairs briefed me. *See how you felt today and how tough it was for you!*

"Yes, but that's not helping me!" I retorted.

Amanda, you have to learn about how you use your power and how you can lose it to other people unless you protect yourself.

"I know, I've heard this before" I said, slumping down onto the bed, as if I'd been scolded.

As soon as you say, "I know" you don't know! You still have a lot to learn. Be careful, Amanda. All is not what it seems!

The pilot show went out over Christmas after being advertised to the hilt with a mention in numerous ad breaks on Channel 5, leading up to the series starting the following month. Although Terry had been dismissive before, as soon as I started to appear on the TV ads, he couldn't advocate what I did enough. My mother's husband too, was more supportive of my work and proudly told his friends I was on TV. He didn't understand it still, but seemed to appreciate something was there for me to be involved in such a project. Chris went quiet which saddened me, but I stayed focused on what I had to do.

When we started to film the first show, Anna, Diane, and I met several other contestants who were also going to take part. Austin was the baby of the pack, a sweetheart, and an old and wise soul. Dennis was funny, very protective and became our father figure. Dave was a gentleman with a cheeky side and was always grounded. Mary was a little trooper, a strong cookie and brutally honest. Soleira was very sensitive, and I could really understand her as she worked predominantly with energy. The whole group had an amazing dynamic, although I still wasn't sure about Diane.

The morning before filming the first programme, all the contestants were sitting in the dining room having breakfast when Deborah asked me to join her. We went to a separate table, and she asked if I could give her a reading of what I was picking up on all the other contestants. I was surprised but assumed she was doing this to see how we were tuning in to each other. I ran through each one until I got to Diane. I told Deborah she'd win. "It's already decided!" I said.

"What makes you say that?"

"Things are not what they seem."

Gradually some of the contestants sensed there was something not right and I sensed there was cheating going on but said nothing. Diane and I started to clash. The more I tried to connect with her, the more she seemed to block me, which unnerved me as I felt the rest of the group were bonding so well. I wondered why we were all feeling the same concerns. After the first programme, Soleira was voted off and we all felt very sad. By then, we'd noticed cheating, and we discussed what we should do. On a number of occasions, crew members had given clues to a certain contestant. We felt we should tell Deborah, but no one wanted to put her under pressure, nor be ousted for being a grass. Instead, we all turned our heads and hoped it was just our imagination. On the second programme, some of the contestants became very angry with what was going on and so the bond deepened. It was becoming obvious the crew were manoeuvring things to their advantage. Dennis in particular was very vocal and said the whole set up was a farce, but we tried to reassure him and said we just had to stay calm and do the best we could. I witnessed it the day I was taken into a marquee and given ten photographs. I was told each one was a picture of a bride or groom on their wedding day, and I had to match the pairs and place them on the table. I knew I'd got them all right.

Then the group of people in the photos were ushered into the marquee. I was told by the host to match up the couples by moving them physically to stand with each other. I managed to move three of the couples as I had paired up with the photos, but then I suddenly felt a brick wall and couldn't speak. I looked at Philip Escoffey and felt his energy deflecting mine. I had no idea why, but I couldn't move. When I was asked if I'd finished, I just nodded. The last two couples just needed to be swapped as in my photos, but I felt paralysed. I only got three out of the five couples right, regardless of the fact I had them all right in the photographs – which they omitted to film. I left the marquee feeling scared and voiced my concerns to the group. That's when Dennis said, "Well he's a sceptic isn't he? He used to work as a psychic and now gets more money from being sceptical of the whole process. Of course, he's going to know how to block. That's the easy bit."

I was shocked and unnerved by what Dennis had said, but he was right, it was how I felt, blocked. I didn't want the uncomfortable feelings and certainly didn't like being judged at the best of times so the programme was becoming more than a little uncomfortable, but I felt I had no choice but to continue with the process and see it out. I wanted to make peace and tried to connect with Diane, but she kept her guard up. I was feeling out of my depth and fears from my childhood in relation to my stepmother came to the surface. I assumed it was because Diane was a woman.

On the final day of filming, I was feeling low. I no longer wanted to be involved in the programme and had just got back to my room after going to the hotel gym when someone knocked on my door and shouted. "Amanda, can you be in reception in ten minutes for filming?"

I threw open the door astounded and said to the runner, "You can't be serious. You've got to be wrong! I was told I wouldn't be filming until this afternoon and had three hours spare."

"Sorry, it's just what I've been told."

In a panic, I rushed into the bathroom, put the shower on and ran back into the room to grab some clothes. I hadn't noticed I'd left the shower curtain hanging out of the bath and when I ran back in, I slipped and went down like a ton of bricks on the cold wet tiles. My head hit the tiled floor first, followed by my leg, which caught the bath panel tiles as I careered into the bath. It took just a moment to feel the searing pain. I could hardly move. I'd knocked the wind out of myself. My head was throbbing, but even worse was the blood pouring out of my leg. I could see I'd damaged my leg in two places but couldn't work out how I'd cut it. Lumps came up almost instantly on my lower shin and below my knee. I was in agony. Tears poured down my face and I begged The Guys to help me.

"Why has life got to be so damn testing? Why this? Why now?" I cried out.

No reply came. Feeling stupid and angry, I patched my leg up as much as I could and, without bothering to shower, I pulled on some clothes and hobbled down to reception. I daren't tell anyone about my accident, as I knew it would compromise me going ahead with the show. For the rest of the day I was miserable and couldn't shake the dark cloud that hovered over me. My head and leg thumped simultaneously, and I felt homesick. Anna and Mary were lovely when I confided in them and did some healing to help me get through the day. They too said they didn't want to be there.

After a particularly horrible confrontation with Diane, I gave up. We'd been waiting in a room together and Diane made a point of saying jealousy was ugly when aimed at those who were successful. We all felt uncomfortable with what she'd said, but we all knew it was aimed at me especially, and at one point I was visualising arrows being aimed into my back. One of the contestants decided it was about time to release the underlying pressure and asked us to group together, have a hug and send huge amounts of positive energy to each other. That exercise revealed how committed and supportive we all were to each other and likewise, identified the person who was on their own agenda. The Guys seemed to have all but disappeared and a wall of silence prevailed. I was voted off shortly after on the second programme, but the contestants didn't want us to be separated. Anna and I had grown close, and all the contestants asked me to continue working with them energetically to help protect them as they felt they were under psychic attack.

When Deborah approached me to speak for the last time, she hugged me and said, "Amanda, you have to trust everything will be OK and this is for the highest good. I know and you know what happened, but it will all be revealed to us why, in time."

328

I knew she was right, but I was choked as I felt I'd been fooled and abandoned by The Guys and said, "Deborah, I know everything's as it should be but I feel like I've been used and don't know how this will affect me. I didn't expect it to turn out this way. I thought I was supposed to show people their own power."

I cried then as I felt exhausted and as if I'd failed. She hugged me close and said, "Everything's OK, Amanda. You know this more than anyone. Please go home and be with your family and trust all will be well." She just looked at me and hung her head and that's when I knew she knew, too. Somehow, I didn't think it would be the last time I saw her.

The next day, bizarrely, my mother was playing golf in the next county and slipped on a slight incline as it was slightly damp on the course. Amazingly, her leg broke in two places with the bone appearing through the skin in exactly the same places as I'd damaged mine when in the bathroom in the hotel only the day before. As she was looking after the children whilst I was filming, I certainly would have had to come off the programme as she was whisked to hospital and received an emergency operation to have a titanium support inserted from her ankle to her knee. When I went to see Mum in hospital, I realised the two points where the bone had come through her leg were the identical points at where I had the large swellings on mine. Above all though, I knew Mum came first and therefore I let all the fears of the show leave me to allow me to focus on what was best for my family.

From then on, I immersed myself in work and keeping fit and focusing on my loved ones. Entering all the local charity runs I could, kept me focused as I still felt I'd left the programme thinking I'd failed. I had regular texts from the contestants telling me they were seeing cheating going on with crew members feeding information to help Diane win challenges. Mary wanted to walk off, but I encouraged them to do their best and learn from the situation. When it came to the end of the programme, Mary nearly blew their cover, but somehow the crew and Deborah kept it going until the end. Diane won the competition, although everyone on the programme knew the truth. I watched the last programme and knew it wasn't just me who could see there was no surprise on the winner's face. It was also evident how angry Mary was as she moved away from the winner when it was announced, but what was done was done.

Just after this, My Spirit Radio contacted me to record an interview to promote Russell Grant, the famous astrologer. I felt humbled by the opportunity and took up the offer and then Suzanne asked me if I'd like to present my own radio show. Appearing on TV had been a challenge, however hosting an hour's show once a month was more than terrifying. Suzanne said she would like me to create my own show based on my work with clients. It would include interviews with special guests, reviewing the latest books and, of course, giving tips and advice to help people who were developing spiritually. I asked The Guys, who by then were communicating again, and they said, *Of course we want you to fulfil this role, Amanda.*

"Well, that's OK for you to say, but you abandoned me on that TV show."

We never abandoned you, Amanda. We guided you to take the challenge head on, which you did. You came out when you'd learned all you needed to learn. It was never about winning the competition; it was always about seeing how competing can take you down a dark path and you simply had to experience that.

When I started recording my first show, I was very nervous, and it certainly didn't come naturally to me. I travelled down to Maidstone in Kent each month, armed with what I'd written for the programme and over time started to form my own unique show. I felt so lucky as I got to review the latest books in the Mind, Body, Spirit field which helped me research my work further with what was currently being explored. Having the show enabled me to approach specialists in their chosen fields of expertise who were more than willing to speak about their experiences and knowledge. I also contacted and interviewed new authors which helped me on so many levels. I realised I was becoming passionate about writing for the show, loved to source incredible mentors, and was gaining confidence with the whole process.

Clients were flowing to me from all directions, and I drank all the knowledge I could from my new experience at the radio show. I felt it was time to find out what I could achieve with my intuitive abilities through formal training and approached a recommended teacher who started to work with me on a one-to-one basis. It was a great experience, and I learned a lot from her, but, as I was ever the sceptic, I felt I only had her word for it to confirm information I was getting was real. I knew I needed to work in a group dynamic. I signed up at my local spiritual church for a regular development circle. I didn't tell them what I'd been involved with on TV, as I felt it would make them judge me differently and I wanted to be treated as a complete novice.

It was around this time that Chris phoned me. I hadn't heard from him in a while so was surprised, but he said he needed to meet with me. He asked me to come into London and a few days later we met at Trader Vic's Bar at The Hilton Hotel. I'd never been to a bar like that before, but I felt an instant connection with all the memorabilia and Polynesian artefacts. It wasn't what I had been expecting. As I walked in, I could see waiters serving cocktails and exotic cuisine. I was in paradise, or home, I couldn't decide which. I spotted Chris across the restaurant as he stood out a mile. He was still his drop-dead gorgeous self and looked confident and happy. As he spotted me, he smiled as if he was so thrilled to see me. Once I'd arrived at his table, he got up and kissed me. It wasn't a kiss I expected. It felt tender and loving and I pulled back to look into his eyes. We sat down, facing each other and when it was evident, I knew what I was feeling from him, he shook himself back to the reality of where we were.

"So, what's so important you wanted to meet with me then, Chris?" I asked, hoping for once he would just take a leap of faith and ask me what we both wanted to hear.

"Let's order a cocktail first!" he said squeezing my hand and passing me the menu.

I tried to focus but couldn't see anything as the words became a blur. My stomach was in knots and my heart in bits. I wondered if he was going to finally tell me he'd left his partner and he wanted me to honour how we felt about each other. I just told him I'd have what he was having and as soon as he ordered the drinks, he dived into a story about what had happened to him recently in Portugal. I tried desperately not to let him see or feel my disappointment but politely laughed and listened to his story. Eventually he got to the point.

"Can you come to Portugal to help this friend of mine?" he said.

"What do you want me to do?"

"I told him you were a psychic and if anyone could help him find a particular spot in the ocean, you could do it!"

"Chris, I help people, I don't look for spots in the middle of the ocean." I said, disappointed and irritated.

He told me the story from the beginning. Chris had recently gone to Portugal to see how the construction of his new holiday villa was coming along. Disappointed with delays, he'd gone in search of the developer who turned out to be a forty-stone man named Brian. Brian tried to rationalise the delays with Chris, but Chris was having none of it. Brian invited Chris out for lunch to find solutions to their business crisis and during their lunch, Chris discovered more about the man's involvement in other things in Portugal which intrigued him.

Brian was a very wealthy man in his own right, owning a bank, a nightclub, and several property development projects. However, Chris was more fascinated with Brian's hobby – searching for the gateway to Atlantis. Brian lived in Lisbon and had heard about items sold in a market that had turned out to be historical artefacts. He'd flown in a geologist from America to authenticate the items he'd bought, and when asked where they'd come from, Brian told him they'd come to the surface in a particular spot in the Atlantic Ocean, just off the coast of Portugal. The geologist suggested the artefacts were possibly from the era of Atlantis. Brian found the man at the market and asked him where he'd found them. A local man who'd found them whilst out in his boat then took Brian back to the exact spot when the tide was low. Sure enough, there was more to discover so Brian had someone drafted in to collect more until he had filled a room full of different sized and shaped pots.

Brian then spoke to a scientist who came to visit him. The scientist told him he was no longer involved in that kind of research as the British government had pulled the plug on funding to all scientists on Atlantis research and they were told to move onto other fields. Brian wasn't fazed by this, even though he felt he was being encouraged to not bother going further. He decided to go down another route and contacted Michael Moore, the controversial American filmmaker, famous for *Fahrenheit 9/11*, *Bowling for Columbine* and *The Awful Truth*, who was interested in Brian's discovery. Brian felt involving someone controversial to broadcast this through the media would allow the information to still come to the surface.

When Chris met Brian, he'd already bought an ex-hospital ship from the navy to use as a base. He had planned to fly in biologists, geologists, and all matter of other specialists to verify the find and have them stay on board the ship near the site of discovery. He had specialised submerging equipment to record and detect under the water, and divers to help with the project. Chris immediately wanted to be part of the process. Chris told

Brian that for many years he'd had dreams about him finding a treasure he discovers whilst diving and was then involved in overseeing the treasure was protected and given to the rightful people. Brian said he had everything in place; all he had to do was find a way of finding the exact spot – the gateway to Atlantis. This wasn't necessarily where the artefacts were washing up. It could be anywhere around the area. Brian and the specialists had not come up with a solution as how to find the exact spot until Chris suggested perhaps a psychic could find it and save everyone the trouble.

"No pressure then!" I said to Chris when he'd finally finished. "So what you're saying is you want me to fly with you to Portugal to meet this man Brian and find a spot in the whole of the Atlantic Ocean which happens to be the gateway to Atlantis?"

"Yes, that's exactly it," he replied.

I couldn't believe what he was asking me, but his face was so alive and enigmatic, it seemed he was convinced it was a significant historical project of public interest so I told him I had to think about it (what I needed to do was check in with The Guys Upstairs).

I left the bar late. We'd both relaxed and it was almost like being back with him in the early days. My heart was yearning for The Guys to say yes whilst my heart said it was a ridiculous plan. I knew I'd honour whatever they told me regardless of my feelings for Chris. When we left, Chris flagged down two taxis. He paid my driver and told him to drive me all the way out to Hertfordshire and before I got in he, held me tight, kissed me deeply and asked me to consider how this trip to Portugal could change everything for us. Trying to avoid giving away my burning desire to agree, I simply told him I'd let him know. I was in the taxi only five minutes into the journey when The Guys tuned in and spoke to me.

Amanda, you've been asked to uphold this challenge in preparation for new changes ahead. Take the challenge head on and trust you'll get what you need to succeed.

I thanked The Guys without asking further questions and settled back into the taxi with my head resting on the headrest, a deep smile on my face and a hope that at long last I could allow myself to love like never before. I could feel I was on the brink. All I needed was to get out to Portugal with Chris and then all would naturally evolve. Before I left, six numbers came to me and I asked The Guys what they were.

Write these numbers down, Amanda. You'll need them.

"What for?" I asked.

You'll have to work that out yourself.

"Well I guess it isn't the winning numbers for the lottery."

Amanda, please take this seriously. You'll need the numbers as they'll give you the answer you seek in Portugal.

Within a few weeks, and after countless emails and a few phone calls to Brian, Chris and I left Heathrow on an early flight to Lisbon. On the way, we spoke excitedly about our plans. We were due to go and stay at Chris's villa and be met by Brian the next day. When we eventually arrived at his villa, he showed me round and I could see not only did his villa need to be finished, but the whole site did also. I was surprised when Chris showed me my room and told me where he'd be sleeping. He left me to unpack and told me when I was ready to meet him on the patio and then we'd go off for dinner. Disappointed, I wondered if perhaps he was just being a gentleman. When we got back to the villa from the restaurant, Chris said, "Look, we could both do with some sleep as we've got an early start," and wished me goodnight outside my door. He kissed me fondly on the cheek and walked back towards his room. I felt cheated. With him blowing hot one minute and cold the next, I had no idea where I was with him. I resigned myself to thinking he was confused and went into my room to sleep with my sadness.

The next day, Brian arrived with a woman he introduced as his carer. Chris had informed me beforehand he had someone to help him with general things like cooking and shopping as he was around 40 stone in weight. Her name was Julie and she told me she was ex-military and making the most of travelling the world caring for different people in different countries. She'd just started the posting with Brian and was finding him very demanding.

We all got to know each other over a coffee and Brian said he wanted to set out and drive down to the Algarve.

"Why the Algarve?" I asked.

"After looking at possible clues through my own research, I just feel it's where the Atlantis gateway's located."

I didn't feel so convinced, but said, "OK, I guess you know where to start."

He ignored my comment and carried on chatting to Chris. I felt uncomfortable and out of place but tried to supress the negative feelings and chatted happily with Julie instead. Then Brian turned to me and said, "So how do you intend to find the location then?"

"Brian, it doesn't work like that. I just have to wait and see what comes to me when the time is right."

"Well, you must have something if you're supposed to be psychic. Don't you have anything?"

"Brian, impressions don't come through on demand. They come through when it's necessary. Please try and be patient and I will give you what you need when I get it given to me." I said, but sensed he was frustrated with having to wait.

He again lost interest in me and we got into his specially adapted car and set off for the Algarve. Several hours later, we stopped at a restaurant at a beach and had lunch. I was relieved to be out of the car and in the fresh air. That's when I saw my first sign. It was a simple cross in the sky formed by two aircraft contrails, and I instantly turned to Brian and said, "I need a map of Portugal and the Atlantic Ocean."

He suggested we headed for the captain of the port to enquire. The captain said we'd have to go to Lisbon where they had all the proper shipping maps, so we all got back in the car and headed back. I felt the whole drive to the Algarve had been a pointless exercise as The Guys would have shown me that sign anywhere. Once we'd found the address for the shipping maps, Julie and I waited patiently in the car whilst Brian and Chris went to purchase them. Eventually they came out armed with maps of all sizes and threw them into the back for me to look at.

"There you go," Brian declared, "have a sift through that lot. Hope you find something! That little lot cost me over £150!"

I felt a little prickly he was so begrudging.

"We'll head over to my apartment so I can show you what we've got on the computers. I hope you get something soon before you have to head off to the airport!"

The usual phrase came into my head, and I felt like saying to him out loud, *No pressure then!* But I bit my tongue.

Eventually we got to his apartment, which was like a fortress with underground car park and lift straight into his apartment. When we arrived in his oversized living room, he showed us to a large desk with several computers on it. Chris sat down with Brian, and they fired up Google Earth to show me certain points of interest. I left them to it and went over to a glass table in the middle of his dining room and laid out the maps. Immediately, I eliminated the large ones and kept out only two small ones which I felt would give me answers.

Julie had gone off to prepare food, so I was left alone to focus. I took the piece of paper out of my bag and wondered if the numbers had something to do with map coordinates. Having a vague recollection of longitude and latitude at school, I thought I would need only two numbers to pinpoint a place on the map.

What else do you have to go on but the maps? I heard The Guys say to me. *Look again, Amanda. Work out the code!*

It took me half an hour but eventually – bingo! I'd done it. I shuffled the numbers I'd been given round on the map until they all coincided with the longitude and latitude numbers. If I used a pencil and ruler, I could draw a line from each of the numbers until they crossed. It was the cross I'd seen in the sky with the aircraft contrails. Eventually, they formed a triangle, but more interestingly, they formed the exact symbol of the cross that I'd seen off the coast of the south of Portugal.

X marks the spot, Amanda, I heard loud and clear. *X marks the spot.*

I called out to Brian, I'd found it and took over the map I'd made with my markings on. "This is the spot!" I said with great pride.

"What do you mean? You can't possibly have it, I've not given you any idea where to look," he said indignantly.

"It doesn't matter," I said. "I know for sure this is the spot and you need to mark it!"

He looked at the map and looked back at his screen. "OK," he said, "we'll put in the exact coordinates she's got marked here and see if they have any relevance."

Sure enough, once he'd put them into the computer, his mouth dropped, and he looked at me with a shocked expression. "Look Chris, that spot where the cross is marked is the exact location of the 1755 earthquake that occurred in the Atlantic Ocean. She must have it. Amanda, I was drawn to this particular event as it killed nearly 50,000 people. It was on All Saints Day. Three tremors struck out in the ocean within ten minutes. The tremors reached as far as Morocco, but a twenty-foot tsunami hit Portugal. As so many were in church, when the buildings collapsed it devastated the population. Fire broke out over the city and thousands of homes, including the royal palace, were destroyed. Most of the country's cultural history was wiped out. The earthquake involved all four elements of earth, fire, water and air and many religious authorities said it was a result of God's anger as it destroyed eight hundred churches."

After digesting what Brian had told me, I left the room with them both talking ten to the dozen and asked Julie for the time. It was almost time to leave for the airport. She said she too was going to leave but was glad she'd met me. "I'm going to give my notice in and go back to Canada and make a go of it with my partner," she said. "I think it took the journey today for me to realise it. You've made me see I've been running from him for too long and need to accept we love each other and can make it work."

I was thrilled for her and knew the journey had been much more than the search for Atlantis. Julie had discovered where her heart lay and I knew I, too, had to let go of Chris once and for all. Perhaps I'd had to go through the whole experience with Julie in another lifetime to understand it in this one. Chris and I soon rushed back to the airport and headed home. I knew I had discovered so much more on that trip than I had anticipated, and it was time to draw a line and move on from him once and for all. With deep resignation and great sadness I finally had to accept I would meet my soul mate when the time was right, even if it would be years, even decades before that happened.

Chapter 37

Give, but give until it hurts.

Mother Teresa

When I got back home, I spoke to a friend of mine who had just got back from a trip to a holistic event where she had gone to a talk given by a scientist whose speciality was Atlantis. I was astounded when she told me the man started to talk about Brian. She gave me the contact number for his university. Two days later, I spoke to him, and he told me about his involvement.

He asked me if I'd seen the artefacts, but I told him I hadn't and I was to help find a location, not corroborate what was already discovered. He told me he'd seen the artefacts as he'd visited the apartment, and he knew they were quite possibly from the era of Atlantis but had been told like other scientists involved in the research to leave well alone and the plug had been pulled from their funding. To keep his role at the university, he like others had no choice but to do as they were instructed. He told me I should stop investigating and move away from it, too. I felt it was a warning more than anything, and he wasn't telling me everything. I felt uncomfortable after that message and decided to leave well alone.

I felt that going back to the Spiritualist Church would give me focus. I wanted to progress and learn how I got spiritual information. Progression was slow however, and I felt frustrated as I wanted to learn and all we seemed to be doing was covering what I already knew with no real understanding of how it was happening. I finally experienced something different. One night, the group leader had invited a medium, Ben, to the church who did platform work (reading as a medium to an audience). I needed him to do a reading for me.

The husband of our Spiritualist Church development leader happened to be a historian and collector of First and Second World War memorabilia. He came that night to show us photographs that had been taken recently from his visit to the area where the Battle of the Somme had been. He asked us to hand the photographs around to see what impressions we got. Looking at one photograph, both Ben and I noticed the same thing. "I can see there was an underground hospital there during the battle," we said almost at the same time. There was nothing to indicate it in the photo, just grass and what looked like a hole in the ground. Ben and I both looked at each other. Several more photos came round and again, Ben and I seemed to pick up the same information. "I can see men in the trees. It looks like smoke, too." I said.

Ben could see it too, but the others were struggling to see what we were seeing. At the end of the session we were told that Ben could read for a couple of people in the group to show us how mediums worked. I was hoping he'd choose me, but he didn't. It wasn't until I was walking the length of the church to leave, that he suddenly came out of the room he'd been in and almost bumped into me. I blurted out, "Is there any chance you could give me a reading at some point?"

He took a card out of his pocket and asked me to call him to organise a visit. The following evening when the children were in bed, Ben came to my home. We got straight down to the reading. He told me things about my family which were accurate, and he picked up on what type of work I did. As he didn't know me, and I'd kept it secret from the church so I could be treated like a new student, I knew he was genuine. He knew I was an intuitive seeing clients, working on a healing level. He started to talk about how I was changing direction with my work. I felt uncomfortable, as I didn't want things to change. Everything was working so well the way it was. He explained that I was going to change course, and this would take me out of my comfort zone (just when I thought everything was going so well) and start working with a new dynamic. He said he saw me tracking energy and finding people. Then without warning, he jumped back as if he'd avoided a collision with something.

"I see you're in danger. I see you being bundled into a car with officials taking you off somewhere. I've been shown that I need to help you protect yourself as you'll need it." And then he looked at me, deeply concerned.

"What do you mean?" I stammered. "How on earth can I be in danger with what I do? I only see clients to help them and I'm hardly going to be in danger dabbling with love, light and twinkles."

"I know," he said, "but I've been shown I need to put you in touch with someone who'll help you."

When I asked The Guys Upstairs later that night, they told me I needed to trust Ben and that what he'd seen was right. I should be guided by him as they'd sent him to me. Shortly after meeting Ben, I met Neville Thurlbeck, then chief reporter for the *News of the World*. He came to interview me when news finally broke that Britain's Psychic Challenge had been involved in the phone voting scandal. Neville was a very dapper, striking man. Before the interview, we chatted about his childhood experiences of things that seemed odd at the time for him. I simply gave him my interpretation of what he'd experienced and normalised it. He was intrigued. I told him what I'd seen in some recent photos as an example. He looked at me stunned. "That's so odd," he said. "I'm going to the site of the Battle of the Somme next week for a holiday."

Neville and I formed a bond that day. The story never went out in the *News of the World*, but instead the *Daily Mirror* published it. Neville was intrigued by what I did and asked me to stay in touch. I found him to be a warm and open person, although I was a little wary because he was a reporter. He asked me if he could discuss at some stage in the future a possible documentary about the Battle of the Somme. I said I'd consider it.

A few days after that, I went to London with Ben to meet Kizzi Nkwocha in a coffee bar. Kizzi was an agent who'd been one of Max Clifford's biggest rivals back in his day. He'd looked after clients such as the King of Uganda, President Clinton's mistress, the Pakistani cricket Captain, Wasim Akram and Michael Perham, the world record teenage sailor. Kizzi had also become known on radio and television for talk shows (interviewing such names as Lennox Lewis and Muhammad Ali) and had been behind charitable organisations such as the Vass Foundation, which focused on alleviating AIDS and malaria in the Third World. I had no idea how he could help me, but Ben told me to trust, which I did, and said he was more than just an agent. When I first met Kizzi, he was immaculately dressed in a suit with a flamboyant and colourful shirt and tie. He was warm and welcoming, but I felt an awesome power of authority which assured me that he was a man who got things done. Ben explained to Kizzi what he'd got in his reading when he'd come to see me.

He smiled at me and said, "This sounds interesting, I'd like to know more. Perhaps I can explain why Ben's brought you to me. I lived out in Cyprus for some time where I produced a radio show out there, amongst other things and that's how I met Bob Cracknell, who I helped and then became good friends with."

I had no idea what the relevance was nor who Bob Cracknell was.

"Bob Cracknell was known at one point as one of the world's leading psychics. He was trained by the FBI and had their accreditation as a law enforcement officer. He then became a member of the IAATI (The International Association of Auto Theft Investigation), and the IPI (Institute of Professional Investigators)."

I still had no idea where it was leading but listened avidly. Kizzi carried on, "He moved to Cyprus to live a semi-retired life and wrote countless books and continued to help with investigations from there. If you've come to me for help, then you'll need to establish yourself so that you're out there in the public domain. I suggest you set up a website to inform the public what you do so that when we need to deal with this, we have something to guide people to for information."

"But I haven't started to do this work yet," I said, confused.

Kizzi took a sip of his coffee and, as he placed the cup back down gracefully on the saucer, he clasped his hands, looked at me and smiled. "If Ben's brought you to me for my help, then you need to trust me. I'll get in touch with Bob in Cyprus and put him in touch with you. Be warned, though – if Bob thinks you're a fraud or there is anything he's unsure about, he'll have no qualms about saying. He's the equivalent of a heavyweight boxer and if he tells you as it is, you'll know about it."

Before I'd met Ben, life had been moving in the right direction. I had a lovely home, time for my children and trips abroad, great friends and my social life was better than ever – but Terry and I were starting to argue. At first, I thought it was because he didn't like the fact that I spent so much time planning and preparing with Ben, but other things started to change too. I was aware that Ben worked differently to me as a medium. As I worked with the power of positive energy, I'd naturally created a new world of a more positive lifestyle and environment. Ben however was going through terrible traumas with his ex-partner which spilled into our everyday meetings as he vented his anguish, and his energy was coming from a different place. I realised I needed Ben's help, so I brushed aside how it made me feel when his fears came up. It seemed though that his fears about his personal life were starting to compound my own building fears about the unknown future and the warning he'd given me in the reading. Slowly but surely apprehension was leaking into my life once more. I was letting my power diminish again. I had nothing from The Guys to give me any clue as to what was about to happen. I felt I had to honour what was going on and do what I'd been advised to do, so when our website was done and Ben and I went back to see Kizzi, he agreed that we were ready. I then emailed Bob and introduced myself as Kizzi had instructed. Sure enough, I received a curt reply from Cyprus. Bob explained he knew both Kizzi and Ben were credible, but he didn't know me from Adam. He said that both Ben and Kizzi had been in touch with him to explain who I was. If Ben was right, then I had better prepare and he would help me as long as I did everything he advised. I replied that I was grateful for his help, and I was clear about his terms.

Then Ben and I waited. Anxiety ruled, so I worked out in the gym daily. Clients were waning and I spent time going off at weekends when the children were away, to walk for miles alone in the countryside. Terry and I were finding things fraught within our relationship as I spent more and more time searching for solace. He felt threatened and so the spiral of negativity in our relationship deepened.

Chris and I also fell out one day when I telephoned him to announce I couldn't deal with him anymore. I knew he was struggling still with guilt but felt stifled with the growing negativity around me and needed to cut the reins of some of my relationships. Everything we had came to a grinding halt. I guess I pushed him away as I was living in an uncertain phase of my life and having him play with my emotions was the last thing I needed. I felt suddenly alone and vulnerable.

I started to spend time alone at home in the evenings and immersed myself in DVDs, watching films that helped me to move away from my daily concerns. Then, on 3rd May 2007, whilst I was about to watch a DVD, the oddest things started to happen. I'd just started watching a film and an overwhelming feeling washed over me as if The Guys had just stepped into the room. I paused the DVD so I could take stock of what was going on. A large clock was frozen on the screen (It was ten minutes to ten on the film) and as I turned to look at my clock behind me, I was shocked to see it was exactly the same time to the minute – ten to ten. A cold shiver ran through the entire length of my body and The Guys had my full attention. At the same time the phone rang, which was odd as it was late. When I got up to answer it, it rang off. When I dialled to see who the last person to call me was, the automated reply told me that the number had been withheld. I felt cold as if someone had turned the temperature down.

Something wasn't right. I went into the hallway as I had an unexpected unease about the children. All was quiet but I ran up the stairs and went into each of their rooms. They were both sound asleep. I felt frightened but couldn't rationalise why. The image of Ben giving me his reading came into my mind. I tried to shrug it off and went into the kitchen and made myself a cup of tea and then went back into the living room to watch the rest of the DVD.

Having membership at Love Films at that time, I received films randomly in the post, three at a time. On that occasion, I had no idea what I was about to watch as the film title had no clue in it why I'd chosen the film in the first place. Having memory loss as a consequence of the meningitis was a pain at times, so I'd go with whatever I picked randomly and would very often order films I'd already seen. The film I chose that night was about a child going missing. The emotion that came from it was disconcerting as I certainly didn't recall ordering a film that would render me emotionally bereft, reminding me of the loss of my own daughter, but I watched it in tears, hugging my knees to me on my sofa as I felt the depth of my own despair and grief. It was almost thirteen years to the day since I had last seen my little girl. I had never stopped loving her, nor had ever given up hope. Although I had written to her every month, there had never been a response. Ironically, the young girl in the film was four years old and I had an overwhelming feeling of my daughter Georgina surge through me.

That night as I tried to sleep, I lay awake in the dark helplessly searching for hope. When finally I did fall asleep, all I could see was my little girl laughing as I jiggled her up and down on my knee, her blonde curls bouncing around her face, her pink cheeks getting warmer and her giggling growing louder. I woke with a start in the early hours as I saw her falling down a huge hole screaming for me to save her. Though I desperately tried to grab her hand as she fell, she slipped from my grip and fell away from me. I screamed out to her by her nickname, "Maddie!" but she disappeared into the darkness. The dream felt so real I got up and ran to the bathroom and was physically sick.

Throughout that morning, I wasn't able to shake the terrible feeling from the night before, so I phoned Ben to tell him I was feeling out of sorts and couldn't meet him that day. He just went quiet. I asked him if he was OK, but he, too, said he felt odd and that perhaps I should wait to see why I'd gone through that bizarre evening. The next day I saw the news about the disappearance of Maddie McCann. Fear engulfed me and I phoned Ben immediately.

"It's her Ben!" I almost yelled at him. "It's her I was being shown!"

"Slow down," he said. "It's who?"

"A child's gone missing in Portugal. She's on the news right now. Turn it on!"

Ben went quiet and I heard him move into his living room and turn on the news. "Oh my God," he said. "Of course it is."

"I can understand why now Ben," I said as the penny dropped. "Her name is Maddie, the same as my own daughter's nickname. She's been abducted just before her fourth birthday and that was exactly when my daughter was taken. She's even got blonde hair too. What on earth am I going to do Ben?"

"I'm going to come over and see you straight away. Have you got any other information about this? Has anything come to you regarding her disappearance?"

"Yes, but I think that's why I'm in trouble, Ben. It must be what I was warned about in the reading. I can feel it."

Ben came round and we sat over a cup of tea, churning over why it had come to me in particular. As Ben advised, I phoned Kizzi. He told me to inform Bob straight away. When I spoke to Bob and told him what I'd got on the night of her disappearance and since, he also went quiet. He then told me that I would have no choice but to help. I didn't know how, as I was concerned the police would think I was some crackpot. But Bob told me that I had an obligation to help. He also told me he'd help and guide me. However, he like Ben felt my life was in danger. I didn't really need to hear that. It was bad enough with Ben telling me. But Bob was deadly serious and told me to record everything I got and to check with him as he would guide me through the process. Out of the blue, within days, the police announced on the news that they were open to receiving psychic information on Maddie's disappearance. Both Ben and Bob knew then for sure that it was no coincidence.

"You'll have to go out there and find her," Bob told me.

"What do you mean, go out there? I couldn't possibly. Can't I just send to the police what I've got and let them get on with it?"

"You haven't got enough and anyway, you only got back from Portugal less than a month ago. Don't you realise it was a dummy run? Amanda, everything happens for a reason, and you could never be involved in something as major as this unless you were prepared well enough in advance."

I asked Ben to come with me. Bob suggested we had a third person on board to record our findings so we could focus on the job in hand so I chose a lady named Karen (a new friend of mine) who I felt would be helpful but not interfere with the process. I booked the tickets to go out as soon as we could, which I paid for and Bob told me that to cover my arse, as he coarsely put it, we should put it out there in the media to protect us by way of a press release.

Bob warned me over the phone with, "Amanda, you have to go to Portugal. Do what you need without detection and get out as soon as possible for your own safety."

I was frightened but felt obliged to honour the situation.

"I, too, see what Ben saw when he gave you the reading and feel you are in danger unless you follow your guidance. You're to contact me the moment you get out there in Portugal and trust me – you'll be OK! If anything happens, then I'll get you out. Please don't worry about that!" Bob said.

Contacting the press prior to our departure would minimise anything untoward happening to us. Kizzi contacted local press and radio and it became public knowledge Ben and I were going out to Portugal to help with the search for Maddie. Packed and ready to go, I waited for Ben – and waited and waited. When we'd left it so late, I didn't know if we'd make the flight, Ben announced he couldn't do it. All I got was a text saying, *Amanda, it was never meant to be the two of us going to Portugal, but it was the only way to get you to commit if you thought I was going with you.*

I was annoyed and frightened, and pleaded with him to help me but he simply sent me a message saying, *Amanda, it is you that's getting the information, therefore it is inevitable that you have to do this alone so I can't influence you in any way. You have Bob and*

Kizzi, and you will be OK. Trust what you're given and please be careful.

I had no choice but to continue with the journey. Karen and I raced to Heathrow and managed to get there by a whisker before the gate closed for check-in. On arrival, we collected the car and drove straight to our hotel, about four miles outside of Praia da Luz so we could have a base far enough away to not be obvious. I had plenty of insight that had come to me before the trip, which I'd made notes about, so just needed to go to where I was guided, to find the links. As soon as we checked in, I needed to go out and tune into the area. I walked down towards the sea and found a spot to have some quiet time and centre myself. I was shown myself taking part in the car boot challenge on Britain's Psychic Challenge and was shown that I'd had plenty of experiences and training to show I could track energy. I was also shown Portugal and my last visit. *You will follow much of the same route*, I was told, and I thanked The Guys for helping me. They were there loud and clear.

We had an early night to make a good start in the morning. The next day we headed to Praia da Luz and that's where my search began. For the next few days, I followed my guidance and made my links as Karen recorded the experience. Bob had told me it was necessary for clarification and to cover me in the event of anything untoward happening to me. On three occasions, we saw Kate and Gerry. However, we looked nothing more than tourists and kept a low profile. On the last day, I ended up at Lagos Marina and got a call from Kizzi.

We were due to fly back to the UK that afternoon, so he'd arranged for GMTV to interview me. By then I had quite a bit of detail connected with the abduction. However, the Marina was screaming to me that was where I needed to be. I found the exact spot I needed to link with and no sooner had that happened, Kizzi called me. I didn't think we had time for an interview and said I wouldn't hand anything over to the press. It would have to wait until I got back to the UK. But Kizzi said that I needed to talk to GMTV as it was important. At four that afternoon Richard Gaisford, GMTV's chief reporter, met me for the interview. Off camera we walked along the marina as he asked me for my own thoughts on the abduction. I told him what I felt to be true, but I had to explain to him that I wasn't prepared to express it on camera as it was a police matter. He and many of his colleagues and associates down in Portugal had their own take on what had happened to Maddie. Being journalists, they were open and inquisitive. It was as if everyone down there from the British journalism and news fraternity knew what had happened but could not voice it. He told me what questions he would ask and promised to not corner me. He told me the report would be aired on GMTV the following morning. I said it wouldn't as something was about to happen. Sure enough, when I got to the airport and entered the boarding lounge, on the large screen in front of me flashed an image of the man they'd arrested in connection with the case. I phoned Richard immediately and told him the man who was arrested was who I'd seen in my visions. The report never did go out as the arrest, for obvious reasons, superseded the interview.

When I arrived home, the press involvement and news was even more intense. I put my findings together and Kizzi advised me to start a daily blog to report what I was getting. Bob wasn't convinced but advised me how to go about it. A friend of mine, Paul, a policeman, came to see me on my return to see how I was. I explained to him what I'd been involved with as I trusted him. He said he could get his boss to look at what I was getting to see if there was anything they could do with it. So it was passed onto the Metropolitan Police who in turn passed it onto their area controller who had worked with psychics in the past. He advised Paul that it should be looked at in greater detail, so it went up to Scotland Yard and the Leicestershire police. Whilst it was a very serious time out in Portugal, the aftermath was much worse. On my return I had no choice and wished I could let go, but I was bombarded daily with messages spiritually which I recorded as Bob and Kizzi advised. That in itself was attracting a wave of people at all levels.

Some messages I received on the internet were from people wanting to help and steer me down a certain route by offering their own suspicions. I didn't buy into this as I realised that while many had good intentions and wanted to find Maddie, others revelled in other people's misfortune and wanted to stop me from helping. I tried to keep strong and ignore all the negative aspects of the search.

I stayed with the police investigation as long as I could, but it was crippling me financially and emotionally. I hadn't seen clients for months and had been totally focused on searching for Maddie. I had to move away from it when I found myself attracting people who were making threats via the internet to leave the investigation alone. They were never specific, but implied my family and I could suffer if I continued. That's when Deborah Borgen suddenly came back into my life. She phoned me out of the blue. I hadn't heard from her nor seen her for two years since the programme. She asked me if I was ready to become a teacher, "I'm coming to the UK and I'm going to teach you what I teach the Norwegian Police."

Chapter 38

It is the supreme art of the teacher to awaken joy in
creative expression and knowledge.

Albert Einstein

Soon I was meeting with Deborah in London and training every day with her to deepen my work and discover what made me question so many aspects of myself. I had no idea until training with Deborah how powerful the mind really was and how best to use it. Up to that point, I'd only scraped the surface. What she taught me brought all my years of research together. I knew I had so much more to learn.

There were only three of us under Deborah's tuition and, even though we all worked hard, I was the only one who went on to teach. Deborah had come from a background of economics and marketing and had been a high-flying financial director, but her abusive upbringing had led her to question the bigger picture. Despite her financial success, she questioned the reality of her world, and her search began. In Norway, people are far more open compared to in Britain. Deborah explained their education was different to ours. "Our education system works more like the Steiner Schools here in the UK. For the first seven years the child is encouraged to be creative. The second seven is the main crux of when children absorb and retain information and then the third seven is about discipline. This system compliments how the brain develops and therefore is more effective."

For several months we trained intensively until I was ready to travel to Norway and observe her teaching in a class environment. There were over four hundred people in the class – an average for Deborah. People would travel huge distances for her insight and teaching, and I felt humbled she'd asked to pass it on to me. When I returned to the UK, I was supervised in my first class in London in January 2008. I'd tried my utmost to move away from all the negativity the Madeline McCann case had brought into my life and still had no real understanding of what I'd achieved by getting involved. The teaching however was giving me new focus. From January, life seemed to take me on a more positive path. On a much deeper level, I felt I was going through change myself as I was gaining confidence through teaching. I had come a long way since my childhood traumas, but equally felt I was only at the start of finding myself. I felt I was only seeing the tip of the iceberg, but at least I'd found the iceberg to start that journey. The search for Maddie McCann never left me as deep down I'd felt I'd failed, but it spurred me on to discover how I could find the power to find my own daughter. I cautiously moved forward on my new path trusting I was discovering something deeper about myself and my work.

The classes started and I was soon travelling around the country as news spread about what I was teaching. The editor of *Soul & Spirit* magazine attended one class and she wrote a six-page article about her experience. Soon after, she asked me to write a monthly page for her magazine. By March the following year I was involved in many projects including the *Faith of Britain Day*. I gathered six of us women from different backgrounds, to get involved with the project. Angelica was a therapist from Turkey, Marlene a carer from New Zealand, Isabelle a scientist from France, Lisa a scientist from the UK and Marjo a banker from Lapland. The publicity that went out was to get people in the UK to focus at a particular time on a particular day to think only positive thoughts, to help bring about positive change, much like Uri Geller had done on TV in the past. It was a non-profit making endeavour to show people how the power of the mind could bring about change for the better. I wasn't prepared for the barrage of abuse I received via emails from over sixty scientists who claimed it was rubbish. We knew having two scientists on board would create controversy but hadn't realised how much.

And then Lisa called me one evening to say she'd found something disturbing about me on the internet. When I logged on and read the vile comments, I nearly collapsed from the shock. I had no idea what was going on behind my walls of protection but the deeper I looked, the more the vile attacks surfaced. Someone had single-handedly started a hate campaign against me through a sceptics' website. The more I read, the worse it made me feel. I was so distressed that Lisa came to my house at one in the morning. All my years of spiritual training vanished as I went into a decline of panic and fear. It was obvious to us both the saboteur had no qualms about crushing me.

I asked for advice from The Guys and was shown to go to the police. I copied over a hundred pages of vile and critical comments aimed to sabotage and discredit me which I took to Hertfordshire Police. Eventually the sceptics, who relished in pulling a "so-called psychic" to pieces, questioned the morals of the person behind the campaign as they claimed it was far too personal. Eventually the sceptics moved away from fuelling the saboteur's fire further. I felt crushed and sickened by the whole sordid affair and that far too much damage had been done. When I spoke to the police, they were sympathetic and said they'd investigate which they did, but back then it was early days in the cyber bullying awareness stages. It was obvious to me that it was Beverley as the clues in all the comments led to her, which the police and I agreed upon. She had used different computer terminals at cyber cafes. Shocked and hurt that she was motivated to attack me in such a way, I chose to walk away. Clearly, she had so much going on at a deeper level and I had no intention of starting a war with her which was what I assumed she was hoping for. Trying to prosecute would take my family under further and I couldn't put my children at risk.

Shortly after the Faith of Britain Day, I started to get debilitating pain in my right cheek. I thought at first I had terrible toothache, but after seeing the dentist twice for two lots of antibiotics, I was finally referred to my doctor. My GP couldn't pinpoint what it was, but the pain became excruciating. It felt like someone was hitting me with a hammer and splintering my jaw. It occurred when I brushed my teeth, when I was outside, when I ate and if I just happened to turn my head. Something was acutely wrong and even though I struggled to keep my business going forward, it was extremely difficult to predict when the pain would occur. I was finding it tough to see clients, let alone teach. Taking painkillers had no effect. After several months, I realised my quality of life was diminishing. Friends and family were concerned as I was often rendered immobilised by the chronic pain's cruelty. My poor children watched helplessly and had no understanding of what was happening to me. I had to adapt my life to my pain. I felt my body was feeling the aftereffects of all the emotional pain I'd endured with the Maddie investigation, what was brought up with the loss of my own daughter and by the hate campaign to destroy me. I could no longer exercise, and my health was being compromised due to my not being able to do anything to heal.

Out of the blue one day I got an email from a television producer named Charles who asked me if he could film me in a documentary he was making about the truth about the disappearance of Madeline McCann. I thought it was some kind of joke or someone trying to trick me. However, I let him explain and he came across as very genuine. He said he was getting cooperation from Portuguese witnesses as well as those searching for her from a British perspective and had been recommended to include me from an intuitive viewpoint. I eventually agreed to meet him. The crew came to my house and filmed me, but he wanted to dig deeper and asked to book another session. I recognised the man who interviewed me from several documentaries I'd seen in the past, so I knew Charles was serious about the film being aired.

We scheduled for the following month. The pain then had got so bad I was at the end of my tether. I went back to my GP and was diagnosed finally with trigeminal neuralgia. It was apparently nicknamed the "suicide condition" and was a rare debilitating disorder that led many people to take their life due to the incredible sudden pain it caused. Now they'd diagnosed me, I started to get treatment. However the pain was increasing even though the medicine dosage was levelled up almost weekly to compensate. When Charles was due to come back to film, I was prepared to go ahead with filming but at the end of my tolerance levels. They were running late and I desperately wanted to relax and go to bed and let go. Then I got a sudden and distressed phone call from Charles from his mobile.

"They've tried to run us off the road and we've had a serious accident!"

"Sorry, what do you mean?" I asked, confused. I'd expected him an hour before.

"We've been run off the road and the van's overturned. We're OK, but two of the crew are hurt and we're heading back to Manchester to deal with them and the van."

"What do you mean *them*?"

"You know who I mean, Amanda. We've had a warning and there's no way I'm going to let my guys risk this further. We're going back and I'll be in touch." He put the phone down.

My world was spiralling once again through uncertainty, betrayal, and pain, and I was sinking fast. I was angry as this was not what The Guys had promised. I had no idea what to do or where to turn so I retreated inwardly in an attempt to protect myself and my children. Charles did email me and told me his regrets at having taken on a project which had tested him beyond belief, but he wished me well and hoped I'd let it go just as he was going to. I was no longer shocked by what came into my life. As the months passed, the pain increased until I had to see a specialist at the Royal Free Hospital who dealt with my rare condition. It had been almost a year since it had begun, and by then only sleep helped ease the pain. Having been particularly healthy since the meningitis and even having given up alcohol, I was shocked my body was rebelling again.

The surgeon explained to me the condition was rare and usually only affected the elderly. It was also a secondary condition for those who suffered from MS or brain tumours and was perhaps the aftermath of melded tissue fibres that had been damaged from my meningitis. He offered me microvascular decompression (MVD), which in most cases was successful and lasted for up to around five years. He was worried about offering me the operation as I was young. His elderly patients usually only required one procedure due to their age. It was an invasive procedure as it involved drilling into the back of the skull and exposing the trigeminal nerve and placing padding there to protect the nerve. As my condition was acute and I could no longer up the medication, I decided to take the risk. The procedure was booked for 19 January 2010, my birthday. I felt this was symbolic as it marked the end or rebirth.

Shortly after seeing the doctor a friend asked me for a favour to help a friend of hers. She said he was desperate, and she knew I wasn't seeing clients but hoped I would see him. His name was Vince. I wasn't at my best and was bloated from medication; in pain most of the time and living on next to nothing, trying my utmost to get through the days. After seeing Vince, as he was a friend of a friend, I asked if he would come with me to the local theatre shortly before Christmas. I explained I'd paid for two tickets, but a friend had backed out at the last minute through illness, and I needed a plus one to go with. I didn't bank on Vince and me falling for each other. He was splitting up from his wife at the time and very low and likewise I had lost everything dear to me. I didn't think it would be any more than a one-off occasion. The Guys Upstairs had gone quiet, although I prayed daily for help, so he was company and filled a void.

From past experience, if The Guys went quiet it was for me to work out what path to take. When Vince came into my life, all The Guys confirmed was that he was supposed to help me but didn't elaborate further. I certainly wasn't ready to move into a relationship. Vince was the perfect gentleman, taking me out for the odd meal and coming to see me at home. As it got nearer to my hospitalisation, there were practical matters to take care of in relation to the children. Mum and my closest friends were all at hand and Vince convinced me he would be there every step of the way. I was flattered and had too little strength to do more than simply accept. I met his family after Christmas and felt he was just what I needed. He was charismatic and funny, sensitive, and loving. His family were adorable, and I trusted him. On the day of my operation he drove me to the hospital so my family and friends could focus on the children.

The last thing I remember before the surgery was Vince telling me he would take care of me. As I went down to the operating theatre, I prayed my life would change dramatically and I could have the life The Guys had showed me. I knew I couldn't have gone through so much for nothing. I woke in a recovery room in agony. I saw Vince walking towards me and tried to make him go away, but he insisted on staying. I was too tired to argue. Later when I woke again on a ward, Vince was there with my best friend Lisa. I couldn't understand why they were together, but he said, "Amanda, don't worry about a thing. Everything's been taken care of. I went to see your mum at your house, and I told her I'd run people up to the hospital and back to take the pressure off your family."

I didn't want him to take over as I felt I didn't know him well enough, but it was obvious by what he said Mum was grateful for his help. Everyone thought he was great, and whenever anyone came to visit, he was there too. I felt very low when I came out of the operation and could do little besides stare out of the window. It was grey and dreary outside. The only life I saw between visits was from two pigeons that visited daily. They captivated me with their mating ritual and their little dances and interactions on my window ledge. Something stirred in me, and I felt a deep longing for my own soul mate dance of passion and commitment.

When they flew back on to the window ledge, I felt a story emerging in my mind. I wrote a short story all about the love of those two birds, who lived in a grey and bleak world but whose love for each other was filled with colour and light. Vince brought his sister in to see me shortly after and I read my story to them. When I'd finished, they were both in tears. It dawned on me it had touched them like it had touched me. For the next few days I wrote comical poetry about the tea trolley lady to make the nurses and patients laugh and short stories to entertain my fellow bed mates. I had unleashed a creative urge in me I couldn't stifle.

Four days later, the surgeon came to see me. I laughed and joked at how I was getting so much better and I was now entertaining the troops, when he noticed my nose.

"How long has your nose been running like that?" he asked.

"I'm not sure!" I said a little taken back by his concern. "I guess since the op." I'd assumed my constantly streaming nose was due to a cold.

"You should have told someone straight away. That's spinal fluid leakage! I don't want to alarm you but there was always a chance we could have a complication!"

Vince went into meltdown. "What the hell do you mean there's a complication?" he demanded.

"Sometimes there's a risk the operation could go wrong, and, in this case, we have to get her down to surgery immediately. She's losing spinal fluid through her nose which means we'll have to take muscle or fat from another part of her body, re-open the wound and pack up the hole immediately."

I was overcome and felt that this was just another horrid sign in a long line of recent failures, telling me the battle was lost. I felt the years of fighting to distance myself from the permanent resident in my head, the voice of my stepmother Sue, had won and I had succumbed.

Vince was panicky but I assured him I had no choice. It was obvious by then Vince was getting very attached to me, but I didn't need his emotional drama on top of my own fears. I went down for surgery immediately and when I came out the pain was worse than before. They'd taken fat from my stomach leaving a throbbing ache there, too. By the time I got out of hospital, my children were beside themselves, having been worrying if they would still have a mum. Mum and my friends were wonderful, attending to everything we needed at home. Vince though was getting most protective, and I needed space.

While convalescing at home, I started to sell anything I had to earn money on eBay. I couldn't go anywhere so whilst sitting in my living room, decided to only watch television that was positive and effective for my recovery. One day I was watching *Escape to the Country* and saw a couple I knew who'd left Potters Bar where I lived in Hertfordshire, to live in a beautiful new home in Norfolk. Instantly, I felt a huge surge of energy telling me I had to move. The children were at primary school and Millie was due to go up to secondary school. When I told her what I wanted for us, she couldn't deal with it.

"What on earth do you want to move for?" she asked me angrily. "We'll be moving away from all our friends. What about Grandma, Granddad and Dad? What will I do without my friends?"

"I know, sweetheart. I can't explain why, but it's just like when I chose your primary school, and everyone said I was mad until it turned around with the new headmistress and became one of the leading primary schools in the country. You have to trust your mum. It's just one of those mad moments I can't explain, but one day you'll understand why."

My friends and family couldn't understand either, especially with what I'd been through, and they begged me to reconsider. Vince, however, thought it was a great idea as he wanted a fresh start himself, so the two of us decided to take the leap of faith. He had nothing and therefore nothing to lose. I'd lost everything and needed to start over and give myself and the children a new beginning.

Finally, 6 weeks after surgery I decided to take the children to school myself. It was snowing and, on my return, I was travelling down a long country road when I saw a BMW appear out of nowhere behind me. I was pulling up at the junction to turn left and was behind another BMW. Looking in my mirror I noticed four men in the car, but as I looked forward the car in front started to turn left and then instantly stopped even though there was nothing coming from the right, nor the left. I'd assumed the car was going to continue, but as I was concerned by the speed the car behind me had arrived at, I was more focused on that car. The car in front put his brakes on and instantly I slammed my foot on the brake but went into the back of his car. It was hardly a prang but immediately four men got out of each car and ran to me which was incredibly frightening.

"Are you all right, miss?" the first man said. "Don't worry, we're all police officers on a training exercise."

That's when it dawned on me I'd hit the back of an unmarked police car with four policemen in it and the other car behind me happened to be another unmarked police car. The snow was now coming down thick and fast. Police arrived at every door.

"Are you all right, miss? Are you hurt?" he repeated.

"No, but I've just come out of hospital recently so perhaps I misjudged and wasn't ready to drive yet," I said.

I was breathalysed by a police officer and a paramedic who arrived at the scene first started to check me for any problems until an ambulance arrived where I was taken on board to carry out further checks. I was more embarrassed than anything, but they informed me as they were police in a training exercise, each policeman had to be interviewed by another policeman from another jurisdiction. By the time my best friend drove past to travel to my house to see me, she couldn't believe her eyes as she hit what looked like a major incident. She recognised my car and pulled over instantly. When she scrambled onto the ambulance, she couldn't believe it when I relayed to her what had happened. It was obviously too soon for me to drive, so for the next few weeks Vince drove on our trips to Norfolk to find the perfect spot to move to. I felt a need to move to a place that inspired me to write.

We decided Norfolk wasn't right, but whenever we drove back through Suffolk, we felt a lure to the county. One afternoon we stopped at a place to have something to eat in a village. We sat at a table and looked out of the window and instantly knew that this was the village we wanted to move to. Within a month, we'd signed up to rent a beautiful old, thatched cottage with a four-hundred-year history. I knew if I could write anywhere, it would be there. I managed to get two school places in the local catchment area, which my friend who was a special needs teacher said would benefit my son more so than the system in Hertfordshire. My son had been diagnosed with ADD/ADHD when he was around five years old.

The school had spaces for both my children, and we moved to Suffolk with ease. It was spring 2010 and I was feeling much stronger and hoped perhaps my relationship with Vince was going to be rewarding in so many ways. It was early days and we had only just moved in. The kids liked Vince and we all hoped for a fresh start. The day we moved in, we were working on the hundred-foot garden in the glorious sun, cutting the grass and weeding, when Vince displayed a side to him none of us were prepared for. Daisy, our beagle, had strayed next door under a ranch style fence and was sniffing around in next door's garden. Vince suddenly lost all control.

He screamed at the dog to come back, and we watched him go from the laughing, joking man we knew to a monster with no control. He was screaming and threatening Daisy. We tried to get her back by calling her, but she was frightened. He marched into next door's garden, grabbed her by the collar, dragged her back and when he was about ten feet from me, he picked her up and slammed her down on her back, threatening me if ever any of us disobeyed him again we'd pay for it. The children and I couldn't believe what we'd seen. Millie cried and ran to Daisy as she tried to get up.

"What on earth are you doing, Vince? How dare you do that to my dog?" I said, but he grabbed hold of me by my clothes and frogmarched me into the house. The kids ran in after us. Once we were all in the kitchen, he slammed the back door and turned on us.

That's when we saw the monster in Vince emerge. "If you ever disobey me or go against me ever, you will regret it! Do you hear me?" he yelled.

Millie was wild with hatred for Vince. "How dare you," she bellowed at him.

"Shut her up or she'll regret it!" he shouted at me with a demonic gaze I didn't think I could see in a human being.

I wanted to defend my children, but he was nineteen stone and was in a rage and my first concern was to calm him down. That's how it started. I compromised to protect them, and he saw that as vulnerability and weakness. He smiled sadistically, showing me he had power over us and we had none. He knew I'd moved the children to a new home, a new school and new life so couldn't go anywhere as I had no home to go back to. I was shocked and disarmed by his outburst and hoped it was a one-off moment fuelled by too many beers, but over that first week his behaviour towards me changed dramatically. I was beside myself with worry. Surely I was over destructive relationships?

Vince had convinced me he would work as a builder (which was his trade) and let me get on and focus on my book. However, the day we moved in he offered my services to an inquisitive neighbour telling her I was a cleaner and did ironing on the side. I couldn't believe my ears when he told me, but as I had to pay my way, I took in her ironing. As the weeks progressed, Vince found it harder and harder to find work, even though I offered to help build him a website, create flyers, business cards etc. He spent most of his time watching Jeremy Kyle and other daytime programmes whilst I got more and more cleaning jobs from the locals. Within a few months, I was cleaning for several different clients and working longer and longer hours, but still he found it difficult to find work. He never took my advice as he was convinced his line of work was specialist and he would attract it when the time was right. As we had bills to pay, I worked every hour I could to make ends meet but I was working for a pittance compared to my consultancy work. I had no credibility in Suffolk to set up as a consultant and, as I'd moved there to write, I prayed when Vince got work, I would be able to start on what I'd moved there for. At one stage I was working ten and eleven hour days, bringing ironing home to do in the evenings. I was getting a great reputation but becoming a cleaner was not what I'd set out to do.

I carried on looking for light at the end of the tunnel. I couldn't leave Vince for the sake of the children's stability, and he cleverly relied on me more and more financially as he was having health issues with his knees which stopped him from working all together, he said. This made it harder for me to decide what to do about Vince as I couldn't take my children out of the schooling which was creating such a difference and we had no home to return to. The children were resilient and like me they learned how to put their heads down when Vince went into an episode and made the most of their new life, friends, and environment. Vince didn't want me to focus on my book and told me it was a waste of my time when I should be focusing on earning for my children. I couldn't understand how he could convince himself it was acceptable for me to slave over people's toilets when he couldn't even get off his backside.

As the months rolled on, he managed to get the odd job, but it wasn't enough, and it was too late to show any commitment. He wanted us to spend money on the house though it was rented, but the landlord duly accepted as it was in dire need of repair. He would throw parties to show our village and friends how well we were doing. However, it was all for show and just kept putting more and more pressure on me to earn more. He was using my credit card and taking me into debt which unnerved me. He assured me, when he got a proper job, he'd pay it all back. By the following year, I convinced Vince to go back to the doctors where they told him he had to start taking his medication for depression. It took the edge off his manic episodes. When he was good, he was very, very good but when he was bad, he was a monster.

Vince was so charismatic, the life and soul of the party and everyone wanted to know him as he was just one of those characters that lured you in. But his family knew about his shameful behaviour and eventually one night he broke down and cried (which he often did) and said, "OK, I admit I punched my wife in the face, but I was worried she wouldn't let me see my daughter. That's the reason why I'm not allowed to see my little girl without supervision. My family know all about what I've done and yes, I feel deeply ashamed. I also tried to hang myself in front of my daughter which didn't work, so I'm not allowed to look after her without family present."

I was horrified and sickened by his revelation. To think he'd tricked me and made me believe he was a kind and caring man who'd look after me and my children. I felt he'd taken full advantage of me when I was recovering, which was despicable. Going to work was my only time away from his scrutiny and without him knowing, I started to write my book. Whilst working at My Spirit Radio back in 2005, Suzanne one of the Directors had suggested I wrote a book about my life story, but I'd never felt ready. When we moved to Suffolk, my intention was to write the book but had always envisioned it would be an idyllic and inspirational situation. I thought I'd sit in a beautiful garden, letting my book evolve whilst my loving partner worked to support us but instead it had become a guilty secret through the need to keep private the very thing I'd always longed to do.

Every day I'd steal moments to write and store it without him knowing. Working long hours cleaning, I'd find moments to store information on my Blackberry phone notebook to transcribe later when he was sleeping. This went on for nearly two years. It was painstaking and almost like I'd asked for Vince to come into my life so I could submerge into recreating the horror of my upbringing to facilitate my writing.

Amazingly as the book progressed, I could see I was working on some kind of parallel Universe with my childhood self and witnessed my strength building through writing the story. I was developing more and more friendships, credibility, and foundations for the children, albeit as a cleaner. People knew me as Amanda, the cleaner. I told no-one of my past. Nobody knew what I'd done before. The Guys convinced me all was meant to be, and I realised even though I worked my socks off, the beauty of my environment, the community I'd strived to be part of and the schooling my children received far outweighed the harsh reality of my relationship with Vince and the long days of cleaning and ironing. He was starting to find it hard to accept my reputation and how I was perceived by people, so the punishments started to become more frequent. I was becoming immune to his punishment, but the following year I was diagnosed with another condition in my head, occipital neuralgia related to a further complication from my meningitis. I felt resentful I was working such long hours and he was getting all the glory. Everyone assumed we were a happy couple. No one suspected the dark secret that lurked behind our front door, much like my childhood home.

I felt the strong presence of The Guys when writing. They showed me that I had to be taken back to the very beginning of my life, to the pain of being punished and worked as a slave through my childhood so I could relay it with sincerity through the story. Whilst writing, it often felt as if I was going through the whole painful scenario again.

During 2011, out of the blue my daughter, Georgina, who was by then nearly twenty-one, contacted me through a relative of mine who'd been doing genealogy for the family. Utterly overwhelmed to have her find me, and with the realisation this too had come about as the parallel of the book unfolded, I realised change would inevitably occur. Having my daughter contact me and speak to her on the phone for the first time in seventeen years made me feel reborn. I'd prayed every day and written to her for twelve of those years until she'd left home and was no longer traceable. I had waited patiently, and the words of the judge rang out in my head, "One day she'll find her mother with her boyfriend …"

Two weeks later I met her at Crewe train station with her boyfriend. I knew her instantly. We ran to each other and held each other for what seemed to be an eternal moment. As we held each other, we knew we'd never given up hope. I spent one whole day with my baby girl, and it felt as if I'd never lost her. I could see deep into her soul, and I saw her survivor spirit. I knew then we'd never lose each other again. Painful as it was to hear, she too had grown up with her father who ignored the abuse she'd received from her stepmother. History repeating itself rang deep in my family. Tears came easily to us both. However, a bond was there that had never left and she neither blamed me nor grieved over her life. In many ways she seemed so much stronger than I was at her age, and I admired her resolve. She was committed to making her life better and had found a deep spiritual side to herself which had supported her. I knew The Guys Upstairs had looked after her.

Finally, all the pieces were coming together in my life to allow me closure. The sacrifice of our relationship had been the most hard hitting and deepest to cope with. I knew because she was back in my life, my other relationships would change too. Eventually I would come out the other side and, if what The Guys were saying would happen, I would eventually find not only the peace and stability I so desperately wanted but also my soul mate. I had no choice but to finish writing my book. I came home one day however and found even though I'd backed up my book on the computer, several chapters and several files had gone missing. I felt completely and utterly bereft. I felt I couldn't go on suffering any more. Something snapped and suddenly I could no longer tolerate Vince's behaviour. Something exploded inside me, and I knew I would never ever go back to being abused or compromised ever again. Life was changing for the better. I would at long last help others to see their power and never let go. My apprenticeship was finally over, and my real work was about to begin. Vince was gone and was the last person I would ever let abuse me.

Chapter 39

If we must part forever, give me but one kind word to think upon and please myself with while my heart's breaking.

Thomas Otway

Money was short, my working day was long, and Millie needed to make a decision about her new school. She had become a strong independent character and, because of mentors at her school, had been encouraged to be a leader – something she loved. Anthony was excelling at science and had become a book addict, although when we lived in Hertfordshire, he could hardly read or write. The move had been a great success as far as their education was concerned and they'd both found new friends.

Then one day our agents notified me out of the blue that my landlady wanted to move back into her home. I knew we'd never find anything as cheap again, so I asked The Guys to pull out all the stops and find the right home for us. We had to move quickly to get our application in for Millie's new school. After we'd seen a few unsuitable homes, the agents told me about a property that had just come on the market. It was perfect. It was in another village and this time with more space and in even more tranquil surroundings than the last one. I realised it was meant to be. When I phoned up the education department, however, they said I was no longer in the catchment area for the school we'd planned for, but I was for the school Millie and Anthony had originally wanted – the academy school. I put in an application, and we were accepted immediately. I saw that as a sign we were in the flow.

Shortly before we moved, I was leaving a cleaning job when my mobile went off. I pulled over to answer it. It was Paul, my old policeman friend from Hertfordshire. We'd not spoken for a couple of years. Apart from that, I'd changed my mobile and only close friends and family had my new number. He was still his old jokey self but when I asked him how he'd managed to get my number, he became serious. "I went to your house to find you, but your neighbours said you'd moved," he said.

"Yes, I sold it!" I said.

"Well, do you remember you gave me all that information on Maddie McCann in 2007?" he asked. "Scotland Yard had the information but lost it, so they asked me if I'd find you to see if you still have it. I don't understand how, but I lost it off my computer as well."

I knew without doubt that the missing chapters from my part written book and certain files, all missing from my computer, were now no coincidence.

Nervously I said, "Paul, how did you get my number?"

"I'm a policeman, aren't I?"

"I lost so much from being involved in that case. I put my children at risk when I had idiots threatening me. I've lost my home and my children's security because of it. I had cyber bullying which tried to wipe out my credibility and have nothing left in this world apart from my friends and family. You think I'm going to risk what I've got left to help Scotland Yard now? If I've lost what's on my computer, you've lost what's on yours and Scotland Yard's lost the material I sent them too, what does that tell you?" I said angrily.

"I know! I didn't think you'd want any involvement. I'll just tell them I haven't managed to find anything and haven't managed to find you. Is that what you want?"

"Paul, I left Hertfordshire for respite but have never worked harder in my life. I've gone through a turbulent relationship and only came here to write, which has come to nothing, and I'm now focused on other things. One day I hope someone will see what I went through wasn't for nothing. What I wrote about went missing recently, and I've no intention of attracting attention and creating more pain."

Paul was now quiet at the end of the phone.

"Don't you see why I can't possibly get involved? Losing material relating to Maddie was just another warning and frightened the pants off me. To top it all, I haven't been able to pick up a pen since. This is all I have though. If I don't finish this book, I don't see how the story ends and that means my whole life was for nothing!"

Paul asked me to promise not to lose contact with him again, but I knew in my heart I couldn't risk putting myself through more of what had happened in the past. I was going through a new phase of finding myself and had to stand by what I believed in.

We settled into our new village and at last I could start moving towards my dream. I started to get more and more cleaning clients, so I started to share them with other women who were as deeply conscientious as I was and wanted some extra money for their household. Slowly but surely I was starting to build something. I enjoyed my new life, my new environment, walking my dogs in the beautiful countryside and travelling to see friends and family. Even though life was hard work, I had an amazing home in a wonderful community and life was rewarding in so many ways.

Mum and Bob were concerned at how much I'd lost financially because of Vince, but by then they had a remarkable acceptance of how whacky it was at times for me whenever I announced my next move. Bob and I had come a long way in our relationship, and I guess by then my teaching had taken me beyond the fractiousness of our relationship of the past. I'd learned long ago that acceptance releases us from the confines of our own limitations. It helped me to see the good in everyone, even those who'd wronged me. I learned so much from everyone who'd been my enemy, so I could only thank them for deepening my awareness of what we attract into our lives, including those I thought I couldn't connect with. It was those who were more challenging that made me dig deeper to find why I'd attracted them and what they were teaching me about my life. I felt I was moving so much closer to the day I could at last honour a true soul mate relationship.

In the latter part of 2012, I was still juggling with my guilt at having given up with my book. The call from Paul had unnerved me further and I had no desire to attract attention. Instead, I was making the most of living a normal life, going to work, coming home, and immersing myself in East Enders. I'd laughed at that sort of existence before. Life was hard graft to say the least, but I was thankful to be living in a beautiful, tranquil location which more than compensated for the endless toilets I cleaned. Every day I would walk in the countryside and talk to The Guys to help me hold onto hope. They always confirmed I was exactly where I should be, and I had to be patient. I accepted this wholeheartedly.

One year after Vince had left, I felt an urge to sign up to a dating site. One of my best friends, a barrister, had met her soul mate through a dating site and they were moving in together. I'd been told it was more the norm now people were too busy to meet people in a bar. I couldn't do that anyhow with my children, so I decided to dip my toe in the water. I had a flattering number of responses, but none ticked my boxes. However, there were two men I felt an instant connection with. One was called Charlie (a good sign as he had my favourite name, that of my Great Uncle Charlie) and then there was Paul (perhaps a sign he had been sent to look after me like my friend Paul). I responded to both, and it was evident from the onset they were completely different.

Paul wasn't good at messaging and preferred to speak on the phone. I happened to be free at the last minute and during our first conversation he insisted he drove up from Hertfordshire (another coincidence, I felt) to meet at a local pub so I didn't need to travel far. I felt that was most considerate of him and liked the way he insisted he did all the travelling as I had children to consider. He gained a big tick that night and yes, he was a pleasant and funny man who engaged me instantly as he had many stories to tell. He was a custody sergeant and I thought that meant he would be trustworthy and reliable. In fact, he'd put on his profile he was dependable. I needed that more than ever. There was no magic or spark when we first met, but I thought we could become friends and more would happen in time. I was in no rush to get into a relationship; I just wanted to go on the odd date to make myself feel alive again.

Charlie was a wing commander for the RAF and was stationed abroad in Munich. At first, I was disappointed at him living abroad, but it allowed us to write and get to know each other in depth. I'd never read anything from a man as eloquent as he wrote and was drawn by his ability to be so engaging and expressive. We had the same sense of humour and an honesty that allowed us to form a bond, but it was a non-starter due to where he was living.

Paul and I met again over Christmas whilst I was staying at my parents, but he came across as shy when he collected me. As we got to know each other, I discovered he was deeply guarded in front of people. I admired his commitment and passion for his job but could feel his tiredness and yearning to retire after his eighteen arduous years of service. He was due to retire in five years and his vision of retirement seemed very appealing. It certainly ran along the lines I'd envisioned for my own future, and I thought if we took it slowly but surely, he could possibly be the one.

One day he invited me to his apartment in Hertfordshire. We were walking in the grounds when he announced that once he retired, he'd have more than enough in his pension to look after us both. I was taken aback by this statement. It came out of the blue and we'd not been seeing each other for long.

Charlie and I were writing to each other regularly and I looked forward to his emails. A friendship was forming and there was deep trust, so we continued to let that develop. Every time I opened his emails, he made me laugh. He brought light into my life, and I loved the way he tested me to come back to him with something wittier. He certainly pushed my boundaries, and I loved the mental stimulation he provided. Paul was easy going and didn't expect anything from me. In fact, he made a point of wanting to make my life easier.

One day, as I drove past a spot in my local area I'd driven past for two years, I noticed a "for sale" sign at the roadside. I'd been intrigued about what was beyond the hedges as it looked like a little bit of heaven from what I'd glimpsed of the sweeping driveway, bushes, and trees. When I was searching for somewhere for Paul and I to go to celebrate New Year's Eve, the same place came up on my search engine for a local black tie do. It turned out to be the site of a wedding venue set in eighteen acres of beautiful countryside. I was mesmerised by the internet photos of the Georgian mill house, the water gardens, the rivers, brooks, and streams that flowed from the River Brett. I knew instantly I had to go and see it, so I booked our tickets and asked the owner to meet me there.

Serendipity is a beautiful thing and when I walked into the little coffee shop, something familiar washed over me. Over coffee, Alison explained how she and her husband had bought the site recently and were passionate about transforming it back to its former glory. I was fascinated by their project and felt an instant connection to it. When she mentioned they were renting out individual units to small business owners, my ears pricked up. The small unit in the corner of the beautiful Mediterranean gardens had just become available as the rental agreement had fallen through at the last minute. I asked to look at it and when I walked into the unit, I had a vision. I saw myself standing there with customers, laughing, and joking. At that time, it was a bare shell with blue carpet stained from water damage and there was trunking that ran around the entire perimeter. I saw on the mental screen of my mind bright colours and sensed beautiful smells and an air of opulence. It was the boudoir I'd seen in one of my visions on *The Psychic Challenge*. The feeling of being there was so strong it almost choked me with excitement and hope. I told Alison I was interested, but I had no idea how I'd transform my vision into reality.

I had nothing to worry about. Three weeks later I'd signed the lease for my new business and *The Revival Exchange* was born. It was based on *The Treasure Chest*, the dress agency I'd run from home when the children were tiny, although I planned to make it bigger and better than before. Paul was ecstatic as he visualised himself retiring, creating his recycled garden furniture, and selling it from the shop's courtyard garden. Things were falling into place. Paul was a skilled carpenter and offered to build the shop fittings in his time off. I was over the moon that someone was going to help me with my dream. Paul had to be the one.

While I was on my walks, The Guys confirmed I was on track, but when I asked about the book, they told me to be patient. I told them of my concern and confusion. The shop wasn't taking me down the route to finish the book and then go back to teaching and seeing clients like they'd originally said. *All in good time Amanda. Focus on the job in hand.* It was odd, but I trusted The Guys knew more than I could possibly know about the future.

Charlie and I still wrote to each other, and I wondered how I could care about two different men at the same time, especially when I'd never even met Charlie. I told Charlie I was seeing Paul, which he was happy about as our friendship was purely platonic and deepening.

Paul had been married three times and told me each of his wives had betrayed him for another man. He'd lost touch with his two children in the aftermath. He showed so much commitment towards the future, but often reminded me he'd never marry again, let alone let someone get under his skin. People around me said he must have been smitten to dedicate all his spare time to help me with the shop. And he did. He came to stay in between shifts and worked tirelessly to create the shop of my dreams. My opulent boudoir. Two months later we opened with over a hundred women attending our launch party with photographers from a luxury magazine, capturing the occasion. It was outstanding success, but sadly, Paul didn't want to attend and cancelled at the last minute. He said his shyness meant he didn't like to mix in crowds. I felt it was a lie but didn't understand why.

Paul had to be the one, because when he came to stay with me, he completely let go and relaxed. Yes, I had to listen to him download and let go of some horrific and challenging things he had to deal with on a day-to-day basis, but I felt humbled I could support him when he was obviously supporting me. It was a compromise. As I got to know him, I realised how stubborn he was and how he always had to be in control. It was Paul's way or no way. I put it down to his past relationship failures and the role he played at work. I respected that, but the more I got to know him, I found he was more often than not, very serious and bordered on pessimism. Again, I assumed it was due to his work, as that was all he talked about. In fact, that was all he had apart from me and The Mill. He only ever really laughed if we went out for a drink. Alcohol played a big part in opening him up.

I would never have been able to open my shop if it wasn't for the belief Bob had in me. At the beginning, I'd gone to my bank, but they'd refused to risk giving me a loan, so I tried a few other sources and, with one day to go to sign the lease, spoke to one of my best friends who told me to ask my family. I felt it was a non-starter, but amazingly, Bob asked me questions, to which I hoped he'd got the right answers, and astonishingly, just like The Guys confirmed, Bob said he'd help with the set-up costs. Having the support of my family was all I needed to make the dream a reality. People had come and gone in my life, and I felt humbled that my only real family believed in me, but I suspected it was my mother who was funding me.

The shop started on a good footing. Having told no-one what I taught, my intention was not only to make my business successful; I wanted the whole site to be successful to reflect my spiritual beliefs. Community spirit was the foundation to any success. It was inevitable I would start bonding with the other business owners, and soon we started working together as a community.

Paul was a lovely man, and I adored his company when he was relaxed, but he seemed to have money problems and I couldn't help wondering why. He'd told me he had a very expensive apartment, car, and lifestyle, but it was becoming evident the apartment was rented, the car was on monthly payments, and the way he spoke about money showed me he was under pressure. He was showing his exclusivity to me by spending every available bit of time off at mine. However, I had to work seven days a week in the shop, so he'd often go off and help with the renovation of The Mill. He was becoming friends with the owner, Steve, and many of the other owners on site.

Life was exciting and challenging and even though I worked long hours and was earning very little, it was such a beautiful transition from cleaner to proprietor. I started promoting and hosting events through a database of ladies who came to visit on a regular basis. The summer was glorious, and we had our first open day with thousands of visitors on site, with everything from vintage cars, hog roast and golf demonstration to an acoustic guitarist serenading the visitors. I loved being part of the community dynamic.

Paul was becoming more distant. One day when we'd gone out for dinner, I asked him about his grandfather and he hit the roof, telling me to stop prying into his past. I hung my head and said nothing but felt his wrath as he hurled angry comments at me. The next week when he came to stay, we went out to dinner again and this time I made a joke about looking after him when he was old and infirm. He lost it again and told me I was out of order to keep pushing him about the future. It had been a joke, but lately he'd become very tetchy. He'd been very extravagant at the beginning of our relationship but when the shop had started to take shape, he was always staying at mine and relied on me to buy all the shopping which I paid for until I had to drop a hint it was costing me much more to accommodate him.

I was shocked when he said, "Since I've been coming to you on my days off, I've not had to pay out for anything other than my monthly outgoings like rent, utilities and petrol."

"Well I guess that's because I buy all the food when you're staying with me."

"Yeah, well when I'm at home I budget on baked beans and toast."

I was crushed by his selfishness, but he reminded me he was free labour even though he no longer had anything to work on at the shop. I didn't know if he was being insensitive or just plain ignorant. I said he'd have to start contributing, but he got angry.

Charlie and I had stayed in touch, and it was nice to have trust in someone who wasn't on an agenda. I often wondered what would have happened if I'd gone ahead and met Charlie and not Paul, but I knew The Guys Upstairs had led me to Paul because of the shop, so I had to trust all was as it was should be. Also, I felt I wasn't good enough for Charlie. How could anyone who'd gone through what he'd gone through in his life accept me as a partner? Charlie had done two stints in Afghanistan and one in Iraq and he'd received medals. I didn't know what on earth I could bring into his life to compare, and accepted Paul had to be my destiny. Apart from his moodiness, which was starting to get me down, I accepted his faults.

Finally, Paul decided to bring all his tools (which were in a friend's garage) to store in a local store shop. That showed me he was definitely committed, even though he blew hot and cold as far as our relationship was concerned. He'd planned to start making furniture during his rest days which he intended to sell through my shop. Something wasn't right though as our intimacy was waning fast, but I put this down to fatigue. He was fifty-five and doing so much. When he asked to borrow my four-by-four to do the final move of his tools and said he'd lend me his precious BMW Z4 complete with red interior, I felt he must consider me as someone dear to him. He talked nonstop about his precious car, who he nicknamed the whore. I couldn't wait to spend a few days driving it to work and was on the first morning in his car that I had an enormously surreal moment. Déjà vu kicked in and I knew I'd done the journey before. It was only as I arrived at work that I remembered where the memory had come from.

I'd had a dream persistently starting back in 2004, which I'd told many of my class students about as an example of re-occurring dreams. That dream had never had an outcome until that moment. The dream started with me waking and knowing the children were downstairs in the kitchen having breakfast. I was moving from the bathroom to the bedroom where I could see through the open window which opened out onto the back garden. I went downstairs to say goodbye and the children left for school. I realised the house I'd dreamed about years before was the house we currently lived in. In the dream, I got ready for work once they'd left for school. Then I drove to work in a black BMW and up a long driveway. When I got there, I walked to all the various businesses including my own which was managed by someone I trusted. There was a huge community dynamic going on and I was visiting to touch base with everyone. I went to several meetings, which pretty much took up most of the day. Then I went to the gym onsite and worked out before going home. Finally, in the dream I saw myself arrive home at the end of the day. The children were doing their homework and I went to spend time with them. There was a woman there we all trusted (I could not see who she was) and I knew she was there to help me with the children as I was off for the weekend. The children were excited to see me. I went upstairs to shower, pack and change and eventually a man in a dinner suit arrived to take me away for the weekend for my book launch. I couldn't see the man's face, but he was striking and strong, and I knew he was my soul mate. I felt it from the depths of my being.

Sitting there in the car, I felt an incredible connection with everything I'd seen in my dream. My current house, the drive to work in the black BMW, the Mill, and the units on site, were all part of that dream. All I could think was *What the hell is going on?* I knew something dramatic was about to happen. As I was driving Paul's car, I assumed he must be my soul mate. Two weeks later I was supposed to pick him up from Ipswich train station. Oddly he'd driven up without telling me. He knew I had to close the shop early to collect him from the station and this wasn't normal behaviour for him. He'd become irrational of late, snapping at me for the slightest thing and hardly communicating. I was taken aback when he called me to say he was almost at my house.

"Paul, I'm nearly at the station. Why didn't you tell me this hours ago? I needn't have closed the shop early."

I drove home, arriving at the same time as him. When I saw him, I couldn't bear to be near him. I wouldn't let him come near me that evening and slept on the sofa. He didn't question my behaviour, but when I said I was sleeping downstairs, he marched into my living room and said, "Get upstairs now."

I ignored him and slept downstairs anyway. The next morning he was coming to help at the Mill with some renovation work and whilst he was in the shower, I was drawn to look at his mobile which he'd left in the kitchen. He usually kept it with him. I'd never wanted to look at it before, but bells were ringing as my instincts told me to look at his messages. To my utter shock I found messages from a girl – their contents showed they were having an affair. Feeling sick to my stomach, I tried to hold it together. When Paul came down for breakfast, I was cold towards him, and it dawned on me he must have thought I'd already found out.

"Paul, are you having an affair with someone else?" I asked as plainly as I could.

372

"What the hell has made you think that? How could you of all people ask me that knowing all my wives had betrayed me?" he almost spat at me. "If you ever did anything like that to me you wouldn't see me for dust. How dare you!"

He walked out of the kitchen. I was angry, hurt and determined to find out the truth. I still didn't want to believe it, though. I held it together all day and that night we went to a local festival. It was obvious there was distance between us. I waited until he'd had a pint before asking again, "Paul are you having an affair?"

"You're behaving stupidly. What on earth has possessed you to question me like this when I've dedicated my life to you?"

"OK, Paul, so what did you do last Wednesday and Saturday?"

"You know where I was, I was at work. I gave you my work schedule. What's this all about?"

"So what if I told you I have evidence to show you were actually at a pub on one occasion with a woman and a party with her on another?"

He started to backtrack and said, "Yes, I did go to the pub and a party with my friends but it's because you've been working so much lately."

"So who is Kay? Are you having an affair with her?"

"I was lonely. What did you expect?"

I got up and walked straight back to my car. He followed me, not saying anything. We drove home in silence and when we got home, he walked into the kitchen. I stood there and looked at him, but it took him a long while before he spoke. "So what do we do now then?" he asked.

"What do you think, Paul?" I said, and I walked into my living room, sat down, and waited for him to come in and explain.

I heard him walk upstairs and wondered if he was using the bathroom or taking time to work out what to say. A few minutes later, he came downstairs, walked towards the front door, opened it and left. He left without saying a word. I sat there in the dark until midnight.

The next day, I was booked to attend a wedding fair at the Mill. It started at midday and in some ways, I needed to keep busy, but the sight of all the happy couples acted like salt rubbed in an ever-deepening wound. Never had I before chased anyone, but I sent Paul a message that day asking for an explanation. He didn't respond. I wrote him a letter asking for closure to understand what had happened, but still nothing. Those who'd befriended him around me were shocked; he'd disconnected from them, too. Eventually I was sitting one day at my usual meditation spot, and I asked The Guys why he'd done what he'd done. *All's not what it seems Amanda. Paul was not betrayed but was the betrayer.*

Then the truth sank in. Yet another betrayal. No matter how much I had worked at making a good life for myself and loved ones and despite The Guys reassurance, I was 46 and it felt like I had just slipped down yet another snake on my eternal snakes and ladders game of life.

Chapter 40

Dream as if you'll live forever, live as if you'll die today.

James Dean

For months I worked day and night to build a business that I was proud of. I still ran my cleaning business to keep the women in work that I'd taken on and I thought it was perhaps my destiny to live a 'normal' life and leave the 'mission' behind. I supported the other business owners on site, many of which became good friends, and I was driven to not only promote us as a community, but to do whatever I could to help elevate our position in the greater community to put the site on the map.

It worked, for a time, though something in me was missing. The more it nagged me, the further within me I pushed it. I worked harder, smarter, and tougher to achieve success, but it came at a price.

One Friday morning, one of my regular cleaners walked into my shop for her weekly pay. After she'd taken her money, on leaving the shop, she turned around and said "Oh, just to let you know, I won't be coming back Amanda. And I've taken all your clients too. They've all agreed they need me, so you're no longer required."

I stood there in shock, open mouthed, as she shot a sly satisfied smirk at me and waltzed out of my shop. I felt a blow to my solar plexus. It was so left of field that I couldn't fathom out how to react, so I did nothing and stood there in utter amazement with what had just happened.

That was the end of my cleaning business, and as I was still in the early stages of investing in the shop, it had been my income to bolster up my expenses until that business was on its feet. I was more hurt and betrayed by the woman who I had taken on as a favour to a friend, than the loss of my business. And as it was so soon after Paul had betrayed me, I felt I had been played and taken advantage of and utterly foolish to have trusted again.

I wondered if it would ever end at that stage, as my life still followed a pattern, no matter how much effort I made to stop attracting it. But it made me more determined to make the shop a success and build my relationships with those around me. Life was great in so many ways, so I had a lot to be thankful for as I'd put the work in. The shop was getting a wonderful reputation and I was about to take on a lady to help run the shop when I fell ill.

At first it seemed to be just a cold, so I went to my kettle bells class that evening after work thinking I would sweat it out, but the next day it felt like I'd been run over by a truck. I couldn't get out of bed. Worse than that, I was having heart palpitations that wouldn't stop.

The children went off to school and I only managed to drag myself downstairs into the living room. I had managed to call one of the other business owners to put a notice on my shop door to say it was closed temporarily, but I knew I was pretty sick. After several hours and the palpitations were still affecting me, I called my doctor's surgery who told me to call an ambulance.

When they arrived, I was in a huge amount of discomfort but after some tests they concluded that I had flu, and the palpitations were probably muscle spasms that were the result of overdoing it in my class with the onset of flu. I was not convinced, and I felt some kind of foreboding around me as if I was under some kind of curse.

I spent a week in that living room. I couldn't even make it up the stairs to my bedroom, so the children had to help prepare food for themselves and get to school. Thankfully the bus picked them up from outside our house in the village where we lived and dropped them back outside after school.

It was not an ideal house and only a temporary measure, as we'd had to move out of our lovely, thatched cottage when the owners wanted to sell. The chalet style house we'd moved to was small, in desperate need of repair, was filled with damp and the garden was hugely overgrown, but I had to get something quick to keep the kids in school and the business running. We lived on the outskirts of a tiny village surrounded by farms, so it was great for dog walking but very isolating for the children.

When we moved in and Millie's asthma had been exasperated quite badly, I complained to the agents who investigated the damp and concluded the house had no damp course whatsoever and the overgrown garden had made the damp worse. I was looking for another property for us to rent just before I became sick.

The shop remained shut though. When I finally managed to return, I never really recovered, but I was more determined than ever to put everything I had into building the shop like I had something to prove to myself and those who had betrayed me. I was on my own mission, but not the one that I was destined for.

A mysterious set of circumstances seemed to unfold from then on. I was involved in the committee to promote the site and organise open days to invite tourists to come and visit to popularise the mill as a destination site. It was a success to a degree but one thing after another just seemed to happen like a jinx had not only been placed on me, but everyone else on that site.

By Christmas, all the businesses were thriving and looking forward to our big Christmas open day when out of the blue, we were all called early in the morning of the event by the owner of the site's wife, who told us that there had been a major burglary. Every one of the businesses had been burgled except for me. I was in absolute shock and raced to the shop to be met by police and other business owners.

It was carnage. But my instincts told me it was no coincidence why this had happened the very evening before our open day when we were all stocked to the hilt. The police concluded that somehow the perpetrators had been locked in the brick barn where several of the businesses were based and once the site was quiet, they angle grinded out of the barn and broke into every business that way as they ransacked and raided, taking everything they could of any value.

Apparently, nothing was heard or witnessed by the site owner who lived on site. And it was concluded that as I had the most valuable stock, they were planning to raid my shop last as I was near to the entrance where they would have had their vehicle parked. The site plans showed a door into my shop which had been blocked up, so they had intended to burgle me, but had to leave when they realised the error. They had to have worked from a plan to have known the layout in the dark.

That was the beginning of a very slippery slope as I watched my world once more, fall apart at the seams. It was like a slow car crash and even though I took on Katy who became one of my dearest friends, to help me run the shop, I realised I was running on a treadmill made of sand. We had a miraculous turnaround in the spring of 2014 by creating a 'club' for women for event evenings and prosecco and strawberries in our courtyard garden, which kept us afloat. But many of the business owners were badly affected mentally and emotionally as well as financially and never really recovered. And many in the community stopped visiting us through fear of getting attacked themselves once news got out as to how viciously the criminals had behaved.

I was still not well, getting more and more exhausted, feeling nausea, and having headaches constantly, but I battled through like a warrior, determined to fight to the death. With the number of women that came to the shop, something was happening that had occurred when I had my little shop in my house back in Hertfordshire, when the kids were young. The more my customers got to know me, the more they wanted my help in other ways. And so the door opened once more for me to see the odd client in the evening after the shop was closed.

While it was like a breath of fresh air to be back doing what I loved, it was by no means compensating for the long hours, the challenges that came with running so much stock and over 200 clients who supplied the items we sold through the business. The site owner Steve was starting to show his true colours and motives too to all of us, and disputes were coming up left right and centre. It was a mad circus, and I knew at some point, someone was going to get hurt. And they did.

I went to my doctor when the sickness and pain was getting too much, who said I was overworking and should take it easy. So I walked away with the attitude of 'well that isn't going to happen'! But then I put my back out and ended up seeing an Osteopath on site who told me I was very poorly and if I didn't stop working, I was at great risk. I knew he was right, even though I didn't know what I was dealing with. Although I'd always believed that we should listen to our instincts, I ignored mine and carried on through a driven fear of failing. I was incessant and would stop at nothing to push through until I had succeeded in getting the shop to a place where I could pull back.

I worked seven days a week. I saw clients in the evening and then I started running workshops for women again at the weekends while Katy ran the shop. The harder I worked, the more I needed to tap into my spiritual work, but I knew it was only an elixir that would take the sting out of my ridiculous schedule. Apart from work, I had two children, a home and three dogs to look after. I felt that 'destructive work ethic at any cost' of my father coming through, but I ignored it and carried on regardless.

One day in the summer, almost a year to the day that we'd opened, an elderly regular customer of mine fell outside my shop and broke her hip. That was the catalyst to a very frightening time where I was being bullied by the site owner, I was starting to fall apart and I could no longer hold up the enormous weight of my responsibility and in a desperate need for help once more, I reached out and prayed that my angels would have the answers.

A few days later, a woman walked into my shop and asked me about running classes at the mill. I asked her what she did, and she told me she was an astrologer. I knew instinctively she had walked into my shop that day as she had been sent to me. I asked if I could get a reading from her as it felt like something was about to be revealed. I needed to find out what was destined for me as peculiarly I felt time was running out.

When Paul had left, I felt compelled to continue with the book, although I had no idea what I would write about, but my intuition was telling me something was about to conclude which worried me slightly. So with the visit of Felicity, the astrologer, I thought it would give me answers as to how to finish off the book. Did that mean that I was doomed or was I about to start a whole new chapter of my life? Either way, the urgency seemed to take me over and I could hardly sleep before my reading.

I walked into the beautiful town house cottage in Woodbridge on a misty summer morning to have my reading with Felicity Karena, who was a very inciteful woman. As she explained how astrology worked scientifically, I listened, fascinated, even if it was way over my head. When she started to talk about my life, having known nothing about me whatsoever, it made so much sense, like she was relaying my life story. She explained what the planetary positions had created for me throughout my journey, and she was spot on with her analysis. She asked me what connection I had with music, which I couldn't understand at first until The Guys showed me the radio show I'd worked for. That's when she told me I'd have to contact them, and it would be connected with the book. Having racked my brain as to who would eventually publish my book prior to ever meeting her, suddenly it made sense.

"Go back to My Spirit Radio and they will help you to publish." She said. I had no idea if the radio show still existed, but I felt a flutter of excitement and recognition considering that's where the first spark of my writing journey had begun.

When I left her house, I'd just got into the car and was looking down at the recording of the reading, when it dawned on me that Felicity had said nothing whatsoever about my shop. She'd mentioned all about my writing, public speaking, teaching, clients, travel, and huge life changes in the future, but nothing whatsoever about my shop. I was about to go back into the house to ask her, when I felt a force hold me back. *Go to Felixstowe Beach Amanda* I heard. The Guys felt very close to me, and I looked down at my watch which said it was eleven minutes past eleven, the magic number that confirmed they were with me. Without questioning, I called Katy to say I was making a detour and would be back at the shop later in the afternoon.

I walked along the coastline, with hardly anyone, and contemplated the thing that stood out in my mind more than anything. Felicity had told me that around the summer of 2014 everything would change dramatically for me, and my life would never again be the struggle it had been. I found a solitary rock to sit on overlooking the sea and asked The Guys what to do next. *Get on with the book of course!*

I returned to the shop that afternoon and as if the Universe was right on cue, as Katy left to go home for the day and I took over, Steve, the site owner appeared at my shop door. What ensued, will always be indelibly marked on my soul. At the time, I was terrified, but now looking back I see it as a blessing.

This was a landmark moment that created the beginning of a whole new chapter in my life. So much so, it was the catalyst for two more books that have marked the change that Felicity outlined in the most spectacular way.

That day was so significant as I had no preconception that I would walk out of that shop, lock the door, and never return. Everything from then on was a fast-track roller coaster ride which took me beyond what I ever thought was possible.

I was approximately seven chapters from completion of my book, I had no idea how it ended and had certainly no idea how to put together the missing chapters. But I had made a start shortly after Paul had left the previous October.

So, I researched the radio station and saw it was a flourishing news and music station and still found Adam Fronteras to be fronting it. Feeling I had nothing to lose, I contacted Adam and he said he'd send it off to three publishing houses to be read. In a few weeks, I received an email from Adam to say he was interested, and I should contact a recommended editor who'd help me through the vast process of preparing the book for publishing. I was over the moon as I still had a chance to achieve what I was being guided to complete, despite the slow collapsing of the life I knew around me.

Once I'd walked away from the shop, I knew I had to face the music, but I knew it was my truth. My health had declined so much so that I had to get the help I needed. I knew I faced bankruptcy and losing everything I had which included our home, assets, investments, and personal belongings but I knew somehow, I would get through it.

It was the most significant and life changing moment of my life and as I rose out of the debris of my collapsed life feeling battle weary and burned out, I started to learn how to find me again. It was a slow and arduous process, but I had faith in The Guys and my heart felt more connected to my purpose than I had ever felt. I knew that if I trusted, it would be for the highest good and all that mattered to me was that it would be good for those that mattered to me and help me to find the missing part of 'me' that was longing to be found.

I knew by what Felicity had shown me that there was a deadline for everything that would unfold which had been written in my astrological chart. Was I ready for it all? I knew according to my dreams and birth chart that the man who collected me to take me to my book launch, must be my soul mate. I had no idea still who he was as he always appeared as faceless. It was only a matter of time before I would finish the book and he would find me. That was incentive and The Guys assured me *You will know him when you are ready, and the clue is already here waiting for you.*

As I put all my faith in that part written story, my own true divine strength and divinity was finally emerging. No one could really understand my path other than my trusted friends and family who'd watched me over the years go through such dynamic change. They were the ones who'd supported me wholeheartedly and never judged me even when life set challenges against the odds and wasn't pretty. I knew after the many battles that I'd fought throughout my life, this was the most significant one of all and it was finally my time to emerge, ready to leave the colossal mountain I had climbed. My time of sacrifice was over. And though this book ends here, the story had only just begun for me which ultimately showed all the miraculous changes that I would go on to create to show The Guys I was ready.

We come into this life with the hope and promise to learn how to love and be creative. I had no idea how deep that lesson would be for me. Some have the fortunate role of living their existence experiencing so much beauty and never seeing the true extent of the horrors that life can create. I witnessed terror, fear and hatred at the deepest levels and learned how to transmute it all to something beautiful. I didn't ask to suffer for the sake of suffering, I trust I asked so I would be a catalyst to help those who needlessly suffer.

There are eight billion people on this planet and every single one of us goes through our own personal grief, sorrow, war and poverty – some more than most. Does it take the news of suffering of others in war torn countries, third world nations or poverty-stricken communities to open our hearts, or do we see elements of that in our everyday lives?

Many of us have touched the face of fear and longing and have strived to find resolution and hope. I had no choice as a child but to fight to stay alive and through hope I found faith. Whether we are religious, spiritual, or hopeful, we are all created of the same matter. Our physical DNA is created so every cell in our body is programmed to become its best self. As humans, we all have that pre-set programme to keep striving to be the best we can be. Whether we strive to come out of poverty or famine or war, we are resolutely determined at our soul level to find love, peace, and security. These are the fundamentals that make us human.

Long ago when we gravitated towards working in communities, we strove as individuals to work together collectively to create the whole for the greater good. It was a team effort with us pulling together and looking after those who lagged behind or were sick. All were honoured. Our world is not suffering because we are not capable as humans to create the whole; we suffer simply when we do not fulfil our dreams to respect the whole.

When we have those quiet moments alone and respect who we are as individuals (not as parents, siblings, children, friends, or neighbours) we find who we are at the deepest level to know our authentic self. How many of us take the time to seek the true person within us and respect ourselves at that level? How many compromise through fear, persuasion, control, or a lack of self-worth?

One thing I learned from my childhood was I found my true nature in my hour of need, found the strength from my inner core to find a way forward and that stood me in good stead to respect the deep programmes that served my higher nature that were created within me. Many can relate to this but find no help when the system only looks at us as a mass, a statistic, a number. Each one of us asked to come here to honour the true nature of our own self-worth, so why should we compromise? My path led me to understand there is a greater force beyond our comprehension. Whether or not we understand it, honour it, have researched, or conquered it, it exists within everyone and everything around us. Only trust, faith and revering our deeper instincts can highlight that energy and bring it to life.

Those who have had life changing experiences will call it hope. Those who have prayed for answers and received them will call them miracles. We all have a name for that which is inexplicable, when all else fails and arrives in the form of a perfect solution.

I have fifty-six years of solutions behind me now as I no longer see suffering but seek solutions to every challenge. I have seen hope and faith at its extreme. I have had answers appear when all else has failed around me, but above all I have helped others to see what I have seen and have the capability to continue to see like we all have the ability. Sadly it's not in our school curriculum. If it were, we'd all have the tools to deal with anything life delivers regardless of how enduring, how testing or how life threatening.

It is not for us to live this life going to work and coming home each day, binge watching box sets and losing ourselves in reality shows in the hope they will give us faith. Faith exists in the real stuff, in the everyday living of our daily existence. Pushing the parameters of who we are is the most exciting and challenging thing we can do as humans, and through those moments when we believe we are suffering, we are not.

Each of us has an opportunity to grow, to learn, to love. I have not gone through this existence without testing the human condition to its utmost endurance and will never give up trying. The reason I am here is I believe we all have this ability, young and old, male, and female, rich and poor, strong, or weak. Whatever we perceive ourselves to be, we have far more than we realise and above all, to offer. Look at how Olympic athletes train, entrepreneurs have vision, and those who have disabilities see the beauty in their lives.

I have no idea where my life is going but I do know my mission is drawing closer. If I knew what that would be I'd be a fortune teller, and I wouldn't be happy with that. Instead, I have the ability to deal with everything life throws at me and find the right solutions at all times. The difference now, though, is I have the capability to ask for what I want in life and to teach that to others.

So, as this book draws to a close, how did I honour my health and well-being, and how did my financial circumstances pan out considering I compromised all security and threw everything at what I believed in? And finally, how did my relationships pan out considering I was destined to meet my soul mate?

All I can say is, watch this space!

Always be a first-rate version of yourself,
instead of a second-rate version of somebody
else.

Judy Garland

Val Clift, Pat Hart, and Amanda Hart, Christmas 1993

Nora Golledge and Amelia Erotokritou (aged three months),
1999

Amanda Erotokritou (aged thirty-three) and Amelia (aged fifteen months), 2000

Amanda with Anthony and Amelia, Southend, 2001

Amanda, Anthony and Amelia at Race for Life, Trent Park, 2002

Millie and Anthony Erotokritou with Bob and Val Clift, 2002

Amanda (aged thirty-six) with Anthony and Amelia, Cyprus, 2003

Amanda between the paws of the Sphinx, Egypt, 2005

Amanda (aged thirty-eight) on the Ridgeway Walk, 2005

Amanda with Yvonne Simpson at a party, 2009

Amelia, Anthony, and Amanda, Spain, 2011

Amanda with Georgina D'ormain in 2011, reunited after
seventeen years apart

Amanda Hart
Natal Chart
Thursday, January 19, 1967
12:02:00 AM GMT
Croydon, England
Tropical   Koch True Node

Felicity Karena

Birth Chart Summary

by Felicity Karena, Astrologer

www.felicitykarena.co.uk

Amanda was born through challenge and had to fight as she came into this life and then find the courage to go out into the world to bring some kind of harmony, justice, and balance.

Her chart shows she makes a good therapist and seeks the challenge to help other people to make adjustments in their life so they can find their own harmony and sense of fairness. She feels the need to fight for good causes and to communicate. It's through her childhood challenges that she's gained the emotional stability to help others.

Amanda has a deep understanding of emotions and feelings and has the ability to intuit through her deep psychic senses. This she's put into a career and has built something with it, especially to help women. Her work is not just on a one-to-one basis but has been brought out to make the world a better place.

She is a hugely caring person and forms relationships with everyone she meets. This caring nature must be balanced with her family and ability to create foundations. In other words, she has become this all-encompassing nurturing person and created structure and foundations out of this.

Her ability to communicate is very strong and she has a unique quality as she has the most amazing chart. It's very complex but there's a continuing theme through it as she is the most remarkably sensitive, feeling, psychic and intuitive person – it's all there. She's become an initiator and leader as it's been easier for her to fight for other people than it is for herself.

There's a lovely harmony between what she values, what she desires and how she goes out and gets it. What she desires and what she values are social welfare and a better world. This is greater than herself and her life's work, why she does the things she does and why she's written her book. Her birth chart says she can make a difference to other people. She has these gifts and talents but equally very earthy and grounded with it.

Amanda's here as a revolutionary to make changes that have a knock-on effect to help other people. These are deep changes but at the same time they're very subtle.

A relationship for Amanda is incredibly significant whether it be as a therapist or in any other capacity. Relationship obviously stimulates her to get on. She has a challenge though and can be a little indecisiveness when she's involved in a personal relationship as she's not quite sure whether she should let them lead or for her to lead. So there's a dilemma there and she's looking for harmony and the perfect mate and perfection. Some people are happy with what's not right but she's always looking for balance and fairness and looking for an equal to her.

Somebody's going to have to be as well balanced and as strong as she is to be her perfect match. It doesn't mean to say doing the same things as her though. She became the healer in her younger adult relationships and didn't get nurtured herself, so she needs to find someone who's equally as strong as her now. This person maybe in another part of the world doing different things to her but can stand up for himself and can give her the nurturing she wants. She desires someone quite courageous, strong, and dynamic.

She may go for a fiery kind of male who needs her earthiness and equally she needs that fire as it will lift her out of herself. This will address the balance as sometimes she can get bogged down in the emotions and feelings of dealing with other people's stuff.

So the fire element and communication are the foremost things for her in a relationship because if she can't communicate, the relationship can't even get off the ground and it doesn't necessarily have to be in the field she works in. They must be unusual, artistic, creative, and different in some way.

Amanda is now achieving her goal to make this world a better place to live in, through her understanding and guidance, which she's honoured since the day she was born.

About The Author

Amanda Hart Intuitive Consultant has helped countless people to overcome adversity, to find their power, purpose, and voice for over 27 years, through her highly developed intuitive faculty, discovered from early childhood.

Amanda trained for many years in numerous holistic practices to understand how the energy world affects us. But she found the key to unlocking negative programmes and behaviours through studying under internationally acclaimed psychologist and media spokesperson, Dr Keith Hearne.

Her memoir '*The Guys Upstairs*,' quite unexpectedly changed her life, having battled with a turbulent childhood, years of domestic violence, addictions, depression and debilitating conditions post-meningitis.

Endorsed by key experts such as Professor Evan Stark (author of '*Coercive Control*') and DCI Steve Jackson (National Domestic Abuse Co-Ordinator, College of Policing), she had no idea of the impact that book would have on her personally, as well as others.

Some may know her as one of the finalists on Britain's Psychic Challenge on Channel 5, a presenter on My Spirit Radio and a columnist for Soul & Spirit Magazine. Today she speaks publicly about her story, to help others make sense of theirs.

As an author, she was invited to write a 3-book series for Orion Publishing and has contributed as co-author to 4 other titles and writes for a variety of publications about her expertise.

Amanda works collaboratively with other inspirers from around the world and passionately supports a large global network of women, helping to elevate and empower them to stand out and fully embrace their unique purpose, to make this a better world to live in.

Her message is clear – *"Our purpose unlocks our power and voice. Embracing vulnerability leads us to fear less and love more."*

If you would like to work with Amanda, then please do get in touch: www.amanda-hart.co.uk.

Testimonials

"Amanda is the embodiment of what the human spirit is all about and her courageous efforts to fight through adversity are the qualities many of us dream of and desire to have." **Theo Paraskevaidis, Australia**

"This book elevates you to a pitch of heightened self-awareness. It promotes self-belief and courage to achieve our goals and dreams in life." **Esther A, UK**

"It is without doubt the best written book of personal and spiritual growth I have read. It was addictive reading from the start." **Julie Marie, UK**

"This is one of the truest, raw and most heart wrenching true life stories I have ever read. I was gripped from the first page, a harrowing and inspirational read." **Rebecca Legate, UK**

"Beautifully written and could not put it down. She is an outstanding author with a real talent for writing." **Elizabeth, UK**

"Amanda's journey is incredible. She crafted words to relate her life story while transforming that of her readers. A fab read!" **C. A. Gaudry, UK**

"10/10 for Amanda's honesty, vulnerability and for her courage to stand up for, and to ask for what she wants in life." **Marie, UK**

"Truly stunning and inspirational. I adored every minute and found it so hard to put down." ***Majda Elaboudi, UK***

"What an amazing story of courage and commitment - a truly inspiring story which shows that life has no limitations." **Nikki Bloss, UK**

"This book will leave you feeling you can conquer anything in life." ***Bally Bainbridge, UK***

"This is a totally addictive read." ***Yasmin, UK***

"Could not wait to get my copy of this book and once I got it, I couldn't put it down!" ***Menchu Soriano, UK***

"HUGELY moving and HUGELY inspirational. My faith in the Universe has been duly reinforced." ***Marc-John B. UK***

Printed in Great Britain
by Amazon

32937672R00225